SOUTHEAST ASIAN

TRIBES, MINORITIES,

AND NATIONS

PUBLISHED FOR THE PRINCETON CENTER OF

INTERNATIONAL STUDIES

A LIST OF OTHER CENTER PUBLICATIONS

APPEARS AT THE BACK OF VOLUME II

VOLUME I

SOUTHEAST ASIAN TRIBES, MINORITIES, AND NATIONS

EDITED BY

PETER KUNSTADTER

PRINCETON NEW JERSEY

PRINCETON UNIVERSITY PRESS

1967

PREFACE

THE PAPERS in this volume are from several distinct sources. Most of them grew out of a conference held in Princeton in May 1965; other contributions were solicited after this conference, and still others came out of a session at the annual convention of the American Anthropological Association in Denver in November 1965.

The conference, on the subject of tribes, minorities, and central governments in Southeast Asia, was held at Princeton University, under the auspices of the Center of International Studies, between May 10 and May 15, 1965. The conference was conducted under a contract from the Advanced Research Projects Agency of the Department of Defense. People were brought together at this conference who had had extensive direct experience with tribal or rural minority peoples or who had been engaged in projects sponsored by central governments which dealt with those people. Papers were prepared in advance of the conference, and these formed the basis for discussion. The papers, as they appear in this volume, have been modified as a result of these discussions, and some of the conclusions of the discussions are also contained in the introductory chapter.

Participants in the conference at Princeton included Dr. William R. Geddes, SEATO Adviser to the Tribal Research Centre in Chiengmai, Thailand, and Department of Anthropology, University of Sydney; Mr. Tom Harrisson, Curator and Government Ethnologist, Sarawak Museum; Dr. Lee W. Huff, Director for Behavioral Sciences, Advanced Research Projects Agency of the U.S. Department of Defense; Mr. Peter Kandre, doctoral candidate, University of Göteborg; Dr. Peter Kunstadter, Department of Sociology and Anthropology, Princeton University; Mr. Charles Henry Ley, Sabah Border Scouts, and Assistant Protector of Aborigines, Department of Aborigine Affairs, Malaysia; Dr. Hans Manndorff, Anthropological Adviser to the Hill Tribes Division of the Department of Public Welfare, Government of Thailand, and Museum für Völkerkunde, Vienna; Mr. Maran La Raw, Anthropological Research Officer, Government of Burma, and doctoral candidate, University of Illinois; Dr. Michael Moerman, Department of Anthropology, University of California, Los Angeles; Mr. John B. O'Donnell, U.S. Agency for International Development, formerly Province Representative, Kien Hoa and Long An Provinces, Republic of Vietnam; Mr. Myles Osborn, Colombo Plan Hill Tribes Adviser to the Royal Laotian Government; Mr. James Thomas Ward, U.S. Agency for International Development, formerly Rural Development Advisor, Refugee Relief Program, Laos.

Mr. Harry Pierson, of the Asia Foundation,[1] Mr. Richard Diao, of the Union Research Institute (Hong Kong), Dr. Frederick K. Lehman of the University of Illinois, and Dr. Gerald C. Hickey of The RAND Corporation submitted papers, but were unable to attend the conference. At the request of the editor, Professor F. W. Mote and Dr. John T. McAlister of Princeton University prepared papers after the conference was held.

Other papers grew out of a panel session on the future of upland tribal peoples in Southeast Asia at the 1965 meetings of the American Anthropological Association in Denver. This panel, which was not connected with the conference held earlier at Princeton, was organized by Professor Lucien Hanks (of Bennington College) and Professor Lauriston Sharp (of Cornell University). The contributions of Dr. Robbins Burling (Department of Anthropology, University of Michigan) and Dr. Joel M. Halpern (Russian Research Center, Harvard University) were a result of this session. Dr. Lehman, who also participated, expanded and elaborated his original paper as a result of this session. The paper by Mr. G. Linwood Barney (Nyack Missionary College, and doctoral candidate, Department of Anthropology, University of Minnesota) was solicited by the editor as a result of Halpern's suggestion following the Denver meetings.

All books growing out of conferences, especially those which have not laid down rigid outlines, may lack consistency. This book suffers from an inevitable lack of uniformity, given the

---

[1] Mr. Pierson and the Asia Foundation were represented at the conference by Mr. James Basche.

diverse training, experience, and interests of our authors. Also, since many of the authors hold official positions, their remarks have sometimes been limited by considerations of security and diplomacy. The views of the authors should not be taken as official representations of the organizations which employ them, nor do they necessarily represent views of Princeton University, the American Anthropological Association, or the Department of Defense.

This book is not so complete as it might have been. It would have been desirable to cover Cambodia and the Malay Peninsula, not to mention Indonesia and the Philippines.[2] No excuse is offered for these omissions, save that it is impossible to cover everything. Mainland China has been included, not because it is a part of Southeast Asia, but because many of the minorities in Southeast Asia are also to be found in China, because China's policies of establishing autonomous minority regions are being copied in Southeast Asia, and because China has openly avowed her intentions of influencing Southeast Asian minorities. Eastern India was included because of the examples of ethnically Southeast Asian tribal peoples being integrated into a central government quite different from those found in Southeast Asia. The greatest concentration in the book (perhaps too great) is on Thailand. The reason for this is simply that information is more readily available from Thailand at the present time, and it proved possible to cover a fairly complete range of topics there.

The conference in Princeton, the session in Denver, and the papers in this book were limited to rural minorities rather than urban ones; and in general the emphasis was on cultural or ethnic minorities, rather than religious or racial ones. O'Donnell's paper on the South Vietnamese Strategic Hamlet Program deals with people who are ethnically a part of the national majority, but their social distance from the central government makes them resemble a minority in many ways. The Chinese, who are the primary urban minority in Southeast Asia, are well covered in a large body of specialized literature of their own. Therefore we have included references to the Chinese minority only when they were appropriate to the main subject under discussion, or, as in Mote's paper, when they were a rural minority.

[2] See Appendix for Cambodian population figures.

Events have moved rapidly in Southeast Asia (particularly in Vietnam, Thailand, and Malaysia) since these papers were prepared for publication in 1965. Many changes in the position of minorities in Vietnam have resulted from the great expansion of American military efforts there, the accelerated fighting in the highlands, and the elections held in South Vietnam early in September 1966 (in which minorities including montagnards, Catholics, and sects like the Hoa Hao received about twice as many seats as would have been prescribed by their proportions in the population). The American presence in Thailand has increased, and has been accompanied by greatly expanded Thai and U.S. programs for minorities, particularly in the Northeast and among the northern hill tribes. The whole matter of "Confrontation" of Malaysia by Indonesia has been dropped as a result of political changes in Indonesia, but the problems of integrating the large non-Islamic population of Sarawak with the rest of Malaysia continue to be among the most vexing difficulties facing that nation. Thus, although some of the conditions described in these papers have been outdated, the background setting of minorities and tribes remains important in national and international developments of the region.

Peter Kunstadter

Chiengmai, Thailand
October 1, 1966

ACKNOWLEDGMENTS

I GRATEFULLY acknowledge the assistance of the many people who aided in the preparation of this book for publication. I of course thank the authors for the speed of the preparation of their papers, and for their patience in making numerous editorial changes. I particularly want to thank Dr. John T. McAlister and Dr. Joel Halpern for their numerous and valuable bibliographic suggestions, and Professor Lucien Hanks and Professor Lauriston Sharp for organizing a panel from which several of the papers in this volume came, and for assisting me in obtaining these papers for publication.

Dr. Robbins Burling, Dr. William J. Gedney, Dr. William A. Smalley, Dr. G. William Skinner, and Mr. David D. Thomas kindly provided me with unpublished materials on linguistic classification and populations, and tried to straighten out for me the very confused systems of linguistic classification which exist in the literature. They are in no way to be blamed for the inadequacies of the linguistic classifications presented in the book.

The large and burdensome secretarial job of preparing this book for publication was shared by a number of persons, including especially Mrs. Diane Appelbaum, Mrs. Anne Birrell, Mrs. Eva Crltz, Miss Risa Rosloff, Mrs. Barbara Salmone, and Mrs. Judy Winkler, who typed, researched, and arranged; Mrs. Charlotte Carlson, Mrs. Judy Getis, and Mr. Ed Lippitt, who assisted in preparation of the maps; and Mrs. Jean Lilly, who assisted with copy editing.

I wish to thank the National Geographic Society for cameras, film, and other support which helped me to take most of my pictures which appear in this volume.

Finally, I wish to acknowledge the assistance of the Center of International Studies, especially Professor Klaus Knorr, Director, for assistance with the many bureaucratic details involved in completing this task, and the Office for Survey Research and Statistical Studies of Princeton University for space in which to work.

CONTENTS

[xi]

CONTENTS

CONTENTS VOLUME II

PART I.   INTRODUCTION

CHAPTER 1

Introduction

PETER KUNSTADTER

THE PROBLEM

This book is addressed to problems of relationships between tribal and rural minority peoples and central governments of Southeast Asia. The questions with which this volume deals are many and varied. First are the questions of what is a tribe, a minority, a dominant majority? How are these people distributed, and how do they come to be where they are? Second, what is the nature of the relationships between these sorts of groups? Third, how are these relationships affected by the general processes of modernization, by current political situations within the nations, and by international disputes? Fourth, in their attempts to promote national solidarity and to build modern nations, how have the central governments and other organizations proceeded with regard to the minority and tribal populations? What programs have been directed toward these people, and how have these programs succeeded? Finally, what recommendations can be made for developing programs and for doing research on the problems uncovered?

GENERAL BACKGROUND

These are problems of nation-building in a modernizing world, made more urgent and more complicated today by warfare or the threat of warfare. But the press of present-day events should not blind us to the fact that the existing patterns of relationship are the results of many centuries of development. The groups

[3]

TABLE 1
POPULATION, DENSITY, AND ETHNIC MINORITIES
IN SOUTHEAST ASIA AND CHINA[a]

Country (& National Majority)	Total 1963 Estimated Population	1963 Estimated Persons per Square Mile	Approx. Percent Minority & Tribal
Burma (Burman)[b]	23,664,000	90.3	44
Cambodia (Khmer)[c]	5,740,000	86.1	14
Laos (Lao)[d]	1,882,000	20.6	47
Malaysia (Malay)[e]	8,200,000	64.0	60
Thailand (Central Thai)[f]	28,835,000	145.3	30
Vietnam, North (Vietnamese)[g]	15,917,000	254.6	15
Vietnam, South (Vietnamese)[h]	14,900,000	225.9	13
China, mainland (Han Chinese,[i] all dialects)	700,000,000	189.6	6

[a] Source: UNESCO (1964: Table 9); *Information Please Almanac*, 1965; individual tables in this book. For details on composition of tribal and minority populations see chapters on the various countries. Because of the very questionable census figures and classifications of minorities, *this table should be used with extreme caution.*

[b] Figure for national majority (Burman) also includes Arakan and Tenasserim dialect speakers and is therefore an overestimate of the national majority population (LeBar *et al.* 1964:38).

[c] Figure for national majority (Khmer) is estimated by subtracting *known* minority populations from the 1962 census total. Therefore, percentage of minority population is underestimated.

[d] Estimate of national majority (Lao) is from LeBar *et al.* (1964:215).

[e] Estimate of total and minority populations for Federation of Malaya are based on 1957 census; for Sabah and Sarawak they are based on 1960 census.

[f] Estimate for total minority population is based on subtraction of the figure for "Siamese Thai" (LeBar *et al.* 1964:197) from the 1960 census total. "Siamese Thai" does not distinguish among the various Thai dialect groups and is therefore a gross overestimate for the national majority population. If "Central Thai" is taken to mean "Buddhist Thais living in the Central region of Thailand," the minority population given by the census would be approximately 71 percent.

[g] Minority and majority figures from 1960 census.

[h] Estimate for total minority population includes only *known* populations and is therefore an underestimate.

[i] Estimate of minority percentage from Bruk (1959:15).

[4]

in question have never been completely isolated nor have they been entirely independent of the dominant political and economic structures of their regions. Many of their cultural features reflect long-term contact with the great civilizations of China and India and with the developing nation-states of Southeast Asia. They are not isolated today, though they live in relatively remote regions; and they are changing today, as they have for centuries, in response to outside contacts. In spite of the relative isolation of these people, their minds are not closed to the introduction of new ideas or new material items. Many of the so-called tribes or minorities in any one country actually turn out to be representatives of cultures which have been highly developed in their own right in some other locality or at some other time, and many of them are highly sophisticated in their dealings with central authority.

Although, as we shall see, it is difficult to generalize about the tribes and minorities,[1] there are features which allow us to distinguish them from the dominant majorities. In each of the countries with which we deal there is one dominant group from which that country derives its name and, at least nominally, the leaders of its central government, in spite of the fact that in some of these countries the dominant group is not actually a numerical majority. In Burma we have the Burmans, in Thailand, the Central Thais, in Laos, the Lao, in Cambodia, the Khmers, in Vietnam, the Vietnamese, and in Malaysia, the Malays. The civilizations of these states are all based in lowland plains areas, broad river valleys, deltas, or coastal regions, where the people make their livelihood primarily from irrigated-rice agriculture;[2] and there they have been accessible to outside influence from the predominantly seaborne contact with the Chinese and Indian traders and missionaries and later with the Arab and

[1] Contrast, for example, the individualistic, money-oriented Iu Mien (Yao), who have little village organization, no communal attachment to the land, but an extremely wide-ranging concept of the identity of the Iu Mien socio-religio-political system (Kandre's paper), with the communally oriented, subsistence farming Lua?, who have a strongly developed village structure, elaborate rules of village land ownership, and great variety of culture patterns between villages (Kunstadter's paper).

[2] The Malays are somewhat of an exception to this in that they have depended on fishing and trading and a coastal economy much more than the other groups mentioned. The Han Chinese, at least in southern China, are also a river-valley people, though living at a fairly high altitude in some places.

European ones. Overland trade with the Chinese has also been important for several centuries in some areas, especially in northern Burma, Laos, and Thailand.

In spite of its obvious cultural debts to China and India, Southeast Asia has developed rather independently of the rest of Asia. With the exception of Vietnam, which was occupied and ruled by the Chinese from about 100 B.C. to about A.D. 940, the area was not subject to large-scale military invasions and control by "outsiders" until the colonial period of the nineteenth century. Even then, although military force was sometimes used to conquer and pacify, large numbers of foreigners were not involved until the Second World War.

As already mentioned, cultural influences did come into the area, largely by sea. The earliest influences came from Indian and Chinese sources and, after the fifteenth century, European ones. If we trace back the history of the region two thousand years or so, we can see that there have been gradual overland migrations of peoples moving generally southward from the hilly regions of China's southern and southwestern frontiers. Usually these invaders did not come in large, well-organized groups, but moved gradually, absorbing the cultures and some of the populations of the people who were already in Southeast Asia. The Vietnamese are again a major exception, as they expanded southward from the Red River Delta region. By military force they conquered the Malayo-Polynesian speaking people of the Cham Kingdom, and threatened the Khmer Kingdom. Once the populations became established in the area, there was considerable warfare as the newcomers set up kingdoms in imitation of those which were already there—this was true especially of the Tai peoples.*

The lowland-based civilizations have sporadically attempted to extend their control over, and sometimes expand their population into, the hill areas. This process has generally accelerated in recent years, as the press of population and improvements in technology have forced and allowed them to move out of

---

* As used in this book, the term *Tai* refers to a group of languages and the tribal and minority people who speak them, such as the Black Tai, White Tai, Tho, etc., and *Thai* refers to the people of Thailand and the varieties of Tai languages which they speak.

their usual ecological setting. The reasons for these movements are obvious when population figures are examined. The countries in question have all had tremendous increases in their populations, especially in the nineteenth and twentieth centuries, mainly in the regions of most intense cultivation. Meanwhile, the minority and tribal areas have been relatively underpopulated, and their resources underexploited. In China, for example, the "National Minorities" (not including Tibet) comprise only 6 percent of the total population, but occupy 60 percent of the territory (Bruk 1959:15), mostly in the border areas of the southwest, west, and north. The figures for South Vietnam are roughly the same. The overpopulation of Java and relative underpopulation of most of the other islands of Indonesia are well-known facts. Thus we find in Kalimantan (Indonesian Borneo), China, Vietnam, and even in Cambodia, Burma, and Thailand, government-sponsored programs to resettle majority peoples (members of the dominant group) in the hills and previously remote border regions which were once the more or less exclusive domain of tribal and minority peoples.[3]

It is only in recent years that control of the hill areas has been technically possible and that the lowland-based states have seriously attempted to extend their control to these areas. In the past, though tribute may have been collected, these were

[3] Diao in this volume discusses some of the aspects of these programs in China and the gerrymandering of national minority zones so as to include majorities of the dominant Han population. See also Bruk (1959:17). Some of the background for the Indonesian resettlement programs is discussed in Pelzer (1948:Chs. 6, 7). The Vietnamese resettlement program is discussed briefly by Henderson (1961) and Ladejinsky (1961). The rather unsuccessful program here was clearly based on strategic considerations (especially control of the mountain minorities) and failed to take into account the differences between lowland and upland environments (Henderson 1961:123, 125 ff.). The Cambodian project involves resettlement of army veterans in sparsely settled areas, apparently for the dual purposes of economic development and control (Smith 1965:169–170). The Burmese army has a similar project for resettlement of army veterans in the Shan and Kachin states (see Pierson's paper). Thailand has not embarked on deliberate policy of resettlement of the population in minority areas for purposes of control, but some of the resettlement and development projects (nikhom), especially those associated with relocation of populations in areas affected by dams, have had this effect. See Kaufman (1963) for a discussion of resettlement of tribal and minority refugees from the civil war in Laos, and Pelzer (1963) for a brief description of the resettlement of Chinese during the Malayan Emergency.

[7]

areas which were not really a part of any nation (Leach 1960). Only within the past half-century, or, more accurately, only since the beginning of the 1950's, have the hill and border minorities become a matter of direct concern to the central governments.[4] They have also become sources of increasing conflict *between* central governments.[5]

In general, then, until quite recently the lowland civilizations did not extend their control very high up into the hills. Ecologically and culturally the mountain and hill regions of Southeast Asia, including the great mass of tangled territory separating valley and lowland China from lowland Burma, Laos, and Vietnam, and the ridges extending from this mass which separate the major river systems from one another, can all be considered as a single unit. The peoples in this area represent several distinct major language groups, but these linguistic divisions correspond neither to present-day political boundaries nor to the basic patterns of life, which in these hills are everywhere rather similar. In contrast to the pattern of lowland civilizations, the pattern in the hills is one of swidden* (slash-and-burn, shifting) cultivation and generally independent villages.[6]

[4] Certainly, in the case of China, attempts have been made for centuries to control the southern and southwestern hill areas, but these areas have remained a refuge for "wild barbarians." Only with modern transportation and communication technology has the government been able to establish real control over much of the country's southern border highlands. Taking a clue from Soviet policies, the Chinese Communists have been much more conscious than most Southeast Asian governments of potential problems and political possibilities of minority groups. (For an example of Soviet policies in action see Armstrong 1965.) This concern has also been taken up by the Vietnamese Communists (including the South Vietnam Liberation Front) and the Pathet Lao, who have been far more sensitive to minority and tribal peoples than has the government of South Vietnam or the Royal Lao Government.

[5] Minorities and tribes have become important internationally on the Thailand-Burma border (Shan and Karen rebels); on the Thailand-Malaya border (problems of Thai Malays and Communist Chinese terrorists); on the Thailand-Cambodia border (Cambodian minority in Thailand and the Khmer Serei movement); on the Thailand-Laos border (Pathet Lao influence among Northeastern Thais, movement of Meo and Yao tribesmen across the border; the Cambodia-South Vietnam border (Khmer minority in Vietnam, Vietnamese minority in Cambodia); North Vietnam-South Vietnam border (various tribal groups); and the Sarawak-Sabah-Kalimantan border (various tribal groups). See the related papers in this volume for details of some of these conflicts.

* Swidden agriculture (also called by the term "slash and burn agriculture," and a variety of other local names) is a system whereby fields are cleared by cutting, drying, and burning the vegetation and are cultivated for only a short period before allowing the fields to return to fallow.

[6] The independence of these villages should not be overemphasized. Some

The fact that these people are relatively remote from the present-day seats of government does not mean that they are necessarily downtrodden or unsophisticated: Harrisson has indicated the relatively high standard of living enjoyed by some of the inland groups in Sarawak; some of the Yao and Meo opium-growing hill tribesmen in Thailand and Laos evidently enjoy a higher income than do some of the rural Thai and Lao in the valleys below them (see Barney's, Kandre's, and Geddes' papers); some of the minority groups in Burma, such as the Shan, are quite sophisticated politically (see Maran's paper); the rural Chinese ("Haw") people in the North Thailand hills serve as a model for the diffusion of technological innovations to both lowland and tribal peoples (see Mote's paper). Although it is true that in some countries (e.g. Laos and Vietnam) tribal people have been subject to informal patterns of discrimination and are known by names which mean "slave," in other areas they have not been in direct enough contact with the "majority" populations to have been effectively dominated. In areas such as Thailand, Sabah, and Sarawak, many of the tribal and minority peoples are quite proud of their cultures, including the features which make them different from the politically dominant populations.

Although the territory looks rugged to Westerners used to the comforts of automobile and air travel, it is by no means impassable to men and women on foot—especially to men and women accustomed to making their living by cultivating the mountainsides. For thousands of years there have been movements of these people along the few narrow valleys which transect this mass and through and across the mountains themselves. Occasionally, the mountain peoples have reached the lowlands and have become transformed there into lowland-type people. But for the lowlanders, once established in the valleys, the mountains have proved to be effective barriers to large-scale movements of populations except during short periods when the area has

---

groups, like the Yao and Meo, have extensive inter-village political structures. Other groups, like the Rhadé and Jarai of Indochina and the Karen and Lahu of Burma and Thailand, have had extensive inter-village religio-political structures, usually centered around a charismatic religious leader or spirit doctor. The question of feudal connections between tribal villages and lowland governments is discussed on pp. 29 ff., and in Lehman's and Kunstadter's papers.

been under the pressures of warfare; and invasions rarely, if ever, have led to large-scale resettlement from one major lowland area to the next.[7]

Political control, however, was extended from time to time from the central areas to more remote regions both by the expansion of native political systems and by colonial regimes. As the hegemony of the central governments expanded, three choices were available to the vanquished: fleeing to the hills, becoming absorbed into the newly dominant group, or establishing, and in some way maintaining, boundaries around themselves so that their identity could be preserved in spite of their loss of political independence. The first choice, fleeing to the hills, seems to have been characteristic of many of the Khmer-speaking peoples in Vietnam, Laos, and Thailand and many of the Malayo-Polynesian speakers in Vietnam; the second choice, absorption, has been the lot of many of the Mon- and Khmer-speaking peoples of what is now Northern Thailand; erection of cultural boundaries for the preservation of identity has been the way for many of the groups which we have called minorities. This brief and overgeneralized account will at least allow us to characterize the peoples with whom this book deals.

DISTRIBUTION OF PEOPLES AND CULTURES IN SOUTHEAST ASIA

The present distribution of peoples and cultures in Southeast Asia can be accounted for in terms of several processes. In the plains, coasts, deltas, and broad river valleys we find the basis for centralized governments: Burma proper is essentially the lower and middle Irrawaddy Valley and Delta; Thailand is based on the Maenam Valley and Delta; Laos, which, except for its international complications, is hardly more than a principality, is really only the plains along the middle Mekong Valley; Cambodia's base is the lower Mekong Valley around the great lake of Tonle Sap; North and South Vietnam are based on the Red River Delta and the Mekong Delta, respectively; the coast of the Malay Peninsula and the lower reaches of the rivers draining

[7] The Thais, for example, invaded and sacked the ancient Khmer kingdom and its capital at Angkor, but they did not stay there to settle, nor did the Burmese, who repeatedly invaded the central plains and northern valleys of Thailand, ever stay there in large numbers once the battles were over. Again, excepting the Vietnamese, the objectives of these wars were usually loot and captives, not territory.

[10]

what was once the British portion of Borneo form the basis for Malaysia. The interiors of these countries and the borderlands between them are the homes of the minority and tribal peoples.

Several different kinds of movements of peoples and cultures are represented in the present arrangement. There have been direct invasions, where territory has been taken and native populations displaced, destroyed, absorbed, or encapsulated. One example of this process has been the southward movement of the Vietnamese along the Annamese coast, in which the kingdom of the Malayo-Polynesian-speaking Chams was destroyed and those Chams who were not killed or absorbed were reduced to an unimportant minority. The northern Mon-Khmer speakers were forced into the inland hills where they are today referred to as *moi* (slave) or *montagnard* (mountaineer). The southward expansion of the Vietnamese continued into Khmer (Cambodian) territory in the Mekong Delta region, a process which continues to the present day.

But by far the most common pattern has been a more gradual movement, not highly organized, including at any one time only a small number of people. The best example of this is that of the Tai-speaking peoples who have been spreading out from the border regions of southern and southwestern China and northern Burma, Laos, and Vietnam. Where these Tai speakers reached large river valleys, as in Assam, Thailand, and Laos, and even in the upland valleys of the Shan States in Burma, they formed kingdoms or principalities. Where they have remained in the hills, they have come to be considered as minority or tribal people, like the Lue, the Red Tai, White Tai, and Black Tai, and so forth. A similar situation is seen with the Viet-Muong, upland groups of Vietnamese who escaped the sinicization which affected their lowland cousins in the Red River Delta in North Vietnam. The process of gradual movement continues with the present-day movements of Meo and Yao into Thailand from Laos (see Kandre's and Barney's papers) and movements of Lahu from Burma into Thailand. Likewise, some of the Tai speakers are still moving southward in Laos and Vietnam. Settlements of these peoples are scattered through the hills as village communities which shift their location in response to the needs of swidden agriculture or to escape oppressive governments or insurgents. Similar movements have taken place from Kalimantan (Indonesian Borneo) into Sarawak and Sabah until recently.

A third process has been the deliberate relocation of populations, often through capture in warfare or as tribute from one prince to his superior. Thus the Mon are scattered remnants of an early kingdom in southern Burma and Thailand, and various fragments of Tai-speaking groups have been moved from place to place within Thailand as the result of a series of conquests.

A fourth process, similar in some ways to the third, has been the deliberate encouragement of migration of certain peoples for special purposes: Chinese migration into Thailand was encouraged for building irrigation canals; into Borneo for work in gold mines and on pepper plantations; and the Chinese and Indian migration was encouraged on the Malay Peninsula for work on rubber plantations and in tin mines. At a rather different level, the British encouraged Indians in the Civil Service to migrate into Burma at the time when Burma was administered as a part of India. Such migrants have formed the bases for very large populations of overseas Chinese who have become integrated in different ways in the countries in which they now find themselves. Often they have become *urban* minorities, and we have not concerned ourselves with them to any great extent in this book. The Chinese in Southeast Asia are treated in an extensive literature of their own (see bibliography in Purcell 1965).

Still another type of movement has involved relatively few people, but has had great cultural impact—the movement of traders and missionaries including Chinese traders bearing a variety of cultural traits, crop plants, and ideas about social structure and religion; Indian missionaries bringing Buddhism and ideas about the organization of states; later traders bringing Islam as well as commerce; and finally, European and American missionaries and traders bringing Christianity, colonialism, crop plants, and world commerce. Again, these people, when they settled in Southeast Asia, were predominantly urban dwellers, but their cultural influence penetrated far inland and has had profound effects on people they have never seen (for example, tobacco and maize, originally New World crop plants, have become ubiquitous in the farthest and most isolated hill regions).

[12]

The result of these processes is not just one but a series of patchworks of language, race, ethnic identification, religion, and distribution of cultural traits. In general, however, the patches on the quilts are larger in the valley-coast-delta-plains areas, reflecting the multi-dimensional dominance of the central governments. The patches are smaller (and sometimes, as in the northern Thailand hills, reduced to the size of single villages) in the folds and creases of the more remote or isolated refuge areas of tribal groups (Bennington-Cornell 1964).

One result of the great diversity in historical backgrounds of the tribal and minority peoples is that the names which are applied to them may not be accurate, in that they lump together a number of people with very different characteristics. The so-called Kha of Laos, for example, are actually composed of a number of distinct cultural groups. Differences among Lua? and Karen groups may also be striking (see Kunstadter's paper). This means that tribal names should not be accepted uncritically as implying cultural uniformity (see Lehman's paper).

Such confusions may have important political consequences in areas where the tribal or minority peoples are representatives of different national majorities. One example of this is the so-called KMT (Kuomintang, Nationalist Chinese) in Burma and Thailand.[8]

It should not come as a surprise that traditional alliances based on family or extended kinship ties continue to function among the tribal and minority peoples in the modern world. We have evidence in this book from Burma (Lehman's paper), Laos (Barney's paper), and Vietnam (McAlister's paper) of the persistent importance in modern politics of these traditional patterns. We see repeatedly the importance of knowledge of local history for an understanding of contemporary alignments, and we learn that not all Karen, or Meo, or Tai tribes are the same in their political relationships, despite the fact that they may share language and many other cultural features with people who are called by the same name.

Despite the diversity of origins, there are many general characteristics of the people which can be listed to show a consistent

[8] See Mote's paper for a discussion of the various distinct groups to which this single label has been applied indiscriminately.

pattern of difference between what we have called dominant majorities, urban minorities, rural minorities, and tribes, as shown in Table 2. A table such as this emphasizes the differences between these kinds of groups, but it should not be used uncritically. The ecological distinction between the upland and remote areas on the one hand and the lowland-plains-valley-coast-delta areas on the other has already been mentioned, but it should be pointed out that ecology alone is not a sufficient explanation for the distribution of types of social organizations or types of groups. For example, the Thai-Lue, of whom Moerman writes, live in a valley area once the seat of the Prince of Chiengkham, a very important cultural and political center in the early history of Thailand, but now a backwater region. Changes in technology can rapidly and radically alter the patterns of ecological adaptation and can make otherwise useless areas available for intensive exploitation (e.g. the vast water-control projects in the Central Thai plains which made wet-rice cultivation possible there on a large scale).

In fact, the boxes into which Table 2 is divided should not be taken too literally. As Lehman and Maran have pointed out, it is extremely difficult to use any set of attributes as defining characteristics for a tribe-minority-majority classification. The lines between the different types are not sharp, and there are numerous exceptions to this summary classification which are discussed in the papers which follow.

Even more important, from a theoretical point of view, is the caveat that a table of this type should not obscure the connections between groups at the various levels represented in the table. We must not view tribes, minorities, and central governments as discrete entities—they are not now, and never have been, separate and distinct. In fact, we find for many purposes that the important thing about tribes and minorities is the nature of their relationships with the central governments or with the dominant majorities. The groups with which we are concerned very often define themselves not only in terms of their uniqueness and isolation (which is one of the traditional anthropological approaches) but in terms of their relationships to other groups. The situation which Leach first (1954) described so well for highland Burma, in which Kachins, for example, define

TABLE 2
TRIBES, MINORITIES, AND CENTRAL GOVERNMENTS
IN SOUTHEAST ASIA

Group	Burma	Cambodia	Laos	Malaysia Sabah	Sarawak	Thailand	North Vietnam	South Vietnam	China, Mainland[b]
				Percentage of Population in Each Category[a]					
Dominant national majority	Burman 55	Khmer 85	Lao 50	Malay 0.3	Malay 19	Central Thai 30	Vietnamese 85	Vietnamese 88	Han Chinese North dialects 67 Other dialects (26.5)
Urban minorities	Indian 0.8 Chinese 1.7	Chinese 7 Vietnamese 7 French 0.1	Chinese 2 Vietnamese ? Thai ?	Chinese 23 British 0.2	Chinese 31 British 0.1	Chinese 10	Chinese 1.1	Chinese 5.7	Hui 0.6 Tibetan 0.5 Manchurian 0.4 Mongolian Korean 0.2
Rural minorities	Shan 6 Mon 1.7 Arakanese ?	Cham ?	Black Tai ? Red Tai ?	Kadazan (Dusun) 32 Bajau 12 Others	Dayak 40	Minority Thai 50 ? Malay 3.9 Kui 0.4	Muong 2.6 Tay (Tho) 3.2 Thai 2.4	Khmer 2.6 Cham 0.3	Chuang 1.1 Uighur 0.6
"Tribes"	Karen 7 Kachin 7 Chin 2 Others	Stieng Rhadé Total tribes 1	"Kha" Meo Man (Yao) Total tribes 16+	Murut 4 Others	Kenyah Kelabit Others Total 11	Karen Meo Akha Htin Others Total tribes 0.8	Nung 1.9 Meo 1.4 Yao 1.1 Others	Jarai 1.1 Rhadé 0.8 Hre 0.7 Bahnar 0.6 Sedang 0.4 Total "tribe" 6.5	Yi 0.6 Meo 0.4 Puyi 0.2 Tung 0.1 Yao 0.1 Pai 0.1

(continued)

[a] Figures are estimates from sources cited in tables for individual countries. Where basis for classification is unknown, proportions may not equal 100 percent.

[b] This classification is not particularly appropriate for China. The Hui, for example, are a religious, not an ethnic, minority, although they are classified by the Chinese as a "minority nationality," and the Tibetans have claimed to an independent nation. Many of the minority nationality populations in China have a more diversified population than is characteristic of many of the groups in Southeast Asia.

TABLE 2
(continued)

Group	Terrain, Ecology	Degree of Cultural Development	Language and Education	Political Structure	Economy
Dominant national majority	Lowland, plains, broad valleys, coasts	Writing, "Great Tradition" religion, (Buddhism or Islam), cities cultivated arts and crafts, specialists, usually national religious hierarchy	Standardized dialect, most people monolingual; public schools	Kingdoms, nation-states; borders set or stabilized by colonial powers; bureaucracies nominally in hands of dominant population, but frequently with foreign minority "advice"; loyalties to nation	Wet rice for consumption and commercial sale; seaborne trade with world market, modern money, and market exchange system; large irrigation and drainage projects; commercial agricultural development; industrial development
Urban minorities	Lowland cities, market towns	Writing, "Great Tradition" religion, but usually not that of the dominant group, traditions consciously related to another country, area, or time, cities, specialists	Different from standard dialect, most people bilingual; often have special schools	Not organized politically, participate overtly or covertly in central government; loyalties to nation and to ethnic group often in conflict; loyalties cross national borders	Often in specialized positions in economy, in commecial and banking enterprises, often restricted from some occupations by law or custom
Rural minorities	Remote or isolated lowland areas poor communication and transportation to dominant areas, low hills, rain, shadow, or poor soil areas	Marginal literacy, usually only for religion usually not the modern form, "Little Tradition" religion, much animism; villages, few specialists, specialities imported	Usually dialect of same language family as majority group, but may not be mutually intelligible; educated people know "standard" form; perpetuation of dialects not encouraged in schools by central government	Contact with lowest bureaucratic levels; little communication to central government; local political organization at village level, position by personal qualities; loyalties primarily to village and to holder of real power	Subsistence agriculturists, wet and dry rice, some production for sale, small-time trade, no industrialization; little wage work, if any
"Tribes"	Hills, jungle, interior away from major rivers	Literacy nil or archaic variety, or missionary-supplied for religious purposes; religion is usually animism, sometimes "Little Tradition," religious leaders rarely have more than local following, but occasional charismatic cults develop: few specialists, except religious	Usually a different language family from dominant group, often strong emotional attachment to language, people often multilingual in tribal and dominant languages, little or no schooling	Contact with lowest bureaucratic levels, if any; little or no communication to central government, only ritual participation in central government, if any; local political organization at village level, very rarely higher; vague loyalties to fellow tribesmen; little if any loyalty to nation, loyalties may cross national borders	Predominantly subsistence dry rice, shifting cultivation (opium growers produce for sale, small-scale terracing or irrigation, if any; trade with local market town or itinerant traders, purchase some manufactured goods, no industrialization; little or not wage work

(continued)

TABLE 2
(continued)

Group	Population	
	Distribution	Dynamics
Dominant national majority	Dominant ethnic group concentrated mainly in one country	Rapid population growth due to recent public health measures and modern medicine; rapid growth of cities, especially growth of "primate" cities
Urban minorities	In large cities and market towns, sometimes itinerant traders, major concentration in some other country	Shares rapid population growth of dominant majority, but immigration controlled or shut off in most countries, outmigration sometimes encouraged; degree of intermarriage varies
Rural minorities	In remote or isolated rural areas, population distribution often does not correspond to national borders	Rapid population growth as public health measures are extended to rural regions; temporary or permanent migration to urban centers as rural economic opportunities diminish or for accumulation of bride-price, generally endogamous
"Tribes"	Often distributed without regard to modern political boundaries, usually discontinuous distribution mixed with other groups	Population growth just beginning to accelerate as public health services and modern medicine become available; very little urban migration, generally endogamous

themselves vis-à-vis Shans, and in which they make rather conscious decisions to become Shan or remain Kachin, is apparently quite widespread in Southeast Asia (see below, pp. 34; 42 ff. for further discussion of this point). This is not merely a matter of "passing," by which an individual decides that his social position should be judged by others in terms of his physical appearance: the process has involved whole villages or communities and their social structures as well as their physical appearance.

Finally, it should be remarked that there is frequently little difference between the ways of life of tribal or rural minority people and that of the rural part of the national majority, despite superficial cultural differences that are often striking. There is usually a fairly substantial social and cultural gap between the urban centers and all rural villages; much of the production of all rural peoples is for subsistence rather than cash; most of the rural people have fairly limited participation in markets, though they depend on them for essential tools and prestige goods; and, until recently, the governmental services have not penetrated very far into any rural areas. Like the rural members of the national majority, most of the minority and tribal people recognize the existence and power of the central governments, and many have been subject for *corvée* labor. Rural people and tribesmen base most of their cooperative action on ties of family and kinship, and rural majority, minority, and tribal villages are bound together as religious communities. Thus it is proper to speak of many of the tribal people as "hill peasants" (Izikowitz 1951).[9]

CHARACTERISTICS OF SOUTHEAST ASIAN NATIONS

Boundaries. Like the distribution of peoples, the present political borders in Southeast Asia represent a series of events. Although the region is old in history, the nations, except for Thailand, which retained its independence throughout the colonial period, are new. They were created mainly during the colonial era by powers quite remote from the scene, primarily as the result of competition among the British, Dutch, and French, and with little reference to the realities of ethnic distributions or the realities of existing political relationships on the ground. The events of the Second World War and the end of the colonial period, with the consequent withdrawal of the European colonial powers, led to some minor realignments (e.g. the Burma-China border); consolidation, or attempted consolidation of nations out of colonial administrative units (Indonesia, Burma, Malaysia) which had not enjoyed political solidarity prior to the colonial

[9] The distinction made by Sahlins (1960:408) and Wolf (1966:2–4) between peasants and primitives does not hold in most of Southeast Asia. They argue that peasants, unlike primitives, do not control their own means of production (land and labor). Though sometimes subject to *corvée* labor, most of the people in the greater part of Southeast Asia own their own land (Lower Burma, the large Malayan plantations and much of lowland Vietnam—the areas of most intensive Western colonialism—are exceptions to this generalization). Otherwise the conditions of life of the tribal and rural minorities and the majority rural population resemble quite closely those described by Wolf (1966).

CHINESE PENETRATION OF MINORITY AREAS

Upper left: Traditional use of forest products—Yao women gather bamboo shoots on Tayao Mountain, Kwangsi Chuang Aut. Region. "The Yao people use bamboo, abundant in their mountains, to build houses and to make tables, chairs, beds and other articles for daily use. The shoots are a prized food." China Reconstructs [CR] July 1964.

Upper right: "Members of the Kunming Botany Research Institute of the Chinese Academy of Sciences investigating fruit tree resources in the Hsishuangpanna Tai Autonomous *Chou*." The team gathered information on all varieties of fruits to provide a "scientific foundation for the full utilization of China's fruit tree resources." CR October 1963. Hou Chung-hsien photo.

Lower left: "Telephone lines being installed in a national minority area in Yunnan Province. . . Telephone services are now available in more than nine-tenths of the communes. . . In remote market towns where regular post and telegraph offices have not yet been established, travelling postal workers appear on days when fairs are held." CR February 1964. Chou Tzu-yu photo.

Lower right: Highway construction developed most rapidly between 1958 and 1961. "The Miao people of the Miao-Tung Autonomous *Chou* in southeast Kweichow welcoming the first lorries to arrive after the opening of a new highway in their area." CR October 1962.

Upper and middle left: Rural fairs
persist under socialism. Communiza-
tion of the tribal economies is said to
have reduced prices and increased incomes and demands for local products
at this traditional spring fair in the
Tali Pai Autonomous *Chou.* CR August 1963. Chu Yu-hu photo.

Lower left: Minority people are being
trained in modern medicine. "A Ching-
po woman health worker gives a patient an injection," Tehung Thai-
Ching–po Autonomous *Chou*, Yunnan.
CR September 1959. Cheng Kuang-
hua photo.

Lower right: "Typical Tai houses . . .
half-hidden in groves of plantain.
Everything is made of Bamboo." Pic-
ture probably taken in Chinghung,
Hsi–shuang Pan–na Thai Autonomous
Chou. CR July 1962.

Opposite page

Upper left: Traditional farming practices remain in parts of the Hsi–shuang
Pan–na Thai Autonomous *Chou.*
"Girls of the Aini nationality picking
tea on Nannuo Mountain, 1,400 metres
above sea level." CR July 1962.

Upper right: Elsewhere in Yunnan
"modern methods have replaced the
most primitive farming technique—
Pai women get ready to spray insecticide." CR December 1961. Chi Kuan-
shan photo.

MODERNIZATION OF NATIONAL
MINORITIES, CONT.

Middle left: Minority peoples have
traditionally had contacts with Chinese markets. Visitors from the surrounding highlands come to the Kunming market. Martin Hürlimann photo
in *Burma, Ceylon, Indo-China* . . .
Landscape, Architecture, Inhabitants.
New York, B. Westermann Co., Inc.,
1930, p. 281.

Middle right: "New housing in Ching-
hung is designed to fit Tai customs."
CR April 1959. Yi Tieh-shih photo.

Lower right: Heavier industries are
also being introduced. "Yang Kuei-
fen (left) of the Miao nationality and
Chin Tsu-huan of the Tung nationality are both lathe operators at the
new General Machine Factory built
in the Puyi-Miao Autonomous *Chou*
in southern Kweichow." CR October
1959. Wang Fu-tsun photo.

MODERNIZATION OF TRADITIONAL
CRAFTS IN CHINA

Upper left: Tai woman spinning
cotton on the porch of her home
in Hsi–shuang Pan–na Thai Autonomous *Chou.* CR July 1962.

Upper right: "Miao girls [from
Kweichow] working at their em-
broidery." Miao clothing is dec-
orated with wax-resist dyed patterns as well. "Fine examples of
designs and handwork are being
collected, studied, exhibited and
published in albums. Some of
them, adapted for rugs, tablecloths
and cushion covers, are greatly ap-
preciated in other parts of China."
CR August 1963. Ho Shi-yao photo.

Middle left: "The silk-screen printing workshop at the Yunnan Printing and Dyeing works, where gay
cotton prints are made for minority peoples." These are sold at the
Kunming Nationalities' Department
Store, where traditional costumes
and ornaments are stocked. Commercial production of clothing has
freed minority nationality women
for other tasks. CR March 1960.

Lower left: "Woollen and cotton
textiles for the minority nationalities made in a co-op in Yunnan
Province." Handicrafts have become a part of the socialist economy. CR October 1962.

Upper left: Literacy and modernization programs start as teams of linguists, anthropologists and historians from the Central Academy of Nationalities and the Academy of Sciences visit minority areas. "An old man of the Miao nationality relates a legend to members of a minority languages investigation team touring the Miao districts in South China to study the sounds of the language." CR August 1962. Ho Shih-yao photo.

Center left: After the languages have been analysed a standard dialect is picked, and instruction is given in the new script. "Members of the Tung nationality in Kweichow study their new alphabet during a rest break." CR August 1962. Yen Mao-jen photo.

Lower left: The skills of literacy are passed on to the younger generation. "In the Yi Autonomous *Chou* in the Liangshan Mountains, Szechuan province, a woman teaches her daughter the script devised for her people." CR June 1964. Hsu Hsin-yao photo.

Lower right: "Chang Pao of the Lahu nationality in Yunnan province notes down the work he has just done in the Lahu script." By 1902 twelve minority nationality publishing houses had been set up and were publishing books and newspapers. CR August 1962. Wang Chuan-kuo photo.

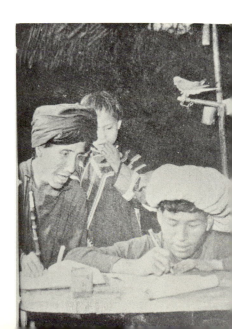

MOBILIZATION OF MINORITIES IN CHINA

Upper left: Minority literature is compiled and used for political purposes. "Delegates from Yunnan holding a group discussion during the session of the National Conference of Outstanding Groups and Individuals in Education and Culture in Peking in June 1960. Hanan Zuai, famous Tai bard, is seated second from right." CR December 1960. Huang Chang photo.

Upper right: The students are mobilized for political action. Under their banner "students of many nationalities march in Peking's annual May Day Parade." CR October 1959. Tu Hsiu-hsien photo.

Lower left: "People of China's national minorities demand: 'U.S. imperialists, get out of Panama!'" CR March 1964. Huang Ching-ta photo.

Lower right: The Central Academy of Nationalities was established in Peking in 1951, and within ten years had more than 3,000 students and faculty members belonging to 50 nationalities. Here they study their own cultural histories before being sent back home as leaders. "Students . . . get together on the campus to dance and sing." CR November 1961. Fu Chun photo.

COMMERCE IN THE GARO HILLS, INDIA

Upper left: Bamboo from the hills finds a ready market in the plains. Rafts of bamboo bundles are poled down stream and sold by tribesmen who then walk home.

Center left: Tribesmen carry huge bundles of cotton to market.

Lower left: Dried fish on display at the Nakam market.

Upper right: As he weighs portions for sale in his Indian type balance, a Garo man hopes to make a profit from his investment in a bag of salt. Robbins Burling photos, 1954-1955.

Upper left and middle left: Garos displaying fruits and vegetables for sale. Most purchases are between plainsmen and Garos—either cash crops that are exported to the plains, or imported manufactured goods. The latter will probably be purchased by other Garos, bringing a cash economy into relations among tribesmen.

Lower left: A trader from the plains displays goods he offers for sale to tribesmen in the Garo Hills: soap, thread, combs, etc. He carries his goods from one market to the next in the wooden chest. Markets are held once every seven days in each locality.

Lower right: Permanent shop in Tura, the administrative center and largest town in the Garo Hills. Pots, pans, and lamps on display are of Indian manufacture and are widely used by Garos. Robbins Burling photos 1954-1955.

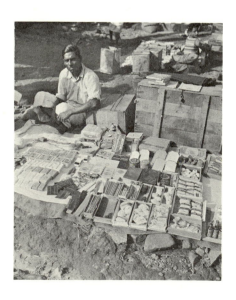

MEO SETTLEMENT IN LAOS

Upper left. Air view of a Meo village in the Luang Prabang district.

Upper right: Meo youths, Keo Katchoum village.

Middle left: Keo Katchoum, a Meo village.

Middle right: Young Meo man with homemade rifle, in Lao trading village.

Lower right: Meo opium field about 100 km. south of Luang Prabang on the road to Vientiane, near Keo Katchoum. Tree stumps remaining after slash and burn clearing are visible in the field. Joel Halpern photos 1957-1959.

MEO SETTLEMENT IN LAOS, CONT.

Upper left: Meo weighing opium in a Lao trading village.

Upper right: Ancestor spirits are invoked during a Meo curing ceremony, Keo Katchoum village.

Middle right: Young Meo women, Keo Katchoum village.

Middle left: Meo girl carrying water in bamboo tubes, Keo Katchoum village.

Lower right: The Lao Inspector of Education for Luang Prabang Province shows Meo villagers in Keo Katchoum the first school map of Laos in the Lao language. This map was produced by the U.S. Information Service. Joel Halpern photos 1957-1959.

Upper left: This Lao trading village, near Sala Pou Khoun on the Vientiane-Luang Prabang road, is a center for trade with upland villages.

Middle left: Khmuʔ women selling packets of banana leaves to Lao women in Luang Prabang town.

Lower left: Lao woman peddling cotton in prosperous Khmuʔ village, Luang Prabang district.

Lowest left: Black Tai mother and children in Nam Tha town. Joel Halpern photos 1957-1959.

Lower right: Khmuʔ boy with baskets of charcoal for the Luang Prabang power plant awaits truck transport.

Upper left: Yao women and girls waiting at the Nam Tha clinic operated by Dr. Tom Dooley. Woman in foreground has infected goiter, a disease common among Yao and Meo.

Lower left: Thai-Lue women who have come to trade in Muong Sai, Luang Prabang Province.

Lower right: Black Tai refugees in Vientiane. Tall hairdo on woman at right signifies that she is married. Joel Halpern photos 1957-1959.

A typical Northeast Thailand village—water shortage contributes to economic problems of this area.

Nikhom Chiengpin, a land settlement community in the Northeast. Note widely dispersed houses.

Middle left: Prosperity of this Northeast village is shown by extensive use of wood in houses.

Middle right: A neat house made of inexpensive materials—thatched roof and woven bamboo walls.

Lower left: A poorer house.

Lower right: A very poor house. Lee W. Huff photos, March 1963.

NORTHEAST THAILAND MDU PROGRAM

Upper left: Villagers gather to see helicopter which has brought part of the MDU team.

Upper right: After speaking with village officials MDU workers make spot checks of economic conditions.

Middle left and right: MDU team helped Ban Klang villagers cut up trees to straighten and widen their street. The work was completed after the team left, and some team members returned to inspect cleared and straightened street.

Lower right: Altar for ceremony to be conducted by MDU team leader at village assembly. The Thai flag, image of Buddha, and picture of Thai King and Queen symbolize country, religion, and royalty, the three sources of Thai national unity. Lee W. Huff photos, March 1963.

Lower left: MDU clinic, under an improvised shelter, is a popular attraction.

NORTHEAST THAILAND MDU PROGRAM, CONT.

Upper left and right: Water used to be drawn by hand from a shallow well in Kut Rua Kham. A well drilling crew was brought in by the MDU team to improve the well.

Middle left: Newly installed hand pump in Kut Rua Kham.

Lower right: The MDU team has set up its motion picture screen in the grounds of a temple.

Lower left: Team leader speaks with school children who will be given school uniforms, notebooks, and pencils. Lee W. Huff photos, March 1963.

Upper left: Fifty-year old Yao village in the mid-level hills, three miles west of Wan Yang. Yao residents stand in front of typical house.

Center: Main street of Wan Yang, a Yunnanese "Haw" refugee village on the lower margin of the hills, southwest of Fang.

Lower left: The closest Northern Thai village lies in the valley about four miles east of Wan Yang.

Lower right: Wan Yang residents have rented fields belonging to Thais, and have hired the owners as laborers to grow winter crops (garlic). Wan Yang lies at the foot of the hills in center of picture. F. W. Mote photos, January 1965.

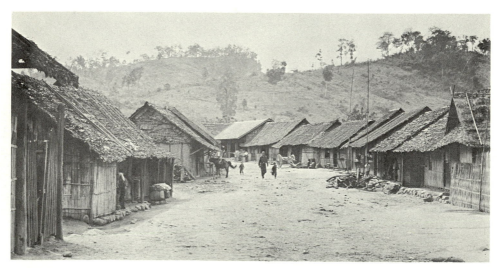

YUNNANESE REFUGEE ("HAW") SETTLEMENT IN NORTHERN THAILAND

Upper: Students assemble at 9:30 for flag-raising at the Border Patrol school in Ban Yang, where policemen-teachers instruct in Thai. Chinese instructors use the same school for classes beginning at 8:00.

Middle: The Chinese temple lies on the highest land in Wan Yang. The Yao headman from a neighboring village has contributed to its construction, and has erected a spirit tablet alongside three Chinese tablets within. Religion here is a Taoist-Buddhist Chinese folk religion from which the Yao religion has been derived. There is also a mosque in this village.

Lower: Wan Yang village, looking northeast toward Thai-settled lowlands. Bamboo pipe carries irrigation water for gardens, and supplies kitchens and bath houses. Meat is drying on rack in center of picture. F. W. Mote photos, January 1965.

Upper left: Meo headman of village near Doi Suthep, Chiengmai Province. Silver necklace and gold teeth indicate his wealth. August 1963.

Middle left: Meo village near Meto, Amphur Hot, Chiengmai Province, surrounded by corn fields in which opium has also been planted. September 1963.

Middle right: Meo village in Thailand, ca. 1900. From *Surveying and Exploring in Siam*, by James McCarthy. London, John Murray, 1900, p. 183.

Lower left: Meo woman and child in village near Meto, September 1963.

Lower right: Meo headman of village near Meto wears Thai style clothes and a Meo sash; on his right his son wears Meo clothing, his other son is dressed in Chinese fashion. September 1963. P. Kunstadter photos except as noted.

KAREN MOUNTAIN-LOWLAND DIFFERENCES, THAILAND

Upper left: Ban Huaj Pyng, a Skaw Karen mountain village. May 1964.

Upper right: Summoning souls to Skaw Karen mountain home, Ban Hak Maj. March 1964.

Middle left: Mountain Skaw Karen woman. March 1964.

Middle right: Pwo Karen house in valley near Thai town of Wang Lung, Amphur Hot, Chiengmai Province. August 1963.

Lower right: Karen women (second, third, and fourth from right) participate in cremation ceremony for Thai Buddhist abbot of Maesariang temple. January 1964. P. Kunstadter photos.

LUA^ꞌ MOUNTAIN-LOWLAND DIFFERENCES,
THAILAND

Upper left: Pa Pae, a traditional mountain village. Border Patrol school is at left. June 1964

Upper right: Men of Pa Pae help to repair Border Patrol school. Writing on blackboard is in Thai and phonetic Lua^ꞌ script. April 1964.

Middle left: A Chinese store-keeper has erected a flag beside a new bridge in Kawng Loi, a Thai-ized Lua^ꞌ mountain village. September 1963.

Middle right: Ban Tun's headman wears his badge of office. He receives a small monthly salary for keeping village records and reporting to the district officer in Amphur Hot. September 1963.

Lower right: Thai-style house and rice barn in Thai-ized Lua^ꞌ valley town of Ban Hua Lin. November 1963. P. Kunstadter photos.

LUAᵖ MOUNTAIN-LOWLAND DIFFERENCES, CONT.

Above: Ban Tun, a traditional mountain village. Woman and girl carry firewood past porch on which rice is spread to dry. Cotton yarn hangs from another porch on which firewood is drying. September 1963.

Middle right: Recent Luaᵖ migrant to Ban Phaeᵖ, just outside of Maesariang, has built his house of materials he could gather from the jungle. September 1963.

Lower left: Recent Luaᵖ migrant to valley wears Thai clothing and weaves Karen-style carrying bag which finds a readier market in Maesariang than do Luaᵖ bags. Ban Phaeᵖ, September 1963.

Lower right: Relatively prosperous Luaᵖ in Ban Ton Phrao, near Maesariang, has wooden house in traditional Luaᵖ style. January 1964. P. Kunstadter photos.

LUAꞱ UPLAND AGRICULTURE, THAILAND

Upper left: Clearing the upland fields with a machete after about nine years of fallow. February 1964.

Upper center: Larger trees are not felled, but their branches are lopped so sun will reach the crops. February 1964.

Upper right: Girls and women help in the clearing. February 1964.

Middle right: Firebreak is made to prevent the fire from burning out of control. Karen fields adjoin those of the LuaꞱ here, and Karens (background) help in the work. March 1964.

Lower left: Older women summon the ancestors to the edge of Pa Pae to make an offering to them before the fields are burned. Older men sacrifice a pig or buffalo on the trail leading to the fields to assure a successful fire. March 1964.

Lower right: Young men carry torches along the bottom of fields to ignite them. Fields near Pa Pae, late March 1964. P. Kunstadter photos.

LUAᵖ UPLAND AGRICULTURE, CONT.

Upper left: While fields still smolder, Luaᵖ man plants woven bamboo *talia* to tell the forest spirits that the field belongs to him.

Upper right: Root crops are planted before any further clearing and burning is done.

Middle right: Young men use long iron-tipped digging sticks to make holes for the rice seed.

Lower left: Girls and women follow and throw seed into the holes.

Lower right: A buffalo is sacrificed to help the rice midway through the growing season.

Lowest right: Rice growing in upland field near Luaᵖ village of Ban Dong, September 1963. Other pictures near Pa Pae, March-June 1964. P. Kunstadter photos.

Upper left: Bed is prepared carefully for rice seedlings which will later be transplanted.

Middle left: Seed is broadcast sown in bed.

Lower left: Hired Karen laborer leads buffalo while LuaꝬ field-owner plows.

Middle right: Hoeing the terraces before harrowing.

Lower right: The final harrowing. Pa Pae, late May to early July, 1964. P. **Kunstadter** photos.

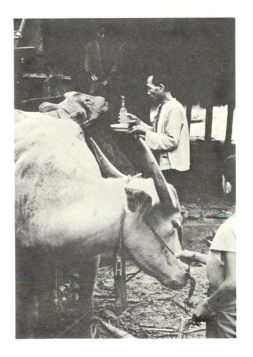

LUAᵖ IRRIGATED AGRICULTURE, CONT.

Upper left: Libation of rice liquor is poured on sacrifice to ancestor spirits of field owner, of collateral relatives, and of the previous owners of the field. Similar ceremony is held at each upland field prior to planting.

Upper right: Transplanting the fields.

Middle left: Young children help by twisting tops off rice seedlings before they are transplanted.

Middle right: After the transplanting is completed, a ceremony is held to prevent the buffaloes from losing their souls. If this ceremony were not held, the buffaloes would weaken and die after the strenuous work of plowing and harrowing. Pa Pae, July 1964.

Lower right: Irrigated fields near Luaᵖ village of Ban Tun, September 1963. P. Kunstadter photos.

Upper left: Water is carried from spring or stream and stored in bamboo tubes. March 1964.

Middle and lower left: Rice is milled daily in a foot-powered mill. The bran and chaff are fed to pigs and chickens. Chickens and pigs are fed and penned under the house every night. Water buffaloes are turned out to graze, and may be tied up at night or left out in the fields. March 1964.

Middle right: Almost every house in Pa Pae has a simple still to make the rice liquor which is required for every social and ritual occasion. July 1964.

Lower right: Fish traps are baited with insects and placed in irrigation ditches. June 1964. P. Kunstadter photos.

Upper left and right, middle right: Fish supplement the diet, and fishing is an enjoyable group activity on a hot day. March 1964.

Lower left and right: Children quickly learn adult roles—splitting firewood and tending younger children. Pa Pae, December 1964. P. Kunstadter photos.

LUAꞌ RITUAL, THAILAND

Upper left: Maidens preparing banana leaves for altar. Ceremony held in Pa Pae during March to honor house spirits.

Middle left: The completed altar. Note Thai King's picture, supplied by Border Patrol, in place of honor to right of altar.

Lower left: Village priest (*lam*) summons spirits to partake in sacrificial meal. Pig lies trussed to his left.

Middle right: Pig is killed with a sharpened stake.

Lower right: Pig has been cooked and small pieces of pork are placed in baskets as offerings. P. Kunstadter photos.

Upper left: Older men of Pa Pae gather to drink, joke, and eat a portion of the sacrificial meal. Man at extreme left is village headman. Girls in background are visitors from nearby Lua^ɂ village of La^ɂup. March 1964.

LUA^ɂ RITUAL AND LOWLAND CONTACTS

Middle left: Lowland-dwelling relatives come to honor their elders at Pa Pae with a headwashing ceremony, and receive a blessing in return. March 1964.

Lower left: Headwashing is also a part of weddings. Lua^ɂ man washes Thai Border Patrol schoolteacher's wife's hand as a sign of respect. Later she dressed in Lua^ɂ clothes and was properly doused. Pa Pae December 1964.

Middle right: Wedding ceremony at Pa Pae culminates as wrists of bride and groom are bound to prevent soul loss and illness. Thais have similar headwashing and wristbinding rituals. December 1964.

Lower right: On Sunday morning Christians play gospel records on phonograph furnished by missionaries, while animistic ritual takes place elsewhere in Pa Pae. On left is the only Karen married into Pa Pae. March 1964. P. Kunstadter photos.

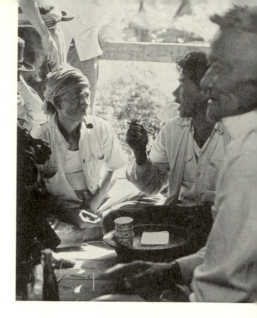

LUAꞋ RITUAL AND LOWLAND CONTACTS, CONT.

Upper left: Lowland relatives, in Thai dress, help guests return to mountains by carrying baskets laden with market goods part way up the trail. Ban Ton Phrao, January 1964.

Upper right: Village expenses are totalled annually and divided evenly among all households. Pa Pae's assistant headman records, while headman (right) supervises. Negotiations are eased with a round of drinks. Taxes owed the government are paid separately. December 1964.

LUAꞋ-KAREN TRADE, THAILAND

Middle right: Two LuaꞋ women of Pa Pae examine a Karen trader's beads. March 1964.

Middle left: Karen trader ladles kerosene which he has carried up from Maesariang into his LuaꞋ customer's bottle. The other kerosene tin contains dried fish, another popular item. LuaꞋ man on right records the transactions and makes change—he received a small commission for allowing the porch of his Pa Pae home to be used as a temporary store. Large cylindrical basket holds household's rice. January 1965.

Lower left: Karen men return an elephant load of rice they have borrowed from Pa Pae householder. January 1965.

Upper right: LuaꞍ man (in dark shirt) has just sold Karen man a piece of paddy land, and seals the bargain with a drink. No written records were kept of the transaction, but all the witnesses had a drink so they would remember the occasion. Pa Pae, May 1964.

TRIBAL TRADE AND MARKETING IN THAILAND

Upper left: Young LuaꞍ man leaves Pa Pae early in the morning, leading a pig to the Maesariang market. January 1965.

Middle left: LuaꞍ man and wife from LaꞍup stop to chat in Pa Pae on their way to sell grass mats in Maesariang. They dress in Thai style for their trip to market. February 1964.

Lower left: LuaꞍ woman, in short striped skirt, buys tobacco in the Maesariang market. March 1964.

Lower right: LuaꞍ man has invested in fermented tea leaves (*miang*) in Maesariang, and peddles the popular mild stimulant to steady customers in Pa Pae on his way home to LaꞍup. He makes this trip every week or so during the dry season. May 1964.

MINORITIES IN NORTH VIETNAM

Upper left: Residents of a newly liberated Tai village take a reading course from a soldier of the Popular Army. From *Lutte contre l'analphabétisme au Viet Nam*. Hanois, Editions en Langues Etrangères, 1959, following p. 8.

Upper right: Class for the formation of montagnard cadres is held in a pagoda. The signboards read: "Death to the aggressor!" and "Death to ignorance!" *Ibid.*

Lower left: Meo tribesmen learn literacy on their bamboo terrace. *Ibid.*, following p. 40.

Lower right: "Women of national minorities voting for the Second legislature of the National Assembly." *The Democratic Republic of Vietnam.* Hanoi, Foreign Languages Publishing House, 1960, following p. 48.

period; and the breakup of colonial units and the reformulation of states supposedly based on ancient principalities or kingdoms (French Indochina).

These nations all have traditions of sacred kingdoms (Heine-Geldern 1956), which have met different fates in the colonial period and its aftermath. Royalty has been retained in Cambodia, Laos, Malaysia, and Thailand, but only in Laos and Cambodia does royalty play a major role in government. Postwar leaders have usually been secular, often military, men, frequently with charismatic qualities. Political power is concentrated in the capital cities.

Prior to the colonial period boundaries between the states, and probably even the concept of precisely delimited territories, did not exist. As we have seen, the boundary or frontier areas were occupied by people who were *not* an integral part of the society of the central government, though they may have been involved as tributaries, as raiders, or sometimes as furnishers of forest products. Not surprisingly, when the borders were drawn, they were not constructed with reference to ethnic distributions. Rather, they were based on questions of administrative convenience and balance between colonial powers. Thus many tribal groups are not confined to a single nation (see e.g. Leach 1960).

The regularization of relationships between these frontier or remote area groups and the central governments often took place for the first time under the colonial regimes, and even then many areas in the hills of French Indochina, the Wa States of Burma, or the interior of Borneo were not effectively controlled. Only recently, with the advent of modern transportation and communication, has control been possible, and only with military emergencies has it been thought to be necessary. This has meant restrictions on patterns of movement for the hill and border populations, irrespective of traditional cultural, linguistic, economic, and social connections.

Economies. The economies of Southeast Asian nations are all largely agricultural, with great dependence on irrigated rice. In "normal" years the area has been agriculturally self-sufficient, and, of the nations we have considered, only Malaysia must import rice. The region has plentiful, but as yet underexploited,

[19]

natural resources. Most of the industry in the area is extractive, with emphasis on the production of such commodities as oil, tin, teak, and rubber, which are usually only slightly processed before export. The population densities for the countries as a whole are relatively low for Asia, but with extreme concentration in the major cities (Rangoon, Bangkok, Singapore, Saigon, and Hanoi). Most of the people are subsistence agriculturalists.

Problems of land tenancy seem highly correlated with the intensity of colonialism (very little absentee ownership in Thailand, which was never colonized; considerable problems in Vietnam and Lower Burma; and in general, few problems of absentee ownership in the more remote regions).

Economic power is concentrated in the hands of relatively few people and is usually localized in the country's major city. The concentration of economic power and the development of industries, along with the concentration of population in the capital cities, have accelerated since the Second World War. Thus, in these countries in general, although some modern manufactured goods are penetrating into the remote regions, economic modernization is taking place primarily in the capital cities, and the economic differences between the central regions and the remote regions are increasing.

Minority Populations and Population Statistics. The proportions of minority and tribal populations vary considerably, from countries like Burma, Laos, and Malaysia with very high proportions to Thailand and Cambodia with quite low proportions. Population figures with adequate breakdowns showing minority and tribal groupings are rarely available for Southeast Asia—the Malaysian censuses represent the only exception. This lack has several causes: political conditions within the country may preclude the taking of a census (there has been no fully reported census in Burma since 1931); tribal and minority people live in remote regions (nomadic hill tribes were not counted in Thailand's census in 1960); and ethnic classifications may be manipulated for political purposes (usually to show greater homogeneity than actually exists in the country, especially if the official attitude is that minorities do not exist). Often this is more than a "head-in-the-sand" reaction and may represent a sincere attempt to build national solidarity by deemphasizing

[20]

ethnic differences. Nonetheless, the absence of accurate census materials means that the extent of the minorities is unknown and that rational planning for them cannot take place. It also means that relatively little reliance should be placed on the population figures which have been reproduced in this book, although they are the best we have.

Religions. Malaysia is predominantly Muslim (though there are substantial Chinese and indigenous minorities, especially on Borneo, which are not Muslim); Burma, Thailand, Laos, and Cambodia are predominantly Buddhist. Vietnam, which has a large number of nominal Buddhists, has a large Catholic minority, and also has many adherents to such sects as the Hoa Hao and Cao Dai. The predominant pattern of religion there defies easy classification and involves considerable ancestor worship and other beliefs drawn from a variety of sources. Hill tribes in all the countries are generally animistic, but Christian missionaries have had considerable success among them, especially in Burma and recently in Borneo. Rural minorities generally belong to one of the "Great Tradition" religions (Buddhism or Islam). Religious differences have formed the basis for factionalism, except in Cambodia, Laos, and Thailand. The Buddhist, Christian, and Muslim bureaucracies, like the political ones, are concentrated in the capital cities, and one or the other of them is more or less officially identified with the political structure of the governments in Thailand, Laos, Cambodia, and Malaysia. In both Burma and South Vietnam, political problems among the minorities have followed when the government threatened to become too closely identified with a particular religion.

In recent years central governments have paid more attention to the potential political role of religion as a device for strengthening (or weakening) national unity. Thus in Laos the Ministry of Religious Affairs conceives of its role as one of controlling the political activities of monks and, specifically, combating Communism among them (see e.g. Halpern 1964:143–146). In Thailand, as an experiment, monks have been sent to hill tribe villages with official approval, adding a religious element to attempts to bring tribesmen into the life of the nation. Proseletyzing missionary activity as an arm of the government has, of course, been much more characteristic of Muslim and Christian areas and during the colonial period played an important role in some colonial policies. Both Muslims and Christians have tended toward a much less tolerant view of religious syncretism than has Buddhism, and the possibilities of religious *integration* of the predominantly animistic hill tribes are probably greater in the Buddhist countries than in Islamic Malaysia.

Relatively little has been said in this volume about the effects of missionaries. One very important aspect of missionary activity, especially the action of foreign missionaries, has been in immensely widening the horizons of people in remote areas through the introduction of literacy and through the missionaries' very presence as representatives of a completely different and obviously advanced material culture. The effects of this are often debated as a matter of national policy. Thus it is quite significant, as Maran has pointed out in the case of the Kachin in Burma, that the Christian Kachin have been among the *strongest* supporters of the central government.[10]

Language. Linguistic variability is very great in most of the countries. Where census figures show extreme uniformity (as in Thailand, where 97 percent are reported to be able to speak Thai), the extent of dialect differentiation has not been revealed. Brown, for example, lists seventy-nine different Thai dialects spoken in Thailand (1965). Governments are only beginning to work out deliberate language policies and to consider the effects of various alternatives. In the former colonies most secular education was carried out in the colonial power's language (English in Burma and Malaysia, French in Indochina). Thus the minority people, in order to become educated, have had to face the burden of trilingualism.[11] With independence a single dialect of the dominant population has been standardized, and the assumption has been that all official business and all public education would

[10] This contrasts with the activities of some missionaries who apparently joined actively in the Karen rebellion (see Cady 1958:591); this led to the charges that foreign missionaries were the cause of tribal rebellions (Cady 1958:596). Cady points out, however, that both Christian and non-Christian elements took part in the rebellion and that missionaries were in no position to control them.

[11] The degree of multilingualism and the ability of different groups to be multilingual are quite varied. Dominant national groups are rarely multilingual; some minority and tribal groups display great talent in this regard. Among the Luaᵖ, for example, most men know Luaᵖ, Karen, and Northern Thai, and

be carried out in that language, although the colonial language might be retained, perhaps temporarily, as the language of higher education and contact with the international community.

Outside of China (see Diao's paper)[12] and North Vietnam, little attention has been devoted to the possibilities of use of native languages as tools for the integration of minority populations. In Thailand, for example, Central Thai is assumed to be the official language for all purposes, and its use in all radio broadcasting was considered to be beneficial for building a Thai nation—in spite of the fact that minority peoples at whom the broadcasts are directed may not understand the Central dialect. There is now some indication that this attitude is changing and that Central Thai may eventually be taught as a "second language" to ease problems of non-Thai-speaking students in the primary schools (Smalley 1965).

Government Policies toward Minorities. The governments of Southeast Asia have recognized the diversity of their respective populations in different degrees. In Laos the problem has been largely ignored—theoretically, everyone born in Laos is a citizen, and legal distinctions are not made according to differences in ethnic group (see Osborn's paper); nevertheless, there is considerable informal discrimination. Some tribal people in Laos (the

---

some know Shan, Burmese, and Central Thai; their Karen neighbors are generally monolingual. See Smalley (1964, 1965) for some of the linguistic reasons for varying degrees of difficulty in learning second languages.

China's attempts to integrate all of the minorities within its boundaries is apparently also reflected in the taxonomy of minority nationalities and languages. Scholars for many years have recognized the existence of a Tai group of languages and the Tai-speaking peoples and have debated, inconclusively, the relation or non-relation of Tai to the Chinese languages. The Chinese census of 1953 distinguished for the first time a large group of people in southern China, the Chuang, who speak a language related to Tai. The present Chinese classification of languages and peoples, as reported by Bruk (1959:18–19, 25–27), subsumes Chuang under the Chinese-Tibetan family and makes the Tai languages a part of the Chuang-Tai sub-group of the Chuang Tung group. Thus even scientific taxonomies are not immune to political considerations: all Tai speakers (including those outside of China) by the stroke of a pen have become a minor group of a sub-group of a Chinese minority.

[12] See also Lin (1961:27) and Ma (1962) for examples of the Chinese policy, which has involved extensive research, selection of strategic dialects as standard, development of phonetic scripts, publication of primers, newspapers, and the works of Mao, and teaching of the national minority languages, which can then be used for political indoctrination.

so-called Kha) play important ritual functions in state ceremonies where their original claims to the land and their defeat at the hands of the Lao are symbolized (Archaimbault 1964). In Cambodia and South Vietnam the problem has been officially denied existence.[13] In Thailand, until recently, the problem has also been ignored, and at present the policy of the government toward tribes and minorities has not been clearly stated. On the other hand, the former British colonies (Burma, Malaysia) have made careful attempts to give at least formal balance to the various large minority or tribal groups.[14] Burma, for example, did this by recognizing within the Union of Burma such administrative units as the Shan, Karen, and Kachin states and giving

[13] According to Prince Sihanouk (in an interview with correspondents following the Congress of Indochinese Peoples, Phnom Penh, March 1965), who was speaking of the French, Vietnamese, and Chinese populations in Cambodia, "Cambodia is not their homeland, we do not have minorities, only foreigners" (*Réalités Cambodgiennes*, March 19, 1965). In spite of this, the Cambodians clearly recognize the international implications of minority problems. They protest the treatment of the Cambodian minority in Thailand, and, in the same interview mentioned above, Sihanouk stated that the conversations held in Peking in December 1964 between the representatives of Cambodia, North Vietnam, and South Vietnam's National Liberation Front had failed, not over settlement of border questions, but only because the guarantees requested by Cambodia for Khmer minorities in Cochin China were not granted (see also Sihanouk's statements on the unwillingness of the Vietnamese minority in Cambodia to be assimilated, in *Kambuja* 4[19], July 15, 1965).

Cambodia has also specifically recognized the strategic importance of tribal minorities in relation to the war in Vietnam, as the following quotation indicates:

. . . in 1959, Cambodia complained that the Viet Minh were using a portion of northeastern Cambodia to infiltrate into South Vietnam. To forestall further incursions by the Viet Minh, Cambodia carved two new provinces, Ratanakkiri and Mondulkiri from the extreme eastern parts of Stung Treng and Kratié, and set up military administrations there. To effect better control of the nomadic *montagnards* who live in the area and who are potential targets of subversive propaganda the government launched a program to move them away from border areas and to settle them in permanent villages (Smith 1965:169–170).

For a discussion of South Vietnamese policy with regard to minorities see Buttinger (1961), Joiner (1965), and the papers in the Vietnam section of this book.

[14] The aborigines in Malaya consist of only a small number of relatively primitive and politically unsophisticated people, who are protected by the government and are not specially represented in the government. By contrast, a careful balance was attempted for the Chinese "minority" and the Malays in setting up the Federation of Malaysia. Many of the tribal and minority people of the Borneo states (Sabah and Sarawak) were quite sophisticated politically and took their places as normal representatives of their states (see Harrisson's paper). But the attempt at political balance did not work in the case of the predominantly Chinese state of Singapore, which withdrew from Malaysia in August 1965.

some of them, at least theoretically, the right to secede from the Union. This policy has not proved very successful as a means of nation-building in Burma, as the people of the minority states have often wanted more independence than the Union has given them, and it has been difficult to hold the Union together. Thus there have been ethnically based rebellions, for example by the Shan and Karen, ever since the Union was formed (cf. Cady 1958:592 *et seq.*).

China, North Vietnam, and the National Liberation Front of South Vietnam[15] all have similar official policies with respect to minorities and tribes—the similarities are quite apparent when the constitutions of the former two are read together with the proclamation of the latter. They all promise to set up autonomous zones in areas where minorities are concentrated, which, although they are conceived of as integral parts of the nation, are supposed to be internally self-governing. Efforts are supposed to be made to ensure representation from them to the central governing bodies, and internally they are supposed to have the freedom to cultivate their own languages and cultures.

To date there have been relatively few attempts on the part of minority or tribal people either to form pan-tribal independence movements or to call upon their ethnic brothers to unite across national boundaries. The closest thing to a pan-tribal movement seems to be the formation of the Front for the Relief of the Oppressed Races (FULRO), apparently with support from Prince Sihanouk, in Cambodia. The attempt here is to call on the hill tribes of South Vietnam to join with those of northern Cambodia. The National Liberation Front of South Vietnam also has a "High Plateau Autonomy Movement Committee" which apparently aims to set up a minority autonomous zone in the South Vietnam Highlands (see "Introduction: Vietnam" for fur-

---

[15] The program of the Pathet Lao is an interesting exception to this pattern among the Communist political structures. Possibly because they recognize the demographic realities (the population of Laos is at least one-half tribal or minority), the Pathet Lao have not advocated minority autonomous zones. They fully recognize the need to cultivate the favor of the tribal and minority people by giving them economic development and political positions within the central political structure, but they denounce what they say are U.S. efforts to set up a separate Meo political unit in Laos, thus separating the Meo from the Lao, among whom they have lived for many generations (Radio Pathet Lao, July 26, 1965).

ther details). The Karen and Shan rebels in Burma have had
little success in appealing to their relatives across the border
in Thailand to aid them in their attempts to set up an independent state.

In spite of numerous attempts within Burma such as the
United Hill People's Congress (Cady 1958:544; Ying 1965:50)
and the consortium of which Lehman writes (in this volume),
the minority peoples have never succeeded in forming a united
front vis-à-vis the central government. The government has always been able to call on one or more of the minorities in combating the others; for example, the Chins were decisive in defeat-
ing the Karen rebels in their drive toward Rangoon in 1949
(Cady 1958:593).

Numerous ethnic-based politico-military groups such as the
Karen National Defense Organization, the Karen National Union,
and the Mon National Defense Organization have been formed,
but these too have been unable to create and maintain sufficient
unity within the groups they represent to maintain concerted
action against the government: the government has been able
to attract some leaders from the dissident factions within the
rebelling groups. Thus a semblance of national unity has been
preserved in spite of continuous small-scale rebellions.

One recurring feature of the revolts of such people is their
desire to gain independent contact with the outside world. Thus,
for example, the tribesmen rebelling against the South
Vietnamese government demanded the right to direct negotiations with Americans, as did Karen rebels in Burma and some
of the Naga rebels in Assam. Unfortunately, the papers in this
volume do not go into this question at any length—but it seems
clear that one of the things involved in the "tribal revolts" is
the fact that these people are not only concerned about preserving their cultural identity, but at the same time, paradoxically,
anxious to become modernized. Frequently they have become
aware of the outside modern world, not as a result of contacts
with members of the dominant majority of their nation, but by
contact with European or American missionaries or soldiers.

Centralization of Power. Regardless of the form of the central
government as specified by its constitution, the minorities and

tribes generally have not participated in the central governments in proportion to their population or, where they are only small groups, in proportion to the territory which they occupy (North Vietnam, Malaysia, and possibly Burma may be exceptions to this generalization). The governments in question are all quite highly centralized and have depended (often out of necessity resulting from external or internal threats) very extensively on the military and police for many of the normally civil tasks of government (see e.g. Wilson [1962] for a description of the political structure of Thailand and Thomas [1962] for a discussion of problems of social change in this highly centralized system). One of the most common features characterizing the central governments which emerges from the papers in this book is the degree of centralization of politico-military power, centralization of economy, of economic and bureaucratic opportunity, of government services, educational institutions, industry, transportation, decision-making, and in most instances a high degree of centralization of population in the area immediately adjacent to the capital city (development of the "primate city") (Hoselitz 1957). The problems of minorities and tribes in these countries are, of course, one of the symptoms of this overcentralization.

The effects of overcentralization of government are many, and they are reflected at many different levels. Concentration of power in a few urban areas is correlated with the development of increasing social distance between urban and rural populations. One result is that the central governments are out of touch with the minorities and tribes—communication is almost exclusively directed from the top to the bottom of official channels; there is very little chance for communication from the people served by the bureaucracy to the actual decision-makers. Central governments in this area usually lack knowledge of conditions in the more remote areas, and they lack the means of getting that information routinely through the normal governmental channels. We shall have more to say on this point shortly. Overcentralization also tends toward arbitrary uniformity in matters of language (see Moerman's paper in this regard) and at least the threat of uniformity in religion—which has caused unrest among tribal and minority groups in Burma (see

Lehman and Maran in this volume) and in Malaysian Borneo.[16]
There has also been a seemingly needless tendency to make legal
systems conform to the standards of some of the central
governments.[17]

The papers in this volume give some evidence of the sorts
of concessions which minority and tribal people feel are important, the disregard for which may lead to problems of political
disintegration; but we do not yet seem to have reached the point
where we can tell what sorts of conditions must be met in producing cultural uniformity or, if pluralism is accepted, agreement
on a minimum set of desired goals in order to have cohesion
in a nation. It does seem clear, however, from the examples given,
that absolute agreement on all matters is not a necessary condition for national cohesion and that attempts to induce absolute
conformity are liable to cause much more trouble than they are
worth.

We should point out here that only the Chinese and Vietnamese Communists have explicitly recognized this need for making
concessions in the constitutional structure of their governments.
The other governments have been vague, perhaps deliberately
so or perhaps because they have not been conscious of the problems of ethnic diversity. Thus in Laos, for example, the assumption is that everyone is Laotian, an assumption which, depending
on its implementation in policy and practice, might actually be
a basis for national integration. But without some means of implementation, given the existing informal patterns of prejudice
and discrimination against minorities, the assumption will prove
to be as ineffective as the declaration that "all men are created
equal." The nations of Southeast Asia can no longer afford to

[16] This certainly has been one of the underlying reasons for political problems
in South Vietnam, although it is not mentioned specifically in the papers of
O'Donnell and Hickey.

[17] See Hickey's paper with regard to customary law among the hill tribes
of Vietnam, and Furnivall (1948:131 ff.) regarding the application by the British
of Indian law in Burma at a time when Burma was administered as a part
of India.

The Chinese Communists paint an idyllic picture of their national minorities
conserving their own cultures (see Diao's paper), but they also go to pains
to suppress "backward customs" which are contrary to Communist doctrine in
such things as religion and marriage practices (see *China News Analysis* 1965,
563:6), as well as such obvious targets as feudalism.

ignore the question of their tribes and minorities, since it is now clear that the Chinese Communists are quite intent upon exploiting ethnic differences for their own ends.

THE NATURE OF RELATIONSHIPS BETWEEN
CENTRAL GOVERNMENTS, TRIBES, AND MINORITIES

Changing Conditions. The pattern of relationships between tribes, minorities, and central governments has changed rapidly over the past twenty years in response to changed conditions of the politics of the region and the technology of transportation and communication. Today, whether they want to or not, the central governments have found that they must pay attention to the tribes and minorities, especially those located on their borders. Gone also are the times when the tribal groups, discontented with their lot under a particular government, could easily shift countries by crossing over an undefined or uncontrolled border without becoming a matter of concern to their new hosts. The tribes have become important because it is they who have intimate knowledge of the hill and border regions which have become strategically important[18] and also because their fellow tribesmen are distributed on both sides of the borders. This strategic importance has led some governments to offer concessions and services to these people for the first time, in an attempt to win their loyalty. Whereas in the past the governments were content to ignore the tribesmen, provided they were peaceful and paid their taxes occasionally, today the governments are attempting to get a commitment of loyalty from the tribesmen, often trying to promote loyalty to abstract ideals and remote personages.

Historical Perspective—Tribal Feudalism. A look at some of the historical background of the relationships may be instructive. The vast majority of the tribesmen are swidden cultivators of rice and upland crops. Because of the need for large amounts

---

[18] The strategic use of tribal people because of their intimate knowledge of trails in border and jungle areas is nothing new. In 1614 Burmese troops who were marching from Moulmein to Lamphun and Chiengmai exploited the dissatisfaction of the Lawa (Lua?) with the Thai. The Lawa cleared the trails which the Thais had blocked, and scouted for the Burmese invaders (Seidenfaden 1923:101).

of land, swidden cultivation in upland areas has in general limited the concentration of population and the permanence of settlements. Villages have ranged in size from perhaps twenty people up to a thousand or more—the larger villages often were
brought, and held, together by common needs for defense. Prior
to the extension of colonial rule and pacification or, in Thailand,
prior to control of the upcountry principalities by the central
government, tribesmen were often allied into multi-village
groups, sometimes with chiefs having authority over a number
of villages. Such chiefs, or in other cases village headmen, often
owed allegiance in a loose-knit sort of feudalism to higher-level
chiefs, princes, or sultans, who were often representatives of
different ethnic groups in other ecological zones (e.g. the sultans
of the Borneo coast, to whom the inland tribes paid homage,
or the Shan sawbwas [princes] to whom Kachin and Karen tribes
owed allegiance). Such leaders in turn might owe allegiance on
still higher levels to more distant leaders, as for example, in
the case of the Shans, to the King of Burma, or in some cases
the King of Siam, or the Chinese Emperor. As central authority
has grown, the middle levels have been cut out, and, theoretically, the tribesmen now owe allegiance directly to the central
government. Often this has in fact led to *decreased* contact with,
and control of, the tribal people.

It may be helpful at this point to introduce an example of
centralization of political power in northwest Thailand. About
150 years ago the Karen who were moving into this area recognized the Lua? as overlords of the land which they cultivated.
The Karen paid an annual rent of 10 percent of the rice crop to
the chief of the Lua? village whose land they used. The Lua?
in turn recognized the overlordship of the Prince of Chiengmai
or Lamphun and made annual trips to pay him tribute, in return
for which the Prince instructed the Lua? in proper conduct and
the proper care of their land. The Lua? could appeal to the
Prince for a reduction in tribute during years of poor harvest. In
his turn, the Prince journeyed to Bangkok to pay tribute to the
King of Siam, who confirmed the Prince's powers in the North.
With the extension of the central government's control, the
Karen and Lua? now pay taxes (if at all) directly to the agents
of the central government, and the role of the Prince of Chieng-

mai has been reduced to a strictly ceremonial one. The old bonds of allegiance, which were once on a rather personal, or at least face-to-face, basis, have now been cut, often without adequate substitution. In the place of the Prince, who in seasons of poor harvest could magnanimously reduce the amount of tribute to be paid, there is now a low-level bureaucrat whose superiors are unaware of, and unresponsive to, local conditions. This example should not be interpreted as an appeal for a return to feudalism. Rather, its purpose is to point out some features of feudalism as a system of administration which have not yet been adequately replaced by modern centralized bureaucracy.

The Maintenance of Cultural Boundaries. Although cultural distinctions have become blurred and have even vanished in some areas as previously distinct groups became absorbed in larger units (for example some of the Lua? and Thai-Yawng groups around Chiengmai have become virtually indistinguishable from Northern Thai communities), other groups have strengthened their means of preserving a distinctive identity. There are many examples of boundary-maintaining mechanisms in the papers which follow. Perhaps none is as clear and as self-conscious as that of the Yao, described by Kandre. The Yao themselves make a clear distinction between three categories of behavior: first, the essential features of Yao culture, especially those having to do with religion; second, items of individual variation, often things like the regulation of behavior between individuals, such as the amount of bride-price to be paid; and third, items pertaining to relations with the dominant government in the area within which the Yao are living. By making this sort of distinction while living in China, Vietnam, Laos, or Thailand, the Yao feel that they are able to preserve their essential "Yao-ness" in spite of the necessity to conform to quite different legal conditions.

Other groups, though they have not expressed the idea as clearly as the Yao, have also preserved their identity, sometimes, as among the hill tribes, assisted by their location, but always reinforced by differences somewhere in their symbolic systems—their language, religion, and value structures. Maran's paper contains an attempt to formulate a general theory of minority-majority relationships, in which it is clear that a *symbolic* opposition between the two lies at the heart of the matter.

In all of the examples in this book the importance of symbolic differences shows up. Moerman discusses the symbolic importance of customs of eating, dressing, and speaking in defining the relationships between members of the Thai-Lue minority and Central Thai government officials (see also Moerman 1965). Lehman and Maran discuss the reaction in Burma to the threatened interference with the minorities' religious systems through passage of a national religion law. The Chinese and Vietnamese Communists have recognized the importance of native language in developing national integration through minority autonomous zones and regions. The minorities are supposed to be free to cultivate their own languages and literatures within these zones.

Recognition of this attachment to symbolic values is the key to understanding what otherwise appears to be contradictory or paradoxical: the statement that minority or tribal people want nothing more than to be left alone; and that they are eager to become part of the "civilized" world. The solution to this apparent contradiction is that the people want to be selective about the changes which are made, especially when the changes involve direct attacks on the symbolic aspects of their lives. Harrisson has indicated how eager for modern education some of the more isolated Borneo natives have been and how they desire to participate in the Malaysian government, but resist, as they have resisted for hundreds of years, attempts to convert them to Islam. Mote has shown how rapidly both hill tribesmen and rural Thais accept agricultural innovations introduced to them by the "Haw" (rural Yunnanese). We now have too much evidence to accept either the idea that these tribal and minority people are inherently conservative or that they are completely flexible. Quite evidently they base their actions neither on a completely overriding materialism nor on overwhelming renunciations of worldly considerations.

We can also consider the demographic permeability of the boundaries between groups. Two processes deserve particular attention here: intermarriage (or endogamy vs. exogamy of the groups concerned) and migration. The attitudes, or in some cases deliberate policies of the groups regarding intermarriage, may be quite different, and their effects are also quite varied. In some cases there is a clear relationship between village or ethnic endogamy and the maintenance of cultural boundaries. Some of the groups discussed in this book have very strong endogamous tendencies: the Lua? in the mountain villages of Northern Thailand are almost exclusively village-endogamous. This pattern of marriage tends to restrict interaction between villages and is apparently reflected in the rapid development of dialect differences, plus considerable cultural variation between villages. There is a very strong pattern that the customs of the household into which a person has married shall prevail, which tends to maintain even minor intra-village cultural variations (see Kunstadter 1965; 1966). The Karen in the same area are matrilocal. Although almost all marriages involve only Karen, the men quite frequently marry into villages other than their own. There are many minor cultural variations in such items as dress style (the weaving is done by women, who do not move at the time of marriage), but the Karen language apparently is not diversifying into distinct dialects very rapidly, as a result of the considerable inter-village contact. Maintenance of "Karen-ness" is thought by the Karen to be associated with their distinctive language and dress styles, as well as by marriage within the group.

But the conservation of cultural boundaries is not necessarily dependent on the mechanism of endogamy. In fact, some of the most vigorous and expanding cultural groups are able to recruit spouses from the outside and still maintain the identity of the group and its traditions. The Yao, as described in Kandre's paper, often make a deliberate policy of recruiting wives and adopting children from other groups, as do the Chinese—exemplified by Mote's paper on the "Haw." In both the Chinese and the Yao cases the assumptions are made that the in-marrying person will be integrated into the community as fully as possible and that the children will be full members of the community in which they are raised—they do not become "marginal men."

The patterns and effects of rules of exogamy and endogamy and the points at which these rules break down need further study as a part of future research on tribal and minority groups in modern nations. How, for example, are the distinctive patterns of the group's culture transmitted to the younger generation when a substantial portion of the mothers come from different cultures? This situation has been fairly common among the first generation of Chinese immigrants into Thailand and other areas when the initial migrants were too poor to bring their wives with them or were unable to have them sent from the mainland at a later time.

Migration is another important variable; for our present purposes, the important question is what becomes of the cultural identification of the migrants. Migration, or change in ecological setting, sometimes involves the maintenance of cultural boundaries, but sometimes it implies their breakdown. Leach (1954) has discussed the process wherein Kachin (who are Tibeto-Burman-speaking, upland, animistic, swidden agriculturalists with little supra-village political organization) become Shan (who are Tai-speaking, valley-dwelling, wet-rice-cultivating Buddhists, with a developed state system), and has indicated that in part the transformation is one of change in geographical location. A move into the valleys implies a change in the way of life, including not only the adoption of irrigated agriculture, but also the Shan language, Buddhism, literacy, and changed patterns of political structure. But change in cultural identification does not necessarily involve changes in ecological position. The example which comes to mind here is that of Lua? families who have "become Karen." In several cases known to the author, whole families (not just single men or women) moved out of Lua? villages and into Karen villages located in the same ecological zone with the same type of technology. In these cases, the migrants adopted Karen-style dress, habitually spoke Karen, abandoned Lua? spirits, and worshiped Karen ones. Their children have become fully Karen and have married Karens. The religious life of the Lua? is more exacting than that of the Karens and requires many more, and more expensive, ritual sacrifices, and this religio-economic factor was the motivation for the change. Religious conversion to Christianity, while retaining the other aspects of cultural identification, has been made for the same reasons (Kunstadter 1965:27–28).

That migration is not necessary for cultural conversion is also seen in the case in which whole Lua? villages in valley locations have become Thai without moving physically. By contrast, other groups, notably the Chinese, have vigorously maintained their culture in spite of hundreds of years and thousands of miles of separation from their mainland.

The examples given here indicate that we do not yet have an adequate general theory regarding the maintenance or breakdown of cultural boundaries. The Chinese case indicates that a number of factors may be involved, including a writing system, a self-perpetuating system for organization of education along traditional lines, and perhaps a traditional feeling of cultural superiority. The examples also show the inadequacy of theories, especially single-variable ones, involving such factors as geographic isolation vs. contact, and physical distinctiveness vs. racial identity.

Economic Factors. One very important factor determining the relationship between tribal and minority groups and the government is the nature of the tribal or minority economy—specifically, the difference between subsistence and cash cropping. This, of course, affects the relative affluence of the people and therefore their ability to participate in the material aspects of modernization. Most frequently, in the cases examined here, the source of wealth among the hill tribes has been opium, and this crop has colored the relations between tribal people and government officials in many ways. Since opium is both illegal and in great demand, the opportunities for profitable extortion are many. Such problems are much less common among the poorer tribes like the Karen and Lua? as compared with the rich Meo and Yao. Extortion is probably the wrong word, since in many cases the amounts collected seem to be fees (in proportion to ability to pay) for services rendered.

The opium-growing tribes and those who have grown rich on other bases (truck-gardening, pig-raising, tea-growing) clearly have wider world views as a result of their increased travel, more extensive trading contacts with the lowlands, and more material possessions, including radios. But in part the wider world view results from a definite cultural orientation to the recognized superiority of lowland cultures (e.g. among the Meo, Yao, and "Haw"). Affluence can also alter the patterns of relationship among the tribal and minority groups: the relatively rich Yao buy children from other groups (including lowland Thai), not as slaves, but in order to increase the productive capacity of their households (Kandre's paper). The Meo may hire Karens to work for them in the opium fields, using a small payment of opium as an incentive. The truck-gardening "Haw" have transformed themselves from hired laborers to employers of lowland Thais, not on the basis of profits from opium cultivation, but rather from intensive gardening, which they have found to be more profitable (Mote's paper).

The Changing Positions of Tribes and Minorities. We will have failed in our description of the tribal and minority groups if we have left the impression that they are static—they are not. Their material cultures, technologies, social organizations, and views of the world in which they live are changing, and the relationships among them, and between them and the central governments, are subject to constant reshuffling. The pattern of stratification in Southeast Asia is nowhere so rigid as it has been in India, where relations between groups are set by caste rules and where, except in Assam and other portions of eastern India, minority and tribal groups almost invariably enter the national society at the lowest social and economic position (cf. for example, Bailey 1960 and Burling's paper).

The pattern of relationship among the tribal groups in Thailand, for example, continues to change. The Karens were at one time economically subservient to the Lua?, who were lords of the land into which they moved, but today Karens hardly recognize the Lua? rights as landlords, and in fact have acquired much of the Lua? irrigated land (through money-lending) and much of the Lua? swidden area (through squatting) (Kunstadter's paper). This change in Lua?-Karen relations relates in large part to the change in Lua?-Thai relations and the breakdown of feudalism in Northern Thailand. Mote's paper gives us another example of change. The refugee Yunnanese ("Haw") rural population, who arrived in Thailand virtually penniless, in only ten years have been able to establish for themselves a place of influence among surrounding groups, including even rural Thais. The rapid rise of economic influence of urban Chinese immigrants has, of course, been very common in Southeast Asia. The strategic role that the Meo have played in the struggles

over Laos means that their position via-à-vis the central government there will be greatly altered (see Barney's paper and the
other papers in the Laos section of this book).

TRIBES, MINORITIES, AND NATION-BUILDING:
SOME THEORETICAL CONSIDERATIONS

Thus far we have discussed a number of characteristics of
tribal and minority peoples in the nations of Southeast Asia, but
we have not focused specifically on the problems of constructing
modern nations out of these diverse peoples. Groups which are
customarily referred to as tribes or minorities are implicitly labeled as marginal in the countries where they exist. They are
usually marginal economically, politically, culturally, and ecologically. As we have already indicated, there are a variety of reasons
why Southeast Asian nations should have a large number of such
marginal peoples within their national boundaries. Characteristically the boundaries of these nations were not drawn to coincide
with ethnic distributions; and these distributions are extremely
complex. We have indicated that the tribal and minority peoples
are neither isolated from, nor well integrated with, the nations
in which they find themselves, but we still need some theoretical
background before we can discuss the practical effects of programs directed at changing the positions of the tribes and
minorities.

Students of nation-building have frequently neglected
questions of the integration of minorities and tribes into the national entities they study. This seems particularly inappropriate
where there are sizable, politically active tribes and minorities.
For example, Pye, who has devoted considerable attention to
Southeast Asian nations, has written a book specifically on
Burma, on the problems of nation-building (Pye 1962). He discusses these questions in terms of personality formation and the
reaction of individuals to the colonial experience and to independence. But one can read his entire book without learning
that there are minority problems of overwhelming significance
in Burma—problems which simply cannot be ignored in a study
of Burma's "search for identity." The question of the ethnic
identification of the political leaders whom Pye studied is not
mentioned, and the whole history of the tortuous negotiations

with various minority groups, and the influence this had on the Union form of government, is simply omitted.

A glance at the table, "Population and Linguistic Affiliation of Ethnic Groups of Burma" (see the section of this book on Burma), shows that well over 25 percent of Burma's population is "minority or tribal." The political subdivisions of Burma also indicate something about the importance of the non-Burman populations (see map 1). Going around the country clockwise, we start with the Arakan State, then come to the Special Division of the Chins, Kachin State, Shan State, Kayah State (the Kayah are a variety of Karen), Karen State, and Tenasserim State (the Tenasserimese are speakers of a distinctive dialect of Burmese). All told these units comprise about half of the country. Pye is mute on the demographic, geographic, historical, and even political significance of tribes and minorities in Burma, despite the fact that at the time his research was being done tribes and minorities (organized as state governments) were represented in Rangoon, and minority and tribal rebellions had raged for years.

One of the outstanding problems in maintaining the Union was the question of integration of these minorities into the nation, and, as Lehman tells us, one of the precipitating factors in the military take-over in 1962 was the threat posed by a band of "federalists" who wanted to restructure the Union along the lines of a federation of ethnically distinct states. Students of nation-building can no longer afford to ignore such facts.

Anthropological and Political Science Views of Nation-Building. Among political scientists Deutsch has concerned himself extensively with the topic of national integration. His book *Nationalism and Social Communication* (1953) was a landmark in establishing the view among political scientists that nations are more than just padding around the formal skeleton defined by a constitution or some other document. A nation must also involve a certain amount of agreement about values, a recognition of common interests, and ability to communicate. Deutsch suggests that the question of *building* nations must involve the *assimilation* of diverse *peoples*. Assimilation of a distinctive people involves such things as learning the language which is spoken by the central authorities. An assimilated population is able to have full, rapid, and easy communication with the national community. Modern nation-building must also involve the *mobilization* of the predominantly rural masses who have not been articulated with the governing hierarchy. *Mobilization* can be measured by such things as proportion of the population which is urbanized (and therefore is more subject to mass communication and less bound to traditional forms of occupation such as farming) or by more direct indices, such as newspaper readership or education. A mobilized population is one which can be organized and changed rapidly. An assimilated population is one which identifies itself and its eventual fate with the dominant national community.

Many rural people, especially in the developing nations, are considered to be "unmobilized." Wolf (1957), for example, discusses "the closed, corporate community" as *one type* of peasant community which acts to seal itself off from the outside world and preserve its identity and stability. Wolf suggests that their form of community resulted from conditions of colonialism. The peasants are marginal participants in the national economy in that they produce some crops for sale; but they strongly resist change. We have already indicated that this characterization as regards the passivity and immobility of peasants is not necessarily appropriate to many of the people of Southeast Asia who escaped the sort of colonialism described by Wolf for Java and Mesoamerica. Nonetheless, the idea of peasant passivity is evidently shared by many authors writing on Southeast Asia (e.g. Wilson 1963:87–88).

The concept of "a people" requires more detailed examination. Deutsch defines "a people" as follows:

> The community which permits a common history to be experienced as common, is a community of complementary habits and facilities of communication. It requires, so to speak, equipment for a job. This job consists in the storage, recall, transmission, recombination, and reapplication of relatively wide ranges of information; and the "equipment" consists in such learned memories, symbols, habits, operating preferences, and facilities as will in fact be sufficiently complementary to permit the performance of these functions. *A larger group of persons*

linked by such complementary habits and facilities of communication
we may call *a people*. (1953:70, emphasis in original)[19]

Thus "a people" is, in effect, a cultural group, and political scientists and anthropologists are talking about the same sort of thing.

Anthropologists like Steward have argued that nations are not merely agglomerations of a series of communities, but are built as higher levels of socio-cultural integration are constructed. These higher levels take over some of the functions of the older, lower levels, and add new functions, not only in the areas of administration and control, but also in such things as marketing, banking, and large-scale productive enterprises. For example, the family in the more primitive types of societies is usually the unit of economic production, distribution, and consumption, whereas in the more advanced societies, with higher levels of socio-cultural integration, although the family retains some productive, distributive, and consumption functions, new supra-family organizations such as factories or corporations, and banking systems have emerged which span many communities (Steward 1949, 1955). Nation-building thus involves the construction of these higher levels and the articulation of families, communities, and larger groupings by means of these higher levels of organization (see Wolf, 1956, for an example of this type of analysis). This view of a nation as an articulated social organization whose units operate at different levels can be considered supplementary to Deutsch's views.

In Deutsch's terms a "nationality" is a people consciously attempting "to acquire a measure of effective control over the behavior of its members." Once it has achieved power it becomes a "nation" (Deutsch 1953:75 ff.). If we follow this outline, the problems of nation-building are to assimilate a sufficient number of individuals, to mobilize them by establishing methods of communication among themselves, especially channels of communication between different social levels, and to acquire political power in the form of a political-administrative system.

[19] We should note that Deutsch's definition of the "equipment" of "a people" is similar in many ways to Tylor's classic anthropological definition of culture as "that complex whole which includes knowledge, belief, art, morals, law, custom and any other capabilities and habits acquired by man as a member of society" (Tylor 1871:1).

Deutsch developed his theory primarily with reference to recent European and American societies (see also Deutsch in Jacob and Toscano 1964). He uses examples from India as well, but in his discussion of India he touches only briefly on the problems of the "mobilized but unassimilated" category of minorities (e.g. educated caste and language groupings), though he does indicate their existence and their importance for retarding the development of a modern nation within the boundaries of India (1953:109–111).

The situation in Europe is very different from that found in Southeast Asia. In Europe, within any given nation (i.e., bounded political unit organized on a national level), the number of different minorities or "peoples" is generally low—on the order of two or three—and these minorities, at the time the modern nations were formed, tended *not* to be internally organized, and generally were not mobilized, so the processes of mobilization and assimilation proceeded simultaneously and usually toward the same goal. In the U.S. (except for the Spanish Americans of the Southwest, and American Indians) large numbers of generally unorganized representatives of different peoples came into an ongoing system which had been established under the auspices of a single people. Assimilation and mobilization operated on individuals rather than on coherent groups.

How must the general view of nation-building be modified in areas where there are large numbers of different peoples? In Southeast Asia the bounded, diplomatically recognized national units were defined as a result of the colonial period; lines were drawn irrespective of ethnic distributions.[20] Many of the minority peoples in Southeast Asian countries (such as the Shan in Burma and the Tai groups of North Vietnam) were, and still are, internally organized on a level which necessarily brings them into structural opposition with the "central government." Such minorities are already organized at a comparable high level of integration, and their members are equally as mobilized as the representatives of the central government. Their own structures

[20] One of the best (or worst) examples of the nonconformity of political borders to ethnic distributions is the border between Laos and Northeastern Thailand. Linguistically and historically defined, there are nine times as many ethnic Laotians in Thailand as there are in Laos. The expansion of the Laotian principalities from their Mekong River bases was toward the west, not toward the Annamite Mountains, which were, and still are, occupied by a wide variety of non-Lao peoples.

necessarily compete with those of the central government when it comes to questions such as allocation of land, taxation, and relations with other "sovereign" units. This will be discussed in more detail below.

Assimilation and Mobilization at the Tribal Level. In the past much of the literature devoted to the study of tribal peoples emphasized the uniqueness, isolation, stability, and homogeneity of such peoples. This view would have obvious implications for the integration of tribal peoples into nations, and would justify the characterization of such peoples as "immobile" and "passive." But this model of tribal society is no longer generally acceptable. Leach's materials on highland Burma (1954), which we will discuss in detail later, indicate how cautious we must be in attempting to attribute such characteristics to the groups which have traditionally been defined as cultural groups or "tribes." Also, as Lehman and Maran show (in this book), no single attribute or set of attributes consistently sets off minority groups from the majority: language, culture (as defined above), ecological position, religion, literacy, degree of political development all fail to separate minorities from the dominant majority. We take the position that it is not cultural differences which define minority groups, but rather the *patterns of relationship with dominant majorities.* Deutsch has recognized this in his denial that common language by itself defines "a people," or that differences in language necessarily imply the existence of distinct peoples (1953:71; the example he uses is Switzerland).

One book, more than any other, has destroyed the illusion that tribal groups are isolated, independent, homogeneous, self-sufficient stable entities: this is Edmund Leach's *Political Systems of Highland Burma,* published in 1954. His book has many messages, some of which are of considerable importance to the study of development of nation-states in areas such as Burma, where "tribal" and "minority" people form an important part of the population and occupy a major portion of the land. The basic Leachian view is one of *interacting social systems* (though not phrased in exactly these terms).

The Homogeneous Tribal Society—An Outmoded Model. Leach has given us a picture of a series of related types of political structure within the so-called Kachin tribe. (The

"Kachin tribal" population lives primarily in the northern bulge of Burma, in Kachin State.) The several social systems portrayed by Leach are *very* different from one another indeed: from "democratic" unstratified, undifferentiated, independent upland village groups within which the leadership is non-hereditary, to quite "autocratic," distinctly stratified, large lowland village communities, with well-defined ties with other communities, and hereditary leaders. The different types are recognized by the Kachin themselves (who have names for them). Still, all Kachin recognize that they *are* Kachin, and identify themselves as such. Such a situation immediately destroys the commonly held idea of cultural homogeneity within a single "tribal" unit.

The Isolated Tribal Society—An Outmoded Model. Another part of the picture which Leach draws shows that the variation in types of Kachin social structure is related to another supposedly independent and distinct society, that of the Shan. The Shan are typically valley-dwelling, irrigated-rice-growing Buddhists, who have hereditary princes. A system of feudalistic relations prevails between communities and (more relevantly for the present purposes) between the supposedly independent Shan and Kachin. Not only are "Kachin tribes" *not* homogeneous, but it also turns out that they are not independent or isolated, and in fact we cannot understand the variations in Kachin social systems without understanding the connections between Kachin and Shan.

Tribal Societies and the Concept of Integration. Political scientists talking about "national integration" have discussed two basic kinds of things: integration in terms of values, attitudes, feeling of community, etc., and integration in terms of structured relationships such as the provision of governmental services, kinds and amounts of patterned interaction among sub-groups, and so forth (see Weiner 1965 for an expanded list of meanings attached to the term "integration"). When we look at Leach's analysis of Kachin and Shan social systems, we can discuss "integration" in terms of both of these concepts. In the first place, Shan society forms a model upon which some Kachin groups attempt to shape their own patterns of social relations, and second, some Kachin groups have feudatory relationships with Shan princes. In some cases there was (and is) quite a conscious process of assimilation, with Kachin deliberately setting out to imitate Shan economy (irrigated agriculture), Shan religion (Buddhism), Shan political structure (princely families), Shan family structure, and Shan language. Ultimately some *groups* of Kachin succeed in "becoming Shan"—their leaders may even intermarry with princely Shan families. We also learn that the movement from the extreme Kachin form of life (upland, slash-and-burn agriculture, animist, small migratory village groups, non-hereditary leadership) to lowland Shan life is not all one way. Groups or individuals may oscillate between the poles. More highly organized irrigated-agriculturalists may again take to upland farming, and traditional Kachin communities even have customary ceremonies for the reintegration of such individuals (data from Maran's paper). This sort of data destroys the idea of tribal societies as stable. Tribal societies are not necessarily stable, and the direction of their instability depends on their relations with other groups.

Non-Isolated, Non-Homogeneous Tribes—Some Additional Examples. How typical is the situation described by Leach? In Burma and in parts of Thailand (wherever it has been looked for) it seems quite common. In the hill area of northwestern Thailand for example (Kunstadter's paper), there are Karen villages whose structure is very much like that described by Leach for the extreme upland form of Kachin. These villages consist of only ten to twenty households, and they are not permanent agglomerations, as they often split up to take advantage of small areas of agricultural land. But there is a whole range of Karen social organizational types: in the valley within a few miles of the hill villages just mentioned, there are larger, permanent villages of irrigated-agriculturalists, many of whom are Buddhists, and in eastern Burma, in Kayah State, less than a hundred miles away, there are still "Shan-ized" Karen *principalities,* with feudatory relationships to Shan princes. In the days before the British destroyed the Burmese kingdom these connections ultimately tied them feudally to the Burmese king (Lehman's paper). A similar situation apparently existed among some Karen groups in the upper Khwae Noi drainage of western Thailand (Stern 1965). Thus Leach's general idea of variability within "tribes" and the relationship of this variability to connections between "tribes" and other groups seems to hold for the Karen as well as for the Kachin.

So far we have mentioned Shan, Kachin, and Karen, and have indicated that, though these groups may be distinct in some features (their languages and religions are very different), their social systems are linked together in a variety of ways. They are linked both structurally (by patterned systems of relationship implied in the term *feudalism*) and in terms of values and attitudes (in the cases mentioned above the Shan way of life is highly valued and serves as a model upon which individuals of other groups shape their behavior).

The Chin give us another illustration of these processes. Working in a theoretical framework similar to that of Leach, F. K. Lehman (1963, and in this volume) has examined the relationships between the society of the lowland Burma kingdom and the Chin, who live on the western side of Burma in the border area of East Pakistan and the southern extension of Assam. The Chin organized themselves into ranked lineages and oriented much of their behavior toward achieving equality with the lowland Burmans. In fact, as Lehman has shown, one cannot understand the structure of Chin society without understanding its relationship to Burman society—and he has indicated (in his paper in this volume) that the present relationship of Chin to Burman is based on the Chin recognition of these past patterns.[21]

Minorities and National Integration—Cultural Orientation. How does a knowledge of minorities help us in understanding some of the problems of national integration? I have already indicated that at least two kinds of information seem important: one is the cultural orientation of the minority—what might be called its reference group—and the other is the preexistent patterns of relationship to other groups. With regard to cultural orientation, the situation in a country like Burma is a bit more

[21] It might be argued that the examples used here are arbitrary, that the people are too sophisticated and do not fit into the class of "typical tribes." What happens if you look for relationships between really wild tribes and more highly organized groups? The Wild Wa, noted headhunters of northeastern Burma, are surely as savage a group as could be found anywhere. But there is evidence to indicate that the Wa headhunting, in addition to serving religious functions, was at least partially political and inter-societal in nature. After all, the Wa preferred Chinese heads, and Lehman (in this volume) suggests that the Wa may have been used by the Shan in regulating trade with Chinese caravans traveling between Yunnan and the Shan principalities.

complicated than in those countries subjected to detailed examination by Deutsch. We find in Burma (for example in the case of the Kachin) that a "people" may have for a reference group another "people" who are participants in a supposedly distinct social system.

The materials in this book allow us to suggest several generalizations concerning the "assimilability" of groups under various conditions. Two preliminary hypotheses emerge from the observation that the Chin generally have been extremely loyal to the central government of Burma, whereas Shan and Karen rebellions against the Union of Burma have been going on ever since the Union was formed (Lehman's and Maran's papers). As we have already noted, much of Chin behavior was consciously modeled on the positively valued system of the Burmese kings. The model for Karen behavior (at least for some of the Karen groups) has been the Shan. The Shan themselves are in many *structural* ways very similar to the Burmans (their economy is based on irrigated agriculture, there are permanent settlements, they have a hierarchical government system, and a form of Buddhism similar to that of the Burmans, including Buddhist schools and a hierarchy of Buddhist monks). In fact, as Lehman has pointed out, the Shan had pretensions to the throne of Burma, and their present desire is to maintain control over their own fate. They believe themselves already to be as civilized as the Burmans and think of proposed Burman influences (e.g. within the Shan Buddhist hierarchy) as unwarranted invasions of their social structure. The hypotheses, then, are that a preexistent positive valuation of the culture of a particular group will lead to loyalty (or assimilation) to a national government which is manned by representatives of that culture; and that a people who consider themselves to be culturally the equal of another people, and who are organized, are not likely to be easily assimilated.

The case of the Kachin lends partial support to these hypotheses. The Kachin have generally been loyal to the central Burma government in spite of long-standing Kachin relations with Shan principalities. Maran argues that this loyalty has largely been the result of the fact that the Kachin were brought to awareness of the existence of the outside modern world through use of Burmese language and literature. It was Western missionaries who first brought literacy to the Kachin, but, unlike most missionaries, those dealing with the Kachin elected to teach literacy in Burmese, not English. This case further suggests the hypothesis that the agent of change (and the culture of which he is a representative) is not so important in determining the direction of nationalistic sentiments as the door which he opens to the outside world.

Minorities and National Integration—Preexisting Relationships. What is the importance of preexistent relationships for the building of new nations? Deutsch argues for the possibility of the existence of nationalism (or "community") despite the existence of structural differentiation between the forms of government of two or more representatives of the same "people" (he uses the example of nationalism—based on easy communication—among members of different American colonies before the revolution [1953:74]). This hypothesis has important implications for irredentism and international relations, which we will discuss later, but for the time being we will consider only nation-building. The data from Southeast Asia indicate some of the difficulties in testing the hypothesis which we will overstate as "nations can be built despite preexistent structural arrangements if easy communication is possible between the members."

We have already cited enough information to indicate that minorities and tribes have related to one another and to the central authorities in *structured, non-passive ways;* they are neither ignorant of, nor isolated from, central authority, and members of *all* such groups apparently realize that central authority is something to be reckoned with. But there is tremendous variation in the patterns of relationship: there is a range from such groups as the Shan in Burma, whose own organization and size allow them to challenge central authority directly, to smaller and more dispersed groups in Thailand, as, for example, the Lua? (see above, pp. 30 ff., and Kunstadter's paper), the Thai-Lue (studied by Moerman), and the Yao (on whom Kandre has reported), who must accommodate in various ways to superior power.

The Lua?, a Mon-Khmer-speaking group, believe that they were once the lords of Northern Thailand (historical and archeological evidence tend to confirm this view), and they can recount stories of the decline of their preeminent position through a period of feudal obligation to the Northern Thai princes, and finally to their present position as taxpayers and citizens of Thailand. "We used to own the land," they say, "but now we belong to Thailand." Lua? principalities have not existed for hundreds of years, and no supra-village Lua? organization exists today. Thousands of Lua? in the lowlands, both as individuals and whole communities, have "become Thai"—they have given up their own language and much of their worship of spirits, which they feel is inappropriate to the conditions of lowland life, and they now are Thai-speaking Buddhists. Ten thousand or so retain still their distinct "tribal" identity in the hills.

In their attitude toward the central government the tribal Lua? are rather like the Thai-Lue, described by Moerman. The Thai-Lue (found in Yunnan, Burma, Laos, and Northern Thailand) once had kingdoms, but the upper layers of their socio-political organization have been lost. Like the Siamese Thai, the Thai-Lue have long been Buddhists. They are conscious of their linguistic distinctiveness (their dialect is not mutually intelligible with Central Thai, which is the official language of Thailand), but they no longer have pretensions to separate political status. Moerman reports that in the past they have recognized, and in the future they will probably recognize, the superiority of any strong power which presents itself—be it Northern Thai princes, Central Thai troops, or Meo invaders from Laos.

Kandre has described a rather different pattern among the Yao. The Yao are an extremely widespread people found in southern China, North Vietnam, northern Laos, and Thailand, with a total population in these areas of over one million. They are quite self-conscious about maintaining their own socio-politico-religious identity, and have deliberately developed a philosophy and political structure which allows them to deal with the central government of any country within which they happen to be, while preserving their basic loyalty to their concept of Yao-ness. They maintain contacts between villages by visiting, trading, intermarriage, and by exchange of letters. In some areas the villages (which are scattered on mountaintops and interspersed with settlements of other ethnic groups) are held together by higher- and lower-level Yao chiefs. Some of these networks also encompass villages of other ethnic groups.

The purpose of this ethnographic discussion has been to indicate the *variety* of adjustments made by minority and tribal peoples to the problem of relationship with superior political power. What are the implications of such diversity for nation-building, and what are the probable outcomes of the processes of modernization which we can observe at the present time?

An examination of most of the *national* societies in Southeast Asia indicates that they are relatively unmodernized (see Levy 1965, for a systematic discussion of some of the dimensions of modernization). Their "specialized" organizations are largely confined to the political organization itself (either the civilian government bureaucracy, or the military). Industrialization, in the sense of large industrial complexes, or even single corporations with many specializations are relatively rare; such inter-communal networks as exist are often based on kinship (e.g. among Chinese businessmen or bankers). Functional specificity paralleling that of the government may exist only in religious organization, and where most highly developed (e.g. Burma, Thailand) the religious hierarchy itself is government-sponsored. If this generalization is correct, it has two implications; first, it means that there may be very little difference in social structure between what is usually called the rural mass of the society and some of those units referred to as "tribes" or "minorities"— except perhaps for different degrees of penetration of the government's agencies. Second, it means that nominally political agencies (the army, the police) will have to assume a variety of non-political activities.

It follows from the first implication that, from the standpoint of social structure, the problem of administration of the *village-based* (e.g. Lua?, Thai-Lue) tribes and minorities may not be much different from that of administration of the general rural population. Obviously, a well-organized group such as the Shan, and some of the similarly organized Tai peoples of North Vietnam, cannot be simply encompassed within a routine pattern of rural administration. Perhaps because of such considerations, Burma has adopted a system of political pluralism which roughly parallels its ethnic pluralism.

The second implication manifests itself in what is often referred to as "overcentralization." The central governments have no rivals in organization, except for such organization as exists in the mobilized but unassimilated ethnic minorities. Also, there is little in these countries, except the governmental structure, which serves as a cross-cutting, multi-community tie holding the various sub-groups of the population together. In a country like Thailand, which is at least superficially homogeneous, ethnically and culturally, adherence to the values of Buddhism is usually offered as an explanation for such national cohesion as there is. The case of the Shan of Burma shows that common religion alone is insufficient: both Shan and Burman are Buddhist, but the Shan resent any attempt by the Burmans to interfere with the Shan Buddhist hierarchy. The case of the Buddhist Thai-Lue indicates it may be dangerous in Thailand to assume that mere adherence to Buddhism is sufficient to lead to loyalty to the nation.

Because the administrative structure is such an important feature in maintaining national cohesion, it is worthwhile examining some of the effects of variation within and between administrative systems. The pattern of administration within any country has tended to be uniform (this generalization does not apply to the colonial period). The Shan, Chin, Kachin, Kayah (Red Karen or Karenni), and Karen, for example, all have states or special districts of their own within Burma, irrespective of the fact that they were, and apparently still are, very different in indigenous socio-political structure. One of the problems for the other Burma minorities (who are often geographically more dispersed, e.g. the Mon) is that they have not been granted similar recognition. Also, some of the minorities which have been given states are not confined entirely to their state (e.g. there are large numbers of Karen in the delta area who receive no special recognition). And, as Maran tells us, there are liable to be minorities within minority states (ethnic Burmans are a legal minority in the Kachin State). Another problem is that some of the minority or tribal groups which have been recognized by being given states do not form cohesive, politically unified wholes (e.g. the Kachin).

In Thailand, which does not have special states for minorities, old feudal relationships and even existent community structures are ignored, or perhaps deliberately destroyed, in imposing a uniform bureaucratic structure on the country as a whole. The

Thai government's model for the local administrative structure has apparently been developed in the central plains, where community structures are only weakly defined (settlements are generally under a hundred years old, houses are strung out along irrigation canals, unoccupied land for exploitation has been readily available, kinship is non-unilineal, patterns of rural leadership are not hereditary, there is great social and physical mobility). This situation in the central plains is in strong contrast to many other areas of Thailand where villages are old, where there is a strong sense of community, where communities may have been linked by feudal ties with local princes, and where (until the mid-1950's, when large modern dams and irrigation facilities started to become available) new land for exploitation was limited.

The effects of these different administrative systems may be very different indeed: political pluralism may feed upon itself. Both the Chin and the Kachin have apparently wanted to "become Burman," but the minority state system of Burma seems to be forcing them into opposition to the central Burma states (which are predominantly ethnic Burman in composition). This opposition in the form of ethnic blocs is seemingly the only way in which the minorities and tribes can receive their share of taxes and government services from the central government, which is seated in a Burman area, and is largely Burman-controlled. Also, central government attempts to enforce cultural uniformity (e.g. in the matters of language and religion) further reinforce the feelings of minority identity.[22]

In Thailand the effect seems to be quite contrary. Uniform treatment in imposing a rural administrative system and tolerantly ignoring cultural differences seems to have a homogenizing effect. For example, the structural differences between Karen and Lua? are decreasing (though culturally and linguistically they remain quite distinct). The Lua? no longer enjoy their position as landlords, cannot collect taxes from the Karen, and have even lost title of their upland fields to the central government. This homogenization of tribal peoples does not necessarily mean

[22] This situation seems analogous to the creation of tribes as politically unified corporate groups, out of previously acephalous, non-property-holding cultural-linguistic units, by the reservation system and the Indian Reorganization Act in the United States.

increased integration with the national majority, or increased mobilization. As the regions where tribal people live become more integrated with the nation as a whole (by means of highways, expansion of trade, expansion of modern techniques of lumbering, etc., which are run by Thai businessmen from big cities), the Lua? and Karen also come to share poverty vis-à-vis the incoming Thai. Traditional jobs (elephant-driving, caravaning) are lost to buses and trucks, and traditional products (e.g. medicinal plants, or slightly quicker-ripening rice) lose their value to a larger market which can bring modern medicine and cheaper rice from other areas (see Condominas 1951 for a description of a similar economic situation among Vietnamese tribes). Flow of transactions between minority and majority (in Deutsch's terms) may very well decrease in frequency, variety, and intensity, and the interactions are at relatively lower levels in the hierarchy of the dominant group. For example, in the past the Lua? headmen reported directly to the Northern Thai Prince in Chiengmai or Lamphun. In other areas Karen headmen forty years ago or more took the post of district headman, but in recent years they have lost this position to Central Thai civil servants (Stern 1965). Now tribal village headmen deal with low-level civil servants who are concerned primarily with administration. They no longer deal with princes who were also concerned with the moral and economic well-being of their subjects.[23]

The process of tribal homogenization may be helpful in reducing the potential opposition to the government, but there are also dangers in this type of administration. Non-recognition of existing community structures (through artificially constructed administrative boundaries, through failure to deal with the effective village leaders, through failure to use existing patterns of village organization in promoting and carrying out local development projects)[24] may lead to the weakening of local community structure. This is a dangerous strategy, even though it may be

---

[23] The Prince of Chiengmai used to lecture his Lua? and Karen subjects about proper behavior and proper methods of upland cultivation, which would conserve forest resources.

[24] For a discussion of political administrative structure as applied to rural villages in the central plains of Thailand see Sharp *et al.* (1953); for discussions of the importance of real communities in Northeastern Thailand see Huff's paper; and for the importance of dealing with the existing patterns of community leadership in a Thai minority group (the Thai-Lue) see Moerman's paper.

appropriate to the need to mobilize the population in order to take advantage of modern economic opportunities. A balance must be established between community disorganization (which nowhere seems to have been beneficial in nation-building) and mobilization of the population for economic development.

International Implications of Minorities and Tribes in Southeast Asia. We have already indicated that national boundaries in Southeast Asia were drawn irrespective of ethnic distributions. This has meant that all Southeast Asian nations have been faced with potential or actual problems of irredentism. Problems of irredentism will probably increase in the future rather than decrease: the minorities have already become targets for mobilization (by both Communists and non-Communists), and mobilization has generally proceeded more rapidly than assimilation.

The situation within Vietnam and vis-à-vis Cambodia is a good example of this. Much of the military action in the Vietnamese wars has taken place in highland areas which are occupied almost exclusively by tribal and minority peoples. These mountain minorities have been caught in the middle of international conflict, and attempts are being made by outside agents (North Vietnamese, U.S. Special Forces) to influence them to participate in what has become an increasingly international struggle. The small degree of assimilation of these minorities is obvious from the facts that several rebellions have broken out among the hill tribe troops against the South Vietnamese and that the South Vietnamese have recently disarmed hill populations who were fighting against the Viet Cong for fear that the tribesmen would turn against the South Vietnamese as well (Anon. 1965A; 1965B; Mohr 1965).[25]

Meanwhile, in Cambodia efforts have been launched (under FULRO—the Front for the Relief of the Oppressed Races) to promote unification of the southern Indochina hill peoples, including those in Cambodia and South Vietnam. (This attempt has used the ethnographically incorrect argument that all these

---

[25] The tribal revolts in 1965 were practically identical with the one in October 1964. The tribesmen again were reported to want to enter into direct negotiations with the United States, and, though it was later denied, the South Vietnamese government was reported to have asked for the removal of U.S. advisers to the tribesmen because of the advisers' role in strengthening the self-consciousness and articulating the demands of the tribesmen for greater autonomy.

tribal people are related to the Khmer, the national majority of Cambodia. In fact many of the tribesmen, including the strategically important Rhadé and Jarai, are speakers of Malayo-Polynesian, not Mon-Khmer languages.) Cambodian support for this movement naturally affects the relationship between Cambodia and South Vietnam, since most of the tribal people involved are located in South Vietnam.

Relations between Cambodia and South Vietnam are further complicated by the sizable Khmer minority in South Vietnam and the large Vietnamese minority in Cambodia. Prince Sihanouk of Cambodia has taken the position that the Vietnamese minority in Cambodia refuses to be assimilated, and likewise argues that the Khmer minority in South Vietnam cannot and will not be incorporated into the South Vietnamese national community because of "the nationalist sentiments of our forefathers which enabled the Khmer race to resist all attempts made to exterminate it, and to survive the genocidal tactics employed to that end by the Siamese and Annamites for a period of five hundred years" (1965:19). Evidently the minority problems related to nationalism will continue to color the relations between Southeast Asian countries for a long time to come.

ACTION PROGRAMS DIRECTED AT TRIBES AND MINORITIES

We can turn now to an examination of the effects of various action programs on majority-minority relations. First we should try to understand some of the motivations behind these programs. We can ask what has been the general philosophy underlying such programs and, in particular, what has been the underlying conception concerning the place of minorities and tribes in the national societies of the countries where the programs have operated. It is perhaps not surprising that the programs described in this book have been motivated almost exclusively by strategic considerations or desires to benefit the economy of the national majority. Often it has been overemphasis of strategic considerations which has led to the failure of the programs. In general, the programs have been designed for several purposes: to achieve political control; to promote the loyalty of the groups to the nation (or liberation front); to prevent infiltration or subversion of the groups; to gather intelligence; and to protect the population from outside aggression. Often an additional motivation has been to open up the remote areas for economic exploitation for the benefit of the dominant group.

A Vietnamese Example. The effects of action programs have not always been those intended or desired. An example from Vietnam is appropriate here. Most of the battles between the Viet Minh and the French were fought in the hills, in areas occupied by minority and tribal groups, and often with troops recruited (on both sides) from minority and tribal groups (see McAlister's paper). In the late 1950's and early 1960's, after the reopening of hostilities in the South, it became obvious that the hill areas and tribal groups would again be of the greatest strategic importance in controlling infiltration of troops and supplies from the North and through the Laotian and Cambodian border areas. Also of great importance was the maintenance of supply and communication lines between the major areas of Vietnamese settlement in the South, often separated by minority and tribal areas. The hill tribes (*montagnards*) had largely been ignored by the Diem government, which was concerned with the hill areas primarily as a place for the resettlement of ethnic Vietnamese refugees from the North (see Ladejinsky 1961:163–164).

A program for the Vietnamese hill tribes by the U.S. Army Special Forces (Sochurek 1965), apparently under the administrative direction of the Central Intelligence Agency (Jumper and Normand 1964:456; Joiner 1965:29–31), was started in 1961. The purposes of this project were to advise, train, and assist indigenous forces in counter-insurgency and to organize, develop, equip, train, and direct indigenous forces in guerrilla operations. In carrying out their tasks, the Special Forces established dispensaries and trained and assisted the tribesmen in building schools, repairing roads and dams, and digging wells, in addition to their military and defense activities. The tribesmen were paid for their work, and stores were established in the camps, in which were sold the manufactured items, such as cloth and fish sauce, which have become essential to hill tribe life. The military and civic action programs of the Special Forces were supplemented by American Volunteer Service projects in such fields as agriculture. By June of 1962 Darlac Province, in which the Rhadé are concentrated, was reported to be cleared of Viet Cong. By mid-

1964, a Montagnard Strike Force of almost 10,000 men had been armed and trained.

In July 1963, the effectiveness of the program having been demonstrated, it was expanded as the Special Forces took control over the Civil Irregular Defense Groups. It should be noted that between 1961 and 1964 lowland Vietnamese participation in the program was strictly curtailed.

The effectiveness of the program was reduced by the political unrest which culminated in the overthrow of the Diem regime in November 1963. In May 1964 the Special Forces unit was transferred from the control of the CIA and placed under the Military Advisory Command. This meant that lowland Vietnamese were placed in command of the mountaineers. Shortly thereafter, in September 1964, following several mass desertions, 3,000 of the armed and trained tribesmen rebelled against their Vietnamese officers, killed some of them, and took twenty American members of the Special Forces as hostages. The revolt was brought to a speedy end, primarily by the persuasive talk of a few of the American Special Forces officers (Sochurek 1965). The outcome of this brief rebellion was the conference of tribal leaders and General Khanh held in Pleiku in October 1964, the results of which are discussed in Hickey's paper in this volume.

The experience in this case is a classic one for illustrating the dilemmas in dealing with hill tribes. The basic objective of the Americans was to increase the integration and viability of the South Vietnamese state. The reason that the hill tribes received attention was their immediate tactical and strategic importance. In general, the people who have proved most able to deal successfully with the tribesmen have been outsiders, Americans, with whom the hill tribesmen had no experience of discrimination or exploitation. The interposition of Americans outside of normal central government channels no doubt had the desired effect of strengthening the tribesmen's ability to protect themselves against the Viet Cong. But it also made them more of a threat to the central government by arming them and giving them a means of organization on a scale much larger than had ever before been accomplished, thus raising fears in Saigon of "balkanization" of the highlands.

"Winning Hearts and Minds." Economic, social, and political

development have usually been offered as inducements, sometimes, as in Vietnam, very late in the game, in order to win the cooperation of the people involved. As experience has been gained, the importance of "winning the hearts and minds" of (or, in social science jargon, establishing common values with) the local population has come to be recognized, but this lesson seems to be quickly forgotten under the pressure of military emergency, when, in fact, it is of the greatest importance. The overall lack of success of the Strategic Hamlet Program in South Vietnam, where, for a variety of historical reasons, there has been an almost complete breakdown of meaningful communications between rural areas and the central government, is the best example of this (see O'Donnell's paper). One successful example of the "hearts and minds" idea seems to be in Borneo, in the face of the Indonesian Confrontation, where Harrisson and Ley both report that a few simple rules of behavior showing respect for local customs make a great difference in winning the respect of the native peoples with whom the military forces are working. But, of course, here the central government was starting with a reservoir of good will among the tribal people. And even here one is unsure whether the loyalty which has been demonstrated is being manifested toward the British advisers or toward the idea of a unified nation of Malaysia, which they represent.

The "winning of hearts and minds" is difficult to measure, and the difficulty increases in proportion to the lack of communication between government and people. Accomplishments of programs tend to be measured in terms of material objects—numbers of schools or latrines built or number of pills administered—without regard to the effectiveness of such measures for reaching the real objectives of the programs: Are the children learning in the schools? Are latrines and pills seen by the people as evidence of the government's interest in their welfare? Are they effective as health measures?

Philosophy of Development. Underlying the ineffectiveness of many of the U.S. and other government assistance programs, and also those of private foundations, has been the lack of a clearly developed theory of social-political-economic development, or perhaps an unwillingness to consider the basic and ultimate aim of economic, technical, and military aid. It has become a commonplace now to point out the failure of viable, well-integrated, popular, effective, free governments to develop in Latin America, the Congo, Burma, Vietnam, or Indonesia in spite of sizable, or even massive, investments of money, material, and talented manpower. Political *stability* has often been the goal in spite of the fact that the world is changing, and in contradiction to the facts that basic changes in economy and popular outlook are being generated by economic aid programs and that there has been a natural and uncontrollable spread of the industrial revolution throughout the world.

It has been true in the past that a concept like "public opinion on national and international affairs" was practically meaningless in a country like Thailand. The people have not known about, and have not cared about, situations beyond their immediate view. Thus Moerman's example from the Thai-Lue of Northern Thailand is neither surprising nor atypical: the people expect to render what is due unto whatever Caesar happens to be in power. Things are changing, however. The existence of roads, buses, transistor radios, the beginnings of literacy, and the cousins who have been drafted or who have gone to the big city to find work mean that the countryside is no longer completely remote—even in the absence of deliberate agents of change and unrest. Public opinion will develop—the only questions are who will be listening and who will be molding it as it develops. The lack of an adequate philosophy results in paralysis or in uncoordinated efforts at political development.

The lack of a clear policy for political development is actually a policy for *laissez-faire;* but it is a *laissez-faire* policy in a far different set of conditions than that under which *laissez-faire* was originally developed. The situation of international competition for men's minds is today far different from that of the eighteenth century. Major political changes are bound to take place as archaic feudalism and the remnants of colonialism prove incapable of dealing with the modern world.

One searches in vain in the experience of the non-Communist programs described in this book for deeper motivations than the general idea of "doing good" and "winning the loyalty of the people." What is to become of the people once their loyalty has been won? The questions of integration vs. assimilation vs. reservation (to name three possibilities) have not been aired; only the Communist-dominated parties of East and Southeast Asia have made reasonably clear statements concerning the rights of the minorities to organize themselves and to preserve or change their cultures (see Elwin 1960 for an attempt to develop such a philosophy for tribal areas of India).

The lack of a philosophic basis for nation-building underlying the programs results in several conditions underlying the lack of success in many aid and assistance programs. First is the inability to plan coordinated programs, since no consistent set of goals exists. Second, is the inability to measure the effectiveness of a total program. Third, is the inability to instill an appropriate set of motivations in field workers or to present a consistent, reasonable, and relevant set of ideas to the target population. This problem becomes clear in O'Donnell's paper on the Strategic Hamlet Program in Vietnam, where ideas regarding fiscal responsibilities were made a basic part of the administration of the program, but where there was no clear philosophy for the political development of the villages and their relations to the Saigon government and no clear reason offered why the villagers should fight to protect themselves. Fourth, there has been a focus on primarily *negative* goals, such as political stability, prevention of subversion, or the control of movement of populations, coupled with economic and medical aid programs which are sure to upset any stability which might once have been achieved.

The lack of an underlying philosophy or theory of political, economic, and social development also contributes to a lack of focus in much of the research being done on the attempts to administer economic change. What *are* the effects of a reservation system, an assimilation policy, or attempts to induce the integration of diverse peoples? (See Colson 1953 for one of the few monographs directed specifically at the effects of the reservation system among American Indians.) How can a nation best be built out of a set of disparate tribes or minorities? Is the experience of the United States "melting pot" relevant for the rest of the world or, in fact, are theories on minority group relationships developed in the United States applicable at all to minority relationships in the rest of the world? Instead of being asked and answered, these questions have been ignored, and the programs have been run on a largely *ad hoc* basis without a continuing effort at using this experience to develop and test general theories of economic, political, and social development.

Lack of coordination *among* programs is another problem, especially when programs involve many different agencies, as they do in Thailand and Vietnam (See Introduction to the Thailand section of this book for a listing of some of the many agencies involved). There are two aspects of this lack of coordination: first, the bureaucratic problem of allocation of responsibility; and second, the problem of developing a total program which is not self-defeating because of its internal contradictions. Two examples may be mentioned in this connection. The first is the relative ease of control of mortality through the use of modern medicine and public health measures, which leads to rapid population growth. This problem, of course, is not limited to Southeast Asia, but it is felt there especially acutely in the more remote areas where the economy is already marginal, where the population is far from the regions where economic development is taking place, where land is already scarce (given existing techniques of cultivation), and where, because of lack of education and cultural differences, internal migration is not much of a possibility. The lack of coordination in the development of an overall plan is evident here in the failure to develop new economic resources and to introduce birth-control devices at the same time as mortality control is introduced.

Another type of uncoordinated program, which has in general been abandoned, but not until it has been tried in turn by each country, is the permanent settlement of nomadic tribesmen in the absence of adequate economic opportunities. It has now been recognized that such programs are likely to antagonize the tribesmen and lead to economic decline which would outweigh any benefits resulting from ease of administration of the settled population. Manndorff's paper on the Thai experience with hill tribe settlement programs is illustrative in this regard. The lesson could have been learned from the disastrous experience among Malayan aborigines during the Emergency, to which Osborn refers, but the experience was repeated in South Vietnam.[26]

[26] See Williams-Hunt (1953) for a description of programs dealing with the

The argument here is not for a completely monolithic system, but rather for the development of a consistent set of goals for the larger problem of nation-building and for attempts to eliminate some of the glaring inconsistencies.

The attempts to induce change have not been entirely unsuccessful. Several things emerge from the papers in this regard. First are the facts that communities *do* exist among the tribal and minority peoples and that they can be the basis for effective action. It is important to emphasize the point because of the rather unfortunate characterization of Thailand, for example, as a "loosely structured society" (Embree 1950), which was partially confirmed in earlier studies of Central Plains villages (e.g. Kaufman 1960, DeYoung 1958, Sharp *et al.* 1953). Moerman, for example, argues effectively for the existence of *real* communities (not just artificial administrative units) among the Thai-Lue and gives an example of the community acting as a whole in response to an outside threat. Huff, in his discussion of the Mobile Development Unit program among Northeastern Thais, shows the effectiveness of a few outsiders as catalysts for inducing action within an existing community structure. Border Patrol Police, operating in relatively small numbers, have had similar effect in stimulating the activity of tribal communities in Thailand. The question remains, how do these community activities, such as building small bridges, or forming a temporary sentry system, or constructing a schoolhouse, relate to the large problem of developing the nations?

Research and Action Programs. One conclusion, after examining these cases, is the need for coordination of research with action programs. In the past research has not been built routinely into economic and political development programs, and as a result we have few good studies of the effects of various kinds of programs on the integration of tribal and minority groups into the nations of Southeast Asia. Mr. Maran's position in the Burmese government, the existence of an anthropological adviser to the Thai Department of Public Welfare, and the creation in

---

aborigines of Malay during the Emergency. Henderson describes some of the problems of highland resettlement in South Vietnam, which proceeded without adequate technical know-how and with deliberate disregard for traditional patterns of social structure (1961).

Chiengmai of the Tribal Research Centre, are evidence that this situation is changing, but the mechanisms for coordinating research findings with program planning still need much work. Successful programs seem to require long-term commitment by dedicated individuals—but under what institutional circumstances can we expect to find these people? In the first place, there are far too few trained scholars in the countries in question. The universities in Southeast Asia are not yet able to turn out locally trained experts, which means that reliance must be placed on foreign experts and foreign training for local personnel, at least for the time being.

Foreign Experts. Although at present foreign experts are absolutely necessary, they are by no means the ideal solution. Usually they arrive not knowing the national and local languages, and the amount of time they can spend in the area, given their career commitments elsewhere, does not enable them to learn the two or more languages or dialects they need to know in order to work both with the local people and within the government structure, to do enough research to become familiar with the local situation, and to give relevant and meaningful advice. The careers of university people depend on the judgments of their home universities, so they must publish in fields relevant to their professions (which may or may not be the areas of most importance for the action programs). The careers of government experts depend on their national bureaucracy, and promotion there again depends on being close to the source.

Another problem with foreign experts is that they can, usually unintentionally, foster separatism among the groups with which they work. If the first and only good treatment the people get is from foreigners, it is not surprising if they want to ally themselves with the foreigners in preference to their "own" country. Examples of this from Vietnam and Burma have already been cited. Ley indicates a sensitivity to precisely this problem when he speaks of the desirability of including Malay personnel in the medical teams designed to serve the Sabah hill tribes. If the objectives are to build national unity and to have a self-perpetuating system to do so, then obviously local expertise must be developed.

Local Experts. But local experts also have problems under

present circumstances. The role of the trained expert adviser or researcher among tribes or minorities is relatively unrewarding in countries where trained people are at a premium. Here again, opportunities lie in the central, not the remote, areas. Also, bureaus dealing with minorities and tribes are low in the bureaucratic structure, which means that opportunities for significant decision-making, for advancement, and even for effective work based on local initiative in the remote areas are strictly limited. Furthermore, if the local expert's job is to evaluate a program within a government of which he is necessarily a very minor official, his lot cannot be a very happy one.

Universities and the Institutional Setting of Research and Action. Likewise, until the local universities are better developed, students must go overseas for the best training, and the types of training available overseas are not necessarily the most appropriate for local conditions. The situation of the universities in Southeast Asia is such as to limit the chance that they will change very rapidly. The universities are arms of the governments, which has meant that opportunities for advancement generally lie outside of the academic world and that the necessary freedom for enquiry, especially in the social or policy sciences, has often been lacking. Also, the universities are small, the countries are small and their resources are limited, and not every country can or should spend its resources on developing first-rate departments in all fields.

The problems toward which foreign aid has been directed (other than the purely military ones) include coordination of a large body of knowledge from many fields, training, research, and the spread of innovations. In the Western World, universities have developed as the institutions largely responsible for these tasks. Central governments have done their own organization, training, research, and diffusion of knowledge only when the problems are relatively narrow and well-defined—the atomic bomb, weaponry research in general, or specific medical problems such as those attacked by the various National Institutes of Health.

The advantages of universities as primary agencies of social change include their multi-disciplinary approach (something which is attempted in a very different institutional setting by

U.S. AID missions) and their relative freedom from external political considerations. We have already indicated some of the reasons why Southeast Asian universities have not been too successful in doing these tasks. The primary example of an attempt to involve an American university in a development program (the Michigan State University Advisory Group in Vietnam) has not been studied from this point of view.[27] Nor, despite Mr. Pierson's efforts, have the often piecemeal programs of independent foundations been examined critically. We do not yet have enough documentation on the way in which institutions of foreign aid interact with the social systems of their own countries and those of the recipient countries to be able to do more than point out some of the problem areas and to stress their importance for research.

Several solutions for some of the administrative problems of foreign aid expertise are suggested in the papers of this volume. Dr. Geddes, for example, has proposed a program of internships, or field-research training, in which foreign scholars would be welcomed to do research on relevant problems and given assistance by the Tribal Research Centre, in exchange for field training for one of the Centre's staff. This sort of thing is already being tried in Sarawak, with preliminary training of local personnel carried out by Mr. Harrisson at the Sarawak Museum, and also by the Hill Tribe Division in Thailand. Such programs will undoubtedly serve useful purposes and will help to put an end to one legitimate complaint which has been lodged against foreign scholars, who are often, and justifiably, viewed as intellectual head hunters: they come, collect their prized research materials, and depart to examine them at their leisure in the sanctity of their universities, leaving nothing in return for the country which has offered its hospitality.[28] In spite of these reservations, there are many instances where foreign and local experts have worked together effectively.

[27] The role of the Michigan State University Advisory Group in the aid program for Vietnam has been described by Scigliano (1963:204–206) and Scigliano and Fox (1965), and mentioned briefly by Fall (1963:224). Michigan State has recently received journalistic notoriety because of the alleged use of the University as a "cover" for the Central Intelligence Agency (*New York Times*, April 14, 15, 17, 18, 1966; *Ramparts* magazine, April 1966).

[28] The recent regulations regarding social research by foreign scholars, of the National Research Council of Thailand, are an indication that these countries will not tolerate such behavior indefinitely.

Internationalization of Research and Action. But the research problems are not merely national ones. The discussion which grew out of several of the papers included here indicated the great desirability of internationalization of research efforts and pooling of research results. The problems of tribes, minorities, and central governments have been shown to have much in common among the several countries, yet there has been little coordination of research effort—and little attempt to work out common problems.

Internationalization will not be easy to accomplish, for several political and financial reasons. The existing political situation in Southeast Asia would make international cooperation among the several nations difficult if all were to be included: Indonesia and Malaysia have been practically at war, and tribal people are caught in the middle of the struggle in Borneo; hostilities between Vietnam and Cambodia and between Thailand and Cambodia also involve areas occupied by minority peoples. But perhaps a start could be made in a formal organization involving Burma, Laos, Thailand, and Malaysia (which have common borders and share some ethnic groups), since these countries have friendly relations. Perhaps some sort of informal cooperation could begin among social and political scientists from all countries under a more or less neutral organization, such as the Pacific Science Congress, or perhaps it might be done around an existing regional organization such as the Mekong River Development Scheme.

Another problem is the financial one—finding a sufficiently large source of money, a source which can make long enough commitments to do effective work. In order to function with maximum effectiveness, such an organization must be free of any hint or suspicion of control by an agency of a foreign government, which means that if funds are to come from government sources, they must be channeled through an international organization that has considerable independence.

The need for internationalization both in research and in action programs for minority and tribal groups is based not only on the fact that there are common problems resulting from common features of environment and ways of life, but also on the fact that relationships between central governments and the minority and tribal groups in their territories frequently affect international relations. Also, the lives of the people concerned are in turn affected by relationships between governments. Minority and tribal groups which have traditionally depended on trade routes across international boundaries have found their lives drastically altered by the closing of borders—examples of this from the papers in this book include the loss of traditional sources of trade goods and loss of a natural iodized salt supply to the inland tribes of Sarawak as a result of the Indonesian policy of Confrontation. There has also been a loss of traditional trade routes for the tribal people of northwestern Thailand as a result of the closing of the border with Burma, which was in turn caused by insurrections among the Burmese Shan and Karen. Likewise, the government's treatment of the Cambodian and Malay minorities in Thailand can affect Thailand's relations with Cambodia and Malaya. The Cambodians, for example, naturally resent what they interpret to be hostile political activity among the Cambodian minority in Thailand. The formation of a Front for the Relief of Oppressed Races (meaning the Indochinese *montagnards*) based in Cambodia cannot fail to affect the relationships between Cambodia and South Vietnam. Thus, irrespective of their own intentions, tribal and minority groups have become important factors in international relations in Southeast Asia, and it is therefore appropriate to seek international solutions to their problems.

BIBLIOGRAPHY

The following bibliographic guides may be useful as introductions to the vast literature on Southeast Asia. More specialized references to individual countries will be found in later chapters.

AUVADE, ROBERT
    1965   Bibliographie critique des ouevres parues sur l'Indochine Française; un siècle d'histoire et d'enseigment. Paris, G.-P. Maisonneuve et Larose.
CONDOMINAS, GEORGES
    1953   Bibliographie, Indochine. *In* Ethnologie de l'Union Française (territoires extérieurs), Tome Second: Asie, Océanie, Amerique. Eds. André Leroi-Gourhan and Jean Poirier, with the collaboration of André-Georges Haudricourt and Georges Condominas. Paris, Presses Universitaires de France.

EMBREE, JOHN F., and LILLIAN O. DOTSON
  1950   Bibliography of the peoples and cultures of mainland Southeast
         Asia. New Haven, Yale University, Southeast Asia Studies.
HAY, STEPHEN N., and MARGARET H. CASE, eds.
  1962   Southeast Asian history, a bibliographic guide. New York,
         Frederick A. Praeger.
HOBBS, CECIL C. et al.
  1950   Indochina, a bibliography of the land and people. Washington,
         D.C., Library of Congress, Reference Department.
  1964   Southeast Asia: an annotated bibliography of selected reference
         sources in Western languages. Revised and enlarged. Washing-
         ton, D.C., Library of Congress, Reference Department, Orien-
         talia Division.
JOURNAL OF ASIAN STUDIES
  Annual   Bibliography of Asian studies. (Published yearly in September,
           references to Southeast Asia broken down by country and
           subject.)
WILSON PATRICK
  1959   Bibliographic article: a survey of bibliographies on Southern
         Asia. Journal of Asian Studies 18:365–376.

REFERENCES CITED

ANON.
  1965   National minorities: the policy. China News Analysis, May
          7, 563:1–7.
  1965A   U.S. denies Saigon demanded recall of three officials. New
          York Times, September 15 [story datelined Saigon, South
          Vietnam, September 14].
  1965B   500 tribesmen affirm loyalty to Ky regime. New York Times
          September 16 [story datelined Banmethuot, South Vietnam.
          September 15].
ARCHAIMBAULT, C.
  1964   Religious structures in Laos. Journal of the Siam Society
          52 (1):57–74.
ARMSTRONG, TERENCE
  1965   Russian settlement in the north. Cambridge, Cambridge
          University Press.
BAILEY, F. G.
  1960   Tribe, caste, and nation: a study of political activity and
          political change in Orissa. Manchester, Manchester Univer-
          sity Press.
BENNINGTON-CORNELL ANTHROPOLOGICAL SURVEY OF HILL TRIBES IN
THAILAND
  1964   A report on tribal peoples in Chiengrai Province north of
          the Mae Kok river. Bangkok, The Siam Society, Data Paper 1.

BROWN, J. MARVIN
    1965   From ancient Thai to modern dialects. Bangkok, Social Science Association Press of Thailand.

BRUK, S. I.
    1959   Naseleniye Kitaya, MNR i Korei. Moscow, Publishing House of Academy of Sciences, USSR. ([Peoples of China, Mongolian People's Republic, and Korea] English translation by U.S. Joint Publications Research Service.)

BUTTINGER, J.
    1961   The ethnic minorities in the Republic of Vietnam. *In* Problems of freedom: South Vietnam since independence, Wesley R. Fishel, ed. New York, The Free Press of Glencoe, Inc., Ch. 6.

CADY, J. F.
    1958   A history of modern Burma. Ithaca, Cornell University Press.

COLSON, E.
    1953   The Makah Indians: a study of an Indian tribe in modern American society. Minneapolis, University of Minnesota Press.

CONDOMINAS, GEORGES
    1951   Aspects of a minority problem in Indochina. Pacific Affairs 24:77–82 (March).

DEUTSCH, KARL W.
    1953   Nationalism and social communication: an inquiry into the foundations of nationality. Cambridge, Mass., The M.I.T. Press.

DEYOUNG, J. E.
    1958   Village life in modern Thailand. Berkeley and Los Angeles, University of California Press.

ELWIN, V.
    1960   A philosophy for NEFA. Shillong, Shri J. Chowdhury, 2d revised edn.

EMBREE, J. F.
    1950   Thailand: a loosely structured social system. American Anthropologist 52:181–193.

FALL, B.
    1963   *Review of* Problems of freedom: South Vietnam since independence, Wesley R. Fishel, ed. Journal of Asian Studies 22(2):224–227.

FURNIVALL, J. S.
    1948   Colonial policy and practice. Cambridge, Cambridge University Press.

GOLENPAUL, DAN (ed.)
    1964   Information please almanac: atlas and yearbook, 1965. New York, Simon and Schuster, 19th edn.

HALPERN, J. M.
  1964 Government, politics, and social structure in Laos: a case
        study of tradition and innovation. New Haven, Yale Uni-
        versity, Southeast Asia Studies. Monograph Series, 4.

HEINE-GELDERN, ROBERT
  1956 Conceptions of state and kingship in Southeast Asia. Ithaca,
        Cornell University, Southeast Asia Program, Data Paper 18.

HENDERSON, W.
  1961 Opening of new lands and villages: the Republic of Vietnam
        land development program. In Problems of freedom: South
        Vietnam since independence, Wesley R. Fishel, ed. New
        York, The Free Press of Glencoe, Inc., Ch. 7.

HOSELITZ, B.
  1957 Urbanization and economic growth in Asia. Economic De-
        velopment and Cultural Change 6(1):42–54.

IZIKOWITZ, KARL GUSTAV
  1951 Lamet: hill peasants in French Indochina. Göteborg,
        Etnografiska Museet, Etnologiska Studier 17.

JACOB, PHILIP E., and JAMES V. TOSCANO (eds.)
  1964 The integration of political communities. Philadelphia and
        New York, J. B. Lippincott Company.

JOINER, CHARLES A.
  1965 Administration and political warfare in the highlands. Viet-
        nam Perspectives 1(2):19–37.

JUMPER, R. and M. W. NORMAND
  1964 Vietnam. In Government and politics in Southeast Asia.
        George McTurnan Kahin, ed. Ithaca, Cornell University
        Press, 2d edn.

KAUFMAN, H. K.
  1960 Bangkhuad: a community study in Thailand. Locust Valley,
        N.Y., J. J. Augustin, Inc. Monographs of the Association for
        Asian Studies, X.

  1963 Nationalism and the problems of refugee and ethnic minority
        resettlement. In Proceedings of the Ninth Pacific Science
        Congress, vol. 3, pp. 170–174. Bangkok, Secretariat, Ninth
        Pacific Science Congress.

KUNSTADTER, P.
  1965 The Luaʔ (Lawa) of Northern Thailand: aspects of social
        structural, agriculture, and religion. Princeton, N.J., Prince-
        ton University, Center of International Studies, Research
        Monograph 21.

  1966 Residential and social organization of the Lawa of Northern
        Thailand. Southwestern Journal of Anthropology 22(1):61–
        84.

LADEJINSKY, W.
  1961 The growth of agricultural credit and cooperatives in Vietnam. *In* Problems of freedom: South Vietnam since independence, Wesley R. Fishel, ed. New York, The Free Press of Glencoe, Inc., Ch. 10.
LEACH, E. R.
  1954 Political systems of highland Burma. Cambridge, Mass. Harvard University Press.
  1960 The "frontiers" of Burma. Comparative Studies in Society and History 3:49–73.
LEBAR, F. M., G. C. HICKEY, and J. K. MUSGRAVE
  1964 Ethnic groups of mainland Southeast Asia. New Haven, Human Relations Area Files Press.
LEHMAN, F. K.
  1963 The structure of Chin society: a tribal people of Burma adapted to a non-Western civilization. Urbana, University of Illinois Press.
LE KHAC
  1962 L'écriture des minorités nationales. La Nouvelle Critique (revue mensuelle, special issue, Du colonialisme au socialisme, Mars) 135:154–164.
LEVY, MARION J., JR.
  1965 Patterns (structures) of modernization and political development. The Annals of the American Academy of Political and Social Science 358:29–40 (March).
LIN YUEH-HUA
  1961 The minority peoples of Yunnan. China Reconstructs, December:26–29.
MA HSUEH-LIANG
  1962 New scripts for China's minorities. China Reconstructs, August:24–27.
MOERMAN, MICHAEL
  1965 Ethnic identification in a complex society: who are the Lue? American Anthropologist 67(5):1215–1230.
MOHR, CHARLES
  1965 Saigon said to oust 3 aides of U.S. over tie to tribes. New York Times, September 13 [story datelined Saigon, South Vietnam, September 12].
PELZER, K. J.
  1948 Pioneer settlements in the Asiatic tropics. New York, American Geographical Society, Special Publication 29.
  1963 Mass migrations and resettlement projects in Southeast Asia since 1945. *In* Proceedings of the Ninth Pacific Science Congress, vol. 3, pp. 189–194. Bangkok, Secretariat, Ninth Pacific Science Congress.

PURCELL, V.
1965 The Chinese in Southeast Asia. London, Kuala Lumpur, Hong Kong, Oxford University Press, 2d edn.

PYE, LUCIAN W.
1962 Politics, personality, and nation building: Burma's search for identity. New Haven and London, Yale University Press.

SAHLINS, MARSHALL D.
1960 Political power and the economy in primitive society. *In* Essays in the science of culture, in honor of Leslie A. White. Gertrude E. Dole and Robert Carneiro, eds. New York, Thomas Y. Crowell Company.

SCIGLIANO, R.
1963 South Vietnam: nation under stress. Boston, Houghton Mifflin Company.

SCIGLIANO, ROBERT and GUY H. FOX
1965 Technical assistance in Vietnam: the Michigan State University experience. New York, Frederick A. Praeger.

SEIDENFADEN, ERIK
1923 The Lawa, additional notes. Journal of the Siam Society 17(2):101–102.

SHARP, L. *et al.*
1953 Siamese rice village: a preliminary study of Bang Chan, 1948–1949. Bangkok, Cornell Research Center.

SIHANOUK, Prince NORODOM
1965 Is nationalism anachronistic? Kambuja Monthly Illustrated Review 4:15–20 (July 15).

SMALLEY, W. A.
1061 Orthography studies: articles on new writing systems. London, The United Bible Societies.
1965 Personal communication (unpublished notes on the teaching and learning of Thai in hill-tribe schools, June 21, mimeographed).

SMITH, ROGER M.
1965 Cambodia's foreign policy. Ithaca, Cornell University Press.

SOCHUREK, H.
1965 Americans in action in Viet Nam. National Geographic 127(1):38–65.

STERN, THEODORE
1965 Research upon Karen in village and town, Upper Khwae Noi, western Thailand; selected findings. Bangkok, mimeographed.

STEWARD, JULIAN H.
1949 Cultural causality and law: a trial formulation of the development of early civilizations. American Anthropologist 51(1):1–27.

1955 Theory of culture change. Urbana, University of Illinois Press.

THOMAS, M. LADD
1962 Thai public administration. New Zealand Journal of Public Administration 25(1).

THOMPSON, V., and R. ADLOFF
1955 Minority problems in Southeast Asia. Stanford, Stanford University Press.

TYLOR, EDWARD B.
1871 Primitive culture. London, John Murray and Company, 2 vols.

UNESCO
1964 Demographic yearbook, 1963. New York, United Nations.

WEINER, MYRON
1965 Political integration and political development. The Annals of the American Academy of Political and Social Science 358:52–64.

WILLIAMS-HUNT, P. D. R.
1952 An introduction to the Malayan Aborigines. Kuala Lumpur, The Government Printer.

WILSON, DAVID A.
1962 Politics in Thailand. Ithaca, Cornell University Press.
1963 Nation-building and revolutionary war. In Nation-building, Karl W. Deutsch and William J. Foltz, ed., Ch. 6, New York, Atherton Press.

WOLF, ERIC R.
1956 Aspects of group relations in a complex society: Mexico. American Anthropologist 58:1065–1078.
1957 Closed corporate peasant communities in Mesoamerica and Central Java. Southwestern Journal of Anthropology 13:1–18.
1966 Peasants. Englewood Cliffs, N.J., Prentice-Hall, Inc. Foundations of Modern Anthropology Series.

YING SIDA, Chao
1965 Short History of the Shan States. The Social Science Review (Thailand) 3(1):45–53.

Periodicals

CHINA NEWS ANALYSIS. Hong Kong.
CHINA RECONSTRUCTS. Peking.
KAMBUJA MONTHLY ILLUSTRATED REVIEW. Phnom Penh.
RÉALITÉS CAMBODGIENNES. Phnom Penh.

PART II: BURMA

PART II: BURMA

THE PRESENT political boundaries of the Union of Burma are largely the result of British colonial efforts and British attempts to define a zone of influence as against those of France and China. When by 1885 the series of British conquests led to the final downfall of the Burma Kingdom, the kingdom's firm control was limited primarily to the Irrawaddy Valley, extending not much further north than Bhamo. Just before the conquest, in one of their periods of expansion, the Burmans had raided and claimed areas of Manipur and Assam, which brought them into conflict with British interests in India.

The mountainous regions which now form the international boundaries with East Pakistan, India, China, Laos, and Thailand were occupied by peoples who were not Burmese in speech and who differed in many other aspects of culture. These included such groups as the Chin, Kachin, Wa, Shan, Karen, and Mon. Some of these groups, for example the Shan, rivaled the Burmans in cultural development and political influence. The British recognized this and gave such territories as the Shan States and Kayah (Red Karen) special administrative status within which traditional patterns of leadership were largely maintained or even reinforced under a system of indirect rule. The tribal peoples were put under a special administrative jurisdiction not directly related to the administration of Burma proper (Hill People's Regulation Act of 1889, etc.). They were governed by the British governor through the Frontier Areas Administration.

For a long time the area which has become the Union of Burma was administered as a part of Britain's Indian Empire, including, eventually, Indian members of the Indian Civil Service. At the end of the Second World War, when the British had agreed to independence for Burma, the question arose as to the form of government and the fate of the various "minority" peoples over whom the Burmans had never exercised firm political control.

After many discussions (some of which are described in the papers which follow), it was decided that a Union of Burma would be formed, within which some of the "minority groups" would have their own states. Dissatisfaction with the results of this arrangement has led to many long and violent attempts among such groups as the Shan and Karen to assert their political and cultural independence.

The minorities in Burma ordinarily define themselves and each other as cultural groups. They are not, however, discrete populations. As Lehman and Maran point out, attempts by scholars to devise a consistent set of attributes which distinguish minorities from the majority have failed. What this means is that it is impossible to understand or define minorities without understanding the general question of inter-group relations. The behavior of the minorities (as contrasted with their self-definition) is structured by their relationships with other such groups—not in terms of such attributes as language, religion, race, or place of residence. The people themselves may seize on any one of these attributes for symbolic reasons and ignore the others. This is symptomatic of the relationships between the groups in question, but, as Lehman and Maran show, this does not form an adequate basis for a theoretical understanding of inter-group relations in general.

One of the problems of nation-building is that of promoting identification with the nation by individuals from diverse groups. As Mr. Maran has pointed out, a Kachin considers himself first and foremost a Kachin, as contrasted with being a Shan or a Burman. He identifies himself not as an animist vs. Buddhist vs. Christian, not as a speaker of Jinghpaw as opposed to Burmese or Shan, and not as a hillside dry-rice cultivator as opposed to a valley wet-rice cultivator. In fact he may be a Buddhist, Shan-speaking wet-rice grower, but in establishing his relations with members of other groups, he first identifies himself as a Kachin (see Maran, p. 140). This sort of group identity has implications for political development, some of which Mr. Maran has pointed out. Only when the Kachin begin to see themselves within a larger context of the proposed Union of Burma do they begin to act consciously as an aligned group of tribes. Previously there seemed to have been no correlation between notions of ethnic identity and the awareness of the need for a concerted political movement of some sort.

As Professor Lehman has shown, the same is true of various Karen groups. Although he indicates that all Karen think of themselves as being Karen vs. non-Karen, the meaning of this varies among the particular kinds of Karen (Karenni vs. Sgaw Karen, or even Kyèbogyi Karenni vs. Bawlahkè Karenni). Indeed one of the reasons Karen and other minority group attempts at achieving independence have failed is that the people have not acted as Karen (in opposition to Burman) but as members of some small tribelet of Karen or as adherents to some particular Karen leader in opposition to some other small group at the same level.

Though many authorities have tried to argue that the lack of cohesion between tribe and nation in Burma is due to the heritage of colonialism, Mr. Maran shows convincingly that, at least for the Kachin, this argument is not valid. Most of the people who have argued that tribal unrest is a result of colonialism have not themselves studied the situation among the tribes, but instead seem to have relied on information from non-tribal Burmans.[1]

Unlike some other countries, Burma seems to have little which can act as a tie to crosscut ethnic identification and bind members of the diverse minorities to the central government. In Thailand, for example, religion and the monarchy are used fairly successfully as national symbols. In Burma religion will not work— the Buddhists among the minorities (e.g. the Shan) see a threat to their cultural existence in the nationalization of religion just as do the non-Buddhists.[2] And, as a result of colonialism, there is not even a vestige of the monarchy around which a symbol of national unity could be built, as has been done in Laos, Thailand, and Cambodia. The problem for Burma is one of great magnitude, not only because the minorities are strategically placed on all borders, but also because they form a very large portion of the population.

[1] The heritage of colonialism may still be important in determining the attitude of the Burmans. Nash, for example, who is concerned with the processes of modernization among the Burman peasants, indicates quite clearly that they much prefer to have the Burman government officials who have replaced the British colonial officers (1965:93–103). Likewise, one can guess that the tribal minorities would prefer to have tribal officials to replace the Burman officials in their localities.

[2] For another view of the relationship of religion to national unity in Burma see Smith (1965, esp. pp. 320–322). This treatment fails to take into account the point Lehman has raised concerning the organizational split between Shan and Burman Buddhists.

POPULATION AND LINGUISTIC AFFILIATION
OF ETHNIC GROUPS OF BURMA

GENERAL CONSIDERATIONS:
A NOTE ON LINGUISTIC CLASSIFICATION

Linguists have tried to classify languages in such a way as to indicate genetic (historical) relationships. The most generally accepted modern classifications are based on comparisons of vocabularies and systematic sound correspondences in the basic vocabulary which reflect descent from a common ancestral language. Other measures have been used to show other kinds of historical contacts between languages (e.g. borrowed words or features of linguistic structure such as noun-classifiers).

The area with which this book deals is one of the world's most complicated linguistic regions, and systematic studies of the languages are only just beginning. Speakers of dialects of the same language family are not always contiguously distributed, but are often found in small pockets or enclaves intermingled with speakers of completely different languages. The linguistic boundaries between dialects are not always sharp—differentiation may be more a matter of political boundaries than of linguistic features (e.g. Lao Tai, spoken in Laos, and Northeastern Tai, spoken in the adjacent parts of Thailand). Because of the present state of knowledge, it has proved impossible to be completely consistent in the terminology I have applied, either in levels of classification (taxonomic level), or in the contents of language groups.

One source of confusion is the lack of standardization in application of names to groups or languages—the same term has been applied to quite different languages (e.g. Kachin), and different labels may be attached to the same group (Kayah is the same as Red Karen or Karenni). I have tried to list some of the more common synonyms for the groups, but here again it should be remembered that there is no standard usage. The terms are applied to different ranges of populations by people with different points of reference. Likewise, I have not been able to arrange the listing of sub-groups so as to be on comparable levels. Two examples may illustrate the problems involved: *Tai Dai* is a term which is used by the Burma Shan to refer to the Hkamti Shan or Ahom Shan, but the same term is used by other Tai speakers to refer to the Burma Shan. *Nung* and *Rawang* are both names for sub-groupings of "Kachin Tribes," but the Rawang are actually a sub-group of the Nung (see Lehman's paper for further discussion and examples).

Another confusion results from the fact that census information, where it exists, is rarely consistent in application of linguistic terms, though linguistic criteria are frequently the basis for census groupings of tribes and minorities. The job of the census is made more difficult in that members of one identifiable minority group may speak different languages, and that different groups may speak the same language (this point is discussed at some length in the papers of Lehman and Maran). Finally, it should be noted that linguistic classifications such as the ones presented in the tables in this book do not necessarily correspond to the important and interesting behavioral facts. For example, in this gross form they can say nothing about the patterns of bilingualism which may make it possible to eliminate linguistic boundaries to communication.

In what follows I have tried to indicate the basis of the classification used in this volume (summarized in Table 3, "Classification of Some Mainland Southeast Asian Languages"), and to indicate some of the other points of view. It should be noted that this chart includes detailed breakdowns only on those groups found in Southeast Asia.

THE CHINESE-RELATED LANGUAGES

Although the large family grouping of Sino-Tibetan languages is generally accepted, the contents and order of sub-groupings within this family are matters of dispute. Chinese and Tibeto-Burman are generally considered to be branches of Sino-Tibetan. Karen is usually considered to be a Tibeto-Burman language sub-group, but some consider it to be more distantly related than other branches. In general I have followed Burling (1965A, 1965B) in classifying the members of the Tibeto-Burman group.

TABLE 3
CLASSIFICATION OF SOME MAINLAND SOUTHEAST
ASIAN LANGUAGES*

FAMILY	FAMILY
Group, Sub-group, Sub-sub-group	*Group, Sub-group, Sub-sub-group*
Language	Language
Dialect	Dialect

? KADAI

Kelao (Ch'ilao)

Laqua

Lati

Li

MALAYO-POLYNESIAN

Chamic, Coastal

Cham
Cham, Cambodian
Chru
Noang

Cac Gia Roglai

Roglai

Southern Roglai

Rai

?Hroy
Chamic, Plateau

Jarai

Krung

Rnadé
Bihê

Malay

Indonesian
Malay
Jakun

MIAO-YAO

Miao (Meo)

Yao (Iu Mien, Man)
Lanten
She (Sho)

MON-KHMER

Bahnaric, N. Bahnaric

Bahnar
Rengao
Sedang
? Sayan

Bout

?Brao

Cua
Kayong

Halang
Halang Doan
Jeh
? Strieng

Hrê

? Kasseng

Langya

? Love

Loven

Monam

? Noar

? Sedang Todrah

? Takua.

(continued)

TABLE 3, *continued**

MON-KHMER, continued	MON-KHMER, continued
Bahnaric, S. Bahnaric (Stiengan)	*Khasi*
Biat	*Khmeric*
Chrau	Chong

Koho
   ? Cil
   Lat
   Pru
	Kymer (Cambodian)

	Kui
Kwanh	Pear
Mnong ?? Cil Mnong Gar	? Saoch
	Mon
Rolom	Mon
Stieng *Bahnaric (? Sub-group)*	*N. Laos*
? Duan	Khmu?
Katuic	Lamet
? Alak	? Mrabri
Attaouat	? Sach
Brôu	T'in
Kattang	? Yumbri
Katu	*Palaungic*

Cao
   Pacoh
      ? Ta-oih
   Phuong
? May
	? Chaobon

	Lawa (Lua?)
? Ngeh	? Penglung
	Palaung (Pulang)
? Ruc	Wa (Kawa)
? Van Kieu (? = Brôu)	

(continued)

[81]

TABLE 3, *continued**

MON-KHMER, continued	SINO-TIBETAN, continued

MON-KHMER, continued

(Group unknown)

Cheng

Ngung Bo

Nha Heun

Oy

Sapuan

So

Sork

Sou

Souei

Thap

The

Ven

SENOI-SEMANG

Senoi (Malayan "Negrito")

Che Wong
Jah Hut
Semai
Temiar

SINO-TIBETAN

Chinese

Nung

Yunnanese (Haw, Ho, Panthay)

Many others

SINO-TIBETAN, continued

Tibeto-Burman

Bodo

Bodo
Garo
Kachari
Koch

Chutua
Lalung
Tipera

Konyak

? Jinghpaw ("Kachin" language)

Burmese-Lolo, Burma

? Achang

Burmese

"Kachin languages" (except Jinghpaw)

Atzi
Hpon
Lashi
Maru

Burmese-Lolo, Lolo

Akha
Hani (Woni)

Kutsung

Lahu (Laku, Mussuh)

Lisu

Lolo (Yi)

? Pai

T'uchia

Xa

(continued)

TABLE 3, *continued**

SINO-TIBETAN, continued	TAI
Tibeto-Burman continued	*Southwestern*
Kadu-Kanang-Sak-Thet-Andro	Lü (Lue)
	Tai Blanc
Kuki-Chin	
	Ahom
Chin	Shan
Kuki	
Lushai	Northern
Ao Naga	Phuan
Lhota	
Manipuri (Meithei)	Central
Mikir	
	Tai Noir
Naga	
	Phu Thai
Angami	
Rengma	Lao
Sema	
	Southern Thai
Thankul	
	Neua
North Assam	
	Red
Abor-Adi	
	Various languages in Yunnan
Aka	
	Central
Dafla	
Bangni	Lung-chow
	Nung
Miri	
	Tay
Mismi	Tho
North Burma	T'ien-pao
Nung	Yung-ch'un
Rawang	

Karen

Karenni
Padaung
Pwo
S'kaw (Sgaw)
Others

(continued)

TABLE 3, *continued**

TAI, continued	TAI, continued
Northern	*Kam-Sui*
Hsi-lin	Kam (Tung)
Ling-yun	
T'ien-chow	Sui (Shui)
T'se-heng	
	Mak (Mo)
Ch'ien-chiang	
	T'en (Yanghuang)
Wu-ming (Chuang)	
? Maonan	**VIET-MUONG**
? Molao	
	Muong
Nhang	
	Vietnamese (Annamese,
Puyi	Ching, Kinh)
Po-ai	
Saek	

* The sources from which this table has been taken and the cautions which must be applied to its use are indicated in the body of the text. Closeness of relationship within a family or group of languages is indicated by vertical separation, but the degree of relationship thus specified is not necessarily comparable from one grouping to the next. Where degree of relationship has not been specified, the languages are listed alphabetically. The present table differs at a number of points from the table and list of languages in Census of India 1961, Vol. I, Part II-C (ii), pp. clxv–clxx, and Appendix I, which are apparently based on Grierson's earlier work.

Miao-Yao and Tai are considered by some authorities to be branches of Sino-Tibetan equivalent to Chinese and Tibeto-Burman; other authorities consider them to be unrelated, or very distantly related (Miao-Yao, for example, has sometimes been classed with the Mon-Khmer languages). For present purposes I have followed Downer in considering that Chinese, Tai, and Miao-Yao are separate families (see Downer 1963 for a recent review of some of the evidence for Chinese, Tai, and Miao-Yao relationships). On the other hand, Shafer (1957) has included Miao-Yao and Tai within Sino-Tibetan (see Shafer for further bibliographic references).

AUSTROASIATIC LANGUAGES AND MON-KMHER

It has long been suggested that a very widespread super-family of languages, known as Austroasiatic, is distributed from the southeastern border of China to central India. The supposed branches which concern us in this book are Mon-Khmer, Viet-Muong, and Senoi-Semang. Some authorities consider that Viet-Muong is related to the Tai languages (e.g. Pinnow 1963:141), and not related to Austroasiatic ones. Likewise, some say Senoi-Semang is unrelated to Mon-Khmer. For purposes of this book I have used the term Mon-Khmer to refer to a language grouping which, according to Thomas (1965A, 1965B), contains the following seven equidistant branches: 1) Bahnaric; 2) Katuic; 3) Khasi (found in Assam); 4) Khmeric; 5) Mon; 6) N. Laos; 7) Palaungic. The Munda languages of central India are also evidently related to the Mon-Khmer family (see Pinnow 1963 for a recent review of the general question of relationships within the Austroasiatic group; see Shorto *et al.* 1963 for additional references).

For present purposes I have considered Viet-Muong as an independent family, and that Senoi-Semang (referred to by Pinnow as the Malacca languages) is distantly related to Mon-Khmer.

TAI AND KADAI LANGUAGES

Paul Benedict (1942) suggested that Tai and the Kadai languages (which are little-known dialects spoken by small populations in the North Vietnam-China border area, and the sizable Li population on Hainan Island) are related. This hypothesis has not been confirmed in the intervening years, but some authorities have accepted it as fact (e.g. LeBar *et al.* 1964). Others have suggested that the Tai languages are ultimately related to Chinese, and that the Kam-Sui-Mak languages form a bridge between Chinese and Tai, but I have considered Tai to be an independent family, within which Kam-Sui-Mak is a distinct branch.

In general I have followed the Tai dialect classification suggested by Li (1959, 1960), with valuable advice from Gedney

(1965). Information on Tai dialects spoken in Thailand is taken from Brown (1965). Li divides Tai into three basic branches: Northern, Central, and Southwestern. Some authorities consider Northern and Central to belong to the same branch, and it is quite evident that the boundaries between the branches are not sharp.

The Kam-Sui languages are considered to be distantly related to Tai (see Li 1943; 1965; Nishida 1955). Bruk (1959) has evidently followed Li in this. Bruk has disregarded the Kadai family grouping, and has assigned various members to different families (Li to the Chuang-Tung group, Kelao to the Miao-Yao group). I have followed Benedict in accepting the existence of a Kadai grouping, but consider it distinct from Tai.

MALAYO-POLYNESIAN LANGUAGES

This language family is distributed all the way from Madagascar to Hawaii and the Easter Islands. Representatives of the family of concern to us are found in Indochina (e.g. the Cham), the Malay Peninsula, and Borneo. Although a great deal of work has been done in reconstructing the historical relationships of Malayo-Polynesian languages in Polynesia, Melanesia, and Micronesia, the classification of the Southeast Asian members has received scant attention in recent years. Thomas (1965B) considers that there are two groups of Malayo-Polynesian (Chamic) languages in Indochina: lowland languages including Cham and Roglai, and a plateau group including Rhadé, Jarai, and Bih.

In order to avoid the controversies alluded to above, I have limited the classification categories to those which have been best established, and I have not concerned myself with such ultimate relationships as are implied in super-families like Austroasiatic. Thus, if the classifications have any value for indicating historical relationships between languages, they refer to a relatively recent period. Since glotto-chronological work must await a more detailed classification of the languages, I am unable to assign dates to the dispersion of the various dialects.

It should be noted that classification within the same language group, or even sub-group, does not imply that the languages are mutually intelligible; they may be quite as distinct as German and English.

TABLE 4
POPULATION AND LINGUISTIC AFFILIATION OF
ETHNIC GROUPS OF BURMA[a]

Group [Sub-groups (Synonyms in Parentheses)]	Estimated Population in Burma[b]	Location (in Order of Size of Population)	Language
Burmese [(Burman, Bama), Arakan, Tenasserim]	13,342,000[c]	Burma, Yunnan, Assam	Tibeto-Burman: Burmese-Lolo, Burma group
Karen [(Kariang, Kayin, Yang) Bré, Kayah (Karenni, Red Karen), Manumanaw (Münü), Padaung, Pwo, Taungthu (Pa O), Sgaw (S?kaw), and others]	1,340,000[d]	Burma, Thailand, Yunnan	Sino-Tibetan: probably Tibeto-Burman, Karen
Shan of Burma [(Ngiaw, Shan-Bama, Tai Yai), Chinese Shan (Tai Dau), Hkamti Shan (Ahom Shan, Tai Dai), Tai Nui] [other Tai speakers in this population estimate include the Hkün (Khün) and Lü (Thai-Lue)]	1,200,000[e]	Burma, Yunnan, Thailand	Tai: South-western
Kachin Tribes [Atzi, Jinghpaw, Lisu (Lasaw, Lisaw, Lishaw, Yawyin), Maru, Nung, Rawang]	750,000[f]	Burma, Yunnan, Thailand	Tibeto-Burman: several distinct dialects of Burmese-Lolo, North Burma, and other groups
Chinese	400,000[g]	China, Southeast Asia	Chinese
Chin [(Kuki, Zo)]	344,000+	Burma, Assam	Tibeto-Burman: Kuki-Chin
Mon [(Peguan, Talaing)]	337,000[h]	Burma, Thailand	Mon-Khmer: Mon
Wa [(Kawa)]	334,533[i]	Burma, Yunnan	Mon-Khmer: Palaungic
Indian	100,000[j]	India, Pakistan, Southeast Asia	Dravidian and Indo-European
Lahu [(Mussuh)]	66,000	Yunnan, Burma, Thailand	Tibeto-Burman: Burmese-Lolo, Lolo group

(continued)

TABLE 4
(*continued*)

Group [Sub-groups (Synonyms in Parentheses)]	Estimated Population in Burma[b]	Location (in Order of Size of Population)	Language
Lü [(Thai-Lue)]	[50,000][k]	Yunnan, Burma, Thailand, Laos	Tai: Southwestern
Akha [(Ikaw), Hani, Woni]	40,000+	Yunnan, Burma, Thailand, Laos	Tibeto-Burman: Burmese-Lolo, Lolo group
Kadu	40,000	Burma	Tibeto-Burman: Kadu-Kanang-Sak-Thet-Andro
Lisu [(Lasaw, Lishaw, Lisaw, Yawyin—a "Kachin tribe"—non-Kachin-influenced are known as Shisham)]	[30,000+][l]	Yunnan, Burma, Thailand	Tibeto-Burman: Burmese-Lolo, Lolo group
Moken [(Selon)]	5,000+	Burma, Thailand, Malaya	Malayo-Polynesian: Malay
Panthay [(Ho, Hui[m])]	1,200+	Yunnan, Burma, Thailand	Chinese: Yunnanese
Hpon	1,000−	Burma	Tibeto-Burman: Burmese-Lolo, Burma group (?)
Achang	[unavailable]	Yunnan, Burma	Tibeto-Burman: Burmese-Lolo, Burma group (?)
Naga [many distinct groups]	[unavailable]	Nagaland, Burma	Tibeto-Burman: Naga, and Kuki Chin
Palaung [(Ta-ang)]	[unavailable]	Burma, Yunnan	Mon-Khmer: Palaungic
Burma total (1963 estimate)	23,664,000		

(continued)

[a] Source: Population figures are from LeBar *et al.* (1964), primarily based on 1931 census, except as noted. Linguistic classifications are from Burling (1965, and personal communication), Maran (personal communication), Lehman (personal communication), Li (1959, 1960), and Gedney (personal communications).

[b] Groups have been listed in order of size of population. Where population estimates are unavailable, groups have been listed alphabetically.

ᶜ Figure for Burmese speakers includes Arakan and Tenasserim dialects as well.

ᵈ Total Karen figure for 1931 includes Sgaw, Pwo, Pa O, and Kayah.

ᵉ Figure, from Maran (personal communication), includes all Tai speakers in Burma. LeBar *et al.* (1964:19) give slightly over one million as the number of Tai speakers in Burma in 1931.

ᶠ Estimate from early 1950's. LeBar *et al.* give an estimate of 350,000 to 400,000 from a partial census which did not include all "Kachin tribes." The estimate of 750,000 is from Maran (personal communication). As indicated in Maran's paper, which follows, the term "Kachin tribes" is a grab-bag of different cultural, linguistic, and political groupings. In Burma these people are by no means confined to Kachin State, but are also found concentrated in Kengtung, Kodaung, Lashio, and Mogok districts, Shan State.

ᵍ Figure for Chinese is estimate by Skinner (personal communication).

ʰ In 1931 there were 337,000 Mon by race, 305,000 by language.

ⁱ Post-1946 estimates by H. M. Young (former district officer in the Wa States) were 324,533 Wa in the Wa States and 10,000 in Kengtung Shan State (LeBar *et al.* 1964:130).

ʲ The partial census of 1953 gives 175,000 as the number of Indians in Burma. This is a minimal figure for that date. Personal communication from Lehman (1965) states that there were approximately 250,000 Indians in Burma at the time of the military take-over in 1962. Approximately 150,000 have emigrated in the succeeding three years, leaving about 100,000. Many of the Indians in Burma are from south India, and are speakers of Dravidian languages.

ᵏ This Lü population figure is from a 1923 estimate of the number in Kengtung and Laos (cited in LeBar *et al.* 1964:207).

ˡ This Lisu population figure is from LeBar *et al.* (1964:28). The Lisu population was also included in "Kachin tribes" total, but not all Lisu are "Kachinized."

ᵐ Hui is the Chinese term for Moslems. Some, but not all, of these Yunnanese refugees and traders are Moslem.

REFERENCES CITED

BENEDICT, PAUL
    1942   Thai, Kadai, and Indonesian, a new alignment in Southeast Asia. American Anthropologist 44: 576–601.
BROWN, J. MARVIN
    1965   From ancient Thai to modern dialects. Bangkok, Social Science Association Press of Thailand.
BURLING, ROBBINS
    1965A   Hill farms and padi fields: life in mainland Southeast Asia. Englewood Cliffs, N.J., Prentice Hall, Inc., Spectrum Book S-110.
    1965B   Personal communication, September 15, 1965.

[89]

BURMA, CENTRAL STATISTICAL AND ECONOMICS DEPARTMENT
    1957   First stage census, 1953: population and housing. Rangoon, Superintendent, Government Printing and Stationery.

DOWNER, G. B.
    1963   Chinese, Thai and Miao-Yao. *In* Linguistic comparison in South East Asia and the Pacific, H. L. Shorto, ed. London, School of Oriental and African Studies, University of London.

GEDNEY, WILLIAM J.
    1965   Personal communications.

LEBAR, FRANK M., GERALD C. HICKEY, and JOHN K. MUSGRAVE
    1964   Ethnic groups of mainland Southeast Asia. New Haven, Human Relations Area Files Press.

LEHMAN, F. K.
    1965   Personal communication, September 20, 1965.

LI, FANG-KUEI
    1943   Notes on the Mak language. Academia Sinica, Institute of History and Philology Monograph Series A, No. 20. Shanghai. Republished in Academia Sinica Bulletin of the Institute of History and Philology 19:1–80, 1948.
    1959   Classification by vocabulary: Tai dialects. Anthropological Linguistics 1(2):15–21.
    1960   A tentative classification of Tai dialects. *In* Culture in history: essays in honor of Paul Radin, ed. Stanley Diamond. New York, Columbia University Press.
    1965   The Tai and the Kam-Sui languages. Lingua 14:148–179.

NASH, MANNING
    1965   The golden road to modernity: village life in contemporary Burma. New York, London, and Sydney, John Wiley and Sons, Inc.

NISHIDA, TATSUO
    1955   Mak-Sui languages and Common Tai. Gengo Kenkyu, Journal of the Linguistic Society of Japan 28:30–62. [English summary pp. 59–62.]

PINNOW, HEINZ-JÜRGEN
    1963   The position of the Munda languages within the Austroasiatic language family. *In* Linguistic comparison in South East Asia and the Pacific, H. L. Shorto, ed. London School of Oriental and African Studies, University of London.

SHAFER, ROBERT, *et al.* (eds.)
    1957   Bibliography of Sino-Tibetan languages. Wiesbaden, Otto Harrassowitz.

SHORTO, H. L., JUDITH M. JACOB, and E. H. S. SIMMONDS
    1963   Bibliographies of Mon-Khmer and Tai linguistics. London Oriental Bibliographies vol. 2. London, Oxford University Press.

SKINNER, G. WILLIAM
    1965 Personal communication.
SMITH, DONALD E.
    1965 Religion and politics in Burma. Princeton, N.J., Princeton
        University Press.
THOMAS, DAVID D.
    1965A Vietnam minority languages (July 1965 revision). Saigon,
        Summer Institute of Linguistics.
    1965B Personal communications.

CHAPTER 2

Ethnic Categories in Burma and the
Theory of Social Systems

F. K. LEHMAN

POLITICAL BACKGROUND: THE FEDERALIST MOVEMENT

In this chapter I shall first give some of the recent background for Burma's current minority problems, and then put it in the general context of an appropriate theory.

Burma's minority problems are at least as vexing and complex as those of any country in mainland Southeast Asia. Mr. Maran (in this volume) has summarized in a general way the analyses of the problem which are available to us and has shown that they take us very little distance toward any understanding. He has told us further that Burma's independence in the form of a *Union* was achieved in 1948, in part as a result of decisions reached at the Panglong Conference, following activities of the Frontier Areas Enquiry Commission. Deliberations of that Commission helped to persuade the spokesmen for various minority groups within the colonial territorial boundaries of Burma to opt for union with the Burman majority.[1]

Since independence in 1948 Burma has been beset with various degrees and kinds of insurgency, and among the insurgent groups have been, for example, the Karen National Defense Organization (KNDO), the Mon National Defense Organization, and other groups whose labels show them to be connected with Kachin, Shan, and even Arakanese aspirations for some sort of recognition as "nationalities."

The Constitution of the Union of Burma is such that certain

[1] In this paper, and the one by Mr. Maran which follows, the term "Burman" refers to a native speaker of the Burmese language, who is a member of the dominant national majority group in "Burma." "Burma" means the territory of the Union of Burma. "Burma proper" means the region of Burma, principally the major river-valley region, which is occupied primarily by Burmans.

blocks of minority peoples (Kayah, Karen, Shan, Kachin), along with Burma proper (the heartland of the majority Burman population), have the status of states within the Union. One block, the Chin, constitutes a "special division," which is not quite a state. On the eve of the assumption of political power by the Burma Army Revolutionary Council in March 1962, there was even fairly substantial talk of the possibilities, pro and con, of some sort of similar recognition for the Mon and the Arakanese.

Prominent among the ostensible precipitating causes of this assumption of power by the military was the activity of a consortium of minority blocks. This consortium was holding the so-called Federalist Seminars in Rangoon the very week of the Revolution. This was well reported in the Rangoon press though not in foreign papers. As nearly as I can judge, the consortium did not claim to represent the governments of the minority-block states, but they did represent interests in and of the minority states and the Chin Special Division. As its steering committee was headquartered in the Kayah State Guest House where I was also staying,[2] I can say that a very diverse set of sentiments on minority issues was represented.

The consortium seems to have concentrated very much on Shan nationalist aspirations, and was perhaps led by proponents of Shan nationalism. In fact, much of the force of the argument behind the organization was the not-too-veiled threat of Shan secession from the Union. Documentation for a description of the issues and actors is lacking because the organization's records were quickly impounded by the Revolutionary government. Thus we can only presume that this particularly strong and well-articulated Shan nationalism was associated with the renewed Shan insurgency of the time. Shan nationalist sentiment had been provoked with the abolition of the political status and prerogatives of the traditional Shan sawbwas (princes) in the Shan State during the military Caretaker regime of 1958–1961.

The "representativeness" of the personnel from the various minority blocks differed considerably from group to group. One inference from the location of the steering committee headquarters (in the Kayah State Guest House) is that the Kayah State apparatus was itself involved. Sao Wunna, who was then Kayah State Minister (in the Union government), was subsequently

[2] I was in no way involved in the proceedings of the meeting.

implicated in a rather serious anti-government conspiracy, and this fact tends to confirm the inference that the state government was involved. In any case, Kayah representation, overt or covert, was by persons at the center of ongoing Kayah State politics. I suspect this was true for the Shans as well, but cannot prove it.

In the case of the Kachin, about whom Mr. Maran writes, the Sama Duwa (who was then President-elect of the Union of Burma) was occasionally seen with members of the steering committee at the Kayah State Guest House. But he walked out on them in anger, and perhaps this move explains why he was not arrested when he returned to Rangoon some days after the Revolution.

The Chin were far less involved, being represented at Kayah Guest House by two Northern (Tiddim) Chin politicians, one of whom was a retired army captain, at that time a member of Parliament. Apparently neither of them was more than an observer and neither was a major political figure in the more vocally nationalist parties (e.g. CNO, or Chin National Organization) of the Chin Special Division. Likewise, neither was arrested on the night of the take-over, as were six of the other participants in the Guest House.

I can say nothing about the other groups.

Leaving aside the Shan secessionist threat as unassessable, the Federalist movement brought diverse people together on the common ground of a proposed *federal* constitution for the Union. In this system more autonomy would be given to the minority constituent blocks. Also, in essence, the Union would not be run so much by Burma proper. Up to this time the Burmans had dominated the Union by means of the parliamentary system of government. Among other things, the Union (central) government was also the government of Burma proper (one of the Union's constituents). What the minorities wanted, as a minimum common denominator, was more power to distribute central government revenue to and within the non-Burman states. There was also talk in the Federalist circles (mainly Shan?) of asking for the right of the states to negotiate independently with foreign governments—ostensibly for foreign economic aid—and this must have appeared a very serious threat to the Union.

So much for the Federalist movement and the attendant Shan

insurgency as background to Burma's present internal problems. It was certainly a complicated minority-oriented situation.

RELIGIOUS BACKGROUND: THE STATE RELIGION ACT

During the final couple of years of the civilian government, under U Nu, the religious question was also a complicating factor in the politics of majority-minority relations. Buddhism is, of course, the religion of most of the Burmans, the national majority people of Burma. It is, in fact, a central part of their sense of national-cultural identity, quite apart from technical questions about individual religious beliefs. On the basis of the somewhat vague promises U Nu made during his successful campaign after the first military regime, he was under pressure to make Buddhism, in some way or other, the national religion.

The State Religion Act was passed about three months before the Revolution which removed U Nu from power. What this act might have meant, of course, cannot be known. U Nu insisted that it would not infringe upon the freedom of religion for adherents of other religions. But it did involve official Union government recognition of the preeminent place of Buddhism as the religion of the majority, and it meant the continuation of the financial and organizational support already given to Buddhist missionary activity, Buddhist monastic-hierarchical reform, Buddhist scholarship, and so on.

The "state religion" question affected majority-minority relations adversely in two very different ways. First, let us take the case of the Shan, who are generally Buddhists of the same doctrinal variety as the Burmans. The Shan Buddhist organization has traditionally been formally distinct from that of Burma proper; under the Burmese kings the Shan monasteries appear not to have been subject to the jurisdiction of the Burmese Buddhist primate (Mendelson 1964). The Shan had felt for some time that the central government was trying to impose Burman monks and Burman monastic traditions in the Shan State, and the State Religion policy only exacerbated this fear.

The reaction of other groups had a different basis. Among some of the tribes, notably Chin, Kachin, and Karen, there are large numbers of Christians. Furthermore, much of their nationalistic political leadership comes from the Christian, mission-influenced sections of the population. Mr. Maran has written of this in the case of the Kachin.

Among the Chin, the only group of which I can speak from fairly direct knowledge on this point, the religious issue seriously agitated a large segment of politicians, particularly those not in the government party. It did not precipitate insurgency, but it created a very real, if quiet, panic. Roughly 70 percent of the Chin are non-Christians; most are animists, but some, especially on the Arakan (Kaladan River) side, are at least nominally Buddhists. Only about 22 percent are Baptists, real or nominal, and a few percent more are Protestants of other denominations, or Roman Catholics.

Despite the small proportion of Christians involved, the State Religion Act resulted in a feeling among the Chin that the central government wished to threaten important symbols of Chin *political* identity. This feeling tended to persist even after the State Religion policy ceased to be in effect under the new military Revolutionary government.

One of the important political functions of Christianity for the Chin has been to serve as a symbol of their being a part of a larger world of civilization via the churches and their missions. That world was, necessarily, the Western world. Thus, to the extent that the Revolutionary government has pursued socialist economic policies and neutralist or non aligned foreign policies, the Chin have felt increasingly cut off from this part of their identification with the rest of the world. As a consequence, the panic among the Chin nationalist political leaders has not dissipated. The secular policies of the Revolutionary government have been seen as a threat to just those things that, to the Chin, are symbolized in the issue of religion.

It should be pointed out that Chin identification with a religious institutional link to the outside world of civilization carried little desire for political separation from the Burmans. For the most part it was quite the reverse. Many Chin, and not just the Christians, felt that their age-old claim to be an integral part of the civilized political economy of Burma proper could be expressed only after the education and all sorts of cultural teachings of Christian missions had made it possible for the Chin to appear to the Burmans as something more than mere tribesmen. The missions gave them cultural leverage for asserting themselves as partners equal with the Burmans in the Burmese economic and political network. It is therefore unfortunate that during the past year or so a serious feeling, perhaps even an active movement, for political separation from Burma has begun in the Chin Hills. From my quite fragmentary current information, this seems to be a very different attitude from that of the past. Although there has always been a small and rather passive sentiment favoring Chin independence, the Chin for the most part have been intensely loyal to the Union. Chin troops were largely responsible for keeping Rangoon out of Karen and other insurgent hands during the battle of Insein in 1949. Chin troops were thought so reliable that late in the summer of 1958, when the first military regime was quietly being planned, Chin troops replaced most others in the strategic Motor Pool and in some other key service depots in and around Rangoon.

MINORITY PROBLEMS AND POLICIES

From all the foregoing we can derive general support for Mr. Maran's contention that Burma has not one but many minority problems, and also that there are *intra*-minority problems. We can conclude that the minorities have felt that Burma's policy toward them has been financially niggardly and administratively subordinating, and that it has not allowed adequately for economic development, educational improvement, or self-expression for the minorities in the Union councils. Until the present Revolutionary Council Government, in fact, there seems to have been no overall "minority policy" other than the very general guarantees of the now defunct Union Constitution.

The present government has propagandized widely for the development of the cultures and economies of the tribal and hill areas of the country. For example, the government has established projects for the development of terrace cultivation in the Chin Hills, and has also established an Academy for the Development of National Groups at Sagaing, which seems to have as its major activity the bringing together of groups of about ten people from each of the various minority areas, who will live together and be trained for about two years. It is expected that they will thereby learn to understand each other's customs and also get a feeling for their joint membership in the Burmese nation. In connection with this the Academy will encourage the practice and performance of the folk customs of the various minority groups, in the hope that the separate minority identities will be seen to complement one another. We do not yet know how different this will be from the former annual custom at Union Day, when hill men were brought to Rangoon to sight-see and to perform tribal dances. At the moment it is unclear whether the present policy will continue to reflect the view that minority customs are just collections of oddities useful mainly for arousing Burman curiosity about the remote peoples of the Union.

AN EXAMPLE OF INTRA-MINORITY PROBLEMS: KAYAH, KAREN, AND SHAN

I should like now to give a previously unpublished example from my fieldnotes of intra-minority problems. The example shows how some aspects of a minority's relationship to the majority population can be seriously affected by relations with other minorities.

Kayah State is one of the constituent parts of the Union of Burma. Formerly it was called the Karen-ni (Red Karen) State, though the ruling people of it call themselves Kayah (or, more exactly, Kaya-li = Karen-ni = Red Karen). It is usually stated as a fact that the change of official name, which took place in 1951, was insisted upon by the Kayah, simply because they did not wish to be identified as a kind of Karen, nor with the very serious Karen rebellion in 1949 and the years following. It is further usually stated as a fact that the Kayah insisted on the change because they had no connection with the rebellion and did *not* consider themselves to be any kind of Karen. But the situation is really much more complex.

The Kayah actually define themselves as a very special kind of Karen. In the villages men will discuss differences and similarities between their Kayah customs and the customs of their various Karen neighbors. One central part of Kayah identity in Burma is that they traditionally have had sawbwas (princes). The sawbwa system is a Shan political system, which derived its jural authority mainly from the old Burmese kingdoms.

There are three statelets of Karenni (Kantarawadi, Kyèbogyi, and Bawlahkè), each of which was formerly under a Shan-style sawbwa (prince). The second, which is in the center of Karenni State, was much involved in the beginning in the Karen National Defense Organization (KNDO), the Karen rebel organization. Its young prince, Saw Shwe, himself led his men as a part of the KNDO in the jungle, and in some of the villages of Kyèbogyi virtually all the able-bodied men were at one time with the insurgents.

Because they were under the leadership of their own prince, the Kayah claimed to be a separate force in the Karen insurgency. For one reason or another this antagonized the central body of the KNDO and led to general disaffection of the Kyèbogyi Kayah and their sawbwa. They withdrew from the insurgency, but it appears that Saw Shwe was detained by KNDO leaders somewhere in the jungle, where he subsequently died or was killed.

For a variety of reasons, the internal, and partly inter-dynastic, politics of Kayah State determined that whatever Kyèbogyi did, Kantarawadi and (perhaps with less zeal) Bawlahkè would do the opposite. Kantarawadi had long been recognized, first by the British and later by the Burmans, as the nominal paramount statelet in Kayah. Kyèbogyi, unquestionably the oldest Kayah statelet, had long disputed this position. When Kyèbogyi joined the KNDO, the Kantarawadi and Bawlahkè leaders were persuaded or constrained not to join. With the attendant destruction of the Kyèbogyi royal house and of elements friendly to it in that of Kantarawadi,[3] Kantarawadi was able to secure control of the Kayah State Ministry of the Union government for members and allies of its own royal house.

Thus what we have in Kayah State is a kind of Karen minority whose special position is defined by its identification with the Shan political system. This identification was used by the Kayah *not* to make themselves appear to be Shan, but rather to set themselves apart as a special entity vis-à-vis other Karen. The Shan are Buddhists; the Kayah, generally, are not. But the special affirmation of Kayah loyalty to the Union of Burma was a typical

[3] Traditionally, the Mahadewi, or chief wife, of the Kantarawadi sawbwa was a daughter of the sawbwa of Kyèbogyi. The story of how and why her son was kept from possible succession to the Kantarawadi sawbwaship in the mid-1940's must be written elsewhere.

product of Shan-style (intra-Kayah) politics among princes, as well as a product of inter-Karen relations.

It is not surprising, with this background, that by 1962 the previously loyal Kayah State government was particularly closely identified with the Shan-dominated extreme wing of the Federalist movement. As Mr. Maran says, it is impossible to view a minority as an isolate and to understand its relations with the majority on that basis. The Kayah State loyalty to Burma in the late 1940's and 1950's was loyalty *as against* other Karen (this is also true of Kyèbogyi separatism within the KNDO). It depended on identification *with* the sawbwa system of the Shan, and as the Shan position vis-à-vis the central government changed, so did that of the Kayah. The Kayah do not relate to the Burmans in a vacuum.

PAST AND CURRENT VIEWS OF THE MINORITY PROBLEM

I have no idea what the future role of the tribal people will be in the nation of Burma. I know what it is now and what, given present policy, it must continue to be for some time to come. Discontent characterizes almost all minority regions of Burma today, tribal and non-tribal alike. Active discontent brings government retaliation, and all this aggravates the general state of feud and insurrection in many parts of the country. The other face of insurrection is, of course, the insurrections of the political right and the political left. These are thoroughly mixed up with minority problems in several cases, but I am going to presume that these two faces of civil disorder are at least analytically distinct.

The most serious obstacle to solving Burma's problems of minority-majority relations is the official attitude toward indigenous minorities. Paradoxically, this attitude is nearly identical to many modern social-science approaches toward societies and cultures in general. I propose that this theory is in need of revision because it is unsound, especially for many parts of Southeast Asia, including Burma.

What are some of the fundamental ideas I am objecting to? First is the idea that any territorially localized group of people is *naturally*, exclusively, and definitively a portion, or a whole, of something called *a* society, and that there is in principle a definite, countable number of societies in the world. Ideally, each of them is supposed, on this view, to be a "people" with a culture peculiar to itself. (Note that the terms "naturally" and "ideally" are very important parts of this rhetoric, albeit frequently inexplicit.)

The second idea is that labels such as Chin, Kachin, Karen, Shan, Burman, and the like, have reference to "peoples" in the sense sketched above. Each of these labels is supposed to correspond either to some empirical, real, natural group of people (i.e., a society), or to some closed set of such societies in those cases where the label is a cover term for a class or type of societies. For example, we can take the idea that the term "Kachin" encompasses such labeled categories as Maru, Lashi, Atzi, Jinghpaw, etc. If we accept this view, "Kachin" refers at most to a species of *external* relations between real societies.

Third is the idea that, except under recurrent, transitory, and problematical conditions (variously called culture contact, social change, or similar terms), local groups fall naturally into these labeled categories in a non-overlapping repartition. Any two *ethnic* categories of this sort (if neither is a cover term in the sense given above) are supposed to be mutually exclusive as to local group membership.

These ideas seem to imply that if we can only somehow sort out these labels "correctly," as in a tribal or ethnic synonymy such as appears in books like the recent HRAF ethnographic gazetteer of mainland Southeast Asia (LeBar *et al.* 1964), it must be possible to arrange them in a proper taxonomy (Conklin 1964) of actual local groups or natural societies, together with their respective cultures. As a corollary it also seems to be supposed that any hierarchical element in such taxonomies (e.g. the element according to which there are differently labeled "kinds" of Kachin) is at most only an organization of essentially *foreign* relations, probably nothing more than explicit recognition by outside observers, or by the peoples themselves, that the peoples so grouped have shared a certain amount of history and may also speak closely related languages.

These are ideas that have been central to the formal rhetoric of Western social and political philosophy from at least the time of the Enlightenment. And this very rhetoric as a formal system of argumentation has been borrowed by many different varieties of modern Burmese nationalism, so that Burmese political life today is conducted in terms of the internationally understood language of Left versus Right, Socialism versus Liberal Democracy, and so on. The same political philosophy, of course, has deeply influenced both the notions about nationhood found in the now defunct Constitution of the Union of Burma and the proposals made for its revision, e.g. by the Shan-led Federalist movement of 1961–1962. Leach (1960) has made a convincing case for the disparity between traditional concepts of nationhood and those that European legal and constitutional considerations have imposed upon modern Southeast Asia.

What has not been pointed out with sufficient force and clarity is that many of these same notions have been inherited from the same source by modern social science. Social science has its roots not just generally in Western thought, but to a considerable degree in the social and political philosophies of the eighteenth century as well as German Romanticist thought (Lévi-Strauss 1955; Pocock 1961). Therefore I think it proper, even though this paper is a part of a symposium directed to problems of a delimited region of the world, to address myself to general social-science theory. For, in one way or another, that theory itself, or a branch of it, has played a major role in generating the problems of majority-minority relations in Burma—or at least in obscuring the conditions required for their solution.

I submit that the solution of such practical national problems is unlikely to be discovered until the exact definition of the problems becomes understood. I do not for a moment suppose that this understanding can be achieved only through the ministrations of social science, but that does not serve as an excuse for avoiding the issue. Indeed, I shall point out below that throughout the pre-colonial period of history the Burmans had a reasonably correct tacit understanding of the nature of their relations with bordering peoples, tribal and non-tribal. That Burma seems to have lost this understanding today is almost certainly directly attributable to the importation of very explicit European ideas about nations, societies, and cultures, and the kinds of phenomena that they are taken to be.

I think that such views of societies as I have described above necessarily pose a serious problem for "nation-building" in countries like Burma, where many symbiotic ethnic categories have existed through much of history and where local groups in this symbiosis have been related to each other in a variety of reticulate ways. When applied toward the solution of something called a minority problem in such a country, these views set up two opposite and equally abortive responses. On the one hand, official actions try to erode minority cultural and linguistic distinctiveness by propaganda, education, and plain force, possibly reducing ethnic peculiarities to the level of harmless historical relics or folkways as a transitional sop to regional pride and prejudice. I suspect that this is implicit in the organization of the new Academy for the Development of National Groups set up by the present Revolutionary Government of Burma at Sagaing (*Forward*, III, 7, 11–17, November 1964).

On the other hand, regional "ethnic" differences can be recognized in the medium of Federalism. One can even try to carve out discrete ethnic states for peoples who have not traditionally lived unmixed in compact contiguous territories. Burma has delineated a Karen state in this way and has tried, with no apparent hope of satisfaction, to carve out a similar state for the Mon—in that vast region of southern Burma where most Mon have long ago become thoroughly Burmanized in language and culture.

The first response, as I have noted, often requires the use of force. In any event, it is almost bound to create hostility between numerically and economically unequal local groups. Adherence to a minority cultural tradition is treated as tantamount to subversion of the nation and is branded as a mark of group inferiority within the nation. The second, or federal, response, given the explicit ideological view I have already attributed to the concept of society, is very likely to create a climate of mutually exclusive, regional ethnic nationalism in the sense that federal relations tend to be fixed constitutionally as those between contractually or "voluntarily" associated cultural and social sovereignties inherently foreign to one another. The tragedy is that this climate can be created where in fact no such concept of sovereignties existed before.

I am not, of course, claiming that *modern* nations necessarily have any other choices practically open to them than the two sorts of responses I have just spoken of. I am, however, questioning the view taken of the "peoples" of Burma and other such countries, when these "peoples" are the objects of very particular, concrete policies of nation-building.

THEORETICAL PROPOSITIONS:
CULTURE, SOCIETY, AND "ETHNIC GROUP"

I wish to suggest an alternative theory of the nature of ethnic categories. It is a theory that I believe is at once less mystical and romantic than the traditional one and at the same time much more in line with the facts of human social and cultural life in general and of Burma and Southeast Asia in particular. What I shall propose is by no means altogether novel. I am obviously building upon Leach's work (1954; 1960). But I must go beyond Leach somewhat, insofar as he has rather drastically and unrealistically oversimplified his definitions of ethnic categories and of majority-minority relations between such categories. Nonetheless, he has shown how people who are at one point Kachins can "become" Shan in a systematic way that is part and parcel of the social-structural rules of the Kachin social system itself. He has also shown that sub-categories within Kachin bear no clear or necessary relationship to linguistic categories.

What theoretical assumptions are required to make sense of these and a host of similar examples from the ethnographic literature on Burma and surrounding countries? How will it be possible to *generalize* about inter-group relations in Burma without so oversimplifying the picture as to render impossible the drawing of interesting connections between theory and fact?

In the first place, I assume that social and cultural systems are reference systems—that is, cognitive models at varying levels of awareness. Actual groups of people make selective use of these models, or appeal to them in order to guide their real-life actions in an actual environment that, in most cases, includes groups of peoples using other such systems. These models generate meaningful *interpretations* to situations and things, and to the range of possible sequences of behavior in these contexts. I wish to avoid implying that models of this kind must tend (even ideally) to be cognitively consistent or homogeneous. The limits of cognitive and affective dissonance within which human social life can function is a real problem in psychology; but almost certainly these limits are not vanishingly narrow. Certainly persons have the continuous problem of maintaining their psychological integrity, and, in one sense or another, so do groups. But I can think of nothing that has been more damaging to the development of a formally adequate social anthropological theory than an unfortunate tendency to confuse persons with roles, or groups with models of organization.

We know that systems must have flexibility because we observe that people respond (often experimentally, but in cognitively intelligible and strategically assessable ways) to a variety of real-life exigencies, many of them in a measure novel and unpredictable. With Leach (1961; 1962) I wish to have a sociological theory that will account directly for this flexibility.

I am also not concerned with any *presumptive* "conflict" between so-called ideal and real culture. Culture, we assume, is in this respect rather like language. In actual discourse we often produce utterances that are not fully grammatical or well formed. Usually this does not interfere with communication, because grammatical rules allow us to *impose* an interpretation on actual utterances. To share a language is to share a grammar in precisely this sense. But while this involves quite massive constraints on the shape of our actual utterances, it does not constrain sharers of a common language to speak exactly alike. If, as Chomsky would have it (1957), the grammars which are in people's heads are not utterance-generating devices, but rather interpretation- or structure-generating devices, so too, one supposes, the "norms" or patterns of a culture cannot be expected to account directly for actual behavior.

THEORETICAL PROPOSITIONS:
"ETHNIC" CATEGORIES AS ROLE SYSTEMS

I suggest that when people identify themselves as members of some "ethnic" category, e.g. Jinghpaw, Kayah, Chin, Sgaw Karen, they are taking positions in culturally defined systems of inter-group relations (this particular formulation I owe to P. Kunstadter). These systems of inter-group relations comprise, at least in the case of Burma, complexly interdependent complementary categories. I claim in particular that, in reality, *ethnic categories are formally like roles* and are, in that sense, only very indirectly descriptive of the empirical characteristics of substantive groups of people.

A role is defined, not in absolute terms, but relative to a whole system of other roles. It is perhaps the exceptional role system that consists of either just two roles or just two kinds of roles, i.e., a single kind of relation (*pace* Nadel 1957, where an attempt is made to reduce all role relations to the dimension of superordination/subordination). Again, I claim in particular that it is characteristic of Burma, as of much of the rest of Southeast Asia, that any local or regional group, especially one that is in any sense a minority group, is inherently likely to have recourse to more than one ethnic role system and more than one "identity." I tentatively ascribe this plurality of ethnic role systems and identities to the ecology of state-level polity in this part of the world (cf. Leach 1960), and to the fact that almost any minority group must come to terms with more than one state civilization and a variety of other minorities, themselves differently treated by different states. In any case, a minority's relations with any given civilization are predictably fluid and *ambiguous* (Leach 1954; Lehman 1963).

These claims are serious, because more is involved in them than merely the common observation that people frequently identify themselves alternatively with reference to categories of wide scope in some cases and of narrow scope in others (Burmese vs. Rangonian, American vs. New Yorker, and so on). Roles, we are often told (Goffman 1958; G. H. Mead 1935; Nadel 1957), are regularly played not simply to the person immediately addressed, but also to an implicit audience of other parties—the public which is, so to speak, shared by the immediate parties to the interaction as their common system of reference. I am in fact suggesting that ethnic categories fall into systems in this sense also.

SUBSTANTIVE EVIDENCE OF THE THEORY

If the very general propositions I have put forward so far are correct, we must expect to find in the ethnography of Burma at least five kinds of facts more adequately accounted for by these proposals than by hypotheses more usually put forward in these connections. I shall list these kinds of facts in a somewhat arbitrary order and try to illustrate each one with one or two substantive ethnographic examples from Burma.

(1) There should be evidence that, at least in some cases, ethnic categories were traditionally defined over a long period of Burmese history by role complementation and not absolutely.

Luce (1959) has shown on the basis of Old Burmese inscriptions that the label "Chin" (the Old Burmese word was *khyan*) as used for peoples immediately west of Burma, was originally a term meaning, as it does today, "ally," or "comrade." Under this category the early Burmans recognized peoples ancestral to present-day Chins, who then inhabited not only the western hill country but also much of the plain of the Upper Chindwin. The Burmans considered them as a useful buffer between themselves and the Sak-Kadu, with whose kingdoms the early Burman state was in fundamental competition. The terms of the system of inter-group relations here must then be taken as three: Burman, Sak-Kadu, Chin.

One may compare this usage (cf. Lehman 1963) with the current Haka-Chin pair of complementary category terms, *zo* and *vai*.[4] *Vai* denotes Burma in its aspect as the focal civilization for the Chin, and the word *zo* has the basic meaning of (relatively) "uncultivated," "backward" with reference to *vai*. This system of categories is at least partially to be contrasted with the triplet of terms, *kawl, lai,* and *zo*. In this system the same Haka-Chin set themselves off from Burma much more sharply and proudly. *Kawl* is a somewhat derogatory word for Burmans, and *lai* (its general gloss is "central") is the word that Haka speakers use for themselves, reflecting their view that they are the cultural and political culmination of the cultural tradition. *Zo,* whose general gloss is again "relatively uncultivated," is here opposed to *lai,* reflecting the way in which Haka speakers look down on people of other parts of the Chin Hills.

(2) There should be evidence that we cannot reconstruct any demonstrable discrete ancestral group for some "ethnic category"—no matter whether we define such a possible ancestral group as a discrete dialect group, or as a group with relatively

---

[4] There are equivalent, but not necessarily cognate, words for *vai* in other Chin languages, and cognate words for *zo* in almost every other Chin language.

sharp cultural discontinuities from its neighbors. In this case there should also be evidence that the category has never achieved the degree of cultural and/or linguistic discreteness from its neighbors that it may claim for itself or have claimed for it by observers treating it as having *a* global culture consequent upon a distinctive history. These things would amount to evidence that an "ethnic category" is not *necessarily* ethnic in any usual sense, however much genuine or spurious ethnicity may be appealed to by any group as a justification or rationalization of their "being" such and such a "people." In addition there should be well-attested cases where the membership of an "ethnic category" is not even ideally absolute. It will also be interesting to find evidence that category *terms* need be neither symmetrical with respect to pairs of terms nor unique with respect to a single term.

All the points made under section (2) can be illustrated with a single case. There is a group of Karen dialects and languages which may be properly called Central Karen. It includes groups living in the Kayah State of Burma and in the hill country just west and north of that state, namely groups speaking Karen languages commonly known as Kayah (some of whom also live in Province Mae Hongson in western Thailand), Brè, Manumanaw (or Münü), Geba, Gehku, and maybe one or two others, and also, probably, Padaung and Yeinbaw. In the first sub-set any two adjacent groups speak mutually intelligible dialects, while groups more distant from one another tend to find their dialects mutually unintelligible. This kind of set is what linguists call an L-simplex.

There is a relatively more sharp linguistic break between the first sub-set of dialects and the Padaung-Yeinbaw sub-set. The first sub-set of groups can also be called a cultural and social simplex chain. All parties agree in recognizing that some villages are both Münü and Kayah, others are both Münü and Brè, and so on. For the bulk of the relevant cultural inventory of these groups, there are no sharp distributional discontinuities, but, with few exceptions, only gradual variations from village to village.

The exceptions concern only the Kayah. In the first place, the traditional costume of Kayah women is strikingly different from anything else found in the whole range of Karen groups. The women wear neither smock nor sewn shirt, and on their knees they wear remarkably large and heavy bundles of lacquered cotton rings. This is hard to account for, although it may very well be a fairly recent development, even a self-conscious emblem of the existence among the Kayah alone of something like a real state-level political system of Shan-style princedoms. These princedoms arose about the middle of the nineteenth century, and the peculiar religious cult that is symbolized by the presence in every Kayah village of ceremonial teak poles (*iyluw*) and other apparatus can be shown to be a direct product of the Kayah's Shan-style political system.

Indeed, this apparatus has extraordinary and detailed parallels with Shan-Burmese Buddhist religious paraphernalia. For instance, the *iyluw* is a virtual duplicate of what is called in Burmese *tagundaing*, the Buddhist flagpole of victory found in many Burmese religious precincts. Although the charismatic-political founders of the cult under discussion reinterpreted these things in syncretistic, non-Buddhist terms (Lehman, forthcoming), Kayah legend and myth typically ascribe the power of these leaders (*phre phrow*, or miracle workers) who were founders of the system of princedoms, to a direct though mystical knowledge of the civilization and institutions of kingship of the Burmans. There is also historical evidence (see Stern 1965) that this movement among the Kayah took its origins in part from the semi-Buddhist millenary cults that flourished and spread among the Sgaw and Pwo Karen immediately to the south in the first two decades of the nineteenth century. In fact, one of the earliest reported leaders of such cults disappeared into Karenni, i.e., what is now the Kayah State, at a time just preceding what I have calculated as the period of the founding of the Kayah princedoms.

These apparent exceptions to the existence of a social-cultural simplex chain as a characterization of Central Karen have all to do in one way or another with a rather recently developed political system, by means of which some Central Karen groups literally took over from the Southern Shan the organization controlling inter-tribal and tribal-Shan-Burmese trade (Lehman 1965; forthcoming).

However, in reality there is about as much difference between one dialect of Kayah and another (variation is from west to east) as between some dialects of Kayah and some of Manumanaw or Brè. Moreover, my recent work among the Kayah of western Thailand has shown that as an ethnic label "Kayah" (it is a word for "person," common to most Central Karen dialects) has two rather different meanings. Thus usage of the term belongs to two different systems of ethnic categories and intergroup relations.

The Kayah of Thailand arrived in their present home territories before consolidation of the Shan-style Kayah political system. The older ethnic meaning of Kayah is preserved among them. They lump western Burma Kayah groups and dialects together with those otherwise labeled by us as Manumanaw, that is as "Münü" or "western Central Karen." Thus "Kayah" is in effect a cover term equivalent to our use of "Central Karen." For these Kayah groups, clearly, the distinctive overlay of things like the aforementioned women's dress and ritual complex, which they too possess, is not allowed to obscure the essential simplex-chain character of Central Karen social and cultural variation.

The Burma Kayah, for whom the Kayah statelet system is more significant, profess to find the degree of linguistic difference between one dialect of Kayah and another quite insignificant in comparison with the differences between any Kayah dialect and even Manumanaw. Kayah is for them a much more specific term, and in fact they recognize no category equivalent to Central Karen. The Padaung and Yeinbaw are called by these Kayah *La khi* (la chiə). The Geba, whose language is in actuality so close to western Kayah that the latter people, having no writing system of their own, write Geba in the missionary-developed Romanization, are called by these Burma Kayah, *pakü da neꝑ*, that is a kind of Sgaw Karen (*pakü*). This is quite interesting, inasmuch as the category Central Karen, wherever recognized by the peoples under discussion, is always opposed to the category Sgaw Karen. Thus the Sgaw word "Bwe" meaning "Central Karen" includes, indifferently, Geba and Kayah.[5] This equivalence is again well illustrated in western Thailand where, in places where one finds numerous Sgaw Karen, Kayah answer to the name of Bwe, and Geba answer to the name Kayah.

There is, finally, still another set of ethnic category labels avail-

[5] The Sgaw word for "Central Karen" is "Bghwe" in the Sgaw dialects of Thailand and "Bwe" in the Sgaw dialects around Toungoo in Burma.

able to some Central Karen groups. The Padaung and Gekhu think of themselves as forming a single category. That is, the Padaung call themselves *kekhoŋ*, as do the Yeinbaw, and this word is nothing but a variation of the word Gekhu, which means in all these cases "country-top," that is, people living in the uplands. This category is opposed to Geba, the people living on the slopes on the western side of the range separating the Kayah State from the Toungoo region of Burma proper.

Clearly there is a great deal of asymmetry in these categorial systems. For similar complications in a neighboring region of Southeast Asia, one can look at the system of labels used by the various Northern Thai-speaking groups of themselves (Moerman 1965).

Another case of asymmetry is that of the Lisu (Maran, this volume). This "people" is an element in the Kachin social system when living among Kachin, but not when living elsewhere (e.g. in Thailand). It is, of course, meaningless to ask whether Lisu is or is not a "kind" of Kachin.

(3) There should be evidence that for some groups of people there is a serious *choice* as to what cultural category to adopt for themselves, and in particular that cultural distinctiveness between two groups is not necessarily a simple consequence of either distance or barriers to direct communication and interaction.

I have shown elsewhere (Lehman 1963) that an interesting problem is raised by the fact that the Central Chin, who have for some centuries lived adjacent to a part of Burma proper which is very sparsely inhabited by Burmans, do not generally insist that villagers maintain and exhibit all the traditional external symbols of "being Chin"; whereas the Southern Chin, who have for centuries lived adjacent to plains regions densely inhabited by Burmans are extremely conservative in this respect. This is a state of affairs that has been noticed for many tribes-peoples in and around Burma (cf. Leach 1960; Scott 1900). The closer these groups live with their civilized neighbors, the more conservative they become of the traditional symbols of "being" a different people. This suggests very strongly that they are reacting, more or less self-consciously, to the immediate possibility of being attracted toward trying to adopt Burman cultural standards, an attempt which, furthermore, would put most of them in the position of being at best unsuccessful Burmans as compared with people whose environment allows them reasonable chances for success at meeting Chin-defined cultural standards of living.

(4) There should be evidence that all proposed simple dichotomies based on attributes fail adequately to characterize intergroup and majority-minority relations in Burma in any reasonable way consistent with the facts. In this connection it has to be pointed out that, if indeed we are not classifying either groups or total societies with the use of ethnic category labels, and if instead these categories are parts of one type of role systems, then, if these role systems are at all complex, say in hierarchical ordering, no dichotomy could possibly characterize such systems adequately.

I will here deal one at a time with the dichotomies usually put forward as characterizing majority-minority ethnic relations in Burma and the rest of Southeast Asia.

(a) It is often supposed that minorities generally are hill dwellers and majority peoples are valley or plains dwellers. Many Karen, both Pwo and Sgaw, have for a very long time, however, dwelt in the plains of Lower Burma and western Thailand. The Plains Chin (Stern 1962) have for some centuries dwelt in a large plains region of western Burma, without ceasing to be a minority people even though living in the very midst of areas of dense Burman settlement and having become heavily Burmanized in language, culture, and religion. On the other hand, while the Shan live in river valleys, the fact that these are upland valleys rather than lowland plains can be shown to have important consequences not only for the peculiarly Shan style of economic and political inter-digitation with surrounding hill tribes, but also for such things as the Shan systems of land use and settlement organization. Certainly too, the traditional multiplicity of Shan principalities is itself largely a result of the dispersion of the Shan among often sharply separated upland valleys.

(b) A related dichotomy often put forward is that between peoples who cultivate irrigated rice and those who practice swidden or shifting cultivation. This dichotomy is imprecise in more than one way. For instance, considerable regions of Upper Burma are so situated that there is very little wet farming done. Of the dry farming that replaces it (see Nash 1965), some at least is swidden farming (*taung ya*) and in addition a certain amount of shifting cultivation is practiced at least in the case of supplementary crop production wherever Burmans have to make use of marginal or newly opened land. The Plains Chin, mentioned above, are a tribal minority practicing for the most part wet farming. By contrast, the Yaw, who live nearby between the Ponnyadaung Range and the Chin Hills, often practice dry cultivation, but they are not customarily classed as a minority. They are Buddhists, speaking a non-standard dialect of Burmese. Lowland Karen (who are classed as a minority tribe) practice a great deal of both wet and dry farming. Their dry farming, moreover, as also in the case of the Kayah, is in some cases plough cultivation, in others hoe cultivation, depending upon the steepness or rockiness of the local terrain.

(c) It is often said that, inasmuch as Burmans have traditionally defined their society as inherently Buddhist in character, that is, as having an explicitly Buddhistic institution of kingship (Mendelson 1961), minorities may be defined as non-Buddhist. Obviously, most of the non-tribal indigenous minorities—the Arakanese, Mon, and Shan (all of whom are definitely and inherently adjuncts of Burman civilization rather than independent civilizations on the same level as the Burmese)—are Buddhists. For the most part they have monastic communities following the same rules of ordination as those followed in Burma proper. Yet the Shan have reacted very adversely to attempts by the Burmese government to Burmanize the Sangha of the Shan State. The Palaung, an Austroasiatic-speaking tribal group of the Shan State, are also Buddhists, and have in general become Shan-ized in politics and culture. Most Plains Chin are also Buddhists now.

On the other hand, Burmese Christians do not constitute a distinct sociological minority group in the ethnic sense. Conversely, a non-indigenous minority like the Chinese remain a minority even though many of them are Buddhists—of a kind, however, different from Burman Buddhism.

(d) Leach (1960) has suggested that, whereas the civilized peoples have characteristically cognatic kinship systems, tribal peoples in this part of the world are unilineal, usually patrilineal.

He has also asserted that succession to positions of political leadership among the tribes-peoples is essentially hereditary, while among civilized Burmans and Shans it is fundamentally charismatic. These things he has ascribed tentatively to the fact that the civilizations are built on Hindu-Buddhist Indian models, while the tribal peoples preserve an old Southeast Asian traditional model of social organization that is shared with China.

But one can just as well attribute the cognatic organization of the civilized peoples to the demonstrated fact that these groups have been formed over the centuries as much by recruitment from diverse other groups, notably hill peoples (see Cady 1954), as by natural demographic increase. In any case, most Karen groups are straightforwardly cognatic, and the rest, e.g. the Sgaw and Pwo, are also basically cognatic despite relatively great emphasis upon matrifiliality for purposes of determining post-marital residence and inheritance (cf. Hamilton 1963; also personal discussion with J. W. Hamilton, T. Stern, and S. Iijima). Indeed, Indian kinship systems are not fully cognatic, while Burman and Shan kinship is nearly so.

Furthermore, many hill men have no *distinct* political offices to be succeeded to (e.g. many Sgaw and Pwo Karen). Nor are all hill men (e.g. Karen) necessarily practitioners of unilineal succession, even where, as among the Kayah, they have a kind of state and an office of "prince." Chiefly status, as with the Chin, is by no means always a matter of hereditary succession, even jurally (Lehman 1963; cf. Maran, this volume). Karen, including Kayah, quite generally recruit their leaders on a markedly charismatic basis; or, more precisely, leaders impose themselves by virtue of their claims to be possessed of unusual powers, to be of miraculous birth, or to have special knowledge of the outside world of civilization. By contrast, even though throughout Burmese history succession to the Burmese throne was uniformly erratic both in fact and in law, one of the first things a royal usurper always felt it necessary to do was to establish in the public mind the idea that he was "of the royal bone"; that is, he had to give presumptive evidence that some of his ancestors were of royal birth.

(e) Language is a poor guide to whether a group is or is not either a minority or an ethnic group in any sense. Even speak-

ers of Burmese are sometimes minorities. Of all the dialects of
the Burmese language, only Arakanese is the language of a group
with separate national consciousness. Arakanese is no more different from Standard Burmese than are many other dialects, such
as Yaw, Taungyo, or Tavoyan. Arakan had, of course, a long
history as one or more independent kingdoms which were often
at war with Burma and which had particularly close relations
with kingdoms in what is now East Bengal.

The Mon are descendants of speakers of an Austroasiatic language, who had an important independent kingdom in Lower
Burma, long before that of the Burmans. Since the eleventh century, however, their country, the Irrawady Delta, has been subject to Burman rule much of the time. Mon nationalism still
exists, and there has been from time to time an attempt to create
a Mon state within the Union of Burma. Yet most people claiming to be Mon by ethnic identification are nowadays native
speakers of Burmese; many in fact speak no Mon at all. The
Mon are actually for the most part quite indistinguishable from
the Burmans in culture and language as well as religion.

Many of the sub-categories of Kachin are identified by labels
whose primary reference is to a fairly wide range of very different
languages within the "Tibeto-Burman" spectrum of Sino-Tibetan
(Atzi, Nung-Rawang, Jinghpaw, Gauri, Lashi, etc.). But Leach
(1954) has shown that it is *not* the case that, for example, all
those participating in the Lashi sub-system of political organization are speakers of Lashi, and, conversely, not all Lashi speakers
participate in the Lashi sub-system.

We can, of course, say that in many instances "ethnic" category labels in Burma, if they are labels of wide scope like
"Kachin," apply only (or largely) to speakers of a single language sub-family. Karen is such a label; so are Chin and Burman.
But Kachin, notably, is not confined to a single language sub-
family. It must follow that we cannot include even a language
sub-family criterion in our theory of the definition of "ethnic"
categories.

(f) Level of political development is hardly a better indi-
cator of minority status than is language. The Shan certainly
must be accounted as having a state-level political system. But
this system of princedoms, with very few exceptions, explicitly

derives its legitimacy as well as its titles of royalty conceptually from the Burmese kingdom. The ideological dependence of the Shan civilization upon the civilization of Burma[6] as a focal Buddhist monarchy was in no way diminished by the fact that very often actual Shan rulers were in open conflict with individual Burman kings. This state of affairs, in fact, was probably no more true of Shan princes than of other *de facto* political leaders of many regions of Burma proper during much of Burmese history. Such conflict was in large measure a struggle for the Burmese throne itself, which, of course, was occupied by the Shan from about 1370 to 1555.

(g) There is no single pattern of economic relations between minority and majority in Burma. While the Shan system is clearly an adjunct of Burmese civilization, the Shan social and political system was itself the immediate locus of the economic symbiosis of many north Burma hill tribes with Burmese civilization. Leach (1954) has proved this for the Kachin, and in general the well-known Shan system of five-day markets was an institution for drawing upon surrounding hill peoples as sources of produce and as allies and dependents.

We can examine further this matter of economic interdependence. The Chin, for example, have always had a great deal of trouble in exercising what they felt to be their legitimate claim on the goods and markets of Burma (and of Assamese and Manipuri civilizations). For the most part they had to assert their claims by raiding and looting, because the Burmans showed little interest in trading with them, or even in claiming to rule over them (*contra* Leach 1960).

Among most of the hill tribes the situation is different. The Shan-Chinese trading complex involved tribal peoples in many ways. Wherever there are Shan in Burma, there are petty pack traders as well as periodic markets. This Shan trade draws the hill people into its orbit by means ranging from casual attraction to coercion. The trade is often less important for the tribesmen than for the Shan, as Mr. Maran has indicated for the Kachin. But in the case of the Kachin this was because they were more

[6] In a similar way the Kengtung Shan were ideologically dependent on the old Northern Thai Kingdom of Lanna Thai, and the Chinese Shan were likewise dependent on the Chinese Empire.

dependent themselves for civilized merchandise upon Chinese traders, who were in turn ultimately a part of the Shan-tribal–Chinese-caravan trade cycle.

The Wa were to a remarkable extent a part of the complex economic and political system through which the northern Shan states subsisted upon trade with the Chinese caravaneers from Kweichou and Yunnan. The "Wild Wa" headhunters and their chiefs seem to have been, among other things, bandits and toll collectors along the caravan routes. Quite possibly by informal agreement, they insured that caravan trade belonging to one prince was not encroached upon by other princes while it passed through the remote Wa areas, far from the direct administration of Shan rulers. (The late G. E. Harvey has suggested evidence for this hypothesis in personal communication, but the case is in no way proven yet).

Obviously, some tribal minorities had to force their claims of symbiosis upon their civilized neighbors, while others were in varying degrees forced into formal dependence. It can be shown that the definition of many of the different kinds of Karen, or of the equally many different kinds of Chin, is in part a function of the different positions of relatively restricted localities in the webs of economic and political intercourse with Shan, Burmans, and Chinese (Lehman 1963; forthcoming). There are over forty Chin languages with numerous dialects in each, but these overlap in unpredictable ways with regional Chin political and economic networks. None of these economic or political or linguistic entities, of course, is a "tribe" in any exclusive sense we might wish to impose upon that altogether vague word.

It seems that tribesmen were often buffers or pawns in the incessant rivalry between various Shan princes. The latter consistently played tribesmen and Burmans off against one another. Clearly this had a great deal to do with the organization of intergroup relations among those tribes that happened to be in the orbit of the Shan-Chinese-Burma network.

Nevertheless, there is no simple distinction to be drawn between tribes-people whose connection with civilization is mediated by the Shan and those, such as the Chin, for whom this was not the case. Many sorts of Karen, for instance, traditionally had direct relations with both Shan and Burmans.

(5) Finally, there should be evidence that in at least some cases these ethnic categories had claimed for them by their occupants less sovereignty, closure, and exclusiveness, vis-à-vis one another and vis-à-vis Burma proper, than is commonly supposed by anthropologists or by internal-policy-makers in contemporary Burmese governments. In short, there should be evidence leading us to suspect in at least some cases that in trying to Burmanize minorities for the purpose of nation-building, one may sometimes endanger just the means that local groups have traditionally developed for living as parts of a system of social relations encompassing Burmans together with many of these other "peoples." Illustrations of this kind of evidence will tend to show also that, in the case of Burma in particular, the ultimate dependence of some tribal categories on a system of inter-group relations whose major focus is Burma proper and its civilization has been obscured by the fact that the connection with Burma proper was systematically mediated by some third category, usually Shan. This is, in its way, of course, further evidence of a non-dichotomous and reticulate structuring of these systems of ethnic categories. In effect one can probably show that a Shan-focused inter-ethnic system was itself a part of a larger system focused upon Burma proper.

The Kayah category can in part be understood, as we have seen, as a kind of Karen system which incorporated a Shan-style political order, while retaining animism. The Kayah did this not so much to make themselves independent of civilization, as to give themselves means for asserting a more direct dependency upon Burma. Thus the Kayah "princes" were always most eager to acquire Burmese titles directly and to have it appear that they ruled in their own territories by appointment of the King of Burma.

The traditional Kachin system was, as we know, Shan-oriented. It also had a complementary Chinese orientation. Many Kachin material symbols of political and ritual status and leadership are clearly modeled on, and often directly borrowed from, both Shan and Chinese. The Jinghpaw language has an extremely large vocabulary of Shan loanwords, but relatively few from Burmese. In the 1870's and 1880's (see Maran, this volume) the Kachin in Burma became in some degree cut off from their access to

China. At the same time, the increasingly strong presence of the British in Burma began to replace the Burmese kingdom as a political center of gravity; for the Shan were engaged in attempting to weaken what had increasingly become Burma's direct hold upon administration in the Shan states. This combination of circumstances, which also for the first time brought Burman administrators into the Kachin area (e.g. to Bhamo), opened up for the Kachin a broader vista of their place in the sphere of civilization. They began to define their distinctiveness with more direct reference to Burma itself, where previously it had been defined with reference to the Shan. The Kachin attempt to take Mandalay in the 1890's has precise parallels in what the Shan had tried repeatedly and sometimes successfully to do earlier in history. As Maran tells us (in this volume), the Burmanization of the Kachin continues to become more important. The fact that the Burmans have ignored this reorientation of the Kachin has led to recent unrest among them.

I have shown elsewhere (Lehman 1963) that traditional chiefs among the Central and Northern Chin were always eager to claim that they were allies of the King of Burma, even though, as a matter of fact, their Burman "allies" were nothing but rebels and bandits fleeing Burmese justice or retribution. This does not appear to be a case where the traditional tribal political institutions were inherently obstacles to the creation among the Chin of a sense of belonging in some way or other to the Burman scene—granted of course that a sense of "belonging" of this kind never meant willingness to acknowledge any possible claims by the Burmans to outright rule of the Chin Hills.

I have also pointed out above that in many ways the Chin employed their political identification with mission Christianity as a means of asserting their claims to be a civilized people able to hold their own *within* a Burmese nation. In many respects the current unrest and disaffection in the Chin Hills has its immediate origin in the Chin reaction to the abortive State Religion Act, one of Burma's explicit nation-building schemes.

CONCLUSION

I can conclude this paper with two sets of propositions. First, clearly Burma has quite complex traditional relations of various kinds with her minority groups. She has even had, traditionally, varying models of relations with individual groups, depending upon what such a group presented itself as "being" on any given occasion—that is, what ethnic label it chose to use for itself. Facts like these constitute inherent aspects of "who" minorities are. If this is so, then there is assuredly no single minority problem, just as there is no single kind of relationship to minorities. Therefore no single, blanket minority policy is likely to be capable of solving these minority problems.

Second, it is obviously necessary to find out in each case just what a minority's traditional relation to Burman civilization has been, before one goes about trying to change that relation. Just noticing that a minority's traditional culture is in large measure different from that of the Burmans in no way precludes that culture's having served as a symbol or surrogate for that minority's claim to be included somewhere in the general sphere of Burman civilization (Lehman 1963). Leach, in his "Frontiers" of Burma article (1960), unfortunately either misses this point altogether or seriously underemphasizes it.

BIBLIOGRAPHY

For the most part I have not given references in the first five sections of this paper. To the extent that the facts mentioned there are not from my own field work, they can be documented conveniently in the following places.

Background on the decisions by tribal and minority groups to join in the Union of Burma:

BURMA
    1947   Report of the Frontier Areas Committee of Enquiry, and appendices. Rangoon.

General history of Burma:

HALL, D. G. E.
    1950   Burma. London, Hutchinson's University Library.

On the Burma government's use of religion in national policy before the State Religion Act:

MENDELSON, E. M.
    1964   Buddhism and the Burmese establishment. *In* Archives de Sociologie des Religions (17):85–95. Paris.

Developments leading up to the State Religion Act, and the history of political development between the two military regimes:

BUTTWELL, R.
> 1961   Civilians and soldiers in Burma. *In* Studies on Asia, Robert K. Sakai, ed. Lincoln, University of Nebraska Press.

SARKISYANZ, M.
> 1961   On the place of U Nu's Buddhist Socialism in Burma's history of ideas. *In* Studies on Asia, Robert K. Sakai, ed. Lincoln, University of Nebraska Press.

VON DER MEHDEN, F.
> 1961   The changing pattern of religion and politics in Burma. *In* Studies on Asia, Robert K. Sakai, ed. Lincoln, University of Nebraska Press.

On various tribal peoples and other minorities, on insurgencies, and on the official view of Karenni-Kayah name change:

TRAGER, F. N. (ed.)
> 1956   Burma. New Haven, Human Relations Area Files. Subcontractor's monograph.

Detailed documentation of England's dealings with Burma's frontier and minority issues.

WOODMAN, DOROTHY
> 1962   The making of modern Burma. London, Cressett Press.

Periodicals

For the period immediately before and after the military revolution of March 2, 1962, the only existing sources of any value are the daily newspapers and monthly magazines of Rangoon, notably: *The Nation* (daily, now defunct), *The Guardian* (daily), *The Working People's Daily* (since 1964), *Guardian Magazine,* and *Forward* (the English language magazine of the Revolutionary Council Government since 1963).

REFERENCES CITED

CADY, JOHN
> 1954   Political institutions of Old Burma. Ithaca; Cornell University Southeast Asia Program, Data Paper 12.

CHOMSKY, N. A.
> 1957   Syntactic structures. The Hague, Mouton and Co. (Janua Linguarum, 4.)
> 1965   Aspects of a theory of syntax. Cambridge, Mass., M.I.T. Press.

CONKLIN, H. C.
> 1964   Ethnogenealogical method. *In* Explorations in cultural anthropology, W. H. Goodenough, ed.: 57–94. New York, McGraw-Hill.

GOFFMAN, I.
    1958   The presentation of self in everyday life. New York, Double-
            day.
HAMILTON, J. W.
    1963   Karen social structure. Paper read at the November 1963
            annual meeting of the American Anthropological Association,
            San Francisco.
LEACH, E. R.
    1954   Political systems of highland Burma. Cambridge, Mass.,
            Harvard University Press.
    1960   The "frontiers" of Burma. In Comparative studies in society
            and history III (1):49–68. The Hague, Mouton and Co.
    1961   Pul Eliya: a village in Ceylon. Cambridge, Cambridge Uni-
            versity Press.
    1962   Some unconsidered aspects of double descent systems. Man,
            Vol. 62, Article No. 214.
LEBAR, F. M., G. C. HICKEY, J. MUSGRAVE, et al.
    1964   Ethnic groups of mainland Southeast Asia. New Haven,
            Human Relations Area Files Press.
LEHMAN, F. K.
    1963   The structure of Chin society. Urbana, University of Illinois
            Press. Illinois Studies in Anthropology 3.
    1965   Report of a preliminary survey of the position of the Kayah
            (Red Karen) of Thailand. Dittoed, 16 pages.
    forth- Kayah society as a function of the Shan-Burma-Karen context.
    coming In volume edited by J. H. Steward. Urbana, University of
            Illinois Press. Illinois Studies in Anthropology.
LÉVI-STRAUSS, CLAUDE
    1955   Tristes tropiques. Paris, Plon.
LUCE, G. H.
    1959   Old Kyaukse and the coming of the Burmans. In Journal of
            the Burma Research Society 42 (1):73–109. Rangoon.
MEAD, G. H.
    1935   Mind, self, and society. Chicago, University of Chicago Press.
MENDELSON, E. M.
    1961   The king of the weaving mountain. In Journal of the Royal
            Central Asian Society 48 (3 and 4):229–237. London.
    1964   Buddhism and the Burmese establishment. In Archives de
            Sociologie des Religions (17):85–95. Paris.
MOERMAN, M.
    1965   Ethnic identification in a complex society: who are the Lue?
            American Anthropologist 67(5):1215–1230.
NADEL, S. F.
    1957   Theory of social structure. London, Cohen and West.
NASH, M.
    1965   The golden road to modernity: village life in contemporary
            Burma. New York, John Wiley and Sons.

POCOCK, D.

  1961 Psychological approaches and judgments of reality. *In* Contributions to Indian sociology V:44–96. The Hague, Mouton and Co.

SCOTT, Sir J. G., and J. T. P. HARDIMAN

  1900– "Wa." *In* Gazetteer of the Peoples of Upper Burma and the
  1901 Shan States, 3 vols. Rangoon, Government Printer.

STERN, T.

  1962 Language contact between related languages: Burmese influences upon plains Chin. *In* Anthropological Linguistics, 4 (4):1-28. Bloomington.

  1965 *Ariya* and the *Golden Book:* a millenary Buddhist sect among the Karen. Paper read at the November 1965 annual meeting of the American Anthropological Association, Denver, Colorado.

CHAPTER 3

Toward a Basis for Understanding the Minorities in Burma: The Kachin Example[1]

MARAN LA RAW

INTRODUCTION

This paper is a preliminary survey of some of the problems which concern the majority-minority relations in Burma. Since this task is extremely complex and sensitive, I can only deal with some basic issues as I see them and then attempt to put the problems in a proper perspective for a clearer grasp. I will first review some typical notions about this kind of problem which are found in published literature, mostly by Western scholars. I will then briefly discuss what I consider to be the primary inadequacies in these accounts. While I will try to state my ideas about more adequate bases for understanding the problems, my primary objective will nonetheless remain a description of the problems as I see them.

The seriousness of the problem of national unity, especially in an ethnically heterogeneous society, has emerged from the tragic experience of post-independence Burmese history (see Emerson 1963:11). In this paper I have taken an anthropological approach to the problems, for the obvious reason that I am a student of anthropology. Another justification for this approach is that social scientists have not indicated to any large extent their interest in this sort of problem in Burma. It is my belief that although this type of approach cannot be expected to produce immediate solutions to the problem, it can substantially

[1] I would like to thank Professor Peter Kunstadter for extending the invitation to participate in the conference and to present this paper. I would also like to record my gratitude to him for his suggestions in revising the paper. My sincere gratefulness also goes to Professor F. K. Lehman, at the University of Illinois, for the many stimulating ideas he added while I was assembling my paper. Finally, I wish to thank my fellow conferees for their helpful discussion.

illuminate some of the causes and will therefore increase our level of understanding of the very real problems.

The Minorities—Traditional Interpretations. After a long involvement in the resettlement of minority groups in the aftermath of World War I, Macartney wrote that "in almost every aspect of social existence there will be found a majority and a minority" (1935:1). The Second World War greatly accentuated the problem, and consequently there was produced a large volume of literature pertaining to nationalism, national minorities, and the adverse affects these may have in the new and developing nations. South and Southeast Asian nations have received their fair share of space in bibliographies dealing with the topic, so that an extensive listing of these sources is unnecessary in a paper of this size.

One can easily see the general positions expressed by various authors in a few typical statements which we shall consider below. What emerges from these can be adequately summarized for present purposes under three types of positions.

The first position is a broad and sweeping generalization about the obstacles to achieving national unity. The minority elements may be specifically labeled as irresponsible. To Emerson, the problem in a country like Burma is that "the contradiction between the nation as a territorial entity and as a community of the like-minded or racially akin has thrust itself forward as soon as the people came to political self-assertion or achieved independence" (1960:112). Of the divisive tendencies inherent in nationalism, Professor Emerson says: "The coming of nationalism to a society which is politically united but made up of communities divided from each other by race, language, religion, or historical development often works to produce very much the same effect, emphasizing inner cleavages and setting one community against the other" (1963:328).

Brecher is more specific in naming the cause of disunity. "Whatever their distinctive traits, these minorities are often unassimilable and, at best, are sources of irritation and instability" (1963:66). He further observes that other kinds of causes may bring about other kinds of disunity, where the pattern is not cut out to conform to the lines of ethnic differences. These are political parties which contributed to instability because "through their ignoble behavior, almost all national movements ceased to aggregate and articulate interests after independence. Rather, they degenerated into factional strife and corruption" (1963:66).

The second kind of feeling which has appeared in print deals with the historical reasons for alienation among the citizens of the new Asian countries. To this end the writers specifically point at Western colonialism and its legacy as the source of conflict. Purcell states the line which is most common. "The contention of the governments of Burma and Indonesia, in which they are supported in principle by Mr. Nehru, is that separatism of the minorities is merely a legacy of the colonial policy of divide and rule" (1956:236). Kyaw Thet is in complete agreement with the above quotation and cites an example from British colonial policy to amplify the point. "[The British Government] set out to fossilize the many quaintnesses of the primitive culture . . . . The Kachins were encouraged to consider themselves apart and the administrative system was adapted toward that end" (1956: 161–162).

The third kind of position which is expressed by students of this region is the belief that the answers lie dormant in history and that the only thing one must do to find them is to project history into the future and make recommendations in that context. These people attempt analytical interpretation of historical facts and prescribe steps for the assimilation of the minority elements into the national stream of life. One must immediately admit that their interpretations often cease to be analytical treatments of history; they become conjectural and speculative. They merely serve the analysts' pursuit of personal ideals, and their long-run prescriptions serve the same end. At least this is undeniably the case in the printed sources, where one seeks a basis for understanding the problems of ethnic minority elements in a country like Burma. Thus we read in Tinker, concerning Burma's constitutional provisions for minorities: "The chapters setting up the state, together with the concession of a right of secession (under stringent safeguards) were inserted to assuage the doubts of frontier leaders rather than to meet actual or administrative requirements: a form of atonement for that age-old suspicion of the Burmese which the hill peoples could not at once discard" (1961:30). This sort of interpretation carries its own momentum, and it generally becomes very awkward not to offer a set of prescriptions as to what ought to be done with the problem of cultural and political integration. Hence, we read Professor Tinker's suggestion: "The policy of deliberately replacing the lesser languages by Burmese may be somewhat arbitrary, and will somewhat accentuate the difficulties of the frontier areas in finding equality with their Burmese cousins, but it is certainly the right policy for the long haul. There is no place for parochialism and clannishness in Burma today, and nothing will create a true sense of solidarity so surely as the acceptance of a common language" (1961:179).

I am not implying that Professor Tinker inclines toward the kind of preoccupation I mentioned earlier, but it is clear that he has made a lot of assumptions about historical facts concerning the relationship between the Burman majority and the elements which constitute today's minorities.

In the section below I ask some questions regarding the positions of the writers to whom I have already referred.

SOME PROBLEMS OF METHODOLOGY AND INTERPRETATION

Probably no one will dispute the conclusion that the writers I have quoted have realized that there are minority problems. However, insofar as our primary concern is to understand the nature of the problem, several questions immediately arise. Have the views mentioned above substantially enhanced our understanding of the minorities? Or have the authors dealt with the minority problems in such a way that we can use their views as a general basis for ferreting out a way of dealing with the minorities? Upon close examination of these sources, the answer is clearly negative.

Professor Emerson makes very general statements about intergroup differences in such aspects as race, language, religion, or historical development. He argues that the condition of heterogeneity is the source of divisive tendencies (Emerson 1963:13). The generality of the statement shrouds the basic questions. Are we to assume that *all* minority groups are passing through the same disintegrative processes? Is the divisive tendency inherent in all societies which are not completely homogeneous? Or should divisiveness be regarded as the outcome of certain kinds of historical developmental features and therefore not the problem to be explained in that context? What sort of *nationalism* are we speaking of, if it can be attributed so indiscriminately to minorities? These questions seem relevant in light of the fact that we seem to have gotten nowhere nearer to understanding the problem by merely making general statements about nationalism in the emerging nations.

Similarly, the belief that the "divisive tendency of the minorities" derives from the colonial legacy of the West falls short on several serious points as an explanation of minority problems. Although it is politically popular to blame Western colonialism for most troubles, there is only partial truth in this belief, and hence it is only partially accurate as an assessment of the problem. There is, of course, a need for understanding the actual historical development of the distinctness of the minority, and colonialism is only one part of the story. The vehemence with which the case against Western colonial history has been argued has only served to obscure the other factors which were involved. For instance, Kyaw Thet disregards the political relations between the Kachin and the last Burmese monarch at the time the British annexed the Kachin area. The British tried to preserve the obvious political *status quo* and did not begin plans for the cultural and political integration of the Kachin into Burman civilization as soon as they had annexed Upper Burma. Is this sufficient justification for Kyaw Thet's position that the British "merely set out to fossilize the many quaintnesses of primitive culture"? The history is otherwise. When the British were annexing Upper Burma, the Kachin had already risen en masse against the Burmese king. It took the British more than ten years after the fall of the Mandalay Empire to subdue the tribesmen (Woodman 1962:373–379), and the Kachin did not finally give up resistance against the British until 1935. It therefore becomes absurd to insist that the British colonial government should have begun immediate steps to assimilate the Kachin tribes in these circumstances.

It is very apparent that we *cannot* expect a full understanding of the Kachin minority problem to arise from our conviction that the British colonialism is the root of all "fissiparous" tendencies.

It is inherently futile to regard the agent (British colonialism) as the basis for an analysis of the problem. We must understand *what* happened: who did it is a relatively trivial matter. The argument for anti-colonialism has been pursued with such exaggerated proportion that it has served as a convenient distraction for many. But the result has been that we do not know enough about the minority elements in our own country to work out a basis for cooperation and eventual assimilation. We have, in this blindness, lost touch with the real fact: that Western missionaries introduced Burmanization to the Kachin, starting in the 1880's, long before the Burmans were even in a position to do so (see below, pp. 141 ff.).

In commenting on Professor Tinker's position, quoted above, I remarked that he has made many assumptions about the historical facts concerning Burma's minorities. To be more specific, it may be pointed out that the "age-old suspicion" of which he speaks is very unlikely to be a historically constant feature among the tribes in the "frontier areas." The occurrence of suspicion can only be explained in terms of historical events antecedent to independence, a fact which Professor Tinker has failed to provide. He also suggests that "in the long haul" the acceptance of Burmese as the national language is the right policy. He implies that this act would erase "parochialism and clannishness." How one wishes in Burma today that this were the case! There are too many contrary examples. The Arakanese are speakers of a dialect of Burmese, but they shattered this "national language brings national unity" myth quite some time ago by taking to the jungle to try to remove themselves from Burman control. The Mon are certainly the minority group which has been culturally most assimilated, but this fact has not brought about harmony and acceptance of equality with the Burmans. Among the Kachin tribes active Burmanization and the acceptance of the Burmese language began in the 1880's—but are the Kachin happily integrated today? (See Butwell 1963:227; Silverstein 1964:149.)

Surely we have not gotten very far using the kinds of statements that scholars have made on the problem of minorities. They have simply recognized the problematic nature of unassimilated minorities. For a general answer to the predicament they have only resorted to sweeping generalizations. It is not apparent that they have given any serious thought to *why* the minorities are problematic in each case, or whether or not each case is different. The result of this inadequacy has been a lack of depth and perspective in our approach to the whole topic. They have tried to argue from the position that the basic differences between groups of people who claim to be dissimilar can be neatly bundled into categories like language, race, religion, and historical development. Since they do not examine cases critically, they have not realized that their a priori criteria for determining intergroup differences are often very relative, and even ineffective. They have inadvertently implied that the differences may be absolute, when in actual cases the criteria may be impossible to apply. To any serious student of the problem, this inadequacy becomes an overwhelming problem in methodology.

In what follows I will argue that the referents of such terms as Kachin, Shan, and Chin are not neat bundles, and that to deal with them as if they were is only begging the issue. I will claim that such an approach is not only imprecise, but that it is also a serious nuisance. I will also propose alternatives based on a definition of "minority group" which will in turn rest on a wider observation of the problem.

It is my belief that the term "minority" has too often been used in a very loose sense and without any characterization of the nature of the group to which it is supposed to refer. Consequently, it has tended to create the false notion that some sort of universal similarity in fact exists in every case and at every level of analysis of "minorities." In actuality there is no empirical basis to justify such assumptions. Since our concern here requires a more detailed and rigorous approach to this problem, we shall henceforth insist that the use of this term is misleading without contextual qualification. By contextual qualification we shall mean diachronic, synchronic, and comparative points of view that may be stated for any particular group of people or any type of social organization we happen to discuss. In what follows we introduce an example of the type of complexity that is usually encountered in characterizing actual human societies.

The Non-Homogeneous Kachin State. Because language differ-ence has often been cited as one principal criterion for inter-group dissimilarity, we will now look into the languages spoken in Kachin State. *Kachin* is a term covering seven linguistic groups, of which two members belong to branches distant from the others within the Tibeto-Burman family. These are Rawang and Jinghpaw. The Jinghpaw language is spoken by the largest group and, in its role as the lingua franca in north Burma, is spread over a linguistic area far larger than the political bounda-ries of Kachin State. Jinghpaw is broken down into three broad dialect regions, one of which falls in the nothern Shan State. Each dialect region has at least five sub-dialect groups.

The three languages of the groups of Kachin who are culturally and politically inseparable from the Jinghpaw speakers have been classified as being immediate cognates of Proto-Burman (see Kyaw Thet 1956:229; and *Linguistic Survey of India*). These are the Atzi, Maru, and Lashi. Each of these has at least three dialects, which are largely mutually unintelligible. Added to this there are three known groups of Lisu dialects and two Rawang dialects. Thus a linguistic classification of minorities would give us a full twenty-nine "minority groups" who turn out to be inter-twined culturally and politically, and for many practical purposes are unified.

Another consideration is that a vital section of the Kachin State population is Shan-Tai in speech. These people speak Tai Nui, Tai Dai, Tai Dau, Tai Lung, and Tai Leng dialects, which are only slightly mutually intelligible. The Tai Dai speakers have claimed for the last seventy-five years that they have "become Burmans," and prefer to be known as *Shan-gyi* (literally "bigger or superior kind of Shan") on the basis of their identification with Burman civilization.

The Burmans divide themselves into two main groups: the "real Burmans" (*bama siʔ*), who trace their origin to the south; and others who claim to have "passed for Burmans," notably the Shan-gyi.

In addition we have a number of very small and scattered languages, such as those spoken by the professional elephant-drivers who claim the status of a full-fledged minority on the basis of their distinct form of communication with the elephants.

Since we cannot dispute language loyalty which the user himself defines, they must be regarded as one more separate group.

What is the result? Falling within one political entity (Kachin State) are such diverse language groups that we have no less than forty minorities (linguistically defined) in a minority political state. But the complexities of definition have just begun. The Kachin speakers, in spite of their linguistic differences, all share notions of common ancestry, practice the same form of marriage system, have an almost homogeneous customary law and social-control system, use only Jinghpaw for ritual purposes, and are largely polyglots, in the full sense of the term. Genetically the languages are divergent; culturally and bilingually the groups of speakers converge.

This phenomenon not only indicates an intricately woven situation, but it also raises the fundamental question of the relevance of language difference as a criterion for defining minorities. This question has received insufficient attention in many studies of minority peoples. It is premature, without having explored the actual situation, to make a statement such as "groups A and B are different in the languages spoken by each." Such a statement tells us little about the features of the socio-linguistic relationship that may link the groups together in a way that makes genetic differences of language unimportant for the analysis of inter-group relationships.

The same argument applies to the other generalized and abstract notions used by historians, political scientists, and others in defining or describing minority groups. By resorting to a general criterion of inter-group difference such as language, one can hardly expect to derive any substantive adequacy in the analysis until it has been qualified with facts pertaining to the context in which language is used—such issues as language attitude and loyalty, bilingualism and its socio-cultural basis, the nature of specialized borrowing between the contacting languages, patterns of dialectal variation, etc. Earlier we argued for contextual qualification of the criteria for inter-group differences, and we repeat this plea here. Undoubtedly, such insistence must reduce the generality of the statements we make about inter-group differences. But it is not generality in sets of formal criteria that we are interested in. Rather, it is the understanding of the context within which language, for example, functions as a meaningful reason for difference between the groups that is our real objective.

The terms "minority" and "majority" themselves indicate that they cannot be mutually exclusive entities. Each is what it is because of what each is to the other. Inasmuch as a majority implies attached minorities, then an adequate observation of the relation between them must treat them as related systems. The distinctiveness of one element can only be properly understood when it is viewed against other related units. This applies to the characterization of the relationship between the majority and the minority, and equally to the relationship between the string of minorities, such as the Kachin tribes, which together form one minority in a larger political context.

With these methodological problems in mind we can make a tentative set of prescriptions as the basis for deriving an adequate understanding of a minority element in a state or a nation. *First,* a plausible policy for dealing with minority elements must be based on an understanding of each element as a functioning socio-cultural system. *Second,* such a basis must exclude the treatment of each element as a formal, discrete isolate. In other words, an element (or system) under study must be viewed within the context of its relations to other elements (or other systems) in all relevant aspects. *Third,* such a basis must take into account the circumstantial factors or developmental features in the general historical process which underlie the present distinctiveness. The present distinctiveness of an element (or system) should not be the starting point for designing a policy of relationship with the state or the majority element.

Now that a broader context has been outlined within which we can deal with the problem of understanding a minority group, we can suggest what we mean by "minority." We must first state that this definition applies only to the limited scope of this paper and the methodological needs we have considered. We can now commit a logical circularity and define a "minority" as *any human group whose cultural and political interests are overshadowed by those of a numerically larger group entertaining a different set of cultural and political interests.* We have thus defined a minority as any group to which we can apply

the three claims we made in the paragraph above. Our requirement is the understanding of the pertinent details, and hence
our approach is microcosmic. We need not worry about the fal-
lacy of logical circularity, since we do not pretend that our approach is macrocosmic. We may also add at this point that the
first two of the claims concern a synchronic description, while
the third claim relates to the problem of a diachronic description
of a minority group.

THE KACHIN: A MINORITY GROUP

We will now list briefly the features which should be included
in the adequate description of the Kachin as a minority. We
can only outline the main features of the circumstances which
have a direct bearing on the present distinctiveness of the
Kachin. Brevity is required by the scope of the paper.

The first significant feature is that the political matrix of
Burma's Kachin State area does not correspond to the boundary
of cultural influences. There are Kachin in other parts of Burma,
in Indian Assam, and in Chinese Yunnan. What appears as one
general cultural picture involves international political
implications.

This irredentist status has been politically important, but culturally irrelevant. In terms of cultural influences, the area is much
further enlarged, for it is only through contact with the Chinese
and Shan systems that the Kachin system becomes distinctive
and meaningful. Throughout the entire Kachin area, lowland
agriculture, accompanied by varying degrees of bilingualism, has
come from the Shan. The extent of the influence can be illustrated by the fact that in 1960, 15 percent of lowland agricultural
land passed from Shan to Kachin hands in Bhamo District alone
(author's fieldnotes 1958–1961, Bhamo). And, as Leach (1954:9)
has pointed out, one of the two ideal models of political systems
(the *gumsa*) between which the empirical Kachin societies oscillate has been derived from the Shan (see below).

Free movement across the national boundary with China persisted until 1958. For centuries the only source of agricultural
implements like plow-blades and hoes, other goods like swords,
and pots and pans has been from China, through seasonal trading
and migratory smiths. Added to these are the many items of

ritual wealth which are borrowed lock, stock, and barrel from the Chinese material inventory, and the practice of ancestor worship, with its great effect on Kachin cultural life.

Clearly, any notion of Kachin cultural distinctiveness must refer in part to the characteristic ritual-symbolic use of such items and traits which have come from their neighbors. The functional importance of this dependence will confirm our earlier statement that a minority element, while itself a functioning entity, can be understood only in relation to surrounding systems with which it has entered into significant relations.

The problem of definition is enlarged because the relation between the majority and minority may involve other minorities or systems whose political boundaries do not correspond to cultural relations. In such cases it may be impossible to analyze the systems separately. The status of minority groups within minority elements (Shan in Kachin), or the minor segments of a majority within a minority element (Chinese in Kachin), and the considerable functional dependence of one group on the other are some of the least understood aspects of the whole problem in Burma today. For example, in Kachin State there is a Burman population, which is protected as a minority element. Whether this protection actually affects the influence of the Burman on the Kachin is another question, but at least this is an indication of the presence of carriers of majority influence within the system of a minority, in the form of still another protected minority.

As noted earlier, linguistic boundaries and areas of cultural influence, or the presence of functional interdependence, can hardly correspond. The division of entities into neat categories like Shan vs. Kachin, or valley culture vs. hill culture, and the argument that these entities conform to ecological zones and types of cultivation hardly conforms to reality today in Kachin State. By contrast with our expectations on the basis of such categorization, the results of long contact between highland and lowland in the Kachin area are wide cultural borrowing, extensive social change, an acutely imprecise delimitation of the two as exclusive societies, and a great deal of Kachin integration with the lowlanders. Some Kachin are well adapted and long established in the valleys.

What are the results of this for the Shan who live in Kachin State? The governmental structure is such that little could be done for the Shan by approaching their problems directly or from their point of view. This is because the Shan are a minority within the Kachin State, and because there is a Shan State where the Shan are the ruling majority. Thus, although the Shan are far more numerous in Burma than the Kachin, they are domiciled as a minority in a Kachin political domain. At the same time, Shan cultural influence on the Kachin far outweighs the significance of Kachin political privilege. The Shan are not alone in this; we have already mentioned the anomalous position of the Burman as a protected minority in the Kachin State.

Apparently the Kachin are not a discrete society, nor are they conceivable as a discrete political unit, despite the existence of Kachin State. However, there are indications that a pluralistic type of organization may eventually emerge, the lines of which would be drawn on a Kachin vs. non-Kachin basis.

Because the various categories of language, political structure, and cultural influence fail to correspond, and because we have already postulated that each minority element is to be regarded as a functioning entity in relation to other such entities, we are forced to use the boundaries of cultural influence as our units of analysis and to consider related systems in this context.

Let us now pursue the circumstantial factors of a distinctive minority group. We have argued that such distinctiveness falls into a pattern only when we view it in the wider context of the boundaries of cultural influence. F. K. Lehman's analysis of the Chin is one such example. Here,

> . . . the elaborate material culture, the prestige economy, the panoply of social gradation, and the persistent tendency to form supralocal realms all serve as symbols of the Chin claim to a place in the scheme of civilization.
>
> This symbolic incorporation of Burman civilization, or of Chin notions of it, is necessary because of the difficulty and instability of substantive Northern Chin contacts with Burman markets and communities (1964:103–104).

The customary treatment of the distinctiveness of the Chin as an entity would refer only to the first part of the above quotation. But a social scientist can regard such analysis only as a surface description and will not find it of value for much more than simple classification. Lehman, however, has not stopped with classification. He sees emerging from his description, and within the larger context of Chin-Burman contact, a "symbolic incorporation of Burman civilization" by the Chin. They have taken an ideal model from their contact with another group, but they have apparently made it inherently Chin in expression. Chin distinctiveness falls into a pattern and becomes meaningful, but only in the broader context. The Chin notion of civilization is a distinctive feature only to the extent of the *factual* importance of the dependent role that the Chin entered into with the Burmans. The fact that cultural or political aspects of the Burman civilization fall within the purview of the Chin cultural or political life is made manifest in the Chin's symbolic incorporation. This is the kind of analysis which we have claimed is necessary as an adequate basis for understanding a minority element.

Kachin social structure has developed in relation to the Shan in a manner analogous to the way the Chin symbolically incorporated Burman civilization. E. R. Leach (1954) describes the Kachin political system as having two *ideal* models. One of these, *gumlao,* is a type which is chiefless. The other ideal, *gumsa,* was derived from the Shan princely state model and has traditional chiefs. Leach asserts that *actual* Kachin societies tend to oscillate between these two ideals, which, he says, are antithetical to one another. While my own field work tends to substantiate much of Dr. Leach's interpretation, I must disagree with him on a number of technical points.[2] For instance, the chiefless *gumlao* type and the *gumsa* type are not at all antithetical to each other. Instead, it is variant forms of the *gumsa*-type society which have become antithetical to one another.

The adherents to the *gumlao* political system have not been influenced by the Shan in any substantial way. Instead, their deviation from *gumchying gumsa,* the traditional, original Kachin ideal model, has coincided with their progressively

---

[2] My disagreements with Professor Leach are dealt with in a paper to appear shortly. I show there that *gumlao* societies are not really chiefless, although among them chieftainship is not strictly hereditary.

greater reliance on upland opium-poppy (cash crop) cultivation, in place of subsistence upland-rice agriculture. This contrasts with some units having a *gumsa*-type society, whose members have imitated irrigated Shan-type rice agriculture on a large scale.

In fact, three kinds of *gumsa*-type societies have emerged. The first is the *gumchying gumsa,* the original, traditional ideal Kachin model, whose adherents are upland farmers, confined to the Triangle Region of extreme northern Burma. Second is the *gumrawng gumsa,* an intermediate type, whose chiefs generally become powerless figureheads. Most of the lowland settlers seem to derive from this type of society. It is associated with the practice of terraced cultivation on mountainsides, but nonetheless the villagers are generally mobile. The third type, *gumsa,* has Shan-type feudatory chiefdoms. All examples are practitioners of lowland irrigated agriculture, with large, concentrated, settled communities.

The third *gumsa* type displays the greatest amount of symbolic incorporation of Shan civilization. In contrast, the *gumchying gumsa* system maintains the requirement of a ritual purification of each lowland *gumsa* adherent before he is allowed to settle in a *gumchying gumsa* domain again. The reason given for this requirement is that members of the lowland *gumsa* society have been exposed to Shan influence and witchcraft and have stopped being real Kachins. This contention is supported on a ritual level, because Kachin animism has no ceremonial-ritual prescription for lowland (irrigated) cultivation. Agricultural ritual is confined strictly to swidden (slash-and-burn) agriculture, the type practiced by the *gumchying gumsa* people. In order to be provided with the protection of the Kachin priests, the lowland *gumsa* adherent must have a swidden field alongside his permanent irrigated field. This is a purely symbolic and non-economic requirement, necessitated by his not yet having taken on all aspects of Shan society.

While *gumchying gumsa* and *gumsa* are antithetical to each other in that each approximates a polar type of society, the middle variant, *gumrawng gumsa,* is in a general state of disorganization. We can return now to Leach's generalization concerning

Kachin political behavior, in which he states that larger aggregates will disintegrate into smaller ones, and that smaller units will re-integrate into larger ones (1954:6). This generalization seems more meaningful when applied to the *gumrawng gumsa* type, which must serve as the intermediate stage in an oscillation between the ideal Shan-type *gumsa* and the ideal Kachin-type *gumchying gumsa* societies.

It is now clear that, in the final analysis, we must view Kachin distinctiveness not only in relation to the Shan, but also in terms of what the Kachin at both ends or poles of the oscillating system regard as the distinguishing features which typify them as Kachin. In other words, we must now ask what features exist which the Kachin regards as marking him off as "Kachin" in spite of the broad range of variation of Kachin social types—a range in which one type has taken a great deal from the Shan.

The next developmental features which we consider, the influences of geography and education, have generally been overlooked by historians and other writers on the subject. Consider the following situation. Kachins were traditionally mountain-dwelling people; lowland Kachin settlements were unusual. The population density of the general area could not have been more than five per square mile (in the 1931 census it was five to seven persons per square mile). Mountain terrain generally made communication and transportation difficult. The Burmese kings had armies which conquered by sheer weight of numbers, not by specialization of units and weapons. Is it likely then that these mountain populations would have been subdued and put under Burman suzerainty for any length of time?

In the past a large ribbon of Shan population has meandered around the Kachin mountain areas and has stood in the way of Kachin contacts with other lowlanders. Evidence of borrowing from the Shan in Kachin language and material culture is substantial, whereas borrowing from the Burmans is negligible. This sort of evidence means that we can discount some claims (e.g. Furnivall 1960:4) of direct Burman control of the Kachin which did not involve the Shan as well. For centuries there have been symbiotic relations between the Shan and the Kachin for food and for protection against other marauding feudatories. Thus we must understand something of the Shan in order to understand the Kachin. Likewise, the Shan must define himself in relation to the Kachin and the Burman.

How has the distinctiveness of the Kachin as a minority affected relations with the central government? In 1947, when the British Parliament required a Frontier Areas Enquiry Commission to collect tribal opinions concerning their possible amalgamation into an independent Union of Burma, the Kachin witnesses were almost unanimously in favor of joining. Reliable records exist (Burma 1947), so we can see what kinds of witnesses were examined. The first group of witnesses was made up of military personnel, on the average more widely traveled and knowledgeable than other Kachin. The second group was composed of professional people, mostly school teachers, clerical workers, Christian missionaries, and some frontier chiefs. At that time public schools were a rarity in the Kachin area, and, to a man, this group had been trained in Christian mission schools.

The history of education among the Kachin is important because it contradicts some of the commonly held notions about the effects of missionaries in tribal areas. The Burman was not the first to teach Burmese language to the Kachin. Instead, the language was taught as a part of missionary education. The first mission school was set up in 1878 in Bhamo, the northernmost town having some contact with Burman civilization. There were no resident Kachin in Bhamo, so the missionaries brought them from the hills and started settlement units. This area became the principal location for education of the Kachin, and it is notable that Burmese was used as the language of instruction. There was very little teaching of English. Graduates from this school spread over the whole Kachin area.

The window through which an educational awakening came to the Kachin was the Burman language and literature. When in 1947 Kachin witnesses gave their approval for a state of some sort within the independent Union of Burma, all but one of the witnesses were products of the Bhamo missionary schools. These were the people who decided that the fate of the Kachin should be with the rest of Burma. Thus it is correct to say that the real beginning of active Burmanization of the Kachin came with the Western Christian missionaries. It is also true that Burmese was accepted as a kind of national language by these educated

Kachin. At the time of the Second World War there were only about twenty-five Kachin who had some command of the English language, and among these were three college graduates, the first and only Kachin to be so educated until then.

The decision to become part of Burma is highly significant because there are now active sections within the Kachin who see the Kachin only as a system within the larger system which is Burma. This start of Burmanization implies, among other things, that the older "symbolic incorporation of Shan civilization" is in the early stages of being outgrown. Education has led to a wider view of geography, politics, language, and culture, which brings to the Kachin the need for a new orientation. This partially explains why the provincialism of the mountain-dwelling outlook was shed and how a Kachin State within a Union of Burma could be conceived as reasonable and agreeable.

In summary, the following developmental factors may be regarded as the principal functional features which have shaped the Kachin today. In the past the Kachin were culturally distinctive only in relation to the Shan and the Chinese, and the boundary of cultural influences emanating from these neighbors delimited the Kachin's distinctive area. Today Kachin distinctiveness lies within the total Burmese system. In the past all Kachin awareness of the Burman was filtered through the Shan, and, of course, the Shan have historically been identified in the larger Burman political and ideological context. It was not until the reign of the Burmese King Thibaw, when the political situation was in a condition of rapid deterioration, the British annexation was imminent, and the Shan had thrown off the Burman yoke and consolidated their states, that Burma came within the purview of Kachin political ambition. This attempt was stopped by the British in 1895, a decade after the rest of Burma fell (Woodman 1962:339–379).

The next developmental factor was the introduction and acceptance of Burmese language and literature, which came with Christian missionaries. Their educational work was largely responsible for the decision to put the future of the Kachin with the rest of Burma (*Kachin Youth League Magazine* No. 1, Vols. 1–3, 1947). In the post-independence years, the acceptance of Burmese and the early stages of Burmanization were viewed as too small and too slow by the central government, while the Kachin appear to emphasize the opposite opinion.

Obviously there has been a tremendous shift in Kachin outlook, especially in view of the history of contact with the modern world. The Kachin continued to resist the British until 1935 and then resisted the Japanese from the beginning to the end of the Second World War. They, along with the Chin, were the only two Burma nationalities to organize resistance and never to give the Japanese suzerainty over them. Following the war they willingly agreed to become a part of an independent Burma.

As an anthropologist I can offer no plausible interpretation for this sudden decision to become a part of Burma other than that it indicates an acceptance of a certain degree of Burmanization. This Burmanization has now, apparently, become functionally more important in the light of the enlarged world view of the Kachin. If this is the case, then the recent indications of unrest in the Kachin area must be traced to a misjudgment on the part of the Burmans of an acceptance which was already there. If the Kachin agreed to the formation of a Kachin state within the Union, what was implied was that he saw his political system within the larger orbit of Burman civilization; he defined his distinctness in relation to the Burman. The acceptance of the Burmese language has substantially enlarged the Kachin world view.

The policy toward minorities, as set forth in the Constitution of Burma, and the actual practices of the bureaucracy are often widely disparate. Perhaps the rapid changes in Burman society have prevented the Burman majority from correctly assessing the Kachin situation. It is clear that the actions of the Kachin in accepting the Burmese language and political union were misunderstood, and signs of friction have recently broken out in the open.

We may quote a pertinent view of the question of integration of minorities from Silverstein. "Little attention has yet been given to the corollary problem of persuading the dominant Burmans to accept the minorities as equals, and convincing them that Burmese culture and history is the product of all people" (1964:152). Prolonged failure to realize the bilaterality of integration or integrative procedure can only result in the greatest obstacle to an eventual solution: crippling suspicion and mistrust on the part of the minority, contempt and intolerance on the part of the majority.[3]

Have we constructed too stringent requirements for the adequate understanding of a minority group? Must we know everything about all things, and therefore is our prescription to be dismissed as arrogant and unworkable? I think not. Wagley and Harris (1958:239), for example, have made a similar set of suggestions for the study of New World minorities. The essence of research in any empirical science lies in the ability to sort out the variable from the constant factors and in the ability to sort out factors which are needlessly redundant. At the outset the task may be formidable, but I anticipate that a concerted attack on the problem, using several disciplines, will lead us to an adequate and concise idea of its nature and implications. Whether we look at the problems of minorities from a purely academic point of view, or actually try to give advice for their alleviation, the problems are too demanding to be left untouched. We cannot be absolved by continuing to ignore the problems, no matter what convictions we hold.

CONCLUSION

If any significant conclusion can be drawn from the example of the Kachin, it comes in the form of three related questions.

---

[3] The picture of relationships between the Kachin and the Burmese government is not as grim as I may have implied. The following case shows a great sensitivity to some of the cultural problems involved in resettlement of some Kachin groups.

Between 1959 and 1961 the Sino-Burmese border settlement was worked out, and the territory of three Kachin villages was ceded to the People's Republic of China (see Silverstein 1964: 165, Map 3). The responsibility for relocation of the villages was given jointly to the Kachin State government and the Frontier Areas Administration of the Burma army. The government officials made all arrangements to enable an almost literal transplanting of the villages. The village chiefs, village councils, ownership and distribution of land, and other institutions were all transferred to the new sites. I visited the resettled villages twice in 1961–1962, to obtain firsthand information about the attempted transplant. The transfer was handled so thoroughly that even the blueprints for the layout of the new villages were made in consultation with the village councils.

This willingness on the part of the government to treat each community as a functioning socio-cultural entity seems to have paid off. The transplanted villages have taken root, and there is every reason for optimism. The government also took the opportunity to introduce some changes as well. These involved a public school system, a hospital, semi-mechanized farming, and the orderly planning of the settlement pattern.

First, do we, in Southeast Asia, understand the minority elements sufficiently to formulate a workable policy? Or do we still punch the colonial sandbag for every appearance of separatism? Second, have we looked wide and deep enough: have we paid sufficient attention to the factors underlying the distinctiveness of minority elements in relation to other elements? Third, assuming that sufficient understanding exists, how far is the central government willing to go to accommodate minority interests?

This last question implies that one can put up a rational superstructure only on a rational basis. A lack of complete cultural integration becomes a problem only if complete integration is the expressed objective of the majority. If we realize that stringent requirements for rapid assimilation will only intensify a delicate situation, we can note that pluralism is an alternate policy to that of complete integration. However, in some situations, the minority and majority interests must coincide. We agree with Kyaw Thet that "the first salient issue must be how to [impress the fact] that in many spheres of activity and at certain levels of association and organization, the whole nation-state is the minimal unit if it is to survive in the condition of the present day world" (1956:166).

The next fundamental concern is how far the recognition of differences could at the same time be designed as a strategy in the integration of loyalties. Is it possible to develop a policy to encourage and preserve different traditions and at the same time discourage disintegrative tendencies? This is a difficult question; and when I make the claim that no two minority elements are, or can be, exactly alike in terms of their requirements for integration with the majority, I have already denied the possibility of a single, universal solution. At a later date I hope to be able to indicate what I feel to be the next step in dealing with the minorities. I shall then suggest what further steps may be feasible for Burma and indicate how some of these steps might be taken.

REFERENCES CITED

BRECHER, MICHAEL
    1963   The new states of Asia: a political analysis. New York, Oxford University Press.

BURMA
  1947   Report of the Frontier Areas Committee of Enquiry, and ap-
         pendices. Rangoon.
BUTWELL, RICHARD
  1963   U Nu of Burma. Stanford, Stanford University Press.
EMERSON, RUPERT
  1960   From empire to nation: the rise of self-assertion of Asian and
         African peoples. Cambridge, Mass., Harvard University Press.
  1963   Political modernization: the single party system. Denver, Uni-
         versity of Denver Monograph Series in World Affairs, 1.
FURNIVALL, JOHN S.
  1948   Colonial policy and practice. Cambridge, Cambridge University
         Press.
  1960   The governance of Burma. New York, Institute of Pacific
         Relations.
KYAW THET
  1956   Burma: the political integration of linguistic and minority
         groups. In Nationalism and progress in free Asia, Philip W.
         Thayer, ed. Baltimore, Johns Hopkins Press, 156–168.
LEACH, E. R.
  1954   Political systems of highland Burma: a study of Kachin social
         structure. Cambridge, Mass., Harvard University Press.
LEHMAN, F. K.
  1963   The structure of Chin society: a tribal people of Burma adapted
         to a non-Western civilization. Urbana, University of Illinois
         Press.
MACARTNEY, C. A.
  1934   National states and national minorities. London, Oxford Uni-
         versity Press.
PURCELL, VICTOR
  1956   The influence of racial minorities. In Nationalism and progress
         in free Asia, Philip W. Thayer, ed. Baltimore, Johns Hopkins
         Press, 234–245.
SILVERSTEIN, JOSEF
  1964   Burma. In Governments and politics of Southeast Asia, 2d
         edn., George McTurnan Kahin, ed. Ithaca, Cornell University
         Press, 75–179.
TINKER, HUGH
  1961   The Union of Burma. London, Oxford University Press.
WAGLEY, CHARLES, and MARVIN HARRIS
  1958   Minorities in the New World: six case studies. New York,
         Columbia University Press.
WOODMAN, DOROTHY
  1962   The making of Burma. London, Cressett Press.

PART III: CHINA

THERE ARE many reasons to include China in a study of Southeast Asian tribes and minorities. China has long been a source both for cultural innovations and for populations which have filtered down through the mountains which form the northern and northwestern boundaries of Southeast Asia. In the past basic patterns of relationships between tribes and lowland governments have been set in China, and these patterns have persisted in Southeast Asia (see, for example, Kandre's discussion of Chinese-Yao relations and Lehman's discussion of Chinese-Wa contacts). Likewise the present Chinese system of establishing autonomous areas for minority groups has been copied in North Vietnam.

Many of the important Southeast Asian hill tribes, such as Meo, Yao, Akha, Ching-po (or Jinghpaw, a Kachin tribe), Kawa (or Wa), and some of the lowland peoples, especially the Tai speakers, have close linguistic and cultural bonds, and some even have kin living within the boundaries of China. In fact, there are many more Meo and Yao in China than within all of Southeast Asia.

Within China the minority populations form only about 6 percent of the total population, but, as the map of autonomous administrative units shows, these peoples are often very strategically located, especially along the border with Southeast Asia (minorities form 20 percent of the population of Southwest China). Disputed international boundaries with Burma (primarily Kachin State) and India (in the North East Frontier) involve areas occupied primarily by minority or tribal people.

For thousands of years the Chinese have shown a talent for influencing and absorbing alien peoples while retaining their own culture. But the process of absorption has been slower in China's southwestern border regions than most other places; the hills of Yunnan and Kwangsi have remained the refuge of millions of Tai-speaking, Tibeto-Burman, and even Mon-Khmer-speaking people who have retained their cultural identification through centuries of Chinese influence.

Chinese policies for subduing or controlling and assimilating its minorities have varied. In the past the Chinese were largely content to maintain order, suppress bandits, extract a bit of tribute, and then ignore the border hill minorities or "barbarians" (for an example of Chinese-tribal relations in the pre-Communist era see Lin 1961). Unless there was some specific issue worth contesting, they were allowed to live pretty much as they were, and only when Han Chinese population became large in a minority area was central government administration extended to the area.

Following the Communist take-over in 1950, much more self-conscious and deliberate policies have been developed for influence and control over the minority peoples. The Communists got support from some of the minorities as early as the Long March in the 1930's, when many Lolo (Yi, I) joined the Red Army as it passed through their territory (*China News Analysis* [*CNA*] 573:3). In the late 1950's a "war [was] declared against backward customs"; attempts were made to ban religious feasts and to eliminate the cultural differences of the minorities (see China 1953 for summary of Communist policies to that date; see Chang 1956, Pasternak 1962, and Moseley 1965 for more recent summaries and further bibliographic references). In 1961–1962 a milder policy was pursued; respect was to be shown for cultural and linguistic differences, and no use of force was to be allowed in attempts to change customs. By 1964 the policy had changed again: minority problems were phrased in terms of "class struggle," and the elimination of cultural differences was again proclaimed as the goal (*CNA* 563:1–2). In part this rephrasing of minority policy as a class struggle was related to problems of suppressing the rebellion of the Tibetan minority.

Regardless of the changes in policy, the Communists have continued to follow certain common practices in their attempts to control the national minorities. The principal method used to incorporate the minorities has been the establishment of nominally autonomous political-geographical units in areas where minority populations are concentrated. As Mr. Diao points out, the autonomy of these units has been deliberately undermined by the introduction of Han Chinese cadres into strategic political positions and by encouraging the immigration of large numbers of Han Chinese into the minority areas.

Quite significant from the standpoint of the Southeast Asian nations is the fact that the Chinese have embarked on a fairly well-coordinated program of research, education, and political development among the minority nationalities. Research has been done on the languages of minorities, and students have been selected from the minority groups, including those along the Southeast Asian borders, for special training and indoctrination before being returned to their homes to act as sources of influence among their own people. The Chinese also have been sensitive to the symbolic value of ceremonies, such as The East Is Red Festival (October 1964), in which representatives of the minority nationalities joined in singing the praises of the Peking regime.

In spite of the fact that the Han form a very clear majority of the Chinese population and hold political power very tightly, they have managed to give the impression that the rights of minorities are being protected. The appearance of autonomy has been used effectively as a propaganda device and as a model for programs in North Vietnam (the setting up of the Viet Bac and Tai Bac Autonomous zones).

REFERENCES CITED

CHANG, CHI JEN
    1956   The minority groups of Yunnan and political expansion into Southeast Asia. Ann Arbor, Michigan, University of Michigan, doctoral dissertation.

CHINA, PEOPLE'S REPUBLIC
    1953   Policy toward nationalities of the People's Republic of China. Peking, Foreign Languages Press.

LIN YUEH-HUA
    1961   The Lolo of Liang Shan. New Haven, HRAF Press, translation by Ju-shu Pan.

MOSELEY, GEORGE
    1965   China's fresh approach to the national minority question. China Quarterly 24:15–27 (October–December).

PASTERNAK, BURTON
    1962   Continuity and discontinuity in Chinese policy toward southwestern tribes since 1911. New York, Columbia University, Department of East Asian Studies and Department of Anthropology, master's degree essay.

Periodicals

CHINA NEWS ANALYSIS. Hong Kong.

TABLE 5
POPULATION, GEOGRAPHICAL DISTRIBUTION, OCCUPATION, RELIGION, AND LANGUAGE OF NATIONAL MINORITIES OF MAINLAND CHINA[a]

Name [Wade-Giles Romanization] Synonym	Chinese Character	Est. Population in China	Distribution (in Order of Population Size)	Distribution in China, in Order of Population Size	Occupation	Religion	Language and Script[†]
Chuang [Chuang] Tho, T'u, T'u-jen, Wu-ming	僮	6,611,455[b] (7,785,414)[c]	China	Kwangsi Chuang Aut. Region, Wen-shan Chuang and Miao Aut. *Chou* of Yunnan, Tung-hsiang Multi-national Aut. County of Kwangtung, Lien-shan Chuang and Yao Aut. County of Kwangtung, and in Kweichow	Agriculture	Pantheism	Tai: Northern. Wu-ming dialect selected as standard; Latin alphabet with six additional letters being introduced[d]
Uighur [Wei-wu-erh] Uygur, Ughuri, Hui-hu, Kao-ch'e, Wei-ur		3,640,125[b] (3,901,205)	China, Russia	Kashgaria, and I-li regions of Dzungaria in Sinkiang Uighur Aut. Region, a few settled in T'ao-yüan County of Hunan	Agriculture, horticulture, animal husbandry, and handicrafts	Islam	Altaic: Turkic. Latin alphabet, with eight extra letters being introduced to supersede Arabic script
Chinese Muslim [Hui] Hui, Ho, Hui-tze, Hwei, Khuei, Panghse, Panthay, Panthe, Panthee		3,559,350[b] (3,934,335)	China, Russia, Burma, Thailand, Laos	Ning-hsia Hui Aut. *Chou* of Kansu, Honan, Hopeh, Tsinghai, Shantung, and Yunnan, and in most other provinces of China	Agriculture; few merchants.	Islam	Chinese, no special dialect. Chinese script: Arabic religious language and script
Yi [I] Lolo, Hei-i, Hei Ku T'ou, I, I-chia, Leisu, Lo-kuei, Man-chia, Man-tzu, Mosu, Neisu, Nesu, Ngosu, No, Norsu, Nosu, Pei-i, Pei, Ku T'ou	彝	3,254,269[b] (3,264,432)	China, Laos, North Vietnam	Yunnan and Liang-shan I Aut. *Chou* in Szechwan, also in Kweichow, and Kwangsi Chuang Aut. Region	Agriculture; some animal husbandry	Pantheism	Tibeto-Burman: Burmese-Lolo, Lolo group. Newly invented romanized script. These people and their language have usually been referred to as Lolo; Yi is the new Communist designation

Tibetan [Tsang] Bod, Bodpa, Kamba, Panaka, Tangut	2,775,622[b] (2,775,622)	China, Nepal, India	Tibet (including Chamdo), Tibetan Aut. *Chou* of Szechwan, Kansu, and Yunnan provinces	Animal husbandry; but more income from agricultural production	Lamaism of yellow and red sects	Tibeto-Burman: Tibetan[k]
Miao [Miao] Hmong, Hmu, Hmung, Meo	2,511,339[b] (2,687,590)	China, North Vietnam, Laos, Thailand	Kweichow, Hunan, Yunnan provinces, Kwangsi Chuang Aut. Region, Szechwan, Chekiang, Kwangtung, Fukien, and Hupeh provinces	Agriculture, also lumbering	Pantheism	Miao-Yao: Miao. Newly invented script being introduced
Manchurian [Man] Manchu, Man	2,418,931[b] (2,430,561)	China	Liaoning, Heilungkiang, Kirin, Hopeh provinces, Peking City, Inner Mongolian Aut. Region, scattered in Shantung, Hupeh, Szechwan, Kansu, Hunan, Kwangtung, and other provinces	Agriculture; urban residents in business	Pantheism, some Buddhism, and Christianity	Altaic: Tunguso-Manchurian. Chinese language and script also widely used
Mongolian [Meng] Meng	1,462,956[b] (1,645,695)	China, Mongolian People's Republic, Russia	Inner Mongolian Aut. Region, Liaoning, Sinkiang Uighur Aut. Region, Kirin, Heilungkiang, Tsinghai, Hopeh, Honan, Szechwan, Peking City, Yunnan, Kansu, Kiangsu, Hupeh	Agriculture and animal husbandry	Lamaism	Altaic: Mongolian language and script[k]
Puyi [Pu-i] Chung-chia, Dioi, I-chia, I-jen, Jao-chia, Jui, Pu-i, Pu-yüeh, Shui-hu, Pen-ti, Yoi	1,247,883[b] (1,313,015)	China	Pu-i and Miao Aut. *Chou* of Kweichow, other counties in Kweichow, Yunnan, Szechwan	Agriculture	Pantheism	Tai: Northern. New Chuang script being introduced
Korean [Ch'ao-hsien]	1,120,405[b] (1,255,551)	South Korea, North Korea, China, Russia	Yen-pien Korean Aut. *Chou*, Ch'ang-pai Aut. County in Kirin province and scattered in Kirin, Heilungkiang and Liaoning provinces and Inner Mongolia	Agriculture (specialize in paddy-rice cultivation)	Buddhism and Christianity	Korean language and script[k]

(continued)

[153]

TABLE 5
(continued)

Name [Wade-Giles Romanization] Synonym	Chinese Character	Est. Population in China	Distribution (in Order of Population Size)	Distribution in China in Order of Population Size	Occupation	Religion	Language and Script¹
Tung [Tung] Kam, Nin Kam, Tung-chia, Tung-jen	侗	710,000d (825,323)	China	Miao and Tung Aut. Chou in Kweichow, San-chiang T'ung Aut. County in Kwangsi Chuang Aut. Region, Hsin-huang T'ung and T'ung-tao T'ung aut. counties in Hunan	Agriculture; also lumbering	Pantheism	Kam-Sui-Mak, possibly related to Tai. New script being introduced. These people and their language have usually been referred to as Kam
Yao [Yao] In Mien, Kim Mien, Kim Mun, Lingnan Yao, Man, Yu Mien	猺 傜	660,000d (747,985)	China, North Vietnam, Laos, Thailand	Kwangsi Chuang Aut. Region, Yunnan, Hunan, Kwangtung, and Kweichow provinces	Agriculture; also lumbering	Pantheism	Miao-Yao: Yao. Spoken dialects vary considerably. New script being introduced
Pai [Pai] Ber Dser, Ber Wa Dser, La Bhu, Minchia, Minchia-tzu, Pai-jen, Pai-man, Per-mu-tuu, Per-tsu, Pe-tsen, Pe-tso, Petsu Shua Ber Ni	白 民家	500,000d (684,386)	China	Ta-li Pai Aut. Chou in Yunnan, and other parts of Yunnan	Agriculture; some industry and commerce	Pantheism, some converts to Christianity	Tibeto-Burman: Burmese-Lolo (?). New script similar to Yi, being introduced
T'uchia [T'u-chia] Piseka	土家	300,000d (603,773)	China	T'u-chia and Miao Aut. Chou in Hunan, Lai-feng, Ho-feng, and Yien counties in Hupeh Province	Agriculture; also handicrafts	Islam	Tibeto-Burman; Lolo group¹
Kazakh [Ha-sa-k'o]		500,000d (533,160)	Russia, China	I-li Kazakh Aut. Chou in Sinkiang Uighur Aut. Region, Kansu and Singhai provinces	Animal husbandry; some agriculture	Islam	Altaic: Turkic.k Latin alphabet with eight extra letters being introduced to replace Arabic scriptl
Hani [Ha-ni] Houni, Woni	哈尼	480,000d (549,362)	China, North Vietnam, Burma	Hung-ho Ha-ni and I Aut. Chou and Chiang-ch'eng Ha-ni and I Aut. County in Yunnan, scattered in Hsi-shuang Pan-na Thai Aut. Chou in Yunnan	Agriculture	Pantheism	Tibeto-Burman: Burmese-Lolo, Lolo group. New script being introduced

Name		Population		Location	Economy	Religion	Notes
Thai [T'ai] Tai, Tai-na, Tai-ni, Tai-li, Tai-peng, Tai-ya, Te-hung Tai, Chinese Shan, Hsi-shuang Pan-na Tai	傣 秦	470,000d (503,616)	China, Thailand, Laos, North Vietnam, Burma	Hsi-shuang Pan-na Thai Aut. *Chou*, and Te-hung Thai and Ching-po Aut. *Chou* in Yunnan, scattered in other counties of Yunnan	Agriculture	Indian sect of Buddhism	Tai: various dialects, probably most y South-western. Tai Leh and Tai Na scripts are being introduced to replace other Tai scripts
Li [Li] B'lai, B'li, Dai Dli, Hiai, K'lai, Lai, Le, Loi, S'lai	黎	360,000d (395,556)	China	Li and Miao Aut. *Chou* on Hainan Island of Kwangtung Province, Kwangsi Chuang Aut. Region, Yunnan, Hunan	Agriculture	Pantheism, some Taoism	Kadai. Newly invented script
Lisu [Li-su] Li-lsaw, Li-shaw, Lisaw, Liso, Lutzu, Yaoyen, Yawyen, Yawyin, Yehjen	傈僳	310,000d (317,465)	China, Burma, Thailand	Nu-chiang Li-su Aut. *Chou* in Yunnan, scattered in Yunnan and Szechwan provinces	Agriculture, some animal husbandry	Pantheism and Christianity	Tibeto-Burman: Burmese-Lolo, Lolo group. Incomplete phonetic script being improved
Kawa [K'a-wa] Hai, Hkawa, Hkun Loi, K'a-la, La, Lawa, Loi-la, Nyo, Tai Loi, Vü, Wa Wii	佧佤 佤	280,000d (286,158)	China, Burma	Meng-lien Thai, La-ku, and K'a-wa Aut. County, Lan-ts'ang La-ku Aut. County, Ts'ang-yuan K'a-wa Aut. County, and Hsi-meng K'a-wa Aut. County in Yunnan Province	Agriculture, some hunting	Buddhism and Christianity, some pantheism	Mon-Khmer: Palaungic. Incomplete script being improved. These people and their language are usually known as Wa
She [She] (Bruk translation spells this "Sho")	畲	210,000e (226,697)	China	Fu-an Special District in Fukien, Wen-chow and Chin-hua spec. districts in Che-kiang, scattered in Ch'ien-shan and Kwei-chi in Kiangsi Province and in Ch'ao-an in Kwangtung	Agriculture	Pantheism	Miao-Yao.k "The Sho . . . speak Chinese and partially preserve their language which is related to the Yao language." (Bruk 1960:33). No special script
Nung [Nung]	儂	190,000e (200,000)	China, North Vietnam	Scattered in southeast Yunnan	Agriculture	Pantheism	Tai: Central. Chinese style script. Nung are considered by Bruk (1960:26) to be merely a subgroup of the Chuang
Tunghsiang [Tung-hsiang]		150,000e (159,345)	China	Tung-hsiang Aut. County in Kansu, scattered in Kuang-ho, Ho-cheng, and Lin-hsia counties in Kansu	Agriculture	Islamic customs like the Hui	Altaic: Mongolian.k No script

(continued)

TABLE 5
(continued)

Name [Wade-Giles Romanization] Synonym	Chinese Character	Est. Population in China	Distribution (in Order of Population Size)	Distribution in China in Order of Population Size	Occupation	Religion	Language and Script[l]
Nasi [Na-hsi] Lühsi, Lüikhi, Moso, Nachri, Nahsi, Nakhi, Nashi, Nazo, Wuman	納西 磨些	140,000 (155,748)	China	Li-chiang Aut. County in Yunnan, scattered in Wei-shi, Chung-tien, Ning-lang, and Yung-sheng counties in Yunnan	Agriculture and animal husbandry; some commerce and handicrafts	Pantheism, some Lamaism	Tibeto-Burman. Newly invented script
Laku [La-hu] Lahu, Lohei, Muhso, Musso, Mussuh	倮黑、 拉祜	130,000[d] (188,103)	China, Burma, Thailand, Laos	Lan-ts'ang La-ku Aut. County in the P'u-erh region of Yunnan scattered in Meng-lien and Keng-ma aut. counties and other parts of Yunnan	Agriculture	Buddhism and pantheism, some Christianity	Tibeto-Burman: Burmese-Lolo, Lolo group. Incomplete script being improved
Shui [Sui] Shui-chia, Sui	水 逩 綏	130,000[d] (160,313)	China	San-tu Shui Aut. County in Kweichow Province, Kwangsi Chuang Aut. Region	Agriculture	Pantheism	Kam-Sui-Mak (possibly related to Tai). Newly invented script
Chingpo [Ching-po] Chingpaw, Jinghpaw Kachin, Kakhieng, Singhpo, Thienbaw	景頗	100,000[d] (101,852)	Burma, China, Assam, Thailand	Te-hung Thai and Ching-po Aut. *Chou* in Yunnan	Agriculture	Pantheism, some Christianity	Tibeto-Burman: possibly related to Bodo group. Romanized missionary script being improved
Kirghiz [K'o-erh-k'o-ssu]		70,000[d] (68,862)	Russia, China	K'o-tzu-lo-su Kirghiz Aut. *Chou* in Sinkiang Uighur Aut. Region	Animal husbandry and agriculture	Islam	Altaic: Turkic. Arabic script being replaced with new Romanized script[j]
Tu [T'u] Monguor		53,000[d] (68,259)	China	Hu-chu Tu Aut. County in Tsinghai; scattered in Min-ho and Ta-t'ung counties in Tsinghai, and in Kansu Province, on the banks of the Kwang Ho above Lan-chou	Agriculture	Lamaism	Altaic: Mongolian, Old Mongolian.[k] Chinese language also used in daily life, and Tibetan used in religious ceremonies

Name	Chinese	Population	Country	Location	Economy	Religion	Language
Daghor [Ta-kan-erh, Ta-kuan-erh, Ta-hu-erh] Dagur, Daur		44,100d (50,121)	China	Tsi-tsi-har (Ch'i-ch'i-ha-erh) Municipality and Fu-yü County in Heilungkiang, scattered in Mo-li-ta-wa Daghor Aut. Banner, Pu-t'e-ha Banner, O-wen-k'o Aut. Banner in Inner Mongolia, T'a-ch'eng County in Sinkiang Uighur Aut. Region	Agriculture	Pantheism and Lamaism	Altaic: Mongolian, Old Mongolian.k New script being developed
Molao [Mo-lao] Molo	仫佬	43,100d (44,679)	China	Lo-ch'eng, I-shan, Liu-ch'eng and I-ch'eng counties in Kwangsi Chuang Aut. Region	Agriculture, some handicrafts	Pantheism	Tai: Northern (Chuang-Tai?).k,m No script
Ch'iang [Ch'iang]	羌	30,000d (42,955)	China	A-pa Tibetan Aut. Chou, Mao-wen Ch'iang Aut. County, Sung-p'an and Li counties in Szechwan	Agriculture, handicrafts	Pantheism	Tibeto-Burman: Tibetan.k No script
Pulang [Pu-lang] Humai, Palaung, Rumai	布朗	35,000e (41,595)	Burma, China	Scattered in Hsi-shuang Pan-na Thai Aut. Chou and Lan-ts'ang La-ku Aut. County in Yunnan	Agriculture	Buddhism	Mon-Khmer: Palaungic
Salar [Sa-la]		30,600e (31,923)	China	Hsün-hua Salar County of Tsinghai; Hua-lung Hui Aut. County of Tsinghai, Lin-hsia County, Hsi-ning and Lin-t'an districts of Kansu	Agriculture, secondarily animal husbandry and commerce	Islam	Altaic: Turkic. No script
Russian [O-lo-ssu]		20,000e (9,766)	Russia, China	Scattered in I-ning and Urumchi municipalities, and Ta-ch'eng County in Sinkiang Uighur Aut. Region	Agriculture, some urban residents in business	Russian Orthodox	Indo-European: Slavic. Cyrillic script
Ch'ilao [Ch'i-lao] I-lao, Kei-lao, Kelao, Kha Lao, Khi Lao, Thi, Thii, Xan Lao	仡佬	20,400e (23,000)	China, North Vietnam	Kuan-ling, Lang-tai, Ch'ien-hsi, and Chih-chin counties in Kweichow, Lung-lin Multinational Aut. County in Kwangsi Chuang Aut. Region	Agriculture and handicrafts	Pantheism	Kadai. No script

(continued)

TABLE 5
(*continued*)

Name [Wade-Giles Romanization] Synonym	Chinese Character	Est. Population in China	Distribution (in Order of Population Size)	Distribution in China in Order of Population Size	Occupation	Religion	Language and Script[l]
Sibo [Hsi-po]		19,000d (21,405)	China	Ch'a-pu-ch'a-erh Sibo Aut. County in Sinkiang Uighur Aut. Region, scattered in Kirin and Liaoning provinces	Agriculture	Shamanism	Altaic: Tunguso-Manchuriank
Maonan [Mao-nan]	毛難佳	18,400d (24,239)	China	Scattered in Huan-chiang, Nan-tan, Ho-ch'ih counties of Kwangsi Chuang Aut. Region	Agriculture	Pantheism	Tai: Northern (Chuang Tai?),k,m No script
Achang [A-ch'ang]	阿昌	17,000e (17,741)	China, Burma	Scattered in Te-hung Thai and Ching-po Aut. Chou in Yunnan	Agriculture, some handicrafts	Indian sect of Buddhism	Tibeto-Burman: Burmese-Lolo, Burma group (?). No script
Tadjik [T'a-chi'k'o] Tadzhik, Chieh-pan-to, Selekur		14,000d (15,014)	Russia, China	Tash Kurgan (T'a-shih-k'u-erh-kan) Tadzhik Aut. County, P'i-shan, Yen-ch'eng, and Sha-ch'e counties in Sinkiang Uighur Aut. Region	Nomadic herdsmen	Islam	Indo-European: Iranian, Shugnan (classified by HRAF Handbooks as Turkic) No script
Uzbek [Wu'tzu-pieh-k'o]		13,000 (11,557)	Russia, China	I-ning and Urumchi cities, T'a-ch'eng and Sha-ch'e counties of Sinkiang Uighur Aut. Region, and in Tung-peh	Mostly urban residents in business or handicrafts; some in agriculture	Islam	Altaic: Turkic
Nu [Nu] Anu, Lutze, Lutzu, Noutze, Noutzu, Nusu, Nutsu, Nutzu	怒	12,700d (13,724)	China	Kung-shan, Tu-lung and Nu Aut. County, Pi-chiang, Fu-kung, and Lan-p'ing counties of Yunnan	Agriculture	Lamaism and Christianity	Tibeto-Burman
Tatar [T'a-t'a-erh]		6,000d (4,370)	Russia, China	I-ning Municipality and T'a-ch'eng County of Sinkiang Uighur Aut. Region and in Tung-peh	Mostly urban residents in business and handicrafts	Islam	Altaic: Turkic

[158]

Alwenke Evenki, Owenko Tungus (in Russia)		6,000e (7,245)	Russia, China	Ahwenke Aut. Banner, Mo-li-ta-wa Daghor Aut. Banner, and A-jung Banner in Inner Mongolia, and in No-ho County of Heilungkiang Province	Hunting, secondarily agriculture	Shamanism, some Christianity	Altaic: Tunguso-Manchurian[k]
Solon [So-lun]		4,900d	China	Inner Mongolia and Heilungkiang Province	Nomadic herdsmen	Shamanism	Altaic: Tunguso-Manchurian[n]
Paoan [Pao-an]	保安	4,000e (5,516)	China	Ta-ho Paoan Nationality *Hsiang* in Kansu Province	Agriculture	Islam	Altaic: Mongolian
Ching [Ch'ing]? Vietnamese	京	4,000e (4,444)	South Vietnam, North Vietnam, Cambodia, China	Tung-hsiang Multinational Aut. County in Kwangtung Province	Mainly fishing, secondarily agriculture	Taoism and Catholicism	Viet-Muong: Vietnamese
Yüku [Yü-ku] Sara-Uighur		3,000d (4,617)	China	Su-nan Yü-ku Aut. County and Chiu-ch'üan County of Kansu Province	Nomadic herdsmen	Lamaism	Altaic: Turkic[k]
Penglung [Peng-lung] Pengyu	崩龍	2,900e (6,309)	China	Te-hung Thai and Ching-po Aut. *Chou* of Yunnan Province	Agriculture	Indian sect of Buddhism	Mon-Khmer: Palaungic(?)
Oronchon [O-lun-chun] Ch'ilin, Oronchon	鄂倫春	2,000d (2,459)	China	Oronchon Banner in Inner Mongolia, Huma, Haunke, and Ai hui counties in Heilungkiang Province	Hunting	Pantheism	Altaic: Tunguso-Manchurian.[k]
Tulung [Tu-lung]	獨龍	2,400d (2,763)	China	Kung-shan Tu-lung and Nu Aut. County in Yunnan Province	Agriculture	Pantheism	Tibeto-Burman
Hoche [Ho-chih](?) Khechke, Nanai, Nanaitsi	赫哲	450e (575)	Russia, China	Fu-yüan, Jao-ho and Fu-chin counties in Heilungkiang Province	Mainly fishing and hunting, secondarily agriculture	Shamanism	Altaic: Tunguso-Manchurian
Pumi [Pu-mi](?)	普米	— (15,000)	China, ?	Northwest mountains of Yunnan Province	Agriculture	Pantheism	(?) Use Tibetan and Chinese languages; no script
Kutsung [Ku-tsung] (Woni or Hani tribe)		— (4,000)	China	Scattered in forest regions of southern Yunnan	(unknown)	(unknown)	Tibeto-Burman: Burmese-Lolo, Lolo group

(continued)

TABLE 5
(continued)

Name [Wade-Giles Romanization] Synonym	Chinese Character	Est. Population in China	Distribution (in Order of Population Size)	Distribution in China in Order of Population Size	Occupation	Religion	Language and Script[i]
Monba[f] [?]	門巴	— (3,800)	China, ?	Scattered in the Sino-Indian border area of Tibet	(unknown)	(unknown)	(unknown)
Han Chinese[g] [Han]	漢	387,000,000					
Northern dialect			—	—			
Kiangsu Chekiang dialect		46,000,000	—	—			
Kwangtung dialect		27,000,000	—	—			
Hunan dialect		26,000,000	—	—			
K'e-chia dialect (Hakka)		20,000,000					
South Fukien dialect		15,000,000					
Kiangsi dialect		13,000,000					
North Fukien dialect		7,000,000					
Total Han Chinese		541,000,000					
Total minority (1953 census)		34,757 985					
Total minority (recent data)		38,173,100					
Total China		575,757,985[h]					
Total China (recent data)		(579,017,700)					

(concluded)

ᵃ Source: Figures from sources indicated below. Locations checked and amplified by reference to Bruk (1959) and the *Provisional Atlas of Communist Administrative Units* (CIA 1959). Information on groups found in Russia was checked in *Atlas of the People of the World* (Anon. 1964) and the *Bol'shaia Sovetskaia Entsiklopediia* (1949–1958).

The Kaoshan, who have a population of approximately 200,000, are concentrated primarily in the central, northern, and eastern parts of Taiwan. These, together with some other minorities estimated to number several tens of thousands who have not yet received official recognition, are excluded from this enumeration.

ᵇ Figures from the original Chinese Communist 1953 Census, published in *Jen-min Jih-pao* (*People's Daily*) November 1, 1954.

ᶜ Figures in parentheses are from the 1961 publication *The Nationalities of China* (Peking, Nationalities Publishing House) as reproduced in *China News Analysis* (569:2–3, June 18, 1965), except for figures for Nung, Ch'iao, Pumi, Kutsung, and Monba, which are taken from *Wen-wei-pao*, Hong Kong, November 30, 1964. These figures *may* indicate recent population changes among minorities, but such an interpretation should be made with extreme caution.

d These figures are taken from official Chinese Communist statistics, based on the 1953 census, published in *Shih-shih Shou-ts'e (Handbook on Current Events)*, Peking, September 10, 1956, and *Jen-min Shou-ts'e (People's Handbook)*, 1957.

e These figures are taken from Chinese Communist statistics, published in *People's Handbook*, 1957.

f These minorities have been recently officially recognized. Detailed data are not available.

g These figures are taken from Bruk (1959:22).

h The figure given for the total mainland China population is the total of the 1953 figures listed in this table. This total does not equal the various totals given by Bruk in different places within his paper: 590 195,000 (Bruk 1959:4), or the census count—574,206,000 (*ibid.*). His totals also included 7,591,000 people on the island of Taiwan, who were not counted in this table. Bruk's figures on Han Chinese are not consistent. We have used the breakdown given on p. 22.

i Sources for linguistic identification: LeBar *et al.* (1964); Chen *et al.* (1956A, B, C, D); Wilhelm (1956A, B, C), except as noted. Linguistic classification has been changed to conform with that in the other parts of this book. See notes accompanying "Population and Linguistic Affiliation of Ethnic Groups of Burma" in Introduction to Part II above for details.

j Source: Ma (1962).

k Source: Bruk (1959:18–21).

l Source: *China News Analysis* (573: 6, July 23, 1965).

m *China News Analysis* (573:5, July 23, 1965) states that the Maonan speak "a Chinese-Tibetan language of the Tung-Shui group." Bruk (1959:26) states, "The Molao and Maonan are two small nationalities, the basic area of which is located to the northwest of the city of Lu-chou in the Kwangsi-Chuang Autonomous Ch'u. Being located in the center of Chuang population, they were subjected to the linguistic and cultural influence of the latter, but the ethnic group to which they belong has never been definitively determined."

n Linguistic classification from *Atlas of the Peoples of the World* (Anon. 1964).

TABLE 6
AUTONOMOUS NATIONALITIES GOVERNMENTS
OF MAINLAND CHINA

Name	Location (Province)	Administrative Divisions[i]	Number of Nation- alities	Total Population (1,000's)	Population of Major Tribes (1,000's)	Date of Founding
A. AUTONOMOUS REGIONS						
Inner Mongolia Aut. Region	Inner Mongolia	7 leagues 9 municipalities 22 counties 50 banners 3 autonomous counties	11	11,700	1,213	May 1 1947
Uighur Aut. Region	Sinkiang	6 special districts 5 autonomous chou 4 municipalities 74 counties 6 autonomous counties	13	4,870	3,600	Oct. 1 1955
Chuang Aut. Region	Kwangsi	6 special districts 5 municipalities 68 counties 7 autonomous counties	11	19,500	7,280	Mar. 5 1958
Ningsia Hui Aut. Region	Ningsia	1 special district 2 municipalities 16 counties	4	1,820	600	Oct. 25 1958
Tibetan Aut. Region	Tibet Proper and Chamdo	5 special districts 1 municipality 68 counties	4	1,270	1,200	Apr. 22 1956
B. AUTONOMOUS CHOU (EQUIVALENT TO SPECIAL DISTRICT)						
Yen-pien Korean Aut. *Chou*	Kirin	1 municipality 6 counties	6	1,019	578	Sept. 3 1952
Kan-nan Tibetan Aut. *Chou*	Kansu	7 counties	6	340	166	Oct. 1 1953
Lin-hsia Hui Aut. *Chou*	Kansu	1 municipality 5 counties 1 autonomous county	7	810	312	Nov. 15 1956
Hai-pei Tibetan Aut. *Chou*	Tsinghai	3 counties 1 autonomous county	6	130	26	Dec. 31 1953
Hai-nan Tibetan Aut. *Chou*	Tsinghai	5 counties	6	200	60	Dec. 15 1953
Huang-nan Tibetan Aut. *Chou*	Tsinghai	3 counties	4	77	46	Dec. 22 1953
Yu-shu Tibetan Aut. *Chou*	Tsinghai	6 counties	4	100	85	Feb. 12 1952
Kuo-lo Tibetan Aut. *Chou*	Tsinghai	6 counties	2	65	60	Jan. 1 1954
Hai-hsi Mongolian, Tibetan, and Kazakh Aut. *Chou*	Tsinghai	1 municipality 3 counties	7	100	—	Jan. 25 1954
I-li Kazakh Aut. *Chou*	Sinkiang	2 special districts 1 municipality 21 counties 2 autonomous counties	13	1,000	500	Nov. 29 1954
K'o-tzu-lo-su (Kizilsu) Kirghiz Aut. *Chou*	Sinkiang	4 counties	11	180	54	Jul. 14 1954

(continued)

TABLE 6
(continued)

Name	Location (Province)	Administrative Divisionsⁱ	Number of Nationalities	Total Population (1,000's)	Population of Major Tribes (1,000's)	Date of Founding
B. AUTONOMOUS CHOU						
Ch'ang-chi Hui Aut. Chou	Sinkiang	7 counties 1 autonomous county	13	98	39	Jul. 15 1954
Pa-vin-kuo-leng (Bayan Gol) Mongol Aut. Chou	Sinkiang	7 counties 1 autonomous county	12	57	20	June 23 1954
Po-er-t'a-la (Boro Tala) Mongol Aut. Chou	Sinkiang	3 counties	13	41	10	July 15 1954
Hsiang-hsi T'u-chia and Miao Aut. Chou	Hunan	10 counties	6	1,800	Tuchia: 396 Miao: 342	Sept. 16 1957
Hai-nan Li and Miao Aut. Chou	Kwangtung	8 counties	4	691	Li: 389 Miao: 14	July 1 1952
Kan-tzu Tibetan Aut. Chou	Szechwan	21 counties	4	540	440	Dec. 25 1950
A-pa Tibetan Aut. Chou	Szechwan	12 counties 1 autonomous county	5	520	210	Jan. 1 1953
Liang-shan I Aut. Chou	Szechwan	11 counties	3	860	700	Oct. 1 1952
Ch'ien-tung-nan Miao and T'ung Aut. Chou	Kweichow	16 counties	7	1,960	Miao: 730 T'ung: 470	July 23 1956
Ch'ien-nan Pu-i and Miao Aut. Chou	Kweichow	16 counties 1 autonomous county	8	1,949	Pu-i: 813 Miao: 233	Aug. 8 1956
Te-hung Thai and Ching-po Aut. Chou	Yunnan	5 counties 1 chen	9	400	Thai: 175 Ching-po: 97	July 24 1953
Hsi-shuang Pan-na Aut. Chou	Yunnan	3 counties	14	320	160	Jan. 23 1953
Hung-ho Ha-ni and I Aut. Chou	Yunnan	1 municipality 10 counties 2 autonomous counties	12	1,880	I: 340 Ha-ni: 280	Nov. 18 1957
Nu-chiang Li-su Aut. Chou	Yunnan	4 counties 1 autonomous county	17	220	110	Aug. 23 1954
Ti-ch'ing Tibetan Aut. Chou	Yunnan	3 counties	7	170	90	Sept. 13 1954
Ta-li Pai Aut. Chou	Yunnan	1 municipality 10 counties 2 autonomous counties	9	1,600	670	Nov. 22 1956
Wen-shan Chuang and Miao Aut. Chou	Yunnan	8 counties	7	1,400	Chuang: 449 Miao: 153	Apr. 1 1958
Ch'u-hsung I Aut. Chou	Yunnan	11 counties	10	1,670	390	Apr. 15 1958

(continued)

TABLE 6
(Continued)

Province or Region	Name of Autonomous County or Banner	Date of Founding
C. AUTONOMOUS COUNTY (EQUIVALENT TO COUNTY)		
Hopeh Province	Ta-ch'ang Hui Autonomous County	1954
	Meng-ts'un Hui Autonomous County	1954
Inner Mongolian	O-lun-ch'un (Oronchon) Autonomous Banner	1951
Autonomous Region	Mo-li-ta-wa Ta-hu-erh (Daghor) Autonomous Banner	1958
	O-wen-k'o (Evenki) Autonomous Banner	1958
Liaoning Province	Fou-hsin Hui Autonomous County	1957
	K'o-la-ch'in Tso-i Mongol Autonomous County	1957
Kirin Province	Ch'ang-pai Korean Autonomous County	1958
	Ch'ien-kuo-erh-lo-ssu Mongol Autonomous County	1956
Heilungkiang Province	Tu-erh-po-t'e Mongol Autonomous County	1956
Kansu Province	Chang-chia-ch'uan Hui Autonomous County	1955
	T'ien-chu Tibetan Autonomous County	1955
	Su-nan Yŭ-ku Autonomous County	1954
	Su-pei Mongol Autonomous County	1950
	A-k'o-sai Kazakh Autonomous County	1954
	Tung-hsiang Autonomous County	1950
Tsinghai Province	Hu-chu T'u Autonomous County	1954
	Hua-lung Hui Autonomous County	1954
	Men-yŭan Hui Autonomous County	1953
	Hsŭn-hua Salar Autonomous County	1954
	Ho-nan Mongol Autonomous County	1954
Uighur Autonomous	Pa-li-k'un (Bar Köl) Kazakh Autonomous County	1954
Region, Sinkiang	T'a-shih-k'u-erh-kan (Tash Kurghan) Tadzhik Autonomous County	1954
	Mu-lei-Kazakh Autonomous County	1954
	Yen-ch'i Hui Autonomous County	1954
	Ho-pu-k'o-sai-erh (Kobuk-Saur) Mongol Autonomous County	1954
	Ch'a-pu-ch'a-erh (Chapchal) Sibo Autonomous County	1954
Hunan Province	Chiang-hua Yao Autonomous County	1955
	Ch'eng-pu-Miao Autonomous County	1956
	Hsin-huang T'ung Autonomous County	1956
	T'ung-tao T'ung Autonomous County	
Kwangtung Province	Lien-shan Chuang and Yao Autonomous County	1958
	Lien-nan Yao Autonomous County	1953
	Ju-yuan Yao Autonomous County	1956[a]
	Tung-hsing Multinational Autonomous County	1957
	Ch'in-chow Chuang Autonomous County	1957[b]
Kwangsi Chuang	Tu-an Yao Autonomous County	1955
Autonomous Region	Pa-ma Yao Autonomous County	1955
	Lung-lin Multinational Autonomous County	1953
	Ta-miao-shan Miao Autonomous County	1955
	Ta-yao-shan Yao Autonomous County	1952
	San-chiang T'ung Autonomous County	1952
	Lung-sheng Multinational Autonomous County	1951
Szechwan Province	Mu-li Tibetan Autonomous County	1953
	Mao-wen Ch'iang Autonomous County	1958
	Yen-yuan I Autonomous County	1964[c]
Kweichow Province	Sung-t'ao Miao Autonomous County	1956
	Chen-ning Pu-i and Miao Autonomous County	1963[d]
	Wei-ning I, Hui, and Miao Autonomous County	1954
	San-tu Shui Autonomous County	1956

(continued)

TABLE 6
(Continued)

Province or Region	Name of Autonomous County or Banner	Date of Founding
C. AUTONOMOUS COUNTY (EQUIVALENT TO COUNTY)		
Yunnan Province[e]	O-shan I Autonomous County	1951
	Ts'ang-yuan K'a-wa Autonomous County	1958
	Keng-ma Thai and K'a-wa Autonomous County	1955
	Li-chiang Na-hsi Autonomous County	1958
	Ning-lang I Autonomous County	1956
	Ho-k'ou Yao Autonomous County	1963
	P'ing-pien Miao Autonomous County	1958
	Chiang-ch'eng Ha-ni and I Autonomous County	1954
	Lan-ts'ang La-hu Autonomous County	1953
	Meng-lien Thai, La-hu, and K'a-wa Autonomous County	1954
	Kung-shan Tu-lung and Nu Autonomous County	1956
	Wei-shan I and Hui Autonomous County	1960[f]
	Nan-chien I Autonomous County	1963[g]
	Hsi-meng K'a-wa (Wa) Autonomous County	1965[h]
	Lu-nan I Autonomous County	1957

[a] The Ju-yuan Yao Autonomous County was reorganized under the jurisdiction of Shao-kuan Special District in October 1963 by merging the former Shao-pien Yao Autonomous County and Ju-Yuan County (*Nan-fang Jih Pa*, Canton, October 5, 1963, p. 1; *Nationalities Solidarity*, Peking, January 1964, No. 68:30).

[b] The Ch'in-chow Chuang Autonomous County was renamed in September 1963. It was formerly known as Ch'in-pei Chuang Autonomous County, and is under the jurisdiction of Chan-chiang Special District (*Yang-cheng Wen-pao*, Canton, September 29, 1963).

[c] Yen-yuan I(Yi) Autonomous County was converted from Yen-yuan ordinary county of Hsi-ch'ang Special District in 1964.

[d] The Chen-ning Pu-i and Miao Autonomous County, under the jurisdiction of An-shun Special District, was founded in 1963 (*Nationalities Solidarity*, Peking, January 1964, No. 68:30).

[e] Hsün-tien Hui Autonomous County, founded in 1957, was converted into an ordinary county in 1960 (*People's Daily*, October 30, 1960, p. 4).

[f] The Wei-shan I (Yi) and Hui Autonomous County was formed in 1960 out of the Wei-shan I (Yi) and the Yung-chien Hui Autonomous Counties. The new unit remained under the jurisdiction of Ta-li Pai Autonomous Chou.

[g] The Nan-chien I (Yi) Autonomous County is under the jurisdiction of Ta-li Pai Autonomous Chou.

[h] Hsi-meng K'a-wa (Wa) Autonomous County is under the jurisdiction of the Hsi-shuang Pan-na Thai Autonomous Chou, and was founded March 1, 1965 (*New China News Service*, March 10, 1965).

[i] Information on nationality autonomous areas of various levels revised in accordance with China, Ministry of Interior (1965). (Ed.)

REFERENCES CITED

ANON.

1964   Atlas of the peoples of the world. Moscow, Institute of Ethnography, and Academy of Sciences, U.S.S.R.

BRUK, SOLOMON Il'ICH

1959   Naseleniye Kitaya, MNR i Korei [Peoples of China, Mongolian People's Republic, and Korea]. Moscow, Publishing House of

Academy of Sciences, U.S.S.R. (Translated by U.S. Joint Publications Research Service, New York, 1960.)

CHAN SHAU-WING et al.

1956A North China. New Haven, Human Relations Area Files Press. Subcontractor's Monograph HRAF-27, Stanford-1, Vol. 1.

1956B Central South China. New Haven, Human Relations Area Files Press. Subcontractor's Monograph HRAF-28, Stanford-2, Vol. 1.

1956C East China. New Haven, Human Relations Area Files Press. Subcontractor's Monograph HRAF-29, Stanford-3, Vol. 1.

1956D Southwest China. New Haven, Human Relations Area Files Press. Subcontractor's Monograph HRAF-30, Stanford-4, Vol. 1.

CHINA, PEOPLE'S REPUBLIC, MINISTRY OF INTERIOR

1965 Chung-hua Jen-min Kung-ho-kuo Hsing-cheng. Ch'u-hua Shou-ts'e [Handbook on administrative divisions of the People's Republic of China, 1965]. Peking (English translation by Joint Publications Research Service JPRS:32,223, October 1, 1965. Washington, D.C., U.S. Department of Commerce, Clearinghouse for Federal Scientific and Technical Information.)

LeBAR, FRANK M., GERALD C. HICKEY, and JOHN K. MUSGRAVE

1964 Ethnic groups of mainland Southeast Asia. New Haven, Human Relations Area Files Press.

MA HSUEH-LIANG

1962 New scripts for China's minorities. China Reconstructs, August:24–27. [Peking.]

U.S. CENTRAL INTELLIGENCE AGENCY (CIA)

1959 China: Provisional atlas of communist administrative units (CIA/RR GR 59-20). Washington, D.C., U.S. Department of Commerce, Office of Technical Services.

VVEDENSKII, B. A., et al. (eds.)

1949– Bol'shaia sovetskaia entsiclopediia. Moscow, Government Pub-
1958 lishing House.

WILHELM, HELLMUT, et al.

1956A General handbook of China. New Haven, Human Relations Area Files Press. Subcontractor's Monograph HRAF-55, Washington-4, Vol. 1.

1956B Northwest China. New Haven, Human Relations Area Files Press. Subcontractor's Monograph HRAF-59, Washington-5, Vol. 1.

1956C Northeast China. New Haven, Human Relations Area Files Press. Subcontractor's Monograph HRAF-61, Washington-9.

Periodicals

CHINA NEWS ANALYSIS. Weekly newsletter. Hong Kong.
JEN-MIN JIH-PAO (PEOPLE'S DAILY). Peking.
JEN-MIN SHOU-TS'E (PEOPLE'S HANDBOOK). Peking.

NAN-FANG JIH-PAO. Canton.
NATIONALITIES SOLIDARITY. Peking.
NEW CHINA NEWS SERVICE. Peking.
SHIH-SHIH SHOU-TS'E (HANDBOOK ON CURRENT EVENTS). Peking.
WEN-WEI-PAO. Hong Kong.
YANG-CHENG WEN-PAO. Canton.

CHAPTER 4

The National Minorities of China and Their Relations With the Chinese Communist Regime

RICHARD K. DIAO

INTRODUCTION

China is a multi-nationality state.[1] Besides the Han Chinese who constitute the majority of the population, there are over fifty national minorities. According to official statistics of 1953, the total minority population amounted to more than 35,500,000; the total increased to 38,900,000 by 1957, representing roughly 6 percent of the entire population of China. Those minorities which number over one million include the Chuang, Uighur, Hui (Chinese Muslims), Yi (I, or Lolo), Tibetan, Miao, Man-

---

[1] In the current Chinese Communist terminology, minorities (religious, ethnic, tribal) are referred to as "minority nationalities." The Communist view of minority nationalities is that the problems involved are those of *class struggle*. Thus Liu Ch'un, deputy chairman of the Chinese Cabinet's commission of nationalities and deputy head of the Chinese Communist Party's united-front department of the Central Committee, is quoted as saying, "The question of nationality is connected with the question of classes, in fact the question of nationality is the question of classes. Mao Tse-tung has pointed out that 'national struggle fundamentally is a question of class struggle'" (*China News Analysis* [*CNA*] 563:2, May 7, 1965, citing *Nationalities Solidarity*).

What is to become of cultural differences and age-old antagonisms between the various minorities in China? Liu Ch'un continues in another article: "We must consider the national peculiarities and differences between nationalities since this is advantageous for implementing the democratic reform, socialist revolution and socialist construction among the nationalities. Friction between nationalities should not be taken too seriously. It can be corrected by education . . . . This does not mean that we want to foster national privileges; for that would be a fundamental error" (*CNA* 563:3, May 7, 1965, quoting from an article by Liu Ch'un in *Red Flag*, fortnightly, Peking, No. 12, June 30, 1964, pp. 16–25, reprinted in *Nationalities Solidarity* 6, 1964).

Since minority problems are class struggles, the final solution is obvious: "It is only with the coming of communism and the gradual extinction of classes that by the merging of nationalities, national peculiarities and differences will disappear" (*ibid.*). Although "merging of nationalities" is evidently the ultimate objective, the Communists, as Mr. Diao shows, are willing to allow the minorities at least a temporary period of autonomy. (Ed.)

[169]

churian, Mongolian, Puyi (Pu-i), and Korean; those numbering 500,000 to one million include the Tung, Yao, Pai, T'uchia, and Kazakh; those numbering between 100,000 and 500,000 include the Hani, Thai, Li, Lisu, Kawa (Wa), She, Tunghsiang, Nasi, Laku (Lahu), Shui, and Ching–po (Jinghpaw); the population of the remaining minorities numbers between several tens of thousands, several thousands, or several hundreds. In addition, there are still a few tribes which have not yet received official recognition as minority nationalities (see Introduction: China, Table 5, n. *a*).

Although rather limited in number, the minorities are very widely dispersed. In terms of area, they are scattered over almost 60 percent of China's 9,600,000 square kilometers. Among the national minorities, roughly eight million, or 20 percent, have taken permanent residence in the cities, towns, and villages all over the country. In fact, many members of the minorities reside together with other groups. The Hui, for example, live in more than 1,600 *hsien* (counties), which constitute 70 percent of all *hsien* in the country. The Manchurians are located in 860 *hsien*; most of the Koreans are concentrated in the Yen-pien Autonomous *Chou* ("prefecture"), but a small number of them have taken up residence in many *hsien* and *shih* (municipalities) in the northeast provinces and Inner Mongolia. The Uzbeks, with a population of only 13,000, are scattered over 69 *hsien* and *shih* in the Uighur Autonomous Region in Sinkiang (*Kuang Ming Daily* [*KMD*], Peking, February 22, 1957).

The areas with the heaviest concentration of national minorities are near or in the frontier regions—Inner Mongolia, Sinkiang, Tibet, Yunnan—which are rich in natural resources as well as strategically important.

Each minority has its own traditions and customs, which differ largely from those of the Hans. Furthermore, there exist among some minorities considerable differences in economic and cultural development, and mutual suspicion and racial hatred resulting from disputes are additional factors that aggravate the difficulties in exercising control over them. The problem of handling national minorities has therefore become a vital question in the formulation of Chinese Communist domestic and united-front policies. In fact, the consolidation and further development of the Communist regime depends very much on whether the national minorities can be effectively ruled.

REGIONAL AUTONOMY AS THE BASIS OF THE NATIONALITIES POLICY

The fundamental policy of the Chinese Communist authorities in relation to the national minorities is phrased in terms of regional autonomy. This policy is largely based on experience learned from the Soviet Union, but modified according to conditions in China. The term "regional autonomy" would seem to indicate that national minorities are permitted to set up their own governments and exercise normal governmental powers and functions in conjunction with the leadership of the Chinese Communist Party and of the Communist government. But unlike the Soviet system, which nominally recognizes the right of self-determination and the right of secession, the Chinese Communist policy continues to stress that all territories of the national minorities are integral parts of the land of China.

Types of Autonomous Regions. According to the "Outline of the Principles of Autonomy in the Nationalities Areas" promulgated in 1952, autonomous regions are divided into three types:

1. A region inhabited by one national minority.
2. A region consisting of one major nationality and several minor nationalities.
3. A region consisting of two or more large nationalities.

In the early years of the Chinese Communist regime, all areas of minority concentrations, regardless of their size, were called "autonomous regions." After the promulgation of the Constitution in 1954, the nationality areas were, according to their respective administrative sizes, officially divided into autonomous regions, autonomous *chou,* and autonomous *hsien.* The designations "region," "chou," and "hsien" are equivalent to province, special district, and county respectively. At present, five autonomous regions, twenty-nine autonomous *chou,* and sixty-five autonomous *hsien* have been set up on the China mainland (Table 6).

While outwardly the Chinese Communist authorities appear to show serious interest in the political and social equality of national minorities and in making them "play the role of master," they do not, however, observe the true spirit of the policy. This is illustrated by the following four points:

(1) Those minorities residing in the towns and rural districts do not enjoy the right of autonomy, although such communities are called "nationality *hsiang.*"

(2) The Han Chinese (national majority) are constantly urged to settle down in the autonomous areas with the ultimate objective of securing a Chinese majority. The migration of Han Chinese into the minority areas, according to official explanation, "is beneficial both to nationalities solidarity and to the construction of the autonomous regions."[2] (Quotation from a report by Li Wei-han to the second enlarged conference of the Central Nationalities Affairs Commission, held on December 21, 1951.)

But the true motive of the migration policy obviously is to bring greater Chinese control over the minority peoples and, in the long run, to assimilate them. For instance, in Inner Mongolia the Mongolians comprise about one-eighth of the region's population, while the Han Chinese have grown to over 80 percent and the other minorities number just over 1 percent of the total (see *Jen-min Jih-pao* [*People's Daily:PD*], Peking, January 31, 1963). In the Ha-ni and Yi (I) Autonomous *Chou* in Yunnan Province, the Ha-ni nationality constitutes 14 percent; the Yi 18 percent; each of the other eleven minorities less than 1 or 2 percent, while the Chinese make up nearly 50 percent of the total (see *PD*, May 7, 1959).

(3) The population of the Manchurians totals over one million, but they are the only one of the larger minorities who do not have an autonomous government of their own at any level. The Communist authorities do not forget that the Manchus ruled China for a long time, that they have a close association with the Hans, and that they are comparatively better educated. To prevent them from achieving political independence, it is necessary, from the Chinese Communist point of view, to deny them the right of autonomy.

(4) In order to achieve the objective of "divide and rule,"

[2] The success of the policy of encouraging Han migration to minority regions and also the gerrymandering of the borders of these regions is shown by the fact that by 1960 the total population in autonomous areas was sixty-three million, of which the majority, thirty-six million, was Chinese (*CNA* 563:1). (Ed.)

the Chinese Communist authorities have deliberately placed peo-ple of the same nationality under the jurisdiction of different autonomous governments. One notable case is that of the Tibetans. There are altogether more than 2,700,000 Tibetans in the country, but they are scattered over large parts of Kansu, Tsinghai, Szechwan, Yunnan, and Tibet. Instead of permitting them to concentrate in one area and setting up an autonomous region for all Tibetans, the Communist authorities have settled them in nine neighboring autonomous *chou,* i.e., Kan-nan of Kansu, Hai-pei, Hai-nan, Haung-nan, Yu-shu, and Kuo-lo of Tsinghai, Kan-tzu and A-pa of Szechwan, and Ti-ch'ing of Yun-nan, and in the Tibetan Autonomous Region.

Autonomous Governments and Their Rights of Autonomy. Like any other local government in the hinterland of China, the autonomous government is formed on the basis of "democratic centralism" and the "people's congress." Nominally, an autono-mous government has greater authority than a ruling body of a similar level in a non-minority area. According to the stipula-tion of Article 70 of the Chinese Communist Constitution, the organs of self-government at all three levels (region, *chou,* and *hsien*), apart from enjoying the right of exercising autonomy, may also: (a) administer the finances of their areas within the limits of their authority; (b) organize the public security forces of their areas in accordance with the military system of the state; and (c) in the light of the political, economic, and cultural char-acteristics of the nationality or nationalities in the given area, make regulations on the exercise of autonomy as well as specific regulations, and submit them to the Standing Committee of the National People's Congress (NPC) for approval. In actual prac-tice, such self-government organs often find their hands bound by various restrictions imposed through the Party's manipulation of the NPC and democratic centralism system, the latter provid-ing a ready excuse for placing all government affairs under the unified leadership of the Party. Let us examine closely how the restrictions are imposed on the organs of self-government:

(1) According to the Communist Electoral Law, the people's congresses at all levels are formed through elections, but the allocation of deputies must be based on population. Thus the

number of deputies representing the main nationality is relatively smaller in an area where its population is in the minority, such as in the case of Inner Mongolia. The Mongolian deputies, under such circumstances, naturally cannot do much to make their voices heard at the Congress. The official promise to let them "play the role of master" is consequently an empty slogan.

(2) Deputies of the national minorities are confronted with similar troubles at the local people's councils. In many of the minority communities and areas, many nationalities live together, so that the council usually is composed of members of all nationalities concerned. While the post of regional government chief is taken by a leader of the main minority nationality of the area, most other posts—such as vice-chairman, vice-governor, vice-county magistrate, and department heads—are taken by the Chinese or members of other nationalities. The chairman of the first people's council in Inner Mongolia, for example, is a Mongolian, but of the seven vice-chairmen of the council, only three are Mongolian, the remaining four being Han Chinese. Among the thirty-seven council members, sixteen are Mongolian, one Hui, one Manchurian, and nineteen Chinese (see *PD*, May 6, 1955).[3] The people's council, under such circumstances, can hardly exercise its functions and powers to promote the interest of the national minorities. It is not surprising that the Mongolians tried in the past to regroup the communities in Inner Mongolia into Mongolian districts, Han Chinese-Mongolian districts, and Chinese districts, hoping eventually to eliminate or to detach themselves from the Han Chinese districts, because "the Mongolians have become heads of the household, but cannot run the household as master" (see *Inner Mongolia Daily* [*IMD*], November 14, 1957).

(3) According to the principle of "democratic centralism," the individual obeys the collective, the local organ obeys the central, and all local organs must be placed under the unified leadership of the central government and perform their functions

[3] Mere numbers of representatives do not give the whole picture. Most of the representatives who are supposed to be ethnic Mongols in the Inner Mongolian government have "become Chinese"; they no longer speak Mongolian, and they dress and act like Chinese (Rupen 1964:3). Nonetheless, even the concession of having some nominal Mongols represented in the government is more than the Kuomintang allowed. (Ed.)

and powers under the direction and supervision of the next higher level. This principle also applies to the organization of the national minority autonomous governments. When a decision concerning the interest of a nationality is made by the appropriate level of an autonomous government, it may be vetoed or disapproved at the next higher level. For example, when the people's congress of the Mo-li-ta-wa Banner (equivalent to a county) in Inner Mongolia passed a resolution, requesting the establishment of a Daghor (Ta-hu-erh) nationality autonomous *chou* to be composed of three banners (Mo-li-ta-wa, A-jung, and Pu-t'e-ha in Inner Mongolia, and parts of Tsi-tsi-har, Lungchiang and Fu-ch'iu in Heilungkiang) it was rejected by the next higher level (see *PD*, February 26, 1958).

(4) With the Party remaining in the supreme ruling position, all actual power of the local government, which is nominally run by the people's congress and the people's council, is kept in the hands of the local Party committees. These committees are at all times under the solid control of the Political Bureau and the Central Committee of the Chinese Communist Party. Any local government decision of importance must, therefore, first be approved by the local Party committee. No decision whatsoever can be made without fully complying with the interest and desire of the Communist Party, especially on matters concerning finance and the armed forces. In other words, the local autonomous government may exercise its functions and power only within limits prescribed by the Political Bureau and the Central Committee of the Party, and not by the Constitution. The autonomous government may, on the other hand, exercise its functions and powers with a comparatively greater freedom in such matters as customs and habits, marriage, and religious beliefs; it may work out specific regulations in the light of concrete local conditions and submit them to the Standing Committee of the NPC for approval. Even this concession is granted in the interest of consolidating the Party's united-front operation for the stabilization of the regime.

The Question of Minority Nationalization of the Autonomous Governments. The question of minority nationalization of the autonomous governments has always been regarded as an important link in strengthening relations between the autonomous government and the national minorities, in bringing about the solidarity of the nationalities, and in consolidating the Communist regime as a whole. It embodies three major aspects: the cadre, written and spoken language, and the form of local government.

The Minority Cadres. As early as 1950, the Chinese Communist authorities promulgated "The Trial Proposal for the Cultivation of National Minority Cadres," stipulating that large numbers of minority cadres would be trained by establishing national minority colleges, cadre schools, and training classes, as well as by urging the young people of the minorities to study in all types of senior and junior secondary schools. With government support and promotion, education of the national minorities has been making rapid progress, as evidenced by the steadily increasing number of trained cadres of the minorities. According to official statistics in 1949, minority students attending colleges numbered only approximately 600. By 1963, at the Central Nationality College alone, full-time students had increased to 1,086 (see *China News Service* [*CNS*], Hong Kong, January 29, 1964). By May 1961, the eight nationality colleges in the mainland had already graduated 41,973 full- and part-time students, representing fifty nationalities, while those still in school totaled 12,716 (see *Nationalities Solidarity* [*NS*], monthly, September 6, 1961).

Minority nationality cadres in 1949 numbered approximately 10,000, which in 1952 increased to 100,000, to 480,000 in 1959, and to 500,000 in 1963. This growth represented roughly a fiftyfold increase compared with the total of 1949 (see *NS*, No. 10, 1959, and *CNS*, September 4, 1963). Of the total, over 100,000 were junior- and middle-grade technical cadres, primary and secondary school teachers, medical and public health personnel, literary and artistic workers, and translators; the great majority of them were engaged in government work in the local autonomous organs (see *KMD*, September 28, 1963).

The above figures show that the number of nationality cadres increased by 90,000 between 1950 and 1952; by 300,000 between 1953 and 1957; and by 80,000 in just one year between 1957 and 1958. The speed of increase slowed after 1958, averaging only a few thousand annually. The slowdown after 1958 could have been caused partly by the economic crisis resulting from the failure of the "Great Leap Forward," but it is also possible that the Communist authorities, who had become more cautious in expanding the force of the minority cadres, were compelled to cut down the number of trainees. At present the percentage of minority cadres in some minority areas is already greater than that of the Han Chinese cadres in the same areas. Thus the training of minority cadres may have reached saturation point.[4] In future the training program possibly will switch emphasis to quality instead of quantity. More efforts are likely to be made to turn out "revolutionary successors" among the minority nationalities.

Years of racial discrimination, going back to Kuomintang days and earlier, have turned the national minorities into emotionally explosive and sensitive groups. To them, "Only when a government is run by the cadres of its own people can it be called a government of its own; otherwise, the government may be good, but it is not its own" (see *PD*, June 14, 1951).

For the convenience of ruling the minority areas, certain numbers of minority cadres had to be trained to replace the Han Chinese. The training program, however, always emphasized the importance of "the human factor" and "the class standpoint." In the selection of trainees, the major consideration was "morality," while "ability and qualification" were of secondary importance. The term "morality" refers to the individual's family background, his revolutionary awareness, and the degree of his loyalty to the Party. At present, children of the so-called five elements— landlords, rich peasants, counter-revolutionaries, bad characters, and rightists—stand very little chance of being admitted into schools of higher learning; the same is true for children of bourgeois families.

The first regulation in the admission policy of the national minority colleges stipulates that candidates "must be those who have joined the revolutionary struggle and worked for more than two years." A report carried in *Nationalities Solidarity*, No. 10, 1959, disclosed that "At present, there are over 500,000 national

---

[4] For example, in Tibet, following the rebellion of the late 1950's and early 1960's, the former Tibetan local government was dissolved, and the new policy was to be carried out by the Preparatory Committee for the Autonomous Region of Tibet, with the aid of "a certain number of cadres of Han and other nationalties" (Patterson 1962:192, quoting Chang Ching-wu, Secretary of the Chinese Communist Party in Tibet, and representative of the Peking government in Tibet). (Ed.)

minority Communist Party members and over 900,000 Young Communist League members." These figures were almost three times more than the total of the minority cadres. This might suggest that most of the minority cadres were not chosen from among the ordinary people, but were carefully selected from among the Party and League members or from those having good qualifications for Party or League membership.

In Sinkiang, many of the minority people considered cadres of their own nationalities as "running-dogs of the Chinese" (*PD*, December 26, 1957). The Mongolians called the Mongolian cadres "racial renegades," and even viewed the veteran Mongolian cadres as "actually Chinese who have disguised themselves as Mongolians to exercise control over the Mongolians" (*IMD*, November 14, 1957). In Kansu, the Huis called the Hui cadres "traitors" who "sell their religion for personal glory" (*KMD*, January 17, 1958).

Although the Communist authorities declared that minority nationalization of the autonomous governments must emphasize the use of minority cadres, they also stressed that ". . . the number of minority cadres and workers in relation to that of the local cadres and workers should roughly be in the right proportion to that between the population of the particular minority nationality and the total population of the area" (*KMD*, March 29, 1957).

In view of the facts that most of the minority areas are composed of several nationalities and that the Han Chinese often constitute the majority, the proportion of the Chinese and the minority cadres naturally gave advantage to the Chinese. The minority cadres in such circumstances were given minor posts in the government. Take, for example, the organization of the Inner Mongolian Autonomous Government. Mongolian cadres assigned to the various regional organs and enterprises under the People's Council comprised only 9.9 percent, the Chinese cadres, 90 percent. In the more important organs, the proportions of the Mongolian cadres was even smaller. In the Public Security Department, for instance, the percentage of Mongolian cadres stood at 5.2 percent; in the People's Bank, 5.9 percent; and the Trade Department, 4.3 percent. In the less important organs minority cadres took up a higher percentage: 50.5 percent in the Physical Culture and Sports Commission; 47 percent in the Nationalities Affairs Commission; and 33.3 percent in the Bureau of Religious Affairs (*IMD*, June 24, 1957).

The minority cadres were not only smaller in number and given only minor posts in the less important organs, they also were ignored by the Chinese cadres, who took them to be nothing more than decorations on the façade of "minority nationalization." The Han Chinese cadres think that their minority colleagues owe their positions to the training and care given them by the Chinese. No serious problem arises if all work at the same level. But if one of the minority cadres gets a higher position, then those Han Chinese under him assume an air of superiority and even defy the authority of the higher minority cadre. This situation developed in virtually all minority autonomous areas. The *KMD* reported on December 14, 1956:

> At the T'ien-chu Tibetan Autonomous *Hsien* government [in Kansu Province], there are a county chief and three deputy chiefs. One of the deputy chiefs, a Chinese, monopolizes everything. All cadres under the government must seek instruction from him, so that he keeps busy all day long. The county chief and other deputy chiefs, all being Tibetan, are regarded as inefficient and incapable of solving problems. He never asks for instruction from the chief, so that all of them remain idle all day long.

The same report went on to cite another example:

> Ma Kuo-han, chief of the Tung-hsiang Autonomous *Hsien* [in Kansu Province], is a Tung-hsiang man and quite able in his work; he enjoys great respect among his own people. But Hsueh Chen-wu, a Chinese, the deputy chief, does not trust him, and thinks that the chief can draw his salary and enjoy his meals, but if he works there is bound to be trouble. Although Ma Kuo-han is the chief of the county government, he is seldom informed of what is going on in the government.

Language. The use of popular language or languages in the minority area is another important policy of the Chinese Communists. According to Article 3 of the Constitution, the national minorities are entitled, without discrimination, to use their native languages, both in writing and speaking. Popular minority languages are not only taught in minority area schools for training in literacy, but also used in conjunction with Chinese in official communications by the autonomous governments.

Prior to 1949 there were seventeen written minority languages, among which only Mongolian, Tibetan, Manchurian, and Korean were widely used. As the population of the other minorities was small, the use of their languages was restricted. As a first step in promoting the nationalities policy, the Communist authorities made persistent efforts to invent and reform minority scripts. They decided early in 1951 to form scripts for those languages which had none and to reform those which were incomplete or unsystematic. Due to a lack of trained personnel, however, the program made little headway until 1956, when the necessary investigation and preparation had been made and a sufficient number of trained cadres were available. At present those in charge have invented new phonetic scripts, resembling Chinese Romanization, for the Chuang, Puyi (Pu-i), Li, Tung (Kam), Miao, Yi (Lolo), Lisu, Hani, Kawa (Wa), and Nasi nationalities; and reformed the written languages, using phonetics, of the Thai, Laku, Ching-po, Uighur, and Kazakh. By using a phonetic system which resembles Chinese Romanization, it is hoped the minority peoples can more easily learn the Chinese language someday in the future.[5]

The Communist authorities also paid considerable attention to the popularization of minority languages, including the new and reformed phonetic scripts. From 1952 to 1958, 9,050 books, totaling 97,353,000 copies, were published in such languages as Mongolian, Tibetan, Uighur, Chuang, Puyi, Miao, Korean, Yi (Lolo), Li, Thai, Kazakh, Kirghiz, Sibo, Lisu, Ching-po, Laku, Kawa (Wa), and Hani. In addition, about seventy newspapers and magazines were published in the same period in Mongolian, Tibetan, Uighur, Kazakh, Chuang, Korean, Kirghiz, Thai, Ching-po, Lisu and Sibo (NS, July 6, 1959).

[5] For further details on Communist Chinese language policies, see Rupen's discussion (1964:4–5) of the policy as applied to Inner Mongolia. A Cyrillic script has been standard in the Mongolian People's Republic since 1945 (an evidence of Russian influence), but the traditional Mongol script is still used in Inner Mongolia, where it serves as a symbol of group identification. In 1958 Peking announced that minority languages would be transcribed with a Romanized alphabet, but as of 1964 this directive had not been applied to Mongolian. The retention of the traditional script in Inner Mongolia was a symptom of the confrontation of Chinese and Russian interests in the Mongols. This conflict also included a vilification of Genghis Khan by the Russians, while the Chinese praised his accomplishments in bringing a higher culture to the Russians. For information on the language program as applied to other groups see Ma (1962). (Ed.)

Apart from the above, many minority-language programs were broadcast by central and local radio stations, many films were dubbed in minority languages, and many plays were written in minority languages by the minority scriptwriters and artists.

Contrary to the spirit of this policy, the Huis and Manchurians, who are more numerous in population, were not encouraged to publicize the use of their own scripts or languages, or the study of their cultural heritage. They were encouraged to learn and use the Chinese language, thus speeding the Communist program of assimilation. This different attitude seems to show that the Communist authorities are afraid that with stronger group identification, the Huis and Manchurians might become politically ambitious and fight for independence.

While outwardly the popularization of the minority languages fits well into the nationalization program, the Communists appear, however, to have been more interested in publicizing the thinking of Mao Tse-tung as the chief means for ideological indoctrination.

In order to reduce local resistance to Communist control and to smooth the way for gradual infiltration of Party influence, the Communist authorities allowed the local autonomous governments to be set up generally in forms common to the customs and habits of their respective localities. Nevertheless, in all local autonomous governments, the people's congress and the people's council were forced to perform their duties under the system of democratic centralism. Thus, with the exception of the titles such as *ch'i* ("banner") and *meng* ("league") in Inner Mongolia, and *pan-na* ("valley plain") in Yunnan still bearing token semblance of the old days, there was practically no difference in substance as compared with other local Chinese governments in any part of the country. All elections of the people's congress, and composition of the people's council, and the terms of their service were exactly like those in non-minority areas.

MINORITY REPRESENTATIVES IN THE CENTRAL GOVERNMENT AND UNITED-FRONT ORGANIZATIONS

As a supplementary measure to win over the support and loyalty of the national minorities, the Communist authorities recruited certain pro-Communist minority personages to take part in the central government organs and the united-front bodies.

The National People's Congress. The National People's Congress (NPC) is the highest organ of state power. The allocation of the NPC deputies is decided according to Chapter Three of the Electoral Law:

> The deputies to the NPC are to be elected by the provinces on the basis of one deputy for every 800,000 persons. The number of deputies should not be less than three in a province with an exceptionally small population. In municipalities under the direct control of the central government and in industrial cities of over 500,000 in population under the provincial government, one deputy is to be elected from every 100,000 residents [Article 20]; all minority nationalities should elect 150 deputies to the NPC [Article 21].

At the fourth session of the Second NPC held in November 1963, a resolution on increasing the number of deputies to the Third NPC was passed. The resolution reads:

> Deputies to the NPC to be elected in the provinces and autonomous regions should be on the basis of one deputy for every 400,000 persons. The number of deputies should not be less than 10 in a province or autonomous region with an exceptionally small number of residents. In the municipalities under the direct authority of the central government or provincial government, in industrial cities of over 300,000 in population, and in industrial, mining and lumbering cities of below 300,000 in population, but with workers and their dependents exceeding 200,000, the allocation should be one deputy for every 50,000 persons; the minority nationalities should elect 300 deputies to the NPC.

Consequently, the total number of deputies to the Third NPC held in December 1964, was increased from 1,226 at the previous Congress to 3,040, while the percentage of national minority deputies dropped from 12.23 percent to 9.87 percent. Of the twenty-eight provinces, municipalities, and autonomous regions, eleven provinces and municipalities had no deputies representing the national minorities. In the other seventeen provinces, municipalities, and autonomous regions, national minority deputies ranged from one to fifty. Individual allocations of the seventeen provinces, municipalities, and autonomous regions are listed in Table 7.

The allocation of the minority deputies is not necessarily in correct proportion to the population; but nearly all minority na-

TABLE 7
PERCENTAGE OF MINORITY NATIONALITY DELEGATES
TO THE THIRD NATIONAL PEOPLE'S CONGRESS, 1964

Area	Deputy Total	Number of Minority Nationality Deputies	Percentage
Tibet	24	21	87.5
Sinkiang	53	40	75.45
Tsinghai	18	12	66.66
Kwangsi	87	47	54.02
Yunnan	93	50	53.76
Ningsia	15	7	46.66
Kweichow	67	27	40.29
Inner Mongolia	55	21	38.18
Kansu	52	12	23.07
Kirin	76	9	11.84
Szechwan	240	27	11.25
Heilungkiang	132	12	9.09
Peking	101	4	3.85
Kwangtung	160	6	3.75
Fukien	54	2	3.70
Hupeh	126	2	1.58
Shensi	70	1	1.42

tionalities have deputies to the NPC. Such a method of allocation
speaks well of the care and caution the Chinese Communist authorities have used to win over the loyalty of the minority peoples. The Chuang and the Tibetans, each with forty three deputies, have the most minority allocations; next come the Uighur
with twenty-seven deputies, the Hui with twenty-five, the Yi
with twenty-three, the Mongolians with twenty-one, the Miao
with seventeen, the Koreans with ten, the Manchurians with
nine, the Puyi with eight, the Thai with six, the Kazakh and
Yao with five each, the Tung and Hani with four each, the
Ta-hu-erh and Kawa with three each, the Tung-hsiang, Li, Lisu,
Laku, and Chilao with two each, and the Ahchang, Pulang, and
twenty-seven others with one each.

The total number of vice-chairmen of the Third NPC Standing
Committee was increased from sixteen to eighteen, but the num-
ber of minority vice-chairmen dropped from three to two. Besides
Saifudin being reelected, Ngapo Ngawang Jigme was newly
elected; and the Dalai Lama and Panchen Erdeni were dropped.
The number of Standing Committee members of the Third NPC

[183]

was increased from the previous sixty-two to ninety-six. The two minority members, Lu Han (of the Yi nationality) and Hsieh Fu-min (of the Chuang nationality) were reelected. In terms of percentages, the national minority membership in the NPC Standing Committee was also lowered.

The Central Government and State Organs. According to the official announcement in the *People's Daily,* January 5, 1965, Ulanfu, Vice-Premier and concurrently Chairman of the Nationalities Affairs Commission, is the only representative of minority people in more than fifty high government posts. A Mongolian, Ulanfu is a member of the Chinese Communist Party Central Committee and Alternate Member of the Political Bureau. A man with such a politically strong background can hardly be taken as a true representative of the national minorities.[6] For all intents and purposes, the minorities have no representatives in the higher organs of the central government.

The National Committee of the Chinese People's Political Consultative Conference. The National Committee of the Chinese People's Political Consultative Conference (CPPCC) is the nerve center of the Chinese Communist united-front activities. Before the promulgation of the Constitution, it actually acted as the NPC. Today it exists only as an advisory organ of the central government.

The number of delegates to the present CPPCC has been increased from the previous total of 1,071 to 1,119. Yet the number of delegates representing the minority people remained at thirty-six. The percentage of their representation thus dropped from 3.36 percent to 3 percent, or roughly one-half of what it should be since the minority peoples comprise 6 percent of the total national population. The number of vice-chairmen of the present CPPCC term of office has been increased from fifteen to twenty-two, but the number of the minority vice-chairmen dropped from three to only one, Pebala Golieh-namje, a Tibetan.

Judging from the figures given above, the influence of the minority people in the NPC, the central government, and the CPPCC is gradually being weakened. Thus the true nature of

[6] Cf. Rupen's remarks (1964:6): "The two highest Party leaders in IMAR [Inner Mongolian Autonomous Regional] (Ulanfu and K'uei Pi), and one of the leaders, Chi Ya-t'ai, all three Mongols, attended the Kuomintang's Mongol-Tibetan School in Peking in 1923, suggesting that they were highly Sinified Mongols even then." (Ed.)

the Chinese Communist policy toward the national minorities shows that it does not lie in according due respect to them, but in further tightening government control over them.

THE NATIONALITIES POLICY IN THE THAI AUTONOMOUS AREA

Local Governments in the Thai Autonomous Region. The Thai population totals about 500,000, slightly over 8 percent of Yunnan's minorities population of six million.[7] The Thai people are scattered in the Te-hung region in western Yunnan and Hsi-shuang Pan-na in southern Yunnan. Over 300,000 Thai people are concentrated in these two areas, and the remaining numbers can be found in all parts of Yunnan Province. At present the Thai people have set up two autonomous *chou,* namely, the Hsi-shuang Pan-na Thai Autonomous *Chou* and the Te-hung Thai-Ching-po Autonomous *Chou;* and two autonomous counties, the Meng-lien Thai, Laku, and K'a-wa Autonomous *Hsien* and the Keng-ma Thai and K'a-wa Autonomous *Hsien.*

The Hsi-shuang Pan-na Thai Autonomous *Chou* was the first multi-nationality autonomous government with a fairly large population that the Chinese Communist authorities set up. Situated to the south of latitude 22 degrees, it covers all of Ch'e-li, Fo-hai, Nan-ch'iao, and Chen-yueh *hsien,* with a total area of 25,000 square kilometers. The Thai people comprise one-half of the total population of 320,000. The Han Chinese also take up a large percentage of the population. In addition, more than ten nationalities live there, including the Hani, Pulang, Laku, Yao, Miao, Hui, Kawa, and Ching-po.

In 1950 a preparatory organ for setting up the autonomous government was put into operation, and over two hundred members of a nationality work team were sent out to set up three autonomous *hsiang,* one each located in Ch'e-li, Fo-hai, and Nan-ch'iao *hsien.* On New Year's Day, 1953, an enlarged meeting of the autonomous *chou* preparatory committee was held with over 430 delegates attending. Topics on the agenda included determining the number of members to serve on the autonomous council, boundary demarcation, official title of the autonomous *chou,* and administrative policies. The autonomous government

[7] This discussion of "Thai" refers only to those Tai-speaking peoples in Yunnan who are called "T'ai" by the Chinese Communist authorities. Other Tai-speakers, including the Chuang, Chung-chia, Shan, Nung, and still others, number more than ten million within the boundaries of China. (Ed.)

was formally inaugurated on January 23, 1953. At first it was called the autonomous region government. On June 8, 1955, it was renamed autonomous *chou,* according to the newly promulgated Constitution.

The Tehung Thai-Ching-po Autonomous *Chou,* in Yunnan Province, situated on the Sino-Burmese border, was set up on July 24, 1953. With over 400,000 in population, this government had within its jurisdiction five *hsien:* Lu-hsi, Jui-li, Lung ch'uan, Ying-chiang, and Liang-ho. The Thai and the Ching-po, both being the main nationalities of the area, had populations of 175,000 and 97,000 respectively.

After being renamed on May 1, 1956, as an autonomous *chou,* the *chou's* territory was considerably expanded with the addition of T'eng-ch'ung, Pao-shan, Lung-ling, and Ch'ang-ning, all of which had been under the jurisdiction of the Pao-shan Special District government. The population was thus increased to more than 1.6 million, with a total area amounting to 37,000 square kilometers. At present there are over ten different nationalities living in the area, including the Han Chinese, who comprise 70 percent of the population, the Thai and Ching-po, amounting to 10 percent and 6 percent of the total respectively, and the rest being Ah-chang, Peng-lung, Lisu, Hui, Yi, Miao, Kawa, and Pai. The natives of the area had shown visible resistance to the expansion of the *chou's* territory. They felt that "Once the territory is expanded and more Han Chinese taken in, our 'kingdom' will be eliminated" and that "Regional autonomy is only nominal, with no position and no authority, and the Party takes over the place of the government" (*Yunnan Daily* [*YD*], December 29, 1957).

The Meng-lien Tha'i Laku, and K'a-wa Autonomous *Hsien* and the Keng-ma Thai and K'a-wa Autonomous *Hsien* were respectively set up on October 16, 1954, and October 15, 1955.

Land Reform and the Agricultural Cooperative Movement. The territory of the Thai autonomous area spreads across tropical, sub-tropical and temperate zones, with plentiful rainfall and fertile soil. The area produces in quantity paddy rice, banana, pineapple, and coconut; other products include tea, cotton, camphor, rubber, quinine, and coffee. China's well-known "Pu Erh Tea" grows in the mountainous region in the vicinity of Men Hai in Hsi-shuang Pan-na.

The Thai are mostly farmers. As early as the twelfth century, what the Chinese Communists have come to term the "feudal system" was already dominant in the area. The "feudal" economic system remained, with the exception of some areas where the natives had been thoroughly assimilated by the Chinese, until the establishment of the autonomous government. For instance, all lands in Hsi-shuang Pan-na were owned by the *Hsuang Wei Szu*, (or *Chao-pien-lin*—"lord of vast tracts"). The *Hsuang Wei Szu* allotted his land to the *T'u Szu* (section chief) in the *pan-nas*, and the *T'u Szu* in turn subdivided their share to the village heads, and the village heads shared their portion with the villagers. The tenant farmers, besides surrendering part of their crops to the *T'u Szu* and the village heads as official rent, had to undertake over one hundred different kinds of unpaid physical labor. According to Communist sources, in normal cases the farmers had to surrender 30 percent, and in special cases up to 70 percent, of their earnings to the local overlords (*PD*, June 6, 1957). Private armies and prisons were maintained to suppress any resistance. The serfs could even be put to death at the will of their lord.[8]

Shortly after the autonomous government was set up, the Communist authorities began to carry out social reforms, especially land reform. In practice, the land reform policy in the minority areas differed from that in other parts of the country. Instead of instigating the peasants from the lowest level to carry out struggles against the landlords, as happened in most parts of China, the more moderate method of friendly negotiation with the landlord was adopted. The authorities, by using the mixed tactics of persuasion and intimidation, made the landlords give up their lands for the benefit of all peasants.[9] Thus the so-called peaceful land reform was smoothly carried out in 1955 and 1956.

[8] See also Lin (1961:28). For further information on Tai social structure and relations with the Chinese in Yunnan see, for example, Chiang (1950) and Wiens (1954). (Ed.)

[9] According to Lin (1961:29), "After the oppressed masses were fully awakened to the necessity for such reforms, the government held consultation with the landlords and slaveowners . . . urging them to give up their oppression and exploitation and promising that, if they did, they would be accorded appropriate political positions and a living standard not lower than before. Land was divided up. Then, later, when the individual peasants understood the need for collective farming, the plots were pooled in agricultural producers' cooperatives." The planned cooperativization of farming evidently met with some resistance (see below, pp. 188–189). (Ed.)

Most of the Thai peasants received on the average two *mow* (1 *mow* = .167 acre) of land that could produce from 460 *chin* (1 *chin* = 1.1 lbs.) to 1,200 *chin* of food grain annually (*NS*, July 6, 1959).

Since the Communist revolution and land reform, the "feudal system" has been broken, and the serfs have become masters of their own land, at least briefly. Today, the Thai people, guided by the Communists, have at least nominal self-government through elections. According to the Electoral Law, they elect their representatives to form a local people's congress, and the latter elects members for the local council. This procedure is identical with that for the rest of the country, except some of the administrative units still retain their old names, which are familiar to the local people through long usage.

In the Hsi-shuang Pan-na Thai Autonomous *Chou*, for instance, they still use *pan-na* instead of *hsien* in the names of the counties under the *chou's* jurisdiction. Hsi-shuang Pan-na is the Chinese transliteration of the Thai term *sipsong* ("twelve") *pan* ("thousand") *na* ("irrigated fields"), or *pan-na* ("irrigated valley plain"). Each valley plain (*pan-na*) is equivalent to, or at the same level with, a *hsien* ("county") in the ordinary Chinese regions. The same thing is true in Inner Mongolia, where they still use the Mongolian terms *meng* and *chi* instead of the Chinese *chuan-sh'u* and *hsien* to refer to some special districts and counties. No matter what name or title is used, however, all levels of local minority government in minority areas are like those in other parts of the country and are under strict Communist control through the people's congress and the system of democratic centralism.

The land reform period coincided with the gradual penetration of Party influence. The *People's Daily* reported on January 14, 1957, that 8,500 rural activists were recruited and trained during the land reform period, 582 natives were admitted into the Party, and 1,938 young people into the Young Communist League. Party organs were established in most of the *hsiang* of the area. Consequently, the Thai lords are hardly in a position to dominate as before, although some continue to hold nominal offices in the organs of self-government. Many now work in the fields with the peasants.

Shortly after the land reform was completed, the authorities urged the peasants to take part in mutual-aid teams and started a number of agricultural cooperatives to persuade the people to join the collectivization. But the peasants, who were satisfied with farming the small lots of their own, showed no interest in the government program. Most of them remained cautious, and few decided to join the cooperatives. The *Yunnan Daily* published on October 19, 1957, an editorial entitled "Observations and Suggestions Concerning the Basic Conditions in the Thai area of the Tehung Thai-Ching-po Autonomous *Chou*," which said:

> During the course of the development of agricultural cooperatives, it can be expected that 4 to 5 percent of the rural population will join in the first year, about 10 percent in the second, and 30 percent in the third year. When the total of participating households has reached about 30 percent, it means that all the poor and lower-middle-class peasants in the area who urgently need to take part will have to be absorbed into the cooperatives. By then, the cooperativization movement will have to face an important turning point.

The *Nationalities Solidarity* also reported on July 6, 1958: "One of the two very first cooperatives in Hsishuangpanna, the Su-sheng Agricultural Cooperative of Ching-hung County, which was first formed in May 1956, had to face mass withdrawal from the cooperative in April and May 1957. Twelve of the 30 member households firmly wanted to withdraw."

This appeared to show that the development of the agricultural cooperativization movement had run into considerable resistance. Even the Communist authorities had to admit that "Despite the great effort we made in publicizing the cooperative system, the understanding of the peasant masses was still very poor." The cooperativization movement was not even basically completed until the latter part of 1958, when the "Great Leap Forward" movement was raging all over the country. During that period the Communist authorities also managed to open up a few people's communes and some state farms specializing in planting economic crops. But the percentage of participating households remained very low compared with other parts of the country. In Hsi-shuang Pan-na, only 70.46 percent of the rural households joined the agricultural cooperatives (*KMD*, November 12, 1958).

At present agriculture remains the major occupation in Hsi-shuang Pan-na. Some production progress has been made as a result of expanded acreage, improved farming methods, and a completion of water conservation projects. For example, rice, corn, sweet potato, groundnut, soy bean, and cotton crops all have been increased from one crop a year to two crops, with some areas claiming three crops of paddy rice. The *Kuang-ming Daily* reported on February 23, 1964:

> In the Thai area of the Te-hung Thai and Ching-p'o Autonomous *Chou,* the total of food grain in 1962 gained 49 percent as against that of 1952. In about one-half of the households, each member of the family had over 700 *chin* of food grain, compared with 817 *chin* in the Hsi-shuang Pan-na Thai Autonomous *Chou.* In 1963, production of food grain gained a further 3.6 percent over that of the preceding year.

Economic crops and cattle also gained to a varying degree. The *People's Daily* reported on May 6, 1963: "In comparing the production of 1962 with that of 1952, cotton shows an increase of 80 percent; sugar cane, 141 percent; tea, 63 percent; large cattle, 39 percent; live hogs, 140 percent and sheep, 100 percent."

One important aspect of the Chinese Communist national minorities program is aimed at helping the minorities to achieve economic development, especially in agriculture, which is, of course, still the main occupation in most minority areas. Generally speaking, the traditional farming methods of the minority peoples were extremely backward. To help modernize them, the Communists have done much work in the field, cultivating experimental plots and helping to collect and distribute information from local experience in raising crop yields. The minority farmers have gradually introduced more scientific farming practices, including spreading manure, weeding, top-dressing, and the use of insecticide. Today nearly all the minority populations are farming in the agricultural cooperatives or communes which have been organized in many minority areas.

In addition, the Communist authorities have financed various projects for the minorities, such as water conservation, industry, and transportation, as well as educational and medical services, which had all been badly neglected in their areas. In doing this, the Communist authorities usually leave to the autonomous governments, for their own use, a larger than normal share of the state's revenue which is collected by local governments through taxation. Also, according to the compilation of State Plans, the state gives additional funds from the central government as subsidies to help the minorities. This policy, of course, is integrated with the Marxist-Leninist political doctrine that in order to win over the support of the minorities and gain their trust it is first necessary to help them in economic development. Thus economic development is used to supplement and smooth over the exercise of political control by the central government.

It would seem, therefore, that the living conditions of the Thai people, especially the poor and lower-middle peasants, have improved from the pre-liberation days. An exact measure of the improvement, however, cannot be made from the available data.

Industry, Commerce, Communication, Transportation, and Post and Telecommunications. Fairly good progress has been reported in the development of the area's industry, commerce, communications, transportation, and post and telecommunications. In the past only handicraft industry existed in this area. In recent years, some locally run state mining and factory enterprises have been set up, including machine-making, electricity production, tea-processing, farm-implement manufacturing, paper-making, and sugar-refining factories. According to official reports, the total industrial production in 1962 in the Te-hung Thai and Ching-po Autonomous *Chou* was 8.4 times more than that of 1952, and industrial output advanced from 4.1 percent to 21.9 percent.

In the past motor roads were practically nonexistent in the area. It would take a traveler more than one month to reach Kunming, the capital of Yunnan Province. At present over 1,000 kilometers of road have been built in both the Hsi-shuang Pan-na and Te-hung Thai autonomous areas, and a trip to Kunming takes about three to four days. In addition, an airline has been opened between Pao-shan and Kunming. At the same time, most communes, *hsiang*, and town offices have telephones. Post and telecommunications now cover four times more area than in the past (*NS*, No. 5, May 1963).

Progress in the field of communications and transportation has considerably increased delivery of produce to other parts of the country, and more commodities can now be brought in from the cities in other provinces.

Taxation. The taxation system for minority areas is the same as that for Han-dominated regions. Taxes are generally divided into two categories: the rural or agricultural tax, and the industrial and commercial taxes. From the standpoint of state revenue, industrial and commercial taxes are more important than agricultural tax. However, in the Thai area, as well as in other minority areas, agriculture still remains the dominant occupation. Agricultural tax serves, therefore, as the main source of revenue which Communist authorities can collect from the minority areas.

The levying of agricultural tax is fixed in terms of a certain percentage of the so-called normal year-yield (not actual year-yield) and is paid primarily in grain. The average tax rate for the country as a whole has since 1958 been fixed at 15.5 percent by the Communist authorities. Each local government within its jurisdiction may vary the rate prescribed by the central government from 6 percent to 25 percent as long as it meets the requisition quota. The rate effected in minority areas is usually slightly lower than average, except in areas where the year-yield is high and bumper crops are expected. The rate in Hsi-shuang Pan-na Thai Autonomous *Chou* and Te-hung Thai and Ching-po Autonomous *Chou,* both producing large quantities of paddy rice, is about 14 percent instead of 12 percent, the average rate fixed for Yunnan Province by the central government.

In spite of the Communist authorities' claim that agricultural tax now comprises only 6 to 7 percent of the total revenue in the state budget, the tax has always been a heavy burden on the peasants of China. This is largely because the levying of agricultural tax is supplemented with the state purchase of grain and part of the peasants' burden is actually turned into profits for the foodstuff and commercial departments of the government. Furthermore, agricultural surtaxes levied by local governments are also excluded from both local and central budgets. Actually, of the total state revenue, about one-half comes directly or indirectly from agricultural production.

Commencing in 1964 with the initiation of the nation-wide "Socialist Education Movement," the Communists have persistently urged the peasants to sell "surplus grain" to the state in addition to the official quota as fixed for the agricultural tax and state purchase of grains. Consequently, the peasants have actually gained very little for personal use even in areas where grain production was reported to have increased since 1964. According to information gathered from interviews with recent arrivals from Yunnan Province, the peasants in Hsi-shuang Pan-na Thai Autonomous *Chou* in 1964 had to surrender more than 20 percent of their earnings to the Communist government and about 15 percent to the cooperatives or commune. These two figures together may actually exceed that which the Thai people normally used to surrender to their overlords in pre-liberation days.

In the category of industrial and commercial taxes, the most important one is the Consolidated Industrial and Commercial Tax, which covers nearly all business and transportation activities, such as the manufacture of industrial products, the purchase of agricultural produce, imports and commodity sales, and business sales of state-owned and collective enterprises, but it has rather little significance in the Thai area. In addition, there are several local taxes, such as those on slaughtering, the selling of livestock, ownership of urban properties, licensing of vehicles and boats, and the like. These taxes, used primarily for local budgetary purposes, vary in kind and rate in each area.

Language Reform, Education, and Public Health. The Thai system of writing, based on an Indian script, is partially, but not completely, phonetic. The history of the Thai people shows that legends and poems were discovered to have been written on tree leaves.

In 1957 the Communist language reformers worked out, on the basis of the original Thai spelling, a new phonetic system, and systematic efforts were made to publicize it.[10] By first taking

[10] In discussing reform of national minority writing systems Ma (1962:26) states: "The Tais have two dialects but five scripts. Two of the scripts, the Tai Leh and Tai Na, were chosen for reform, because they are the most widely used in both dialect areas and possess much written literature. These two scripts have their origin in an Indian script but they developed in different ways, the Tai Leh remaining closer to the original Indian while the Tai Na had been much simplified by discarding many useless letters. Their alphabet has had a long history and, as a form of national culture, it is much loved by the Tais. The basic form was therefore retained and only a few letters which had become phonetically obsolete were discarded." (Ed.)

the poor and lower-middle peasants, who were mostly illiterate, into part-time classes, the Communist authorities attempted to eliminate the illiteracy in the area and at the same time to disseminate the Communist revolutionary thought. Starting in 1958 textbooks were written and printed in the new Thai script, and these were followed by the publication of Thai-language newspapers and magazines. At present about 70 percent of the young people have learned to read and write. Up to 1960 there were five secondary schools and 250 primary schools, with over 20,000 students in the Hsi-shuang Pan-na Autonomous *Chou* (*PD*, November 27, 1960).

In the Te-hung Thai and Ching-po Autonomous *Chou,* an article in the May 1963 issue of *Nationalities Solidarity* reported:

> Up to the end of 1962, primary schools increased by 79 percent over the total of 1952, and students 39 percent by the same comparison; among them, the number of frontier schools gained 178 percent, and students 269 percent as against the corresponding figures of 1952. Ordinary and specialized secondary schools more than doubled and students increased by 47 percent; among them, those schools in the frontier regions increased three times over the 1952 total and students increased 2,260 percent.

In the area of public health such epidemics as bubonic plague, malaria, smallpox, and cholera have been basically controlled, and the prevention and treatment of malaria has been particularly successful. According to official reports, the percentage of malaria cases in the population dropped from 7.9 percent in 1953 to 1.5 percent in 1962. The Meng-hai Pa area, which was hardest hit by malaria in the past, had by 1962 cut the incidence from 50 percent in 1953 to 0.03 percent (*KMD*, January 24, 1963).

Again according to official statistics, public health organizations in Hsi-shuang Pan-na were increased from eight to thirty-three in ten years. In the Te-hung Thai and Ching-po Autonomous *Chou,* fourteen public health stations were set up by 1962, an increase of 245 percent over the 1952 figure. The number of hospital beds increased 821 percent over the 1952 total; full-time medical workers increased 300 percent, and among them the number of minority medical workers gained as many as fourteen times over the 1952 total (*NS*, May 1963).

Religious Belief and Marriage. Nearly all villagers in the Thai autonomous area are followers of the Southern or Theravada form of Buddhism. There is a Buddhist temple in nearly every village, and the people spend from 10 to 20 percent of their income in observing Buddhist ritual.

According to local custom, a boy should enter a temple at the age of seven or eight to prepare himself for becoming a monk. He stays in the temple until he is twenty. While living in the temple, the boy does not spend all of his time reciting the Scriptures; he learns to read and write too. In the past the monks were highly respected by the local people. Their food was sent to them by the villagers, and they never took part in physical labor. Even when a monk walked in the sun, it was customary for the villagers to hold an umbrella over his head.

The Chinese Communist authorities in their dealings with this group of Buddhist nationalities were clever enough to show outward respect for the freedom of religious belief, but they also were clever enough to promote the idea of "freedom not to believe." It is now forbidden for any villager to "urge" or "persuade" anyone to become a believer. At the same time the authorities make serious efforts to destroy superstitions in the minds of the young and to instigate them to discriminate against the monks who refuse to work in the fields. In the Thai villages the following sarcastic doggerel has been widely circulated:

> Humming the Scriptures, you don't work;
> You enjoy circling on horseback with an umbrella
> over your head;
> While others perspire profusely in the fields;
> You eat up all the food you exploit;
> But you neither labor nor produce;
> We'll see what you're up to when you return to your
> normal life.

(*New Observation* [*NO*], Gen. No. 197, Nov. 16, 1958)

Unable to continue facing such taunts from the masses, the monks finally are being forced to take off their Buddhist cloaks and join the peasant ranks in the fields.[11]

[11] Buddhism has also been the target for reform in Inner Mongolia. The lamas there are supposed to join cooperatives, and have been required to work 260 days per year, after which they may dispose of the remainder of their time in religious activities if they wish (Rupen 1964:4, citing Ulanfu's speech to the Silingol League lamas, July 10, 1958). (Ed.)

Furthermore, long-established custom formerly prevented the monks from social contact with women until they returned to normal life. But the Communist authorities, under the pretext of publicizing the new form of marriage, openly ordered the villagers not to interfere with monks who wanted to find girl-friends, and, moreover, the girls were encouraged to make friends with the monks. The catch, of course, was that before a monk could approach the girls, he had to become some sort of labor activist. The teasing was strong, and so was the desire. And since the human desire prevailed, even the monks began to work hard in the fields to acquire the necessary qualifications. Gradually religious influence has been weakened among the Thai people, and it is possible that someday soon religious belief may be completely eliminated.

The Thai marriage system has always allowed free courting, and it is strictly a monogamous system. Matchmakers are only required to show respect to the parents, a mere formality. In general, such a system conformed with the Communist idea of marriage, so that there was no major reform in this particular area. But political indoctrination has taught the young to be careful in choosing their life-long partners. Besides finding love, the couples must be sure their class standings match and that neither side is politically backward. Therefore, a monk who does not work hard in the fields can hardly find an ideal partner.[12]

In the past the women were confined to the house and taking care of domestic chores. The villagers superstitiously believed that "When a woman plows the fields, a three-year-long drought will occur; when a woman digs an irrigation ditch, no water will ever come through; and when a woman helps build a dike, it will never be full of water" (KMD, May 18, 1961).

At present the Thai women not only take care of the house and teach their children, but they also take part in farming and freely move about at rural affairs. In many cases they are proving to be more capable than their men.

---

[12] The Communists have interfered with marriage customs in areas where the customs do not conform to Communist ideals. For example, they have attempted to discourage the Ching-po custom of arranged marriage, to reduce the amount of bride-price (which often customarily involves a period of service by the groom to his father-in-law), and to restrict the wedding (which used to involve lengthy feasting) to a simple ceremony (CNA 563:6, May 7, 1965). (Ed.)

Training of Minority Cadres. Training large numbers of minority cadres has been one of the fundamental policies of the Chinese Communist regime. In the last ten years they have trained over 1,300 minority cadres among the fourteen nationalities in the Hsi-shuang Pan-na area, gaining twenty times over the early years of the regime. Impressive progress also has been reported in the Te-hung Thai and Ching-po Autonomous *Chou*. At present full-time minority cadres (excluding those at the *hsiang* offices) comprise 14.1 percent of all cadres in the area; in the frontier regions the number of minority cadres has reached 26.8 percent of the total, and the figure reaches nearly 30 percent if the *hsiang* and town cadres are added (*NS*, May, 1963).

CONCLUSIONS

Theoretically, the Chinese and the Russian Communists take the Marxist-Leninist idea as the foundation of the policies toward the national minorities. That idea is summed up in the expression: "National in form, Socialist in content." In other words, in order to place the minorities politically under the strict control of the Communist Party, it is permissible to accord them a degree of freedom in such matters as economy, culture, language, customs and habits, and religious creeds, as these are minor but psychologically important concessions for winning over the loyalty of the minority people. Such an idea can best be described by an old Chinese saying: "Selling dog-meat behind the trademark of a sheep's head." In the case of the national minorities, the "dog-meat" is the content of the Chinese Communist minority policy, while the "sheep's head trademark"—regional autonomy—is the clever ruse for achieving the objective.

In practice the Chinese Communists differ in methods from the Russian Communists. The Soviet system takes the form of a union which, nominally at least, recognizes the independent status of the participating member units and even accords them the right of self-determination and the right of secession. The Chinese Communists, on the other hand, stress the sovereignty of one government, also that all minority autonomous regions within the national boundaries are component members of the great national family, and that all such regions are inseparable parts of the country. This difference in the way of handling minority problems is largely due to the fact that the population of the minority peoples of China is very small, and historically many of them have had close associations with Han Chinese. In addition, the interests of the Chinese Communist Party dictate a policy of denying the autonomous governments the right of self-determination and the right of secession.

The Chinese Communist nationalities policy also differs from the policy of the Nationalist Chinese government. Although Dr. Sun Yat-sen long expounded the idea of "racial equality," the Nationalist government ignored its importance and even deliberately played down the differences between the government and national minorities. By simplifying the complicated conditions in the minority areas, the Nationalist government adopted the same method of administration that prevailed in non-minority areas. Consequently, racial disputes were aggravated instead of alleviated. The Chinese Communists worked out their policy by adopting the dialectical point of view: "To solve contradictions on the basis of recognizing them." As a result, the first thing they did was to recognize and accept the differences between nationalities, and they then accorded the minorities nominal respect. From that point on they tried to make use of acceptable forms of self-government through which to push forward, step by step, the social reform program in those areas. In practice they did not impose pressure from outside, but stepped up the training of minority cadres who could be used as the medium for disseminating revolutionary ideas.

Results have proved that the Communist way was more clever and practicable than the fact-ignoring approach of the National-ist government.

At present racial discrimination and oppression have been, ostensibly at least, reduced or eliminated. In the Communist Constitution it is clearly stipulated that "all the nationalities are equal" and that "racial friendship, mutual help, and solidarity" should prevail. There have been visible changes in the relations between the minority nationalities and the Han Chinese; and disputes among the minorities themselves have been relatively reduced. Fairly good progress in the economic, cultural, educational, and health fields has been achieved.

But the road to socialist progress is not entirely lined with roses. During the period of social reform, in the minority areas, the Communist authorities sowed many seeds of dissension among the various class elements of the minority communities. From this ground of dissension there has grown a new form of discrimination and oppression. And it is becoming so intolerable that more and more minority peoples are growing apprehensive and cautious, and in some cases fear of the new rulers has been expressed in open resistance. In Yunnan Province, for example, the minority people often openly criticized the Communist social reform program. Among the criticisms frequently heard were: "Class and class struggle in the minority area are created by the Communist Party"; "Democratic reform is to create a racial split"; "The livelihood of the minority people is not as good as in the pre-liberation days" (*YD*, August 22, 1957).

Official Chinese Communist reports naturally have given very little information on the activities of resistance, except in the case of the rebellions on a larger scale that broke out in Tibet and Sinkiang. There is, however, one highly revealing paragraph in an article entitled "The Present Nationalities Problem in Our Country and Class Struggle," by Liu Ch'un, Vice-Chairman of the Nationalities Affairs Commission, published in the June 3, 1964, issue of *Hung Ch'i* (*Red Flag*). It says: "In recent years, the activities of the local nationalist elements have been rampant in many minority nationality areas." In other words, it means that resistance and revolt have not only been prevalent, but perhaps violent also.

In their execution of the nationalities policy, the Chinese Communist authorities have in recent years repeatedly warned the Han Chinese cadres to overcome the undesirable influence of "Great Hanism" as a major step in improving relations with the minority peoples. They have, on the other hand, shown equal attention to the activities of "local nationalist elements" who may have been trying to seek political independence and to free themselves from Communist rule. The Communist authorities have for the past few years never relaxed their efforts in carrying out ideological struggle and criticism against such elements. Harsh criticism and denunciation were widely practiced during the period of "blooming and contending" and the subsequent "anti-rightist" campaign between 1957 and 1958. In that period a number of minority intellectuals launched open attacks against the Communist policy toward the nationalities. Some said the Communists had fouled up socialist reform; still others said they had ruined the cooperativization movement; and there were others who complained that foodstuffs had become more and more scarce and daily commodities had been steadily decreasing (*PD*, December 26, 1957).

Consequently, some minority intellectuals were purged. But the suppressive measures were not strong enough to eliminate the lingering influence of local nationalism. In recent years local disturbances have demanded Communist attention to such an extent that the authorities have, since 1963, taken remedial steps to ensure their control over the nationalities. One such step was the initiation in 1963 of the socialist education movement centered on class struggle. To carry out the struggle in a thorough manner, the Communists purposely created class antagonism and racial discrimination among the nationalities. At the same time they are so determined to eliminate the influence of local nationalism that they have linked it up with the vital question of national defense. An editorial entitled "To Develop All-Out Class Education among the National Minorities," published in the August 1963 issue of *Nationalities Solidarity*, said:

> In order to materialize their dream for a restoration of the old order and to cover up the true nature of their anti-Party and anti-Socialist activities, the reactionary class elements of the national minorities will continue, by making use of the racial and religious cloak, to deceive the masses and to benumb and paralyze the class-consciousness of the masses. Meanwhile, due to the fact that most areas of the national minorities are situated on the frontier regions of the motherland, the imperialists, reactionaries of all countries and modern revisionists will in their plot to overthrow our country exhaust their wits in conspiring with such reactionary elements of the national minorities to kindle the racial emotions and split the racial relations in an attempt to destroy the unity of the motherland and solidarity of the nationalities in order to tempt the minority people to detach themselves from the socialist road.

In fact, the Communist instigation of class hatred and class struggle has backfired. Since an adverse situation has developed, the Communist authorities have tried to direct the attention of the masses against the activities of the "reactionary and exploiting class" and "foreign imperalists." In the process, they certainly hope to get rid of the incorrigible elements of "local nationalism," to further tighten their control over the national minorities, and to consolidate the political power of the regime.

REFERENCES CITED

CHIANG YING-LIANG
  1950 Pai-i te Sheng-huo Wen-hua [The life and culture of the Pai-i]. Shanghai, Chunghua Book Co. (Human Relations Area Files translation.)

LIN YUEH-HUA
  1961 The minority peoples of Yunnan. China Reconstructs, December:26–29.

MA HSUEH-LIANG
  1962 New scripts for China's minorities. China Reconstructs, August: 24–27.

PATTERSON, GEORGE N.
  1962 Recent Chinese policies in Tibet and towards the Himalayan border states. The China Quarterly, December:191–202

RUPEN, ROBERT A.
  1964 The MPR and Inner Mongolia, 1964. China News Analysis 540:1–7 (November 13).

WIENS, HEROLD J.
  1954 China's march toward the tropics. Hamden, Conn., Shoe String Press.

Periodicals

CHINA NEWS ANALYSIS (CNA). Hong Kong.
CHINA NEWS SERVICE (CNS). Hong Kong.
HUNG CH'I [Red Flag]. Peking
INNER MONGOLIA DAILY (IMD).
JEN-MIN JIH-PAO [People's Daily] (PD). Peking.
KUANG MING DAILY (KMD). Peking.
NATIONALITIES SOLIDARITY (NS). Peking.
NEW OBSERVATION (NO).
YUNNAN DAILY (YD).

PART IV: INDIA

THE EASTERN portion of India is included in a book on Southeast Asia for several reasons. The population of eastern India (including Assam, Nagaland, Manipur, Tripura, and the North East Frontier Agency [NEFA]) includes a large proportion of tribal and minority people who speak languages closely related to languages of Southeast Asia rather than to the languages of India proper, and their cultures in many ways resemble the cultures of neighboring Southeast Asian peoples. Just as the southern boundary of China does not mark a cultural or linguistic division, the eastern border of India does not mark off a cultural or linguistic area. Eastern India thus is an area where Southeast Asian highlanders come in contact with a highly stratified lowland society based on caste. It is interesting to compare the reaction of the highlanders of eastern India with the reactions of highlanders elsewhere in Southeast Asia who are in contact with relatively unstratified lowland societies.

The Indian examples indicate a variety of political solutions to the problems of large concentrations of minority and tribal peoples within an already heterogeneous population. As Burling points out, hill tribesmen in eastern India have long been involved in the economy of the lowlands. But in general the hill people of eastern India have refused to enter into the caste system. They have been unwilling to accept the religious and symbolic assumptions, as well as the social stigma of being integrated into the lower levels of the caste system. This is apparently in contrast to the fate of tribesmen elsewhere in India who, for centuries, have been incorporated as individuals and as groups at the lowest caste levels. The conversion of large numbers of eastern India tribesmen to Christianity may be interpreted in part as the ritual symbolization of this attempt to stay out of the caste system.

Burling points out in the paper which follows that it is in the east that India has been faced with some of its most serious political problems in attempting to form a unified nation. The national government has been forced to recognize the cultural distinctness of Nagaland and to give it status as a state for a variety of geographical and politico-military reasons, as well as

[205]

for reasons of cultural difference. And Burling indicates that other cultural groups have been quick to seize on the Nagaland precedent in requesting state recognition.[1]

In a brief survey such as this it has not been possible to spell out the processes by which the Nagas have managed to build sufficient political unity to achieve statehood through fairly well-coordinated political and military action. This is a very real problem, since the Nagas are actually quite diverse culturally and linguistically, traditionally they have rarely been organized above the village level, and they have traditionally been headhunters fighting among themselves just as bitterly as they have fought against the Indians. No doubt in India as in Burma (Lehman's paper), the recognition of the Nagas as something separate and apart both by British and Indian administrations, combined with attempts to force them into the standard Indian social-political model, helped to create political unity where none existed before.

Burling gives an optimistic picture of the success of representative democracy within the state of Assam, where hill tribes and lowlanders are both represented in state government. In areas such as the Garo Hills, where tribesmen have been allowed to participate in government on an equal basis with the lowlanders, where the central government has not been strict in attempting to enforce cultural uniformity, where long-time missionary activity has led to the development of a literate and educated group of people, and where the borders have not been the scene of

---

[1] There has been renewed fighting by Naga and Mizo tribesmen in Nagaland, Manipur, and the Mizo Hills District of Assam since these papers were written. The Nagas, some of whom continue to press for complete independence from India, attacked Indian troops, claiming that aggression against the Nagas continued even after a cease-fire conference between Prime Minister Indira Gandhi and Naga leaders. The Mizo (or Lushai) revolt was evidently organized by the Mizo National Front, one of several Mizo political organizations which is striving for Mizo national independence (*New York Times*, 18 February 1966, "Bombs kill 36 on train in India's Naga area"; 19 February 1966, "Mrs. Gandhi meets with Naga leaders"; 20 February 1966, "India and Naga insurgents agree to expand observers team"; 21 February 1966, "Angry Nagas cancel meeting with Indian leaders"; 3 March 1966, "Indian outposts are attacked by nationalist Mizo tribesmen"; 5 March 1966, "Rebel tribe widens India hill attacks"; 6 March 1966 "Indian Army recaptures outposts from Mizo rebels"; 7 March 1966, "India bans group seeking secession in a tribal revolt"; 9 March 1966, "Mizos hold 6 Indian outposts"; 10 March 1966, "Mizos ambush Indian patrol").

serious international disputes, this approach seems to have worked quite well. It is not at all clear that the same solution can work in NEFA, where the people are much less sophisticated (they are much less likely to be literate in an Indian language or English, and have been kept isolated deliberately by both British and Indian administrations) and where the border has been subject to an important series of recent international battles.

TABLE 8

SCHEDULED TRIBES AND SCHEDULED CASTES IN INDIA, 1961 CENSUS*

| Area | Total Population | Scheduled Tribes | | Scheduled Castes | |
		Number	Percent of Total	Number	Percent of Total
India	439,234,771	30,130,184	6.86	64,449,275	14.67
Assam	11,872,272	2,064,816	17.39	732,756	6.17
Manipur	780,037	249,049	31.93	13,376	1.71
Nagaland	369,200	343,697	93.09	126	0.03
NEFA	336,558	298,167	88.59	—	—
Tripura	1,142,005	360,070	31.53	119,725	10.48

* Source: *Census of India*, 1961, Vol. I, Part II-A (ii).

TABLE 9
POPULATION AND LINGUISTIC AFFILIATION OF ETHNIC GROUPS OF EASTERN INDIA[a] (ASSAM, MANIPUR, NAGALAND, THE NORTH EAST FRONTIER AGENCY, AND TRIPURA)

A. ASSAM

Group	Estimated Population in Assam	Location of Greatest Concentration in Assam	Language
Assam—Non-Tribal			
Assamese	6,780,000	Throughout Assam	Indo-European: Indo-Aryan, Assamese
Bengali	2,089,000	Throughout Assam	Indo-European: Indo-Aryan, Bengali
Hindi	524,000	Throughout Assam	Indo-European: Indo-Aryan, Hindi
Nepali	215,000	Throughout Assam	Indo-European: Indo-Aryan, Nepali
Oriya	146,000	Darrang, Lakhimpur, and scattered	Indo-European: Indo-Aryan, Oriya
Santali	69,000	Throughout Assam	Munda (prob. related to Mon-Khmer)
Assam—Scheduled Tribes			
Khasi	363,000	United Khasi and Jaintia Hills	Mon-Khmer: Khasi
Bodo (Boro, Plains Kachari)	345,000	Goalpara, and scattered	Sino-Tibetan: Tibeto-Burman, Bodo
Garo	301,000	Garo Hills	Sino-Tibetan: Tibeto-Burman, Bodo
Mizo (Lushai)	216,000	Mizo Hills	Sino-Tibetan: Tibeto-Burman, Kuki-Chin
Mikir	154,000	Mikir Hills	Sino-Tibetan: Tibeto-Burman, Naga-Kuki[b]
Miri	136,000	Lakhimpur	Sino-Tibetan: Tibeto-Burman, North Assam
Rabha	38,000	Goalpara, Garo Hills	Sino-Tibetan: Tibeto-Burman, Bodo
Dimasa (Hills Kachari)	32,000	North Cachar Hills	Sino-Tibetan: Tibeto-Burman, Bodo
Lalung	10,600	Nowgong, Khasi Hills, Mikir, and North Cachar Hills	Sino-Tibetan: Tibeto-Burman, Bodo
Hmar	10,000	Cachar, Mikir, and North Cachar Hills	Sino-Tibetan: Tibeto-Burman, Kuki-Chin
Lakher	9,500	Mizo Hills	Sino-Tibetan: Tibeto-Burman, Kuki-Chin

(continued)

TABLE 9
(continued)

A. ASSAM, *cont.*

Group	Estimated Population in Assam	Location of Greatest Concentration in Assam	Language
Deori (Chutiya)	9,100	Lakhimpur	Sino-Tibetan: Tibeto-Burman, Bodo
Koch	8,000	Garo Hills	Sino-Tibetan: Tibeto-Burman, Bodo
Pawi	6,900	Mizo Hills	Sino-Tibetan: Tibeto-Burman, Kuki-Chin
Assam total°	11,872,772		

B. MANIPUR

Group	Estimated Population in Manipur	Language
Manipur—Non-Tribal		
Manipuri-Meithei	502,000	Sino-Tibetan: Tibeto-Burman, Kuki-Chin
Nepali	13,500	Indo-European: Indo-Aryan, Nepali
Bengali	10,000	Indo-European: Indo-Aryan, Bengali
Manipur—Scheduled Tribes		
Tangkhul	44,000	Sino-Tibetan: Tibeto-Burman, Naga-Kuki
Thado	30,000	Sino-Tibetan: Tibeto-Burman, Kuki-Chin
Kabui	29,000	Sino-Tibetan: Tibeto-Burman, Naga-Bodo
Mao	29,000	Sino-Tibetan: Tibeto-Burman, Naga-Kuki
Paite	17,000	Sino-Tibetan: Tibeto-Burman, Kuki-Chin
Hmar	15,000	Sino-Tibetan: Tibeto-Burman, Kuki-Chin
Kacha Naga (Empeo)	9,700	Sino-Tibetan: Tibeto-Burman, Naga-Bodo
Simte	9,500	Sino-Tibetan: Tibeto-Burman, Kuki-Chin
Vaipei (Vaiphui)	8,000	Sino-Tibetan: Tibeto-Burman, Kuki-Chin
Maring	7,700	Sino-Tibetan: Tibeto-Burman, Naga-Kuki
Anal	5,500	Sino-Tibetan: Tibeto-Burman, Kuki-Chin
Kom	5,500	Sino-Tibetan: Tibeto-Burman, Kuki-Chin
Gangte	4,900	Sino-Tibetan: Tibeto-Burman, Kuki-Chin
Maram	4,900	Sino-Tibetan: Tibeto-Burman, Naga-Kuki
Chiru	2,300	Sino-Tibetan: Tibeto-Burman, Kuki-Chin
Lamgang	1,900	Sino-Tibetan: Tibeto-Burman, Kuki-Chin
Khoirao	400	Sino-Tibetan: Tibeto-Burman, Naga-Bodo
Manipur total	780,037	

(continued)

TABLE 9
(continued)

C. NAGALAND

Group	Estimated Population in Nagaland	Location of Greatest Concentration in Nagaland	Language
Nagaland—Non-Tribal			
Nepali	10,000	Scattered (?)	Indo-European: Indo-Aryan, Nepali
Hindi	4,500	Scattered (?)	Indo-European: Indo-Aryan, Hindi
Bengali	3,800	Scattered (?)	Indo-European: Indo-Aryan, Bengali
Assamese	3,600	Scattered (?)	Indo-European: Indo-Aryan, Assamese
Nagaland—Scheduled Tribes			
Konyak	57,000	Tuensang	Sino-Tibetan: Tibeto-Burman, Eastern Naga[d]
Ao	56,000	Mokokchung	Sino-Tibetan: Tibeto-Burman, Central Naga[e]
Sema	47,000	Mokokchung	Sino-Tibetan: Tibeto-Burman, Western Naga[f]
Angami	34,000	Kohima	Sino-Tibetan: Tibeto-Burman, Western Naga[f]
Lotha (Lhota)	26,000	Mokokchung	Sino-Tibetan: Tibeto-Burman, Central Naga[e]
Pochuri (including Sangtam)	18,000	Tuensang and Kohima	Sino-Tibetan: Tibeto-Burman, Western Naga[f]
Phom-Sha	13,000	Tuensang	Sino-Tibetan: Tibeto-Burman, ?
Yimchunger	13,000	Tuensang	Sino-Tibetan: Tibeto-Burman, ?
Khiemnungan	12,000	Tuensang	Sino-Tibetan: Tibeto-Burman, ?
Chang	11,000	Tuensang	Sino-Tibetan: Tibeto-Burman, Eastern Naga[d]
Chakesang	10,000	Kohima	Sino-Tibetan: Tibeto-Burman, Western Naga[f]
Zemi-Zeliang	9,400	Kohima	Sino-Tibetan: Tibeto-Burman, Naga-Bodo
Zheza	8,800	Kohima	Sino-Tibetan: Tibeto-Burman, Western Naga[f]
Chakru	8,000	Kohima	Sino-Tibetan: Tibeto-Burman, Western Naga[f]
Rengma	5,800	Kohima	Sino-Tibetan: Tibeto-Burman, Western Naga[f]
Makware	769	Tuensang	Sino-Tibetan: Tibeto-Burman, ?
Nagaland total	369,200		

(continued)

TABLE 9
(continued)

D. NEFA

Group (Sub-groups or Synonym)	Estimated Population in NEFA	Location of Greatest Concentration in NEFA	Language
NEFA—Scheduled Tribes			
Abor-Adi (Abor-Adi, Ashing, Bokar, Bori, Gallong, Milang, Minyang, Padam, Pailibo Pangi, Pasi, Ramo, Shimong, Tagin)	?	Siang[g]	Sino-Tibetan: Tibeto-Burman, North Assam, Abor-Adi
Aka (Hrusso)	?	Kameng	Sino-Tibetan: Tibeto-Burman, North Assam, Aka
Bangru	?	Kameng, Subansiri	?
Dafla (Apatani, Bangni, Dafla)	?	Subansiri[h]	Sino-Tibetan: Tibeto-Burman, North Assam, Dafla
Karko	?	Siang	?
Khampti (Hkampti)	?	Lohit	Tai: Southwestern, Shan
Lodung	?	Siang	?
Memba	?	Siang	Sino-Tibetan: Tibeto-Burman, Tibetan
Miji	?	Kameng	?
Miri	?	Subansiri	Sino-Tibetan: Tibeto-Burman, North Assam, Miri
Mishmi (Digaru, Idu-Mishmi, Miju)	?	Lohit	Sino-Tibetan: Tibeto-Burman, North Assam, Mishmi
Monpa	?	Kameng	Sino-Tibetan: Tibeto-Burman, Tibetan
Naga (Nocte, Tangsa, Wanchou)	?	Tirap	Sino-Tibetan: Tibeto-Burman, Naga
Singpho (Jinghpaw)	?	Lohit, Tirap	Sino-Tibetan: Tibeto-Burman, Singpho[i]
Solung	?	Kameng, Subansiri	?
NEFA total (1961 census)	336,558[j]		

(continued)

TABLE 9
(continued)

E. TRIPURA

Group	Estimated Population in Tripura	Language
Tripura—Non-Tribal		
Bengali	772,000	Indo-European: Indo-Aryan, Bengali
Manipuri-Meithei	28,000	Sino-Tibetan: Tibeto-Burman, Kuki-Chin
Chakma	22,000	Indo-European: Indo-Aryan, Bengali
Arakanese-Mogh	10,000	Sino-Tibetan: Tibeto-Burman, Burmese-Lolo
Nepali	1,700	Indo-European: Indo-Aryan, Nepali
Tripura—Scheduled Tribes		
Tripuri	284,000	Sino-Tibetan: Tibeto-Burman, Bodo
Halam	16,000	Sino-Tibetan: Tibeto-Burman, Kuki-Chin
Garoo (Garo)	5,000	Sino-Tibetan: Tibeto-Burman, Bodo
Kuki	3,000	Sino-Tibetan: Tibeto-Burman, Kuki-Chin
Lushai (Mizo)	3,000	Sino-Tibetan: Tibeto-Burman, Kuki-Chin
Tripura total	1,142,005	

[a] The material in this table was assembled from *Census of India*, 1961, Vol. I, India, Part II-C (ii), Language Tables. Group names are those given in the census. Information on location of groups in Assam was modified by reference to the 1951 census in the cases where the 1951 census had a more complete breakdown. Linguistic classifications have been modified in a few instances to correspond with usage elsewhere in this book (see notes accompanying the Burma population and linguistic affiliation table for further details on problems of linguistic classification). The designation "Scheduled Tribes" is from the Census, Vol. I, Part II-A (ii). Population figures have been rounded to the nearest thousand (for large groups) or the nearest hundred (for small groups).

[b] The Mikir language is classified as a member of the Kuki-Chin group of the Tibeto-Burman family elsewhere in this book.

[c] A number of small groups of immigrants from other parts of India have not been included in this breakdown, but are included in the Assam total.

[d] The Eastern Naga languages are probably closely related to what is called the Bodo Group of Tibeto-Burman elsewhere in this volume.

[e] The Central Naga languages are probably closely related to what is called the Kuki-Chin Group of Tibeto-Burman elsewhere in this volume.

[f] The Western Naga languages probably fall under what is called the Naga Group of Tibeto-Burman elsewhere in this volume.

[g] The Gallong and Tagin groups are found primarily in Subansiri Frontier District, as well as in Siang; the Padam group is found in Lohit Frontier District as well as in Siang.

[h] The Bangni group is found in Kameng Frontier District.

[i] The Singhpo language is tentatively classified as distantly related to the Bodo group of Tibeto-Burman elsewhere in this volume.

[j] Census data for NEFA are so incomplete that there is little point in giving population figures for the various tribes. Elwin (1960) has estimated that the total NEFA population is about 500,000.

BIBLIOGRAPHY

Bibliographic references to eastern India may be found in Fürer-Haimendorf (1958, 1964) and Patterson and Inden (1962). The general situation of tribal peoples in India and government programs for them is summarized periodically in government reports (e.g. India 1960; 1961). Elwin, who was influential in establishing government policy with respect to tribes throughout India has described his philosophy specifically with respect to the people of the North East Frontier Agency (1960). Some of the British administrative history of the eastern India frontier areas is summarized in Reid (1942) and Elwin (1959).

Classic ethnographic monographs on the peoples of this region include Fürer-Haimendorf (1962), Gurdon (1914), Hodson (1908; 1911), Hutton (1921A; 1921B), Mills (1922; 1926; 1937), Parry (1932), Playfair (1909), and Shakespear (1912). Valuable ethnographic notes are also contained in the various censuses of India, especially the census of 1931. Recent ethnographic studies include Baruah (1960), Dutta (1960), Roy (1960), Sharma (1961), Shukla (1960), Sinha (1962), Srivastava (1962), and Burling (1963). For a study of the integration of tribal people elsewhere in India see Bailey (1960).

BAILEY, F. G.
   1960   Tribe, caste, and nation: a study of political activity and political change in Orissa. Manchester, Manchester University Press.

BARUAH, TAPAN KUMAR M.
   1960   The Idu Mishmis. Shillong, Shri P. C. Dutta, on behalf of the Adviser to the Governor of Assam.

BURLING, ROBBINS
   1963   Rengsanggri: family and kinship in a Garo village. Philadelphia, University of Pennsylvania Press.

DUTTA, P. C.
   1960   The Tangsas. Shillong, P. C. Dutta, on behalf of the Adviser to the Governor of Assam.

ELWIN, VERRIER
   1959   India's Northeast Frontier in the 19th century. London, Oxford University Press.
   1960   A philosophy for NEFA. Shillong, Shri J. N. Chowdhury, on behalf of the Adviser to the Governor of Assam, 2d revised edn.

FÜRER-HAIMENDORF, CHRISTOPH VON
   1962   The naked Nagas. Calcutta. Thacker Spink & Co., 2d revised Indian edn.

FÜRER-HAIMENDORF, ELIZABETH VON
   1958   An anthropological bibliography of South Asia. Paris and La Haye, Mouton and Co.
   1964   An anthropological bibliography of South Asia, Vol. II, 1955–1959. Paris and La Haye, Mouton and Co.

GURDON, PHILLIP RICHARD THORNBAGH
  1914   The Khasis. London, Macmillan, 2d edn.
HODSON, THOMAS CALLAN
  1908   The Meitheis. London, David Nutt.
  1911   The Naga tribes of Manipur. London, Macmillan.
HUTTON, JOHN HENRY
  1921A   The Angami Nagas. London, Macmillan.
  1921B   The Sema Nagas. London, Macmillan.
INDIA, CENSUS COMMISSIONER
  1961   Census of India, 1931.
  1932   Census of India, 1961.
INDIA, MINISTRY OF HOME AFFAIRS
  1960   Report of the Committee on Special Multipurpose Tribal
         Blocks. New Delhi, Government of India Press.
INDIA, SCHEDULED AREAS AND SCHEDULED TRIBES COMMISSION
  1961   Report of the Scheduled Areas and Scheduled Tribes Com-
         mission, 1960–61. Simla, Government of India Press, 2 vols.
MILLS, JAMES PHILLIP
  1922   The Lhota Nagas. London, Macmillan.
  1926   The Ao Nagas. London, Macmillan.
  1937   The Rengma Nagas. London, Macmillan.
PARRY, N. E.
  1932   The Lakhers. London, Macmillan.
PATTERSON, MAUREEN L. P. and RONALD B. INDEN
  1962   South Asia: an introductory bibliography. Chicago, Syllabus
         Division, University of Chicago Press.
PLAYFAIR, ALAN
  1909   The Garos. London, David Nutt.
REID, SIR ROBERT
  1942   History of the frontier areas bordering on Assam, from
         1883–1941. Shillong, Assam Government Press.
ROY, SACHIN
  1960   Aspects of Padam-Minyong culture. Shillong, Sri Sachin Roy,
         on behalf of the North-East Frontier Agency.
SHAKESPEAR, J.
  1912   The Lushei Kuki clans. London, Macmillan.
SHARMA, R. R. P.
  1961   The Sherdukpens. Shillong, P. C. Dutta, for the Research De-
         partment, Adviser's Secretariat.
SHUKLA, B. K.
  1960   The Daflas. Shillong, P. C. Dutta, on behalf of the Adviser
         to the Governor of Assam.
SINHA, RAGHUVIR
  1962   The Akas. Shillong, P. C. Dutta, for the Research Department,
         Adviser's Secretariat.
SRIVASTAVA, L. R. N.
  1962   The Gallongs. Shillong, P. Dutta for the Research Department,
         Adviser's Secretariat.

Tribesmen and Lowlanders of Assam[1]

ROBBINS BURLING

ASSAM AND SOUTHEAST ASIA

As an integral part of the Republic of India, Assam is not conventionally thought of as a part of Southeast Asia, yet it shares many characteristics with the nations to the east and there is justification for including it with Southeast Asia when considering the role of tribal peoples. Like the nations of Southeast Asia, Assam has a minority of tribal mountaineers who differ in many ways from the lowland majority. As in much of Southeast Asia proper, the hill men live largely by swidden agriculture; they are fragmented into dozens of linguistic groups, and until the colonial period no political system based in the plains was able to extend its control consistently into the hills. Except for recent converts to Christianity, the hill men (like most of their cousins to the east) fall under that vague rubric of "animism" and are thus set off from their Hindu neighbors in the valley. And, as in other parts of Southeast Asia, lowlanders tend to look upon the hill people as naive and primitive rustics, while they are often seen in return as wily, sophisticated scoundrels.

This much follows the familiar Southeast Asian contrast between lowlander and mountaineer, but in two respects the contrast in Assam seems even sharper than elsewhere. Only in Assam is the racial difference between the people of the mountains and those of the valley great enough to prevent a hill man from losing himself among the plains population, or to prevent a lowlander from becoming lost in the hills. More important, I think,

---

[1] My first acquaintance with Assam was made possible by a generous grant from the Ford Foundation from 1954 to 1956. The present paper was originally prepared for a symposium on "The Future Role of Tribal Peoples in the Nations of Southeast Asia," held in Denver at the 1965 meeting of the American Anthropological Association.

the lowland Assamese, as participants in the civilization of Hindu India, have cultural patterns quite different from those of the lowland Burmese or Thai or Vietnamese, and these characteristics alter the manner in which hill man and plains man can deal with one another. Although the burdens of caste are said to rest more lightly upon the Assamese than upon most Hindus, caste still creates a barrier of a sort unknown in Southeast Asia proper. The royal Burmese could solidify his position by strategic marriages with chiefly hill families, and at the uppermost levels of Southeast Asian society it seems that ethnic differences tend to dissolve. To the higher-caste Assamese, however, intermarriage with a tribesman is unthinkable. Elsewhere in Southeast Asia, a mountaineer with sufficient wealth and a sufficiently chiefly pedigree can occasionally deal with upperclass plains men on reasonably equal terms. The tribesman in Assam, whatever his status at home, can enter Hindu society only at the bottom.

These special characteristics of Assam seem to me to be relatively minor, however, and for present purposes at least, the more interesting contrasts between Assam and the rest of Southeast Asia arise from the differing political history of the two areas since the Second World War. The fact that Assam has not been part of political Southeast Asia, but has instead been attached to India, has given the tribesmen a unique experience which may possibly have implications for the tribesmen in the smaller nations. In comparison with most of Southeast Asia, independent India has had an orderly political life, and the apparatus of elective parliamentary democracy has, so far, worked with relative success. India has operated under its independent constitution for fifteen years, and with the deaths of Nehru and Shastri it successfully achieved two orderly transitions of power. The nation has, moreover, held three general elections, in which most of the tribal people of Assam have participated.

To characterize Indian political life as tranquil, however, would be going too far, and the integration of Assam's tribal minority has not been the least of the manifold problems besetting the new government. Though they number less than 1 percent of India's population, the tribal people have posed a serious national problem, and within the state of Assam, where they constitute something closer to 15 percent, the relations between tribal and lowland people have been marked by almost unceasing friction. The relations have been governed by three varying political experiments, each of which I will describe briefly in the following pages: 1) the so-called autonomous hill districts within the state of Assam; 2) the separate state of Nagaland; and 3) the centrally administered North East Frontier Agency.

TRIBESMEN IN A CONSTITUTIONAL GOVERNMENT

As befits an intricate nation, the Constitution of India is an intricate document. In the edition I have used it runs to 273 pages even without its amendments.[2] This great (to an American) bulk results from many factors, but among other things the Constitution provides not only for the organization of the central government, but for the state governments as well, and in the case of Assam, it makes explicit and detailed provisions for the tribal areas. These provisions are found in what is known as the "Sixth Schedule," a sixteen-page appendix which with the various other "schedules" follows the main body of the Constitution.

The Sixth Schedule divides the mountainous regions of Assam into two classes. The wilder areas (known at the time the Constitution was framed as Balipara Frontier Tract, Tirap Frontier Tract, Abor Hills District, Mishimi Hills District, and Naga Tribal Area, which constitutes the inner, or wilder part of the Naga Hills) were to be centrally administered as the North East Frontier Agency or NEFA (see below). The less wild hill tracts were apportioned among six districts: the United Khasi-Jaintia Hills, the Garo Hills, the Mizo District (formerly Lushai Hills), the Naga Hills (i.e., the more settled portion of the Naga Hills, which was to be distinct from the wilder Naga Tribal Area included as part of NEFA), the North Cachar Hills, and the Mikir Hills. Each of these six districts was to have a district council whose members would be elected by adult suffrage from territorial constituencies into which the district would be apportioned. These district councils were new, unlike any government bodies that had existed earlier, and they were granted broad local powers and duties, including the right to build roads,

[2] The Constitution of India (as modified up to November 1, 1956).

[217]

set up schools, administer markets, regulate land and agriculture, and the right to collect the most important local taxes. The councils were given jurisdiction over "customary law" (pertaining to marriage, inheritance, the appointment and succession of chiefs or headmen, and what the Constitution calls "social customs"), and they were expected to establish the courts that would decide disputes arising under these headings.

These formal provisions of the Constitution, though possibly somewhat cumbersome, explicitly attempted to reconcile the hill people's desire for autonomy with the requirements of national unity. The unique ethnic position of the tribal people was recognized. They were given the major responsibility for their own customary law, and the hill districts were explicitly exempted from certain national legislation that might infringe upon their traditions. The only provisions that might strike an outsider as superficially unreasonable are those which grant very broad powers to the governor of the state of Assam. Legislation passed by the district councils must be signed by the governor before it becomes law. He can change the boundaries of the districts, and he can even dissolve the district councils and assume their powers. It must be remembered, however, that under the spirit in which the Constitution was written, the office of governor of the state is analogous to that of the Indian president, and the presidency in turn is modeled upon the office of the British monarch. It was clearly the expectation of the writers of the Constitution that short of extraordinary circumstances the actions of the district councils would be approved by the governor.

Of course, writing a formal constitution and putting its provisions into smooth operation are quite different things. Political experience was rare among hill men, and the people had had no experience with direct suffrage. Nevertheless, the district councils were organized, members of the councils were elected in the first general election in 1952, and with varying degrees of efficiency, the councils have grappled with the problems of local government ever since.

Because they were elected from tribal constituencies, it was probably inevitable that the councils would become the focal points of tribal nationalism. The state legislature, whose electorate is largely plains Assamese, has tended itself to be responsive to its own variety of nationalism. Tribal leaders have issued periodic calls for tribal loyalty, so as to rally resistance against the real or imagined encroachment of the ambitious Assamese. Plains leaders have answered by insisting that hill man and plains man in Assam are indissolubly bound by history and sentiment, and they have periodically suggested that only outside agitators could possibly have stirred up the tribesmen to such a point of self-assertion.

The overt disagreements between hill and plains leaders have been caused more by emotional issues than immediately practical issues. There have been occasional disagreements about the jurisdiction of various governmental bodies, competition for the inevitably limited government funds, and rarely someone has become concerned about the future allocation of profit from the potential mineral and hydroelectric wealth of the hills. But issues of language, religion, and cultural tradition have caused far more bitterness. No educated hill man can calmly accept the condescending way in which plains men sometimes refer to the hills as backward, as primitive, and as lagging many centuries behind the more progressive and civilized plains. The hill leader doubts that the average hill farmer is economically worse off than the average lowland farmer, and he knows that some of the hill districts are, by Indian standards, well educated. By one count, in fact, the Mizo Hills turned out to have the highest percentage of literacy of any comparable district in India. Why, then, wonders the hill man, must others persist in describing the tribes as "backward"?

SYMBOLIC DIFFERENCES BETWEEN HILLS AND PLAINS

Plains Assamese like to suggest that it is the conjunction of mountains and lowlands, with the mingling of their contrasting peoples, that gives their state its unique character and sets it off from the rest of India. Convinced that the British deliberately kept the hills isolated from the plains and deliberately fostered naive separatist ambitions among the hill people, the plains Assamese often feel that if only they were given the chance, they could cooperate in building a united and vigorous Assam under

[219]

the leadership of Assamese. They could then gradually draw the hill people within the embrace of their civilization. But the hill people, by and large, act as if they want no part of what the plains men offer. Khasis became annoyed when street markers written in Assamese script appeared in their district, and no issue has more infuriated the tribal people than periodic suggestions by plains men that the Assamese language be used in hill schools.[3] Standards of English have been relatively high in the hills, and the tribals dread having to learn not only English, and perhaps Hindi as a new national language, but the state language of Assamese as well. Phizo, the Naga leader, made political capital out of the refusal of a distinguished Hindu visitor to share a feast of pork and rice beer. "Here," said Phizo, "is a symbol of the unbridgeable gap between the Nagaland and India."[4]

Over the past century many tribesmen have become Christians (the largest number are Baptists), and virtually every tribal leader is a Christian. The differences between hill men and plains men are far older the coming of Christianity to Assam, but both tribals and Hindus have often come to look upon Christianity as the chief symbol of their separation. Indeed, some hill men may become Christians precisely because they feel they need a symbol that will emphasize the feelings of separatism they already have and which, at the same time, will give them a claim to be "civilized." But to the Hindu lowlander, Christianity is often seen as a legacy of the colonial West, a foreign doctrine implanted in their midst.[5]

In spite of emotional issues, in spite of unclear jurisdictional boundaries between various government bodies, and in spite of the occasional inefficiencies of inexperienced officials, the district councils have functioned, and with one tragic exception reason-

[3] Report of a debate in the Assam Legislative Assembly, *Assam Tribune*, December 24, 1963.

[4] Quoted by Verrier Elwin (1960:244).

[5] In late 1963, when thousands of tribal refugees poured into Assam from East Pakistan however, the government of India suddenly found it worthwhile to point out that many of the refugees were Christians. In this way India asserted to the world that India is a secular state which discriminates against no religion, and that the issue between India and Pakistan is not that of Hinduism vs. Islam, but rather the Indian acceptance of the ideal of a secular state vs. Pakistani communalism.

ably orderly government has been carried on. This brings me to the events which led up to the most recent political experiment in India's far northeast, the establishment of Nagaland.

THE FORMATION OF NAGALAND—A TRIBAL STATE

It is difficult to know exactly why the grievances of the Nagas had so much more violent consequences than those of the other tribes. Perhaps the Nagas had a slightly more fierce tradition of warfare than others, traditions which date back to pre-British times. Perhaps they happened to have some unusually able or belligerent leadership. Perhaps too, the fact that the Naga Hills were the only part of India to be occupied by the Japanese during the Second World War meant that the general turmoil caused by passing armies, and the availability of weapons which they abandoned, helped to foment unrest and encourage rebellion. In any event, as early as 1947 Angami Zapu Phizo was demanding complete independence for the Naga Hills, and by the early 1950's Nagas were in open rebellion. The Indian army struggled to assert control, and in a pattern of guerrilla warfare, with which Americans have become all too familiar, government troops burned Naga villages suspected of harboring rebels, and when rebels could not kill Indian trooops, they turned upon "loyal" Nagas instead. As is also not entirely unprecedented in other guerrilla wars, neither side seemed able to achieve real victory. The Nagas staged periodic raids on government posts. They used captured weapons or arms which they smuggled from Pakistan, a hundred miles away.[6] At least one report of Chinese arms appeared in the press, but no substantial ties between Nagas and Chinese have been documented.[7] In fact, when the Chinese invaded India, Phizo, by then living in exile in London, offered to end the rebellion and to organize resistance against the Chinese if Nehru would agree to hold a plebiscite on Naga independence.[8] Foreign missionaries were accused of encouraging the rebellion, but no real evidence for this has ever been given. Of course, the rebel leaders, like all tribal leaders, are Christians. It was reported that Naga delegates brought their Bibles to a

[6] *New York Times*, May 4, 1962. *Assam Tribune*, December 16, 1963.
[7] *New York Times*, September 21, 1957.
[8] *New York Times*, November 16, 1962.

peace conference and knelt in prayer before conferring.[9] To Indians this may smack of Western colonial influence, but to a Naga it may simply be an added ritualization of his deeply felt independence. Nagas tried at one time to bring their case before the United Nations, and they have insisted that their country never was a part of India.

The response of the Indian government was slow and by no means consistent: sometimes it was political and conciliatory, sometimes military and harsh. But as years passed without a military solution, Nehru and the Indian government came slowly to agree to establishing a state of Nagaland, separate from Assam, but still within the Indian Union. Though the rebel leaders did not agree, other "loyal" Nagas did, and it was hoped that this compromise which granted more autonomy than a hill district but less than complete independence would undermine support for the rebel cause.

Bills creating Nagaland passed in Parliament in 1962, and in December 1963 Nagaland, embracing both the older Naga Hills District and the "Naga" areas of NEFA, became the sixteenth and smallest state of the Republic of India. With 370,000 people, Nagaland is supposed to be on a par governmentally with the nine million of Assam, not to mention the sixty million of Uttar Pradesh.[10] When the first state elections were held in January 1964, supporters of the "loyalist" Naga Shilu Ao won the majority of seats in the new forty-six-seat state legislative assembly, and Ao became the chief minister.[11]

Even this did not end the rebellion. Raids continued through March of 1964, but beginning in September negotiations with the rebels brought the first real hope for genuine peace.[12] A truce was arranged, but as late as November 1965, when the truce was due to expire, rebels threatened to renew hostilities unless the government dropped its premise that negotiations be restricted to solutions requiring the Nagas to remain within the Indian Union.[13]

Until recently, no other tribe had taken up arms or seriously

[9] New York Times, September 7, 1964.
[10] Nagaland has its own capital at Kohima, its own legislature and chief minister, and its own representatives in the national parliament.
[11] New York Times, December 2, 1963; January 18, 1964.
[12] New York Times, September 6, 1964.
[13] India Briefing, December 1965.

demanded complete independence, but many demands have been made for separate hill states and the success of the Nagas could only encourage separatist ambitions. In 1965 a party called the Mizo National Front was calling for an independent Mizo land and it scored some electoral successes.[14] By 1966 violence had broken out in the Mizo hills and the threat of a repetition of the Naga conflict hung over that district.

NEFA—TRIBES UNDER DIRECT ADMINISTRATION

The third political experiment for the hill areas is represented by the North East Frontier Agency, or NEFA, as it is generally known. This is the region designated as "Part B Tribal Area" by the Sixth Schedule of the Constitution, and it is the area which was most lightly administered during British times. NEFA constitutes the north and northeastern mountain tracts, the areas which border Bhutan, China, and northern Burma. Its population has been variously estimated at two hundred thousand to a million, Verrier Elwin's (1960) estimate of a half-million being as reasonable as any. The men who framed the Constitution felt, quite rightly no doubt, that it would be impossible to set up elective government there immediately.

NEFA is constititutionally designated as a part of Assam, and it is supposed to be united with the rest of the state when it has reached a "sufficient" stage of development. In the meantime, it is administered by a separate agency, responsible through the Governor of Assam (who is himself a central appointee, not a locally elected officer) to the central government. In effect, therefore, NEFA has been ruled as a centrally administered territory, and a presidential appointee has sat in Parliament to represent its people.

Since the British period travel into NEFA has been strictly controlled. This has been partly to protect the traveler against possible danger in unadministered territory, but the rule is now also quite explicitly designed to protect the tribal people from the encroachment and exploitation they might suffer if outsiders had unlimited access to their hills.[15] So long as it is difficult for anyone not directly connected with the NEFA administration

[14] *India Briefing*, December 1965.
[15] Statement by Prime Minister Nehru reported in the *Assam Tribune*, December 18, 1963.

to gain admission, and in the absence of articulate local leadership, it is difficult to know just what the present situation is. Certainly local violence is being controlled, roads are being built at an accelerating rate, and the government has launched various ambitious schemes for agricultural and educational development. The strategic importance of the region, particularly since the Chinese invasion (the main thrust of which was into NEFA), will surely stimulate the government to push its development schemes as rapidly as possible, though it may discourage elections and the risk of independent political movements such as have characterized the other hill regions.

TRIBESMEN IN A REPRESENTATIVE DEMOCRACY

As citizens of India, the tribal peoples of Assam have not only been subject to local government, but (except for the people of NEFA) they have also participated in the nation's three general elections, and their representatives sit in both the Assam State Legislative Assembly and in the national parliament. Some idea of the ethnic division within the state can be seen in the results of the 1962 elections.[16] In that year, 105 members of the legislative assembly were elected from as many constituencies of the state. By the time of the elections the Naga Hills had been separated from Assam and did not send representatives to the assembly, but the remaining hill districts comprised fifteen of the 105 assembly constituencies. Of these, eleven were won by the "All Party Hill Leaders Conference" (APHLC), a coalition of hill parties from the various districts, and most of these seats were won decisively. The Congress Party, which generally offered the only serious opposition, was soundly defeated, as it had been in earlier elections. Of the four seats which Congresss did win in the hills, three were in the North Cachar and Mikir Hills, districts which I judge to be more like the plains in their general ethnic character and political attitudes than other hill districts. The weak position of the Congress Party in the Assam Hills is shown dramatically by the fact that of the 2,833 legislative assembly seats which were contested in the various states of India in 1962, the only two seats for which Congress did not

[16] The elections in Assam were reported in detail in the *Assam Tribune* between February 25 and March 4, 1962.

offer a candidate were in the Assam Hills.[17] In those constituencies alone Congress admitted it had no chance. The Congress Party has clearly become identified with close ties to other parts of India, and a vote against Congress has come to mean a vote for tribal autonomy.

By contrast, of the remaining ninety seats of the Assam Legislative Assembly, no less than seventy-five were won by Congress, leaving a scant fifteen seats to be distributed among independents and the various other parties. (The Communist Party of India, incidentally, won no seats at all in the Assam Legislative Assembly in 1962, making Assam one of the two states in India without CPI representation. The developing border dispute with nearby China apparently squelched the already weak following of the Communist Party there.)

As the largest single opposition block, the APHLC had the right to become the formal opposition in the Assembly, and there were speculations that they might become allied with certain independents who drew their support from the Bengali minority in Assam.[18] Apparently the APHLC leaders declined to take these opportunities. Having been elected on a platform which demanded a separate state as its major plank, they were apparently unwilling to participate in assembly affairs to the point of forming a "loyal opposition." For a time they even threatened to resign in a block from the Assembly.

Two APHLC candidates also ran for seats in the national parliament in 1962, one of them successfully. (The total Assamese delegation to the Lok Sabha, the lower and more powerful house of Parliament, is twelve.) A few other tribesmen have been elected to earlier parliaments, and others have sat as presidential nominees to represent NEFA. One Khasi lady, a member of an earlier parliament, even came to the United Nations some years ago as a member of the Indian delegation, but the number of tribespeople in the national parliament will inevitably remain miniscule.

Even in Assam the APHLC was outnumbered eleven to seventy-nine by Congress. Preoccupied with the issue of a separate hill state, the APHLC representatives do not seem to have exer-

[17] *Assam Tribune,* January 14, 1962.
[18] The *Statesman,* Calcutta, March 1, 1962.

cised even as much weight as their small numbers might have permitted with respect to other issues facing Assam. Nevertheless, if in no other way than by continual agitation, they have kept the tribes from being a forgotten corner of a large nation, and by creating live electoral issues, they have stimulated new and expanded political horizons for their people. The issues reached the top in late 1963 when APHLC leaders conferred with Nehru. He offered them some hope for a greater measure of local autonomy, though he rejected their demands for a separate hill state.[19]

Though the hill people are badly outnumbered, their representation is not negligible. It may someday be increased by representatives from NEFA, and they might receive support from the leaders of Nagaland. In a nation where everybody belongs to a minority of some sort, there is always the possibility that strategic alliances will allow the tribal votes to decide issues where other votes are divided—and enhance the power of the tribes in the process. So long as the electoral machinery continues to operate, the hill people do, at least, have an institutionalized way of airing their grievances, and they have some means to guide the decisions which affect their territories.

THE INDIRECT EFFECTS OF ECONOMIC CHANGE

Most of this paper has dealt with formal political relationships because I feel it is in these that Assam's experience has been least like the nations to the east. In conclusion, however, a word about economic prospects may not be out of place. As in the rest of India, the government has been increasingly concerned with community development projects. Government officers have encouraged improved agricultural practices, dug wells, opened schools and dispensaries, and taught elementary techniques of sanitation and public health. I am not sure that Indian agronomists know much more about the problems of swidden agriculture than do Americans. As in the nations further east, one hears occasional desperate statements about the wastefulness of swidden, but there has been virtually no official attempt to prohibit burning in the areas where that has been traditional; indeed, official policy seems to have been to try to improve swidden

[19] *Assam Tribune,* December 24, 1964.

agriculture rather than to replace it (e.g. Elwin 1960:82 ff.).

However, many of the hill tracts of Assam are relatively densely settled by comparison with other swidden regions, and population seems to be expanding as rapidly as in other parts of India. Sooner or later the limits of swidden agriculture must be reached.

Perhaps systematic farming encouraged by sophisticated experimentation and government encouragement can keep swidden production ahead of the population, though I am not at all certain. But the steady extension of roads throughout the hill areas may provide a real alternative. It may be that the economic salvation of the hills lies not in subsistence grains, the crops the government is often most concerned with, but in specialized cash crops that grow better at higher altitudes than in the lowlands. Already Khasis export great quantities of potatoes, and Garo oranges have been so successful that it has been profitable to ship them by truck out of the hills and then airfreight them to Calcutta. Many other perennial or orchard crops—areca nuts, betel leaf, tea, pineapples, cashew nuts, pepper—may ultimately make far more valuable crops than hill rice or millet. Of course, to place reliance upon cash crops requires an assured system of distribution and carries with it the danger of complete dependence upon the plains for subsistence grains, but that may be a less frightful alternative than immediate hunger. An increasing shift to perennial crops would also inevitably bring about changes in land tenure practices, and, in all likelihood, a shift in the direction of individual control of land. This could introduce an imbalance in the distribution of wealth, such as I think I was able to observe in those Garo villages where perennial crops or permanent wet-rice fields had begun to rival swiddens in importance (Burling 1963:311–312).

In spite of these dangers, I think that if I were responsible for the agricultural development of the Assam Hills, I would be tempted to encourage cash crops, particularly perennials, but I strongly suspect that the way in which such crops are going to spread most effectively is not through the exhortation of agricultural extension workers, but through the invisible pressures of the market. Hill farmers in Assam are quite astute enough to decide whether they can get more rice by growing it themselves or by growing oranges and then trading them for rice. My guess is that the extension of roads could quite rapidly tip the balance in favor of the cash crops. It may even be that the recent concern for the improvement of swidden agriculture comes at the time when swidden is becoming obsolete, not because it is inherently deleterious to the soil but because other forms of agriculture will become more profitable with the better transportation that is increasingly available.

No hill man wants to bring a halt to continuing economic development, but to become economically more integrated with other parts of the nation implies some sort of continuing political relationship. In spite of my great sympathy for the tribal minority, the Naga notion of complete independence has never seemed realistic to me. I am even doubtful whether it makes a great deal of difference whether a hill region is organized into a separate state or into a semi-autonomous part of another state. Somewhere in the political process compromises have to be made. The main features of the needed compromises seem to me to be obvious. The plains people could grant cultural independence to the hills: let them speak their own languages, eat their own food, brew their own beer, and worship as animists or as Christians, whichever they prefer. If the plains people would stop insisting that they live on a higher level of civilization than their tribal brethren, half the problem would be solved. On the other hand, the hill people must sooner or later admit their geographical proximity to the plains and agree to whatever political and economic compromises are needed to keep the country from coming apart at the seams. The problem lies in persuading people to make these compromises. I am ethnocentric enough to believe that in the long run, the slow and noisy workings of elective parliamentary politics is the best hope, and in its willingness to let people elect their own leaders, I think India deserves our profound admiration.

REFERENCES CITED

BURLING, ROBBINS
    1963   Rengsanggri: family and kinship in a Garo village. Philadelphia, University of Pennsylvania Press.

ELWIN, VERRIER
    1960 A philosophy for NEFA. Shillong, Adviser to the Governor
        of Assam, 2d revised edn.

INDIA
    1956 The Constitution of India. Delhi, Manager of Publications.

Periodicals

ASSAM TRIBUNE. Gauhati.
INDIA BRIEFING. New York, India Council of the Asia Society.
NEW YORK TIMES. New York.
THE STATESMAN. Calcutta.

PART V: LAOS

Laos: Introduction

JOEL HALPERN AND PETER KUNSTADTER

LAOS IS a land in the middle. Her heterogeneous population reflects her position on an ethnic watershed, and her history tells repeatedly of struggles to control the land which lies south of China, northeast of Burma, east of Thailand, and west of Annam. The struggle continues today, more or less openly, despite the "neutralization" of Laos following the 1962 Geneva agreements.

On the one side Thailand gives aid to her allies in the Royal Lao Government (Chalermnit 1961; Murphy 1965:122 ff.), with considerable assistance from the United States. And on the other side, beginning as early as 1951 (Burchett 1959:89–91), the Communists of North Vietnam, the Chinese, and for a time the Russians have given aid to their allies, the Pathet Lao (e.g. Le Kham 1961; Sheehan 1965; broadcast of Radio Pathet Lao, July 26, 1965, October 26, 1965; Radio Peking, December 22, 1965). The Chinese have also had a long interest in Laos. Chinese Hô (Yunnanese) invaders or raiders repeatedly sacked the north of Laos. The successors to the Nationalist Chinese are reported to have troops in the area near Luang Prabang (Radio Pathet Lao, July 26, 1965). Communist Chinese are reported to have supplied advisers to the Pathet Lao and to have sent construction crews to build a road from China to Phong Saly and to Ban Houei Sai on the border with Thailand (Sutherland 1963; Fall 1965:193; Radio Pathet Lao broadcast, August 5, 1965; *New York Times*, December 17, 1965). Fall even claims that Laos now has better road communications with China and North Vietnam than with its non-Communist neighbors (1965:193). The Chinese have also supplied economic and cultural missions in Xieng Khouang Province (report of Radio Pathet Lao, July 27, 1965).

Likewise, though they have been required by the Geneva agreements of 1962 to withdraw their troops, the Americans are involved in backing their Thai allies and in providing continued support to the Royal Lao Government in the form of economic aid and refugee aid programs (Ward's paper) which have allowed the Royal government to retain some control over the mountainous areas where the Pathet Lao have had some of their greatest military and political successes (cf. Fall 1965). Laos also figures importantly in the Vietnamese war, since the Ho Chi Minh trail from North Vietnam passes through Pathet Lao-controlled southeastern Laos, through an area populated predominantly by "Kha" tribesmen (*New York Times*, December 17, 1965, p. 2; January 9, 1966, pp. 1–3).

The present boundaries of the Kingdom of Laos are the result of the French colonial period; in particular their form was set as the result of contests between France, Britain, and Thailand for the territory which lay between Burma and the French interests on the Indochina coast, as well as conflicts over access to China.

Laos was not a unified state when France intervened in 1893. A Laotian kingdom, Lan Xang, with its seat at Luang Prabang, had once ruled over much of the lowlands of what was to become Laos, and also over much of Northern Thailand. The power of Lan Xang had long since declined, as the country was caught in a series of wars and was invaded repeatedly by Burma, Thailand and Annam. There were also wars among three principalities into which Lan Xang had split: Luang Prabang, Vientiane, and Champassak. Xieng Khouang, which was annexed by Annam in 1832 (Mathieu 1959:40; Dommen 1965:8), has had a somewhat different history.

The French were seen as protectors from the incursions of the Siamese, at least initially, when they established their Protectorate of Luang Prabang in 1893.[1] The princely family of

---

[1] The Chinese Hô had recently burned Luang Prabang, which had also been threatened by the Black Flags of the tribal Tai from northwestern Vietnam, when the French established the Protectorate. The Siamese, who had earlier promised protection, had taken hostages to Bangkok and had failed to give the Laotians relief from the raiders (Dommen 1964:9–10; a detailed account of this period is found in Pavie's journal). Thus it is understandable why the elite among the valley Lao considered themselves "Children of the French Peace." In view of the past relationships and present military realities it is not surprising that the Vietnamese on one side and the Siamese Thai on the other hold Laos in rather low esteem as an underdeveloped rural hinterland which needs assistance in throwing off the yoke of its self-appointed protectors. Examples of these attitudes are found in the writing of the North Vietnamese correspondent, Le Kham (1961:2 ff.), who speaks of the "simple" Pathet Lao in the Xieng Khouang "cow country" which lacks paved roads. The editor of the Thai Chalermnit Press in introducing a book by his Laos correspondent (1961) writes of the humble food, poor accommodations, and poor roads with which the correspondent must cope. Later in the book the correspondent goes on to describe how easily the Thai could make money in Laos. "The Thai people . . . crossed over in

Champassak, in southern Laos, was under Siamese influence at this time. These old principalities have retained political significance: Prince Boun Oum of Champassak was Prime Minister at the time of the ascendancy of the Rightist General Phoumi Nosavan between 1960 and 1962 (see Dommen 1965:29 *et seq.* for information on Boun Oum's career). In Xieng Khouang the descendant of the princely family serves as governor under the Royal Lao Government. Evidently he still retains some thoughts of autonomy, and his relations to tribal minorities (specifically Meo) reflect this position (see Barney's paper).

Nominal independence from France was regained after the Second World War, and the conditions of foreign intervention were set at the Geneva Convention which ended the French-Indochina War in 1954, and in the Geneva Agreements of 1962.

The problems of building a modern nation in Laos are complicated not only historically and politically, as already indicated, but also by features of economy, geography, and demography. Laos is landlocked. Her route to the sea via the Mekong River must pass through both Cambodia and South Vietnam, and the way is blocked by the Khone Falls on the border with Cambodia. Goods shipped through Thailand, by rail from the port of Bangkok, must be ferried across the river, since no bridges cross the Mekong into Laos. All other routes to the south are overland across rough country and poor roads. Thus Laos is entirely dependent upon her neighbors for contact with the outside world.

Since Laos has no major industries, she is dependent on foreign sources for almost all manufactured goods, and depends on foreign aid for most of the money with which to purchase them. Laos is even dependent on Thailand for much of the food to supply her capital, Vientiane, which is the largest town in the country. This is not to say that Laos has no potential for economic growth. With proper development of transportation, for example, some areas could become rice exporters, and forests could be exploited. (The prospect of a dam to be constructed

---

big numbers . . . to Vientiane . . . where they found no competition since the Lao were not commercial-minded and Laos still lacked technical men. It was easy therefore for Thai nationals to come and earn a much higher income in Laos . . . . The Lao did not even know how to grow rice and vegetables or raise stock properly . . ." (Chalermnit 1961:71).

near Vientiane, which would supply hydroelectric power under the Mekong River Development Scheme holds promise for Vientiane and other areas of Laos.)

Added to these problems is a great ethnic diversity. The ethnic Lao may well be a minority in their own country, and most of the major ethnic groups, including the Lao themselves, are but parts of much larger populations found across the borders in Thailand, China, and Vietnam.

Although no good census materials are available (see population table below, and Halpern 1961A; 1964B, table 9), about half the population of Laos can be considered "minority" or "tribal." The Lao officials like to speak of four different groups, the Lao, the tribal Tai, the Lao Theng, and the Lao Xung.[2]

The Lao are the politically dominant group, and are found primarily in the valley of the Mekong and its major tributaries, and in Northeastern Thailand. Most Lao are subsistence growers of wet rice. They are Buddhists, and, though princely families exist, the rural villages do not contain hereditary classes. Their social structure is generally bilateral, and thus they characteristically have no widespread lineages nor clans, nor any large-scale social organizations based on kinship.

The tribal Tai, including the Neua, Lue, Red, Black, and Phu Tai are generally found in the higher valleys, and also in adjacent parts of northwestern Vietnam, southwestern China, and Northern Thailand. The Black Tai are generally considered to be "typical" in that they have preserved much of what was apparently the traditional Tai way of life prior to the expansion of the Tai-speaking peoples in Indochina. They live in narrow upland valleys, where they cultivate rice, making use of irrigation and terraces. They also do some swidden farming on mountainsides, and grow some opium as a cash crop. In Laos, as in northern Vietnam (see McAlister's paper), the Black Tai have organized themselves into *muongs* or principalities. These principalities are generally limited to a single valley, and though some of the Tai groups in Laos were nominally involved in the Sip Song Chao

---

[2] As used in this paper, the term Lao refers to the valley Lao, who are also called Lao Lum. The tribal Tai are sometimes called the Lao Tai. The Lao Theng (or Thenh, or Theung), or "mountainside people," are sometimes referred to by the pejorative term "Kha," meaning "slave." Lao Xung (or Sung), the "mountaintop people," include the Meo and Yao (or Man).

Tai (Twelve Tai Principalities) of northwestern Vietnam, this loose federation had little effect on the groups in Laos.

The Black Tai social system has three hereditary classes. The princely class is formed of the members of two large families, the Lo and the Cam, who apparently retain title to all the irrigated land within the muong. Use-rights to swiddens are owned by the people who clear the land. The princely families have ritual functions at the commencement of the planting season, and in worshiping the chief god of the muong. Members of the Luong and Ka families comprise the priestly class, which enjoys high prestige. Priests, of whom there are three ranks, are in charge of other communal rites and individual ceremonies. The other Black Tai families form the commoner class, from which are drawn the farmers, artisans, and soldiers. Commoners who use irrigated land must pay a tax, in labor, to village or muong officials. Most of the Black Tai population live in small villages which are under the control of the *chao muong*, or prince.

The Black Tai are largely self-sufficient, making for themselves most of what they consume. There are Chinese shops in market towns and itinerant Chinese merchants who visit the villages, but the Black Tai have had little cash to spend on manufactured goods.

Hickey (1958) argues that the location of the Black Tai in upland valleys, away from the Vietnamese and lowland Lao, has allowed them to preserve much of their traditional Tai culture and to develop the fragmented principalities which are their characteristic socio-political structure (1958:206, 210). The isolation of the Black Tai from the centers of civilization should not be overemphasized; in spite of the fact that they are not Buddhist, they do have their own Indian-derived script (see Hickey 1958, Izikowitz 1962 for further information on the Black Tai).

Although in many respects the Black Tai may be typical of the tribal Tai, there are a number of important exceptions. The Lue, for example, are Buddhists in addition to worshiping a number of typical Tai spirits (see Moerman's paper and the summary of Lue culture in LeBar *et al.* 1964:206–213). The Lue in Laos are descendants of what was once a fairly highly organized Chinese-influenced state in the Sip Song Pan Na of southwestern Yunnan, and this ancient political structure still has relevance for relations between the Lue and other groups (see Moerman 1965). Though most of the tribal Tai are predominantly subsistence agriculturalists, some have specialized in other occupations. Whole villages of Tai P'ouen (Phuan) in the Tran Ninh Plateau (Xieng Khouang Province) have specialized in blacksmithing. Their villages are located on main trade routes, and they travel widely to sell their wares (Izikowitz 1962:83).

The Lao Theng label is applied to a diverse group of people who are descendants of the indigenous proto-Indochinese. They are Mon-Khmer speakers and include the Khmuʔ, Tʔin, Lamet, and Loven. The majority of them are animists, and they are predominantly dependent on swidden rice agriculture, but some practice irrigated agriculture (e.g. Smalley 1961:8). Though ordinarily they are not organized politically above the village level, some groups, especially in the south, were able to mount large-scale resistance against the French colonial forces.

The Lao Xung include the Meo and Yao. They are generally mountaintop dwellers, dependent on swidden rice agriculture for subsistence, and on opium for cash income, and livestock production for sale as well as for prestige and sacrifice. They are recent migrants from the north. The Meo who have remained in China have evidently become quite acculturated to Han Chinese culture (see Ruey 1960 for a brief account of the Meo in China and Ruey 1962 for a discussion of their southward migration). Those who have moved to Southeast Asia reflect Chinese influence in many aspects of their culture. They may even hire Chinese tutors to live in their villages. The patrilineal social system of the Meo, with its supra-village proliferation, is described in Barney's paper, and the somewhat similar system of the Yao (Iu Mien) is described by Kandre in the Thailand section of the book (see also Iwata 1960).

The lines between the cultures of the various groups are not always sharply drawn. The Lao Theng have frequently "become Lao" in different degrees. For example, Izikowitz (1951:24) refers to people who are "identical with the Khmuʔ [but] have adopted Buddhism," and Smalley (1961:4,8) refers to Khmuʔ who have become Buddhists and adopted the Lao language. Smalley also believes that thousands of fully assimilated Lao are of Khmuˀ descent. The Laotian social system is not closed, and official policy encourages all inhabitants to consider themselves to be Laotian. As Barney suggests, many Meo seem to prefer to maintain their distinct identity, though some individual Meo have also become culturally Lao. Though Laos does not have a unified and cohesive national society, the ethnic groups are by no means independent entities. Historically, they have been related economically and politically with lowland markets and political-administrative systems, and are bound by ritual ties to the lowlands; and they are increasingly involved in the international and internal struggles within Laos.

The Lao population is not evenly distributed throughout the country. The elite Lao are concentrated in the civil capital (Vientiane), in the royal capital (Luang Prabang), and in a few old towns along the Mekong. In addition to the ubiquitous urban Chinese shopkeepers (see Halpern 1961), there are many Siamese Thai or Vietnamese merchants and businessmen. The Siamese Thai are relative newcomers in this role and have taken advantage of the departure of some of the Vietnamese since 1954, plus the intensification of trade which has come with increased foreign aid (see Chalermnit 1961:55). The fact that the urban population is small indicates the limited economic development of Laos; the fact that the urban population is largely non-Lao is a further indication that the fate of the Lao is not completely in their own hands (see Halpern 1964B:15–19 for a discussion of urban patterns).

There is a great gap in Laos between the few wealthy urbanized French-educated elite and the mass of the people who are subsistence agriculturalists (see Halpern 1964B: Table 29 for an exposition of rural-urban differences). The separation is reinforced by poor communication systems, lack of education in rural areas,[3] and lack of economic development.[4] Buddhism and the

[3] Until recently secular public and private school education above the primary level has been confined to urban areas, and has been available to only a small portion of the population. U.S. aid programs have brought schools to some rural, tribal, and refugee areas. See Halpern (1964A:Table 8) for an indication of the geographic limitations of the school system. See Schanche (1962) for a popular account of one of the American aid programs to tribal schools. See Barney's paper for a discussion of Meo schools. The Communists have also been active in promoting education in their "liberated" areas, and have paid special attention to Meo schools and the schooling of other minorities. A recent

symbolic presence of royalty have helped give a feeling of nation-hood to the Laotians,[5] but obviously the country is not a well-integrated unit. Despite a degree of ritual interaction with the lowland Lao, common religion does not serve as a bond for the tribal people, most of whom are animists (see Barney's paper for the role of religion as a symbol of ethnic difference). The Luang Prabang princes fight among themselves, and the ruling family of Champassak contests with them for the allegiance of at least the southern Laotians.

The distribution of ethnic groups of Laos does not correspond to international boundaries. The Laos-Thailand border has been subject to change for centuries, reflecting the relative strengths of the Laotian and Thai princes. The Lao and Northeastern Thai dialects are indistinguishable across the border (in fact there are nine times as many Lao speakers in Thailand as there are in Laos); trade and kinship connections are maintained except as internal and international conditions prohibit them (see Chalermnit 1961:44–45). Indeed, in the last three or four genera-tions people have found themselves living in Laos or Thailand depending on international events of no immediate concern to themselves (i.e., modifications of the border as a result of agree-ments between the British and French in the 1880's, the subse-quent readjustment with the aid of the Japanese in World War II, and a return to the earlier border at the end of the war). As is demonstrated elsewhere in this volume (Kandre's paper), until recently the borders have not proved any barrier to the

---

North Vietnamese publication claims that in 1964 there were 36,200 children enrolled in schools in "liberated areas," with an additional 250 in secondary schools. Presumably most of these are tribal people. Secular schools have been scarce in this area, and these are impressive figures even if exaggerated (Fall 1965:183; *Vietnam Courier* 37:6, October 7, 1965).

[4] The elite of Laos is by no means a completely closed kinship group, but kinship connections may be used to cement other social ties. Position in the elite may be achieved with money, education, and good fortune or power (on structure of the elite see Halpern 1964A:5–7, 28 ff.). Social mobility through the military has become increasingly important. Kong Le, a "Kha" by birth, achieved his meteoric rise through the army. At first he was trained by the French and fought against the Viet Minh. Later he received training from the Americans. He reinforced his social position in 1959 by his third marriage, to the niece of socially prominent Laotian General Ouan Ratikon. Kong Le's base of influence is in the army, not particularly among the southern tribal people (see Dommen 1964:143 ff. for the story of Kong Le's career).

[5] Even the Pathet Lao continue to appeal to the King as a symbol of national unity (e.g. broadcast of Radio Hanoi reporting Pathet Lao manifesto, October 28, 1965).

movement of tribal and minority people (such as Yao, Meo, Khmuʔ, and various Tai groups), and they too maintain kinship and other connections across the boundaries. The same situation has existed along the Chinese and Vietnamese borders, which everywhere cut across ethnic distributions. This is significant when one considers North Vietnamese presence in Laos and influence among the Pathet Lao. Historically, there appears to have been a consistent trend of migration by both Lao and tribal groups southward, particularly to the southeast, as a result of recurrent wars as well as population pressures emanating from Yunnan. The Yao and Meo provide perhaps the most dramatic example of this movement, a trend that continues with current warfare.

The connection between tribe and nation in Laos has varied considerably between different tribes. The prior ownership of the land by the "Kha" tribes is still clearly recognized and symbolized in royal ceremonies, as is the story of the subjection of these autochthons by the Lao (Smalley 1961:6; Archaimbault 1964). "Kha" means "slave" in the Lao language, and "Kha" people, such as the Khmuʔ, have been liable for *corvée* labor. But other than ritual recognition there is little or no participation by the unassimilated "Kha" in the Royal Lao Government above the level of district chief (*tasseng*), the next to lowest level of rural administration. By contrast, the Meo of Xieng Khouang have had representatives and even ministers in the Royal government (Barney's paper).

The French did not go out of their way to develop or reinforce tribal units by setting up separate administrative devices for them as they did in the Vietnamese Central Plateau (where the French attempted direct administration of the tribal people) or in Tonkin (where they encountered strongly organized Tai minorities and preserved traditional political appearances while trying to manipulate elected or appointed leaders). Because of their opium production, tribesmen (in distinction to the Lao lowlanders) were offered some concessions—but these were in the form of relief from taxes, not recognition of tribal sovereignty.[6]

---

[6] See Halpern (1964B:115–118) regarding current features of the opium trade and Reinach (1901:310) for an example of early French interests in expanding opium production. See Barney's paper regarding influence of opium on Meo-Lao relations in Xieng Khouang Province.

The reactions of various groups to the problems of assimilation have often been quite different. Typically the Khmu? have been rather passive and submissive, whereas the Meo have been aggressive in their relations with the Lao. Differences in Khmu? and Meo reactions are reflected in their recent messianic cults, which are supposed to lead them to a better life. Among the Khmu? the messiah is depicted as an omnipotent king for whom they should show respect by stopping all work and consuming all their resources in feasts. The messiah will then appear among them, or they will visit him in his cave, and he will make available to them all the material trappings of Western civilization which are presently denied them. By contrast, the Meo messianic myth foresees Jesus Christ as the messiah, appearing among them in a jeep, giving them arms and summoning them to action. According to this myth, the Meo will depose the local Lao officials, and then will take over the national capital (Halpern 1960:63; see also Smalley 1965).[7]

We can also compare Khmu? and Meo economic and political integration. The Khmu? apparently have had no political participation in the Lao administrative system above the level of the *tasseng*. Though the Khmu? occasionally produce agricultural surpluses for sale, they are primarily subsistence farmers. Their economic relations with the Lao are as subjects for *corvée* labor, sometimes as hired agricultural workers or servants, and as participants in markets for basic commodities and tools (Izikowitz 1951; Smalley 1961). Apparently some of their economic relations have been mediated through the institution of the *lam*, a Lao middleman (Halpern 1964B:94–95). By contrast, the Meo are producers of an important cash crop, opium, and are relatively prosperous. One may guess that the original basis of the special Meo relationship with the Lao Governor of Xieng Khouang may have been control of opium production and trade, since Xieng Khouang was the only province in Laos where production of opium was legalized by the French.

The minority and tribal groups do not appear to be unified political entities in Laos, as some groups in Burma and Annam

[7] The Meo messianic myth may also be a reflection of their instrumental attitude toward the Christian religion and their identification of Christianity with modern Western technology and power.

have been. There is evidently some supra-village organization among some of the groups such as the Meo and Yao (see Barney's and Kandre's papers), who are relative newcomers to Laos, but nothing on the level of the Shan principalities seems to have existed to rival even the limited power of all the Lao princes. The minority Tai in Laos seem not to have been as well organized as were the Sip Song Chao Tai of northern Vietnam (see McAlister's paper and Hickey 1958). Nonetheless, some of the tribal peoples were able to resist French control fiercely during the colonial period (see Halpern 1964:80 ff.). The tribal peoples of Laos historically appear to have been involved in a shifting series of extra-village alliances dependent in large measure on the waxing and waning of local petty states. It is only in this century that unitary state control has begun to be imposed. (The same type of situation has existed in ethnically similar Northern Thailand, where only in the last fifty years has the Bangkok-based Thai government attempted to regulate comprehensively the lives of the tribal peoples.) The preceding period was hardly one of autonomy of individual tribal units, however; such interpretations are founded on lack of historical knowledge, which was admittedly difficult to obtain when documents were lacking, fragmentary, or hard to come by (for historical data on a specific group see e.g. Kunstadter 1965:1-7).

Tribesmen are considered to be citizens of Laos, but most of them have no special representation in the government. A few Meo (for example, Touby Lyfong and General Vang Pao) have reached high office under the Royal Lao Government, but it is unclear whether they have done so as individuals or because they were selected as representatives of minority interests (see Barney's paper). It is clear, however, that the Royal Lao Government has not attempted to organize minority interests; it appears that they do not want the minorities to become organized as such. Tribesmen were not systematically recruited into the Royal Lao Army until 1961, when United States Army Special Forces detachments arrived in Laos; simultaneously the United States was supporting a national army composed largely of ethnic Lao (Dommen 1964:272). Likewise, in the past the government has ruled against the publication of tribal languages, apparently out of fear that this would reduce the possibility of assimilation of tribal populations. Recently, however, a Meo language newspaper has been published (see Barney's paper), and broadcasts are being made in Meo (see Osborn's paper).

Fall (1965:173 ff.) has pointed out that the split between the Pathet Lao and the Rightists follows lines of very old ethnically based antagonisms. Most of the Pathet Lao-controlled areas (generally areas away from the Mekong Valley) have traditionally been inhabited by minority Tai and tribal peoples (Fall 1965:191). The Pathet Lao control Phong Saly and Sam Neua Provinces. In part this is due to geography—these provinces adjoin China and North Vietnam. In part the Pathet Lao control is due to politics—they were forced to withdraw from other provinces but were allowed to stay in Phong Saly and Sam Neua as a result of the 1954 Geneva Accords (Fall 1965:179–180). But their strength also lies in the ethnic composition of the two provinces—about two-thirds of the population of Sam Neua is minority Tai, and over one-half of the population of Phong Saly is "Kha" (see Halpern 1964B:11, and sources listed for Table 9). In fact, the Lao appear to be in the majority only in Vientiane, Khammouane, Savannakhet, and Champassak provinces (*ibid.*).[8] It is in the areas where the ethnic Lao are in the minority that the Pathet Lao have been most successful in creating a Communist administrative structure parallel to that of the Royal Lao Government; the Pathet Lao claimed in 1965 to control two-thirds of the territory of Laos and nearly half the population (Fall 1965:183).

As in North Vietnam (see McAlister's paper), the Communists have generally been quite successful in their appeals to the minority and tribal peoples, who have been mobilized in aiding the revolutionary struggle. Where the Pathet Lao have failed to gain the support of tribal people (e.g. among the followers of Touby Lyfong), it apparently has been due to preexisting alliances and antagonisms among the Meo themselves (see Barney's paper).

By contrast with the Royal Lao Government, the Pathet Lao, from the time of their founding, consciously incorporated minor-

[8] Vientiane Province has been divided into Vientiane and Borikhane provinces, and Champassak into Champassak, Sedone, and Sithdone provinces since these statistics were compiled.

ity interests, and have continued to emphasize appeals to ethnic groups.[9] Whereas the Royal Lao Government officially does not recognize tribal languages, the Pathet Lao have developed a Meo script presumably closely related to that developed for the Meo in adjacent areas of North Vietnam (*Vietnam Courier* 37:6, October 7, 1965). The Pathet Lao have sent specialists from the Meo and other tribal groups to school in North Vietnam, Peking, and Moscow, as well as to their own schools in the Communist-controlled provinces of Laos (Fall 1965:183).

Faydang, a Meo leader who was one of the original founders of the Pathet Lao movement along with Prince Souvannavong, seems to have been used precisely for the purpose of winning Meo support and organizing Meo military units (Burchett 1959:216 ff.).[10] Although the differences between Faydang's and Touby's followers are often referred to in terms of ideology and morality (Burchett describes Faydang's burning commitment to the Communist cause; Le Kham [1961] characterizes Touby's

---

[9] The following is a section of the Action Program adopted at the Second National Congress of the Neo Lao Hak Sat (the political branch of the Pathet Lao) in Sam Neua Province, April 6–11, 1964, as reported by the Vietnam News Agency, Hanoi, April 13, 1964 (cited in Dommen 1964:319):

1. To unite all the people, unite various nationalities (tribal groups), strata, religious communities, political parties, patriotic personalities, and intellectuals, including individuals in the Royal Family and Buddhist monks and nuns who favor peace and neutrality, regardless of their political tendencies, beliefs and religion . . . .

The closest analogous appeal of the Royal government seems to be the following statement by Prime Minister Prince Souvanna Phouma on January 1, 1965, published in a news release of the Royal Embassy of Laos, Washington, February 8, 1965:

We must remember also that a large segment of our rural population lacks many commodities, relief, social security services, that many who live in towns find quite natural to receive from the State. Think of our countrymen in the mountains, the countryside and the plateaus of the interior, who enjoy none of these benefits. We may guess what kind of hostile propaganda can be made of this. It certainly has other objectives, but it vividly exposes all these inequalities . . . we should strive to reduce or eliminate them.

[10] Other tribesmen have also been recruited in large numbers by the Pathet Lao (Fall 1965:187). Pathet Lao Radio (July 26, 1965) acknowledges the effectiveness of Meo fighting on the side of the Royal Lao Government: ". . . Meo bandits are under the direct command of U.S. officers who have trained them with weapons. The U.S. imperialists have used these Meo bandits to carry out destructive acts against the Laotian nation . . . . The U.S. imperialists are now planning to set up a Meo force with a view to partitioning the country and separating the Meo people, who have lived in Laos for generations, from the Laotian people."

followers as "pirates"), Barney informs us that the split between Faydang and Touby is of long standing. Touby's clan had traditionally been allied with the princely family of Xieng Khouang, and Faydang's clan (which is generally located further to the north) had been left out of this arrangement.

Sithone Komadam is another tribal leader in the Pathet Lao, whose influence is largely with the "Kha" peoples in southern Laos. He is the son of a "Kha" chief who led a revolt against the French in the early 1900's. Like Faydang, he is a vice-chairman of the Central Committee of the Neo Lao Hak Sat (see Burchett 1959:208 ff.). It is interesting to note that Prince Boun Oum of Champassak, the Rightist leader, allegedly aided the French in suppressing the rebellion of Sithone's father (Fall 1965:174).

Because most of the recent fighting in Laos has occurred in the hill areas, the minority and tribal people who live there have been deeply affected. Some of the problems of the tribal people in the northern part of Laos are dealt with in the papers that follow. The people in the southeastern part of Laos through which supplies pass from North into South Vietnam must also have been affected. One can easily imagine the massive recruitment of local (tribal) labor required by the Ho Chi Minh Trail. Long-term effects of the building of roads in tribal areas will almost certainly reorient trade patterns, make government services more accessible and control more effective, and will doubtless involve the permanent relocation of many tribal villages.[11] Such effects have already been noted in past years along the Vientiane-Luang Prabang Road. Roads will come to serve the same needs as the Mekong and its tributaries have done for the ethnic Lao. These effects will surely endure after peace has returned.

The magnitude of the dislocation of people as a result of the warfare in Laos can be judged from recent estimates that "about 250,000 people, mostly Meo and Yao hill tribesmen, are partially or fully supported by U.S. aid" (U.S. Senate, Committee on the Judiciary 1965:16, statement of R. M. Poats, Assistant Administrator for the Far East, Agency for International Development).

[11] Japanese films shown recently on American television depict classrooms and workshops located in caves in southeastern Laos, where tribal people are trained and work. This is cited as the Pathet Lao response to American bombings.

This total amounts to an increase of about 110,000 refugees since the Geneva agreements were signed in 1962 (*ibid.* pp. 6–7, statement of Leonard Unger, Deputy Assistant Secretary for Far Eastern Affairs), and represents at least 10 percent of the total population of Laos. Some aspects of the massive U.S. assistance programs for these refugees are discussed by Osborn and Ward, whose estimates of the number of refugees are considerably lower than those cited above.

Paradoxically, it may be in Laos, the least developed of Southeast Asian countries, where the problems of tribal-minority-lowland relations will have to be worked out most rapidly. In the past, minority and tribal populations could solve the problems of pressure from lowland forces simply by fleeing higher into the mountains or further into the jungle. But modern military technology means that today there is nowhere to hide, and recent political developments mean that wherever they go the tribesmen and minorities will be the target for political influence from one or the other side of the Laotian struggle. Thus the tribal and minority people will have to develop some sort of lasting adjustment to more continuous contact with the lowlanders of Laos and their outside allies.

Simultaneously, the lowlanders will have to take a more realistic approach than simply denying the existence of minority problems or conceiving of a slowly and informally evolving Laotianization through adoption of Buddhism and increased education. The refugee relief programs are at best a temporary solution to the problems of the displaced minority and tribal populations.

Though Osborn and Ward speak optimistically about the accomplishments of the refugee relief programs, these programs are obviously dependent on foreign aid not only for material and financial support, but also for the formation of their underlying policies. Similarly the Pathet Lao have called for outside help: "We hail and stand ready to receive specialists and technicians of all countries who, for the sake of justice and peace, would volunteer to help us build and develop our economy and culture in the liberated areas" (Pathet Lao Radio, October 28, 1965). Meanwhile they boast of their new irrigation projects and schools, and denounce United States-supported programs of the Royal Lao Government as ruses to fool the people.

The recognition now being given to tribal and minority peoples in these programs—for the first time many are receiving government-sponsored health, education, and welfare services—the incorporation of some of these people into military and political organizations, and the deliberate cultivation of minorities by the Pathet Lao and North Vietnamese means that formal relations between central government and minorities can never again be simply ignored. The tribes and minorities are increasingly literate, increasingly aware of the outside world, and (with modern military training and weapons) increasingly able to exert real influence.[12] Laotian attitudes and policies toward tribesmen do seem to be changing, at least with respect to the Meo. Touby Lyfong and General Vang Pao hold important positions; in spite of a law against the printing of tribal languages, a Meo newspaper is being distributed, and broadcasts are being made in tribal languages over government radios.

We cannot stress too strongly that as far back as records exist the tribal people of Laos have never lived in isolated static communities. Villages moved every few decades, and longer-term stability was the exception. But, although they were not isolated in the past, the contacts were largely limited to the borders of the tribal communities. Much of the trade took place outside of the community, and was either mediated through an agent such as the *lam* (in the case of the Khmu?) or was carried out by Chinese traders who brought their goods to the mountain villages. Tribesmen such as the Khmu? or Lamet worked for wages among the lowland Lao, or even crossed into Thailand for work—the locus of this work was outside the tribal communities, and the wages were used for traditional purchases of prestige goods or tools which did not disrupt tribal community patterns. Ritually the Khmu? played an important part in lowland Lao state cere-

---

[12] Despite these changes Barney reports that the traditional Meo social structure has survived the rigors of continuous warfare and flourishes even in the refugee camps. This may well mean that the Meo will emerge with an even stronger sense of identity and better means for inter-village social organization than they had before the war. For hundreds of years, starting in China, the Meo have had to cope with centralized governments. Apparently they gave up lowland plow agriculture as they fled Chinese persecution. In the mountainous areas of northern Indochina they have adapted themselves to contact with central governments by living in the mountains and relying on a valuable cash crop, opium, to give them a high standard of living. Now that some of them have been forced by the war into the lowlands, will they be willing to return to the mountains when the war is over?

monies, but again this was outside of the sphere of Khmu? communal religion. If missionaries came to the tribes, they were as representatives of completely alien (Western) societies. Politically the village headmen of the Yao and Meo functioned as intermediaries between the lowland government and the villagers, most of whom had little or no direct contact with the government. Such assimilation as took place (and much did take place both on an individual and a community level) was not the result of deliberate policy on the part of the lowlanders.

The situation has changed radically since the Second World War. Tribal communities are much more directly penetrated by lowlanders, and tribesmen have begun to play a more direct role in lowland society. The tribesmen have been deeply involved in the civil wars of Laos. Their economies, especially in the refugee areas, have been extensively modified—many have become completely dependent on airlifts for subsistence. Politically they have become involved at the top levels of the Pathet Lao, and at least a few Meo have reached high positions in the Royal Lao Government. Even small rural communities have become the particular targets for direct attempts at political influence by both sides.

Apparently the Meo will play a key role in any future developments. It seems to have been recognized by all sides that the Meo are the tribal people most suitable for organization into military and political units, and they have received aid and attention to a much greater extent than have other minority and tribal peoples. In this respect the Pathet Lao have a built-in advantage in their close alliance with North Vietnam, where there are some 220,000 Meo, several times the number in Laos, concentrated in the formally recognized Meo districts of Thua-Chua and Mu Cang Chai in the Tay Bac Autonomous Zone which borders on the Pathet Lao-controlled parts of Laos (Fall 1963:150–151).

The question remains how much either the Royal Lao Government or the Pathet Lao will be willing to accommodate the tribes and minorities in attempting to build national unity when the immediate political-military problems are resolved and massive foreign aid is withdrawn.

If the two opposing governments continue to control their respective territories, contrasting social systems may develop, as has happened for example in North and South Korea or North and South Vietnam. One major contrast which might be expected to develop would be in local governmental institutions, which would deeply affect tribal and minority peoples. If, after the present struggle, one side attains a monopoly of power in Laos, that side will have secured for itself the major rights to grapple with the problems of state formation. In this they will be influenced in large measure by the evolving patterns of their patrons. If Laos manages to avoid incorporation by North Vietnam and/or Thailand, neither the pattern of autonomous zones of the former, nor the basically traditional structures of the latter will suffice as a model for national unity in Laos. This is true because of the preponderance in the population of Laos of ethnic groups without traditions of centralized administration. Looking beyond the contemporary deep involvement in Southeast Asia of Western powers (now mainly the United States), hopefully, some lasting form of regional integration may develop, perhaps based on the most positive program in the area to date, the Lower Mekong development scheme (Schaaf and Fifield 1963).

BIBLIOGRAPHY

There is an extensive body of French literature on the peoples of Indochina, but much of it is devoted to language and religion. Information on economy, social, and political structure of tribal and minority groups in Laos gathered by professional social scientists is scarce. Unfortunately, no economic study exists for the hill areas comparable to that of Gaudillot and Condominas (1959). Izikowitz' landmark monograph on the Lamet (1951) shows what an anthropologist can do when he considers problems of interrelations between tribe and lowland, rather than thinking of tribes as isolates. The lack of publications specifically on Laos is partially compensated for by studies of overlapping populations in neighboring countries (e.g., Abadie 1924, Bernatzik 1946).

Works of special relevance to the subjects covered in this book are listed below.

ABADIE, MAURICE
    1924   Les races du Haut-Tonkin de Phong-Tho à Lang Son. Paris,
                Société d'Editions Géographiques, Maritimes et Coloniales.
ARCHAIMBAULT, CHARLES
    1964   Religious structures in Laos. Journal of the Siam Society
                52(1):57–74. Gives information on the ritual relations between
                "Kha" groups and the Royal government.

AYMÉ, G.
1931   Monographie du Vᵉ Territoire Militaire. Paris, Exposition Coloniale Internationale.

BARNEY, GEORGE LINWOOD
1957   The Meo: an incipient church. Practical Anthropology 4.

BERNATZIK, HUGO ADOLF
1947   Akha und Meau: Probleme der angewanten Völkerkunde in Hinterindien. Innsbruck, Wagnerische Universitäts Buchdruckerei.

BOCK, CARL
1884   Temples and elephants. London.

BURCHETT, W. G.
1959   Mekong upstream: a visit to Laos and Cambodia. Berlin, Seven Seas Publishers. (Presents the Communist view of the Laotian situation with background information on the role of tribal people in the Pathet Lao.)

CHALERMNIT PRESS CORRESPONDENT
1961   Battle of Vientiane 1960 (with historical background leading to battle). Bangkok, Chalermnit Press.

COLONNA, M.
1938   Monographie de la province de Saravane. Bulletin des Amis du Laos, 2.

DOMMEN, ARTHUR J.
1965   Conflict in Laos: the politics of neutralization. New York, Praeger. (A synoptic account of the political events in Laos since the Second World War, with an extensive bibliography.)

FALL, BERNARD
1963   The two Viet-Nams: a political and military analysis. London and Dunmow, Pall Mall Press.
1965   The Pathet Lao: a "liberation party." In The Communist revolution in Asia: Tactics, goals, and achievements, Robert A. Scalapino, ed. Englewood Cliffs, N.J., Prentice-Hall, Inc.

FRAISSE, ANDRE
1951   Les villages du plateau de Bolovens. Bulletin de la Société des Etudes Indochinoises.

GAUDILLOT, CLAUDE and GEORGES CONDOMINAS
1959   La Plaine de Vientiane: rapport d'étude, Tomes I–III, Royaume du Laos, Commissariat au Plan, Octobre 1959. Paris, Bureau pour le Dévelopement de la Production Agricole.

HALPERN, BARBARA and JOEL M. HALPERN
1964   Laos and America—a retrospective view. South Atlantic Quarterly LXIII(2):175–187.

HALPERN, JOEL M.
1960   Laos and her tribal problems. Michigan Alumnus Quarterly Review, 67:59–67.

1961A   Population statistics and associated data. Laos Project Paper No. 3. Los Angeles, University of California, mimeographed.

1961B   The role of the Chinese in Lao society. Journal of the Siam Society 49(1):21–46.

1964A   Government, politics, and social structure in Laos: a study of tradition and innovation. New Haven, Yale University, Southeast Asia Studies. Monograph Series 4.

1964B   Economy and society of Laos: a brief survey. New Haven, Yale University, Southeast Asia Studies. Monograph Series 5. (These two monographs contain much basic data, the second includes an extensive general bibliography.)

1965   Laos, future prospects and their limitations. Asian Survey VI(1):59–65.

HICKEY, GERALD C.

1958   Social systems of northern Vietnam. Chicago, University of Chicago, Department of Anthropology, Ph.D. dissertation. (Contains a description of several northern Vietnam ethnic groups and includes material on the Black Tai of Nam Tha, Laos.)

IWATA, KEIJI

1959   Ethnic groups in the valley of the Nam Song and Nam Lik: their geographic distribution and some aspects of social change. Japanese Journal of Ethnology. Also published in English, in mimeographed form as Laos Project Paper No. 15, Joel M. Halpern, ed. Los Angeles, University of California, 1961.

1960   Kokubu Laos no Shosu Minzoku. Shillin, 1. Also published in English, in mimeographed form as Minority groups in northern Laos, especially the Yao, Laos Project Paper No. 16, Joel M. ed. Los Angeles, University of California, 1961.

IZIKOWITZ, KARL GUSTAV

1951   Lamet: hill peasants in French Indochina. Göteborg, Etnografiska Museet, Etnologiska Studier 17. (The best general ethnography on a Laotian tribal group, giving an extensive account of the relationship between the Lamet hill people and the lowland people of Laos and Thailand.)

1962   Notes about the Tai. The Museum of Far Eastern Antiquities [Stockholm], Bulletin 34:73–91.

KAUFMAN, HOWARD K.

1963   Nationalism and problems of refugee and ethnic minority resettlement. In Proceedings of the Ninth Pacific Science Congress, 1957, 3:170–174.

KENE, THAO

1958   Bibliographie du Laos. Vientiane, Edition du Comité Littéraire.

KUNSTADTER, PETER

1965   The Luaʔ (Lawa) of Northern Thailand: aspects of social structure, agriculture, and religion. Princeton, N.J., Princeton University, Center of International Studies, Research Monograph 21.

LAFONT, PIERRE BERNARD
    1964   Bibliographie du Laos. Publications de l'Ecole Française
            d'Extrème Orient, Vol. 1. Paris, Ecole Française d'Extrème
            Orient. (An extensive critical bibliography, especially for
            French sources.)

LeBAR, F. M., G. C. HICKEY and J. K. MUSGRAVE
    1964   Ethnic groups of mainland Southeast Asia. New Haven, HRAF
            Press.

LeBAR, FRANK M. and ADRIENNE SUDDARD (eds.)
    1960   Laos: its people, its society, its culture. New Haven, HRAF
            Press. A general summary of social science data on Laos.

LE KHAM
    1961   From the Plaine des Jarres to Ban Ban [an article appearing
            in Van Hock (The Letters), No. 135, February 24, 1961,
            pp. 1, 6, 7, 14, and No. 136, March 3, 1961, pp. 14–18].
            Translation by U.S. Joint Publications Research Service, Wash-
            ington, D.C. JPRS: 9307.

MATHIEU, A. R.
    1959   Chronological table of the history of Laos. In Kingdom of
            Laos. France-Asie, English edition, pp. 32–49.

MOERMAN, MICHAEL
    1965   Ethnic identification in a complex civilization: who are the
            Lue? American Anthropologist 67 (5, i):1215–1230.

MURPHY, CHARLES J. V.
    1965   Thailand's fight to the finish. Fortune 72 (4):122–127; 266,
            270, 272, 274, 276 (October).

PAVIE, AUGUSTE
    1898–   Mission Pavie en Indochine. 1879–1895, 10 vols. Paris, Leroux.
    1919

REINACH, LUCIEN DE
    1901   Le Laos. Paris, A. Charles, Librairie-Editeur, 2 vols. (Trans-
            lated by the Human Relations Area Files, Indochina source
            no. 149) (A basic source for the colonial period.)

RUEY YIH-FU
    1960   The Magpie Miao of southern Szechuan. In Social structure
            in Southeast Asia, G. P. Murdock, ed. New York, Wenner-Gren
            Foundation for Anthropological Research, Viking Fund Pub-
            lications in Anthropology, 29:143–155.

    1962   The Miao: their origin and southward migration. Taipei, Inter-
            national Association of Historians of Asia. Second Biennial
            Conference Proceedings, pp. 179–190.

SAVINA, F. M.
    1930   Histoire des Miao. Hongkong, Imprimerie de la Société des
            Missions-étrangères de Paris.

SCHAAF, C. HART and RUSSELL H. FIFIELD
    1963   The Lower Mekong: challenge to cooperation in Southeast
            Asia. Princeton, N.J., Van Nostrand.

SCHANCHE, DON A.

 1962 An American hero: the exclusive story of how an American farmer has devoted his life to a one man crusade for freedom and democracy in war-torn, Communist-infiltrated Laos. Saturday Evening Post 235:15–21; 91–95 (June 2, June 9). (A journalistic account of the work of Edgar "Pop" Buell among the Meo.)

SHEEHAN, NEIL

 1965 North Vietnamese fear B-52's, a deserter reports in Saigon. New York Times, December 21, 1965.

SMALLEY, WILLIAM A.

 1956 The Gospel and the cultures of Laos. Practical Anthropology 3:47–57. Contains a description of the relationship between some tribal groups and the Lao.

 1961 Ethnographic notes on the Khmuˀ of the Northern Laos. Manuscript notes prepared for the Human Relations Area Files, December 15. (These notes are incorporated in part in Ethnic Groups of Mainland Southeast Asia, F. LeBar et al., eds., 1964.)

 1965 Ciaŋ: Khmuˀ culture hero. In Felicitation Volumes of Southeast-Asian Studies, vol. 1, pp. 41–54. Bangkok, The Siam Society.

SUTHERLAND, HENRY

 1963 Dr. Dooley's ex-pilot sees division of Laos; USC graduate student, back from 10-month visit, says nation is lost as neutral. Los Angeles Times, Sunday, May 12, Sec. B, p. 2. (Report of an interview with Ted Werner who gives an account of Chinese penetration into northern Laos.)

U. S. SENATE, COMMITTEE ON THE JUDICIARY

 1965 Refugee problems in South Vietnam and Laos, hearings before the Subcommittee to Investigate Problems Connected with Refugees and Escapees, of the Committee on the Judiciary, United States Senate, 89th Congress, First Session. Washington, D.C., U.S. Government Printing Office.

Periodicals

NEW YORK TIMES. New York.
VIETNAM COURIER. Hanoi.

TABLE 10
POPULATION AND LINGUISTIC AFFILIATION
OF ETHNIC GROUPS OF LAOS[a]

Group [Sub-groups (Synonyms in Parentheses)]	Estimated Population in Laos[b]	Location (in Order of Population Size)	Language
Laotian Tai [(Lao)]	1,000,000	Laos, Thailand	Tai: Southwestern
Khmu' [(Kha Khmu, Khamu, Mou)]	100,000	Laos, Thailand	Mon-Khmer:[c]
Meo [(Miao), Striped Meo, White Meo]	50,000[d,i]	Kweichow, Hunan, Szechwan, Kwangsi, Yunnan, North Vietnam, Laos, Thailand, South Vietnam	Miao-Yao: Miao
Chinese[e]	45,000	China, Southeast Asia	Chinese
Neua	38,500	Laos, North Vietnam	Tai: Southwestern
Loven [(Boloven)]	18,000	Laos[f]	Mon-Khmer: Central Upland
Lü [(Lue Thai)]	16,000	Yunnan, Burma, Thailand, Laos, North Vietnam	Tai: Southwestern
Red Tai [(Tai Daeng)]	15,000	North Vietnam, Laos	Tai: Southwestern
P'u Noi	10,000	Laos	Mon-Khmer? Tibeto-Burman?
Brao [(Lave, Love)]	9,000	Laos, Thailand, Cambodia	Mon-Khmer: Central Upland
Souei	8,600	Laos	Mon-Khmer: Central Upland
Black Tai [(Tai Dam, Tai Noir)]	8,500+	North Vietnam, Laos	Tai: Southwestern
T'in [(Kha Phai, Kha T'in, "Lawa")]	6,000	Thailand, Laos	Mon-Khmer: Northern Upland
Lamet	5,800	Laos	Mon-Khmer: Palaung-Wa
Yao [(called Man in Laos, Iu Mien)]	5,000	Kwangsi, Kwangtung, Hainan, North Vietnam, Laos, Thailand, South Vietnam	Miao-Yao: Yao

(continued)

TABLE 10
(continued)

Group [Sub-groups (Synonyms in Parentheses)]	Estimated Population in Laos[b]	Location (in Order of Population Size)	Language
Yuan [(Khon Myang, Northern Thai)]	5,000	Thailand, Laos	Tai: Southwestern
Oy [(Oi)]	4,500	Laos	Mon-Khmer: Central Upland
Akha [(Ikaw), Hani, Woni]	4,500	Yunnan, Burma, Thailand, Laos	Tibeto-Burman: Burmese-Lolo, Lolo group
Kasseng	4,000	Laos	Mon-Khmer: Central Upland
Nha Heun [(Hoen, Nia Hoen)]	3,000	Laos	Mon-Khmer: Central Upland
Lahu [(Mussuh)]	2,000	Yunnan, Burma, Thailand, Laos	Tibeto-Burman: Burmese-Lolo, Lolo group
Alak	1,750	Laos	Mon-Khmer: Central Upland
The	1,500	Laos	Mon-Khmer: Central Upland
Ngeh [(Nghe), Kieng]	1,000+	Laos[f]	Mon-Khmer: Central Upland (Bahnaric?)
Halang Doan [(Duan)][g]	1,000	Laos, South Vietnam	Mon-Khmer: Central Upland
Sou [(Souk)]	1,000	Laos	Mon-Khmer: Central Upland
Sapuan	900	Laos	Mon-Khmer: Central Upland
Sork	600	Laos	Mon-Khmer: Central Upland
Ataouat [(Attaouat, Katu)]	[not available]	Laos	Mon-Khmer: Katuic
Cao	[not available]	Laos[f]	Mon-Khmer: Central Upland
Cheng	[not available]	Laos	Mon-Khmer: Central Upland
Halang	[not available]	South Vietnam, Laos	Mon-Khmer: Bahnaric
Haw [(Hô, Yunnanese)]	[not available]	Yunnan, Thailand, Burma, Laos	Chinese: Yunnanese
Katang	[not available]	Laos	Mon-Khmer: Central Upland

(continued)

Group [Sub-groups (Synonyms in Parentheses)]	Estimated Population in Laos[b]	Location (in Order of Population Size)	Language
Langya [(a sub-group of Jeh, see under South Vietnam]	[not available]	South Vietnam, Laos	Mon-Khmer: Bahnaric
Monom [(Bonom, Menam)]	[not available]	South Vietnam, Laos	Mon-Khmer: Bahnaric
Noar	[not available]	Laos[f]	Mon-Khmer: Central Upland
Ngung Bo	[not available]	Laos	Mon-Khmer: Central Upland
Pacoh [(Bô River Vân Kiêu)]	[not available]	South Vietnam, Laos	Mon-Khmer: Katuic
Phuan	[not available]	Laos	Tai: Southwestern
Phuthai	[not available]	Laos, North Vietnam, Thailand	Tai: Southwestern
Sayan	[not available]	Laos[f]	Mon-Khmer: Central Upland
Saek [(Sek)]	[not available]	Laos, Thailand	Tai: Northern[h]
So	[not available]	Laos, Thailand	Mon-Khmer: Central Upland
Ta-ôih [(Kantua, Tau-Oi, Ta Hoi)]	[not available]	South Vietnam, Laos	Mon-Khmer: Katuic
Thailand Thai [(Siamese)]	[not available]	Thailand	Tai: Southwestern
Thap	[not available]	Laos	Mon-Khmer: Central Upland
Vietnamese	[not available]	South Vietnam, North Vietnam	Viet-Muong: Vietnamese
Ven [(Veh)]	[not available]	Laos	Mon-Khmer: Central Upland
Laos total (1962 estimate)[i]	1,882,000		

(continued)

[a] See notes accompanying the Burma population figures in this volume for a discussion of the problems of linguistic classification. The primary source used for location and population figures in Laos is LeBar et al. (1964), except as noted. We have used more recent sources where they contradict LeBar et al. The following figures are listed by Halpern (1964, Table 9) for Laos in 1955:

Ethnic Composition of the Population of Laos, 1955

Lao and Tai	856,000–865,000
Kha	210,000–258,000
Meo-Yao	52,300– 52,900
Vietnamese	8,000
Chinese	32,350
European	8,000
Indian and Pakistani	500
Total	1,167,150–1,223,850

TABLE 10
(continued)

Halpern bases his figures on official Laos sources. He notes that these figures do not include Phong Saly and Sam Neua provinces, that they are based on projections of available figures, and that the figure for the Kha (Lao Theng) group appears to be seriously underestimated. On the basis of comparison with earlier figures, the Lao and Tai figure appears to be an overestimate.

ᵇ Groups are listed in order of size of population. Where population of groups is unknown, the groups are listed alphabetically.

ᶜ The Khmu? have usually been classified as one of the Wa-Palaung branch of Mon-Khmer, but Smalley (in LeBar *et al.* 1964:113), who has done the most extensive work with the Khmu?, considers that their language is closer to the Mon-Khmer languages of South Vietnam.

ᵈ Estimate of Meo population from Barney, personal communication, figure for early 1950's. This figure is roughly equivalent to combined figure of 52,300–52,900 for Meo and Yao, given by Halpern (1964:Table 9).

ᵉ Figures for Chinese in Laos are from Skinner (1965).

ᶠ These groups are reported by LeBar *et al.* also to be found in South Vietnam, but are not included in Thomas' list (1965).

ᵍ From the point of view of language, Thomas (1965B) suggests combining Halang and Halang Doan.

ʰ Linguistic classification of the Saek (Sek) is from Gedney (1965), whose recent work indicates that it is definitely not a Mon-Khmer language.

ⁱ Personal communication from U. S. Agency for International Development indicates that in 1966 they use much higher figures for Meo in Laos (88,000), and for total Laos population (2,600,000).

REFERENCES CITED

BARNEY, G. L.
    1965   Personal communication.
GEDNEY, WILLIAM J.
    1965   Personal communication, September 21, 1965.
HALPERN, J. M.
    1964   Economy and society of Laos: a brief survey. New Haven, Yale University, Southeast Asia Studies. Monograph Series 5.
LEBAR, FRANK M., GERALD C. HICKEY, and JOHN K. MUSGRAVE
    1964   Ethnic groups of mainland Southeast Asia. New Haven, Human Relations Area Files Press.
SKINNER, G. WILLIAM
    1965   Personal communication.
THOMAS, DAVID
    1965   Vietnam minority languages—(July 1965 revision). Saigon, Summer Institute of Linguistics.
    1965B   Personal communications, July 21 and September 22, 1965.

CHAPTER 6

Government and the Hill Tribes of Laos

G. M. T. OSBORN

INTRODUCTION

The intention of this paper is to provide a condensed picture of the tribal peoples of Laos—of the conditions they live in today and what is being done to alleviate their hardships resulting from isolation, war, and a traditional lack of interest in their welfare and development. To give the picture its proper perspective, it should be mentioned that the writer has, to date, served twenty months in Laos as an adviser to the Royal Government on the administration of hill tribes. He has, therefore, not been specifically concerned with research and study of tribal groups, but more with their general administration and with bringing them practical help. It should not be inferred from this that the importance of research has been overlooked; on the contrary, the writer is fully aware that ideally and given normal conditions, research and study are necessary precursors to formulating administrative policy for tribal peoples and that, following this, research should continue to run parallel to development planning and its implementation. Regrettably, the situation in Laos has for many years precluded the launching of a balanced research program, and hence the information that is available from past anthropological and social studies devoted specifically to these problems is scarce.

For the purposes of this paper the writer has made the assumption that the readers have a fair understanding of the political vicissitudes of Laos over the past twenty years and have some knowledge of the current situation, which has inevitably affected the tribal peoples.

Although the contents of this paper are largely based on the writer's personal experience and observations, information from other sources has been included (e.g. statistical). In such cases checks for accuracy have been made wherever possible. The opinions expressed, except where otherwise indicated, are personal to the writer. In the text the term "tribal" refers to hill tribes as distinct from the Lao.

POPULATION, ETHNIC DISTRIBUTION, AND LANGUAGES

The population of Laos (all races) is variously estimated in the absence of any formal census at between 1.75 and 2.3 million, of which approximately half are tribal peoples. The latter live at altitudes frequently in excess of 3,000 feet, in contrast to the Lao, who are lowlanders; hence, throughout the region the settlements of hill tribes and the Lao are in general clearly separated, with the Lao inhabiting the flat alluvial land adjacent to the Mekong and its tributaries and the tribal peoples living in or above the high valleys and on the high plateau.

The ethnic distribution of the hill tribes does not break down conveniently into regions, as many of them are scattered throughout the country. An example is the "Kha" (Laotian word for "slave") group of tribes (some fifty different tribal peoples). They form about 25 percent of the total population, and although the largest concentrations are in the northwest and south, small pockets are also found in central Laos. The Meo (Miao) and Yao (Man) tribes, on the other hand, which may total as much as 100,000 or 5 percent of the population, have to date confined themselves exclusively to the portion of Laos north of Vientiane. The so-called Tai tribes comprise about 16 percent, or 320,000 people, and live in widely scattered settlements chiefly in the mountain valleys of northern Laos. The three main tribes are Tai Dam (Black Tai), Tai Daeng (Red Tai), and Tai Khao (White Tai), but there are also Tai Phuan, Tai Neua, and Phou Tai (Phuthai). (These designations are made by the Lao according to the color of traditional costumes, location, or some other characteristics, real or imagined.)

The number of distinct languages and dialects spoken in Laos would be difficult to estimate, but the major division is between those who speak Tai languages and those who speak the Mon-Khmer languages. In the former group are included the Lao and the Tai tribes, and in the latter are the so-called Kha tribes or Lao Theung. The Meo and Yao speak languages of another unrelated family. There is no lingua franca for all these groups other than Lao, which is known only to a relatively small percentage of the "Kha," Meo, and Yao tribal peoples. The Tai tribes, whose dialects may be akin to Lao, may find it easier to understand spoken Lao.

HISTORICAL AND CULTURAL BACKGROUND

The oldest groups in the area, the so-called Kha, are considered by the Lao to be the original inhabitants and owners of the land. Their primary claim to the land is symbolically recognized in ceremonies, like those held at Luang Prabang, in which the Kha are defeated in a game which represents the ancient contest between their ancestors and the Tai-speaking invaders. Other tribal groups, such as the Meo and Yao (or Man), are comparative newcomers to Laos, having arrived from the north, where the bulk of their population still remains, starting in about 1850.

Relationships between the Tribes and with the Government. The considerable differences in background of the multi-ethnic population of Laos, lack of a common culture and language, and economic inequalities inherent in the differences in habitats are not conducive to easy assimilation. For centuries the Lao have provided the governing class; and, although they have developed a degree of cultural, economic, and political unity among themselves (disregarding dynastic rivalries) they have had little interest in assimilating the non-Lao groups. Still, the tribes and minorities have not been isolated. Administrative relations with non-Lao people have been created through official recognition of local village headmen (*nai ban*) and district chiefs (*tasseng*) (see Barney's paper on political connections between Meo and Lao and Kandre's paper on connections between Yao and Lao).

There have also been extensive economic relationships between tribesmen and lowlanders. The role of the *lam* (who is an ethnic Lao middleman) developed to regulate trade between Khmu? and lowland Lao markets (Halpern 1964:94 ff.). The Meo engaged directly in the opium trade with Chinese traders and apparently also with the Lao (see Barney's paper). For years Khmu? and Lamet have worked in the Laotian lowlands and even in Thailand to earn money to buy prestige goods (drums and buffaloes) and other necessities (iron tools) (see

Izikowitz 1951). There are also ritual and symbolic interdependencies betweeen hill people and lowlanders (Archaimbault 1964). But despite these many interconnections, the ethnic groups have tended to remain distinct.

Paradoxically, there is one factor arising from the civil war which may in time lead to a gradual breaking down of these inter-group barriers—the refugee problem and its solution. For the past twenty years or more Laos has been faced with the recurring influx of refugees from within its own borders. More recently this has become seasonal, for it results from Pathet Lao encroachments during the dry season (January to May). Thus in the majority of cases the refugees are tribal people who are ill-equipped to cope with the calamity of loss of home, possessions, and means of livelihood. The hill people, of course, are primarily shifting cultivators, but in the past their moves have been planned and orderly. The dry season is the time when they prepare their fields for planting after the harvest. If they cannot prepare their fields, they cannot plant a crop for the following year. The tribal people now find they have nowhere in the jungle to which they can retreat. Their fields and their homes are always subject to destruction.

In the past the degree of help they could expect depended largely on the region they happened to be in; if it was an area where a foreign agency or mission or its equivalent was operating in conjunction with Lao authorities, they would receive all the assistance available for immediate relief and long-term resettlement. In general this still applies. The U.S. AID refugee program, without which the situation would be disastrous, now supports some 150,000 refugees throughout the country. These are people who would be unable to subsist without periodic supplies of rice, clothing, medical supplies, etc. The majority of the refugees live in isolated areas that can be supplied only by air. U.S. AID and the Royal Lao Government activities are coordinated by the Social Welfare Adviser, U.S. AID, and the Director of the Social Welfare Department, Ministry of Social Welfare.

Outside these areas the circumstances were, and still are to some extent, different. For example, where tribal refugees happen to come to the attention of the local authorites (through fear, ignorance, or pride, many tribal headmen do not take the initiative in reporting their predicament), they receive in theory an initial issue of food and welfare commodities such as rice, blankets, etc.; but after this they are left to fend for themselves. Small wonder then that one finds scattered throughout the country groups of tribal refugees who through Pathet Lao pressure have at some stage been forced to leave their normal habitat and seek refuge in or near the main centers of population. The more developed and industrious tribes endeavor to adapt themselves to their new environment. A few succeed, whereas others who lack strong leadership and assistance are unable to overcome their bewilderment and eke out a miserable existence.

In summary, until quite recently the Laotian government has largely ignored the problems of refugee relief, particularly those involving resettlement and rehabilitation. When it has dealt with them, it has done so on a purely *ad hoc* and regional basis without attempting to coordinate resources or formulate an overall policy. Of course it could be argued, and no doubt has been, that with an acute shortage of funds, bad communications, and many other fundamental deficiencies, refugee relief could not be accorded any priority. Besides, it clearly suited some political factions to discourage the introduction of a proper relief and resettlement program—starving refugees make a good talking point and a soft target for subversion.

However, late in 1962 the Royal Lao Government requested the United Nations to arrange for a survey to be made of refugees and demobilized soldiers; the latter were included because at that time it was hoped to reduce gradually the strength of the armed forces of the country as unification progressed under the Government of National Union. The survey was conducted in early 1963, and some of the recommendations in the subsequent report form the basis of a new national program for resettlement of refugees now being developed by the Ministry of Social Welfare under the guidance of a United Nations Resettlement Adviser.

A modest start has now been made within the limitations imposed by financial support for the program and trained personnel; but more significant is the fact that the importance of resettlement properly planned and executed, and irrespective of the ethnic groups concerned, has at last been recognized by many in authority when hitherto it was understood only by a few.

Generally speaking, the resettlement and agricultural development programs in Laos are primarily for subsistence agriculture, owing to the poor communication system. There are, however, instances where a resettlement is located close enough to a town to make transportation economically feasible. In such cases the goal of agricultural development is a combination of production for both subsistence and for the local market. Virtually nothing has been done to develop markets either for the hill tribesmen or for the Lao, nor has there been any development of agricultural credit.

This particular facet of tribal administration, which is common to all countries of Southeast Asia to a greater or lesser degree, is being dwelt on at some length, since its satisfactory solution, in addition to improving the economy, health, and welfare of the tribal community concerned, can also go some way toward providing the answer to the main problem of bridging the gap between central governments and their tribal peoples. In other words, through the medium of resettlement and its accompanying benefits, the administrative machine becomes directly involved on a personal level with tribal people, possibly for the first time; and if this contact is made and developed with understanding and respect for tribal custom, beliefs, and tradition, it can hardly fail to improve relations.

At this point it seems appropriate to consider briefly what resettlement really means, as its connotation is evidently not always clearly understood. Resettlement is the planned process of bringing the human and land resources of a country together for social economic ends. The social objective is primarily the development of viable communities, and the economic objective is normally agricultural production. There are other temporary objectives in certain circumstances, such as providing security and insulation against militant Communism and subversion. Perhaps the best example of this was the vast resettlement program launched by the Malayan government during the Emergency in 1952: over a period of a few years one million of the rural population (mostly Chinese farmers) were moved from the jungle fringes, where they were soft targets for Communist terrorist subversion, to properly planned New Villages. This not only afforded a reasonable degree of protection (Police, Home Guards, illuminated perimeters, etc.), but, more important, it enabled the civil authorities to introduce to these illiterate people a new way of life in the form of education, medical, and health services and improved agricultural methods. The people have often proved eager to learn. There were difficulties, of course, during the transitional period; but the viability of the concept has been proved and this program was the greatest single factor in the defeat, which took twelve years to accomplish, of the Communist-inspired insurrection.

Included in this mass resettlement were tribal groups (aborigines) living in deep jungle, whom the Communist terrorists were using as screens, sources of intelligence, and food suppliers. Their resettlement posed additional problems, and experience showed that if it was to be a success, very special care and unlimited patience were required. Initially, some small groups were airlifted out of deep jungle; but no one had given sufficient thought to the group's wishes, since the military requirement was considered to be paramount. In some cases this action proved to be a fatal mistake, and the groups were taken back. The lesson was learned, and from then on a technique was evolved whereby small military units with an interpreter were deployed in deep jungle for long periods with the sole task of winning over the aborigines to the point where they would come out voluntarily. The time involved varied from a few weeks to many months, depending on the degree of contact the group had previously had with the Communist terrorists.

It is relevant here to quote the views of the then Adviser to the Department of Aborigines on what he considered after long experience to be fundamental to the success of resettling tribal peoples:

(a) Proper planning. Co-operation of the group concerned and their voluntary (not forced) agreement to the scheme.
(b) Availability of suitable land voluntarily acceptable to the group; and assurance of Government approval to occupy the land.
(c) Government assistance in the form of:
    (i) Rationing until new cultivations are productive;

[265]

(ii) Welfare goods (clothing, tobacco etc.);

(iii) Tools and implements necessary for house building and agriculture;

(iv) Medical attention;

(v) Proper administration and protection once they have moved;

(vi) Assistance to obtain employment if necessary;

(vii) Education for the children.

(d) Unlimited patience; time for the community to adjust itself to its new circumstances and mode of life. Best achieved by arranging for an advance party from the group to move to the new area and prepare the way for the remainder. May take between six and twelve months to complete a move. If a change in agricultural methods is involved, it will take longer.

In concluding this section, it can be said categorically that a good *rapport* between government and tribal peoples can only be achieved through genuine mutual confidence, which may take many months, if not years, of patient effort to establish. Deepseated prejudices must be overcome. Then and then only can a sense of belonging start to take root. If this sense is carefully fostered by all means available, it should lead ultimately to a closer identification with, and participation in, the life and economy of the nation.

GENERAL PLAN OF THE ACTION PROGRAM

Unlike other countries in Southeast Asia with similar tribal problems, there is no ministry, department, or division of the Laotian government specifically responsible for the administration of the hill tribes. This probably arises from the fact that the constitution accords Laotian citizenship to all permanent residents of Laos, regardless of race, who are not already citizens of another country; it also guarantees all citizens the same rights and privileges under the law, as well as the same type of administration. In practice, these constitutional provisions do not generally apply to the tribal peoples, who in many cases still retain their autonomy. One example of the way the system may operate should be illustrative. The official languages of the courts are Lao and French. Tribal languages are barred from the courts, although tribal interpreters are supposed to be admitted. The point at question here is somewhat irrelevant, since under the military conditions which have prevailed in Laos for many years, the normal court procedures have often been suspended.

The main goal of the action program was to forge new and effective administrative links between government and the hill peoples both at central and provincial levels. At the central level it would be done by establishing, initially, the nucleus of a special department for the administration of the hill people; and at the provincial and district levels by closely involving the administrations in specific capital aid and welfare projects for the benefit and development of the tribes.

In addition to these relief and development programs for bringing government to the tribes, the intention is to introduce a radio program devised specifically for the tribal people of Laos and to broadcast in selected tribal languages. The precept here is that to achieve the ultimate goal of gradual assimilation of the tribal peoples into the national life and economy, the first and foremost essential is to be able to communicate with them. If this cannot be done initially through the medium of the national language (Lao) alone, then tribal languages must be utilized in addition.

PROGRESS OF THE ACTION PROGRAM

The concept of a special department for the administration of the tribal peoples in Laos has been generally accepted in principle, together with the policy aim that tribal people should be recruited to posts in the department when this step is found practical. At the present time, the staffing of such a department presents certain fundamental difficulties, the major ones being those of finance and personnel. Without the former, it is obviously not possible even to contemplate recruiting the latter. It would not answer the problem to second or borrow staff from other government departments on either a long-term or temporary basis. The secondment of staff was tried and proved a failure in the Thai government's Hill Tribe Development and Welfare Program, which *inter alia* calls for mobile extension teams. Secondment to the teams was unsatisfactory, and direct recruitment and training had to be used by the Hill Tribes Division of the Department of Public Welfare. Personnel seconded from one department to another feel, with good reason, that their promotion prospects within their home department suffer (out of sight, out of mind). In addition, there are the usual problems of working in the field in areas where communications are poor, such as long delays in the payment of already low salaries.

Ideally, a department administering hill tribes should be largely self-contained, certainly with respect to the everyday needs of the tribes in the fields of agriculture, medicine and health, basic education, welfare, etc. The department should be able to develop and implement its projects independently with the assistance and advice provided by tribal research. There are many reasons for this—the fundamental one is the absolute necessity for the right approach. The wrong one can do irreparable damage. The key executive staff of the department should not only be qualified in their respective fields, but, equally important, should have experience with hill people; and the extension workers who, after training, will often be operating without supervision in remote tribal areas, should be very carefully selected. A sense of dedication, understanding, and hard work is essential for the effective functioning of a department administering tribal peoples.

Within the limitations imposed by finance, the intention would be to establish the nucleus of this department in Laos with a balanced field team of specialists in agriculture (including livestock), medicine and health, community development, and welfare. Since such specialists are not presently available in the country, they would have to be recruited for a limited period from outside; then Laotian counterparts would understudy them in their field work. After acquiring field experience, the Laotians would need further training to fit them for administrative or semi-technical posts in the department. Once the process of establishing the nucleus was well under way, the creation of a cadre of extension workers and research facilities could be considered. Regarding the latter, the Laotian government might well profit from the Thai government's Tribal Research Centre in Chiengmai, where research and studies will cover at least some of the tribal groups common to both territories. Specific problems in which experience might be shared could include methods used to solve such problems as providing alternative cash crops to replace opium, and the development of methods for training field staff. The Meo, Yao, Mussuh (Lahu), and Khmu? are the chief opium cultivators in Laos—all but the latter are large-scale opium producers in Thailand as well. Opium is the mainstay of their economy. As in Thailand, this is very much of a potential problem in Laos, and one of great complexity. Of the many tribal revolts against the French regime in Laos, at least one, that of the Meo in Sam Neua Province in 1918, was caused in part by attempts of the French to collect a tax in the form of opium.

The difficulties of lack of finance and expertise have been touched on, but it would be more than unrealistic to overlook or attempt to minimize the current problems arising from the confused internal political situation in Laos. This has tended to paralyze the administrative machine and deny to the government access to large areas populated by the tribes. A further aggravation is the woefully low salary scale of government employees. High wartime prices, coupled with fixed salaries, means that there is little inducement to hard work and integrity on the part of government workers, and government service no longer attracts the best candidates.

In the light of this somber picture one cannot help but reflect on the advisability of even attempting to create this new department at the present time with so many factors conspiring against its viability. This is not a policy of despair; it is an honest appraisal of the relevant facts, and it represents an equally genuine desire to ensure, as far as possible, that when government is properly introduced to the hill tribes in Laos, it has, at least, a reasonable chance of attaining its aims.

In the meantime, a modest start has been made to generate government interest in tribal matters at the provincial and district levels, by the launching of projects (schools, welfare, and wet-rice cultivation) exclusively benefiting certain tribal groups. Results so far are encouraging. A few radio sets have been distributed to selected tribal villages where Lao is understood, and undoubtedly much enjoyment is derived from the programs. There is an army transmitter at Luang Prabang, not a part of the national network, which broadcasts news in the Meo language for fifteen minutes every weekday, and Meo music for thirty minutes on Sundays. It is too early to evaluate this particular medium, pending the introduction of a special tribal radio program and a larger distribution of receiving sets.

CONCLUSIONS

(a) There are now indications that as a result of the ever present refugee problem in Laos (the majority of refugees being tribal) there is developing awareness in the government of its responsibilities toward the hill people.

(b) If this consciousness can be translated into impartial assistance in the right manner, a big step forward will have been taken in the relations between the government and the hill tribes.

(c) Whereas the importance of establishing a special department for administering the hill peoples is recognized, the continuing political instability and internal strife together with lack of finance, are cogent reasons against creating the department at the present time. The risks of it being stillborn are too great.

(d) Plans for establishing the department should proceed with the firm objective of implementation when circumstances are more propitious.

(e) In the meantime, efforts should be concentrated on developing communications with the hill peoples. Radio seems to be the most practical method. Of course, this development must be carefully synchronized, with increased programming coordinated with the distribution of more radio sets, since at present Radio Peking is already broadcasting extensively in some of the tribal languages.

(f) Where government services (e.g. medical, educational and administrative) exist in predominantly tribal areas, much more could be done to promote a better understanding with the hill people through the medium of these services.

REFERENCES CITED

ARCHAIMBAULT, CHARLES
  1964 Religious structures in Laos. Journal of the Siam Society 52(1):57–74.
HALPERN, JOEL M.
  1964 Economy and society of Laos: a brief survey. New Haven, Yale University, Southeast Asia Studies. Monograph Series 5.
IZIKOWITZ, KARL GUSTAV
  1951 Lamet: hill peasants in French Indochina. Göteborg, Etnografiska Museet, Etnologiska Studier 17.

CHAPTER 7

The Meo of Xieng Khouang Province, Laos

G. LINWOOD BARNEY[1]

THE MEO

The Meo and Laos are representatives of a large group spread over southern China and northeastern Southeast Asia.[2] They number about two and a half million in China, two hundred and twenty thousand in North Vietnam, almost fifty thousand in Thailand, and were estimated at about fifty thousand in Laos over a decade ago.[3] They have gradually moved southward and westward out of China in the past 150 years and generally occupy highlands when they move into Southeast Asia.

XIENG KHOUANG PROVINCE—ETHNIC DISTRIBUTION

Xieng Khouang Province in northern Laos is largely a plateau, with a broad plain, the Plaine des Jarres (also known as the Tran Ninh Plateau), at an elevation of about 4,000 feet, and surrounding mountains rising another 1,000 to 5,000 feet. An estimate, perhaps exaggerated, in 1959 indicated that there were forty-five thousand Meo in this province alone. Village elders state that Meo have been settling in the province for about a

[1] The field work on which most of this paper is based was done between 1950 and 1954, when the author was engaged in linguistic and missionary work in Laos. This is a modification and expansion of a paper entitled "The Meo of Xieng Khouang Province," which was Laos Project Paper 13, Joel Halpern, ed., University of California, Los Angeles, mimeographed. Information was supplemented by Theodore Andrianoff, who has been a missionary in Laos since 1948, and by conversations with Touby Lyfong, Meo leader, when he visited the United States during the spring of 1965.
[2] See Bernatzik (1947), Graham (1954), Morechand (1955), Roux and Tran (1954), and Savina (1930) for descriptions of Meo elsewhere in Southeast Asia.
[3] For sources of population estimates of Meo outside of Laos see the tables of population accompanying the other parts of this book. No accurate count of Meo in Laos has been made, but the estimate of at least fifty thousand seems reasonable, given the observed large numbers of Meo in refugee camps at the present time.

hundred years (Mathieu, 1959:45, states that the Meo came into Laos in 1840).

In Xieng Khouang, as in much of Southeast Asia, there is a fairly orderly topographical distribution of ethnic groups. The Lao, who are Buddhists and wet-rice growers, live primarily in the river valleys. They maintain only a slight margin of authority in Xieng Khouang, although they are the dominant ethnic group of Laos. Minor ethnic groups—Vietnamese artisans, Chinese traders, Indian cloth merchants, Western missionaries, airline personnel, and European colonists—were, before the Communist invasion, concentrated in or near the town of Xieng Khouang.

The Khmu?, who live mainly in the foothills, are primarily dry-rice agriculturalists. Politically they are submissive to the Lao; they give little indication of attempting or desiring to attain political autonomy or recognition. They have long been in contact with the Lao, from whom they have learned many material culture traits, but they have retained their animistic religion (see Smalley 1956).

The Meo are usually located high on the flanks of the mountains, where they are primarily slash-and-burn, dry-rice cultivators. They also grow corn and vegetables, and earn cash through production and sale of opium, livestock, and surplus agricultural goods. Unlike the Khmu?, the Meo have maintained a high degree of social and political solidarity and have retained a distinctive material culture, especially in their dress. They self-consciously perpetuate their cultural distinctiveness from the Lao, though they are quick to accept many items of Laotian culture, including literacy.

The Town of Xieng Khouang. The town of Xieng Khouang was a colonial administrative center for the French and was the seat of the Laotian governor (*Chao Khoueng*). Xieng Khouang has been the location of a daily market (which attracted people from as far as five days' walk away) and the site of a large festival in the twelfth (lunar) month. The town (and the province) were connected by highway with Vinh on the Vietnamese coast to the east, Vientiane on the Mekong border with Thailand to the southwest, and Luang Prabang, the royal Laotian capital to the west. The roads have been closed because of Communist activities most of the time since the early 1950's. The province has been the scene of repeated bitter battles, since it lies in the middle of the invasion route from North Vietnam to the northern Laos lowlands along the Mekong. Though the hill-based Meo have repeatedly prevented the Communists from securing their hold on the Plaine des Jarres (e.g. Warner 1965:35–36), most of the communication with the rest of Laos in recent years has been by air.

The Government of Xieng Khouang. The Governor of Xieng Khouang who is recognized by the Royal Lao Government fled to Vientiane at the time of the first Communist invasion. A provincial government in exile was maintained in Vientiane for a number of years, but administrative offices are now being built in Sam Thong, a refugee center west of Xieng Khouang in a part of the province controlled by the Royal Lao Government (see Ward's paper). The Communists control the town of Xieng Khouang and have installed their own provincial government forty kilometers from there at Khong Khai, in the center of the Plaine des Jarres.

Xieng Khouang was one of four principalities which, at the time the French took control, existed in the area which has now become Laos. It had managed to maintain its independence by paying tribute both to the stronger Laotian principality and to Annam (North Vietnam). Under the French the Luang Prabang "kingdom" was recognized as paramount. However, for purposes of convenience, administrative affairs were set up in Vientiane, and the power of the other three principalities was curtailed. But in Xieng Khouang, unlike other areas of Laos, the traditional patterns of leadership were not drastically altered: the present governor, Chao Sai Kham, is the descendant of the old Prince of Xieng Khouang. Each province in Laos is normally divided into several *muong* (administrative territorial units roughly equivalent to a county), each of which has an appointed *chao muong*, or county officer. Xieng Khouang is divided into four *muong* territories, but there are five *chao muong*. Four are Lao, one for each territorial *muong*. The fifth, Touby Lyfong, is the "chief" of the Meo population which is scattered in the hills of the entire province (see below).

Relations of Meo to Lao. The Meo are not a politically or culturally unified group, even in Xieng Khouang Province. At least two Meo leaders have a following there:[4] Touby Lyfong

---

[4] General Vang Pao, another Xieng Khouang Meo, is also becoming recognized as a Meo leader because of his successful military career (see below).

(presently allied with the Royal Lao Government) and Faydang (allied with the Pathet Lao). The alignment of their followers in their competition for leadership seems based on traditional clan alignments as well as on the general political situation in Laos. Both of these men belong to the White Meo (or *mon tleu*) group. The Striped Meo (*mon len*), who are much less active politically, speak a different dialect. At least one Striped Meo clan claims relationship with the White Meo, but the exact nature of this relationship is not known to the author. The Striped Meo are not favored in receipt of political plums.

Although the details of the historical relationships between the Meo and the Lao of Xieng Khouang are not known to this author, the following seems to be a reasonable reconstruction. An alliance or working agreement seems to have been worked out between the leader of one group (evidently a large and important clan or group of clans) of White Meo and the Governor of Xieng Khouang (this agreement may have been worked out even prior to the French colonial period). Touby Lyfong and *Chao Khoueng* (Governor) Sai Kham are heirs to this arrangement. In addition to this alliance, the two are close personal friends. Touby's father was known as the richest Meo in Xieng Khouang. During his lifetime he held a position vis-à-vis the Lao similar to Touby's. He sent at least three of his sons to school, and Touby was a schoolmate of Chao Sai Kham when they went to school in Hanoi.[5] Both personal friendship and historical alliance seem important in their present relationship.[6]

[5] Touby is the oldest of three surviving educated brothers. His younger brother, Tougou, is one of the leading lawyers in Laos and was educated in France. Toulya, another brother, once served as a deputy from Xieng Khouang Province.

Another version of this story states that Touby's father came from China as a poor young man, and was taken into the household of Faydang's father as a servant. Under Faydang's father's tutelage, Touby's father prospered. Touby's father's children went further in school than did Faydang's father's children. Faydang's brother, Lofang, went to school in Xieng Khouang, where he finished elementary school. He did not go on to high school in Vinh, as did Touby, but returned to his own village, Nong Het, where he became a school master. During the Japanese occupation the French appointed Touby as a district chief (*tasseng*). Faydang's family resented the prominence given to their former servant's son. They identified themselves with the Communists, and allied themselves temporarily with the Japanese, against the French. Touby remained loyal to the French during the occupation, and throughout the Indochina War which followed. In 1956, when elections were held for the National Assembly, Touby ran against Lofang and defeated him. Thus the split between Touby's and Faydang's families has continued. (Ed.)

[6] Following Kong Le's 1960 coup, an attempt was made to ensure the continued loyalty of the Xieng Khouang Meo (one of the best-organized fighting forces

Faydang was at one time a Meo chief (recognized as a district chief) from the northeastern part of Xieng Khouang. He is now the leading Meo member of the Pathet Lao. It is said of his followers that "whatever Touby's people do, Faydang's people will do the opposite." This division is of long standing, though Touby and Faydang are related (Touby's mother is said to be Faydang's father's real sister; she is a member of Faydang's clan, the Lo clan). Touby's present alignment with the Governor assures that Faydang will be aligned with the opposition, in this case the Communists.

General Vang Pao worked his way up through the ranks, first under the French, and later under the Laotians. His base of power is primarily with the army, though he enjoys considerable respect among the Meo as the first of their group to attain a high commissioned rank. He has considerable power since he is military commander in the area where many Meo refugee camps are located. His family is connected with Touby's by kinship ties,[7] and the two are not now in direct competition for leadership of the Meo.

MEO SOCIAL ORGANIZATION—FAMILY AND CLAN

The patrilineal clan system of the Meo dominates their social organization, serving as a primary focus for their culture as a whole by tying together social, political, economic, and religious aspects of behavior. The basic unit of the Meo social structure is the "household" or patrilineal extended family, meaning not only those who live under one roof, but also including all those under the authority of one household head. Thus a single house-

---

in Laos) to the central government. Touby was given a place in the cabinet. Shortly after he took this position, he went to Xieng Khouang to visit his family. Upon arriving there, he—and Chao Sai Kham—called a meeting of all district chiefs (tasseng), both Meo and Lao. The Governor declared that he was breaking away from the central government and asked all his district chiefs to join with him in resisting all enemies. The probable reason for this was that Touby and the Governor feared a Communist take-over of the Laotian government, and the Governor saw a chance to reassert a claim to Xieng Khouang autonomy. An alliance was made with Prince Phoumi Nosavan (the "Rightist"), then based in Savannakhet, who furnished arms and materiel to Chao Sai Kham and Touby. Xieng Khouang repledged its loyalty to Vientiane after a change in the government.

[7] There is a regular pattern of exchange of women between the two clans. Women of Vang Pao's clan (Vang) become wives of men in Touby's clan (Ly), and women of Touby's clan can become wives of men from Vang Pao's clan.

hold could include a man's unmarried daughters, his sons and their wives and children, and possibly his sons' sons' children, and might also include a few other feeble or otherwise dependent relatives. All members of the household carry the clan name of the household head in addition to their given name. The clan name refers to descent from a mythical ancestor, and common membership in a clan serves as a bond of kinship and friendship between people who would otherwise be strangers. Members of the same lineage, who can trace their common descent from a known ancestor, refer to their lineage mates by a common term meaning "my olders and youngers." The lineage does not seem to be a functional social unit.

The actual place of residence is determined by the number of people in the household. If the household gets too large, it may split. The number living in a single house ranges up to thirty-four, but frequently a married son will build his own house near his father's and will remain under his father's authority.

Deep respect for elders is highly valued, so much so that corporal punishment of children need not be resorted to. Even after a son has married, he continues to respect the authority of his father. Women have authority over children, but in all family matters the father's word is final. As soon as it appears that an unreconcilable conflict may break out, the household will split. The result is a tendency for development of "stem families" as residential units. The oldest son usually stays with his father, while younger sons leave the household if the household splits. Overt expressions of conflict within the family are very negatively valued, and a household should split in order to maintain good relations between family members.

A child is always responsible to his father. If the father is not the head of the household, he in turn is responsible to the household head, who is usually his father, grandfather, or elder brother. Although the household head has final authority in household matters, he is not a dictator—his decisions represent his considered opinion after discussions with the adult men under his authority. The authority of the father diminishes with distance: a man who moves out to set up an independent household will become a household head in his own right if he moves far enough away.

The average Meo village contains about eight houses, with the range between one and forty. When there is only one household in the village, the household head is also the village head; when there are several households of the same clan, the eldest household head usually functions as village head. The leadership pattern is more complex where more than one clan is present; this is discussed below under political organizations.

Marriage. Although for some purposes the household is an independent unit, it also operates within the larger context of the patrilineal clan system, as is seen most clearly in the practices of courtship and marriage. Customary law forbids marriage within the clan, and this is backed by a modified "brother-sister" taboo between people of the opposite sex from the same clan. Acquaintance with eligible girls is made at such events as the New Year festival, when whole villages are invited to visit villages belonging to another clan. These festivities are a time of courtship; friendships made at this time are followed up when the boy visits the girl's village. If the girl responds favorably to the boy, the relationship should end in marriage.

Marriage can only be realized after considerable maneuvering. The young man must secure a "go-between," usually an elder brother or paternal uncle, to negotiate with the girl's parents. They may insist that the girl wait until her elder sister marries, or until her younger siblings grow older, or they may want a high bride-price. If a settlement cannot be reached, the young couple may elope, leaving the settlements to be made later, often with the aid of a panel of neutral parties.

If the marriage takes place in the normal fashion, the bride and groom exchange silver neck-bands, and the families of the bride and groom exchange visits and feasts. Such visits and the exchange of gifts which accompany them encourage close relations between the two households and, to some measure, between their two clans.

Although the groom is supposed to provide the bride-wealth necessary for the marriage, his household may assist him in accumulating the necessary amount. Their evaluation of the bride, and the past contributions of the groom to the other householders, will condition their decision. In addition, the young man is expected to accumulate any wealth he can in anticipation of marriage. The household head will sometimes make gifts to him, and he may earn and keep extra amounts for this purpose.

The wedding feasts always involve contributions of the household as a whole. Therefore, the bride and groom incur economic obligations to the entire household, which serve to tie the new couple more firmly to their household and to reinforce the marriage bonds.

By virtue of marriage, the bride gives up her membership in her father's household and clan and her rights to inheritance from her father. She becomes a member of her husband's household and clan, but she may occasionally visit her parents' home.

Polygyny is permitted, and wealthy men often can afford several wives. Often a man will inherit his deceased brother's widow. One of the wives in a polygynous household is considered to be the most important or "big wife," who directs the household activities of other wives. Wives live together under the same roof, sharing the same sleeping area; and no emotional problems appear to result from this arrangement.

Although divorce is possible, it is not frequent, and it is strongly discouraged, since it would disrupt relations between clans. A panel, consisting of a representative of the husband's household, of the wife's parents' household, and of the district chief (see below) may be convened to hear the couple's complaints and to advise them in patching up the quarrel.

Marriage is used by the Meo to create ties between clans; good marital relations are conducive to good clan relations, which in turn are conducive to further marriages between the clans. These relationships are renewed and reinforced by the reciprocal festivals and marriage feasts.

MEO POLITICAL ORGANIZATION

The full scope of the traditional Meo political system has never been present within Xieng Khouang Province. Historically it appears that the Meo had a strongly organized kingdom some time before they entered Laos (see Bernatzik 1947:Chs. 2, 6). During the colonial period they were at first under the rigid authority of the French; the Japanese occupation during World War II broke this pattern, and after the war the French substituted a form of indirect rule. At present they are under the nominal authority of the Royal Lao Government (RLG), but they are caught in the conflict between the RLG and the Pathet Lao. Despite their years of nominal submission to central authority, the Meo have maintained their own local political system.

Units of Meo Political Structure. The basic units of Meo political structure (household and village) and the basis for political action (respect for elders) have already been mentioned. Higher levels of authority have been built largely on the model of the household. The chief of a village is himself a household head, and in multi-house villages he is ordinarily the eldest of the household heads. A few exceptions to this rule which the author has noted seem to have resulted from recognition by the villagers of the military honors which the individual received from the government.

The village chief (*nai ban*) functions between households in much the same manner as does the household head between members of the household. The village chief is an honored leader on the local scene, holding a place of prestige in local festivals, judging inter-household disputes, and also representing the village to the outside world. He is expected to act for the good of the community. He is responsible for maintaining old trails and opening new ones, and for organizing the move of the village to a new location. He has authority in emergencies. During the Communist occupation in the early 1950's the village chief was responsible for the defense of the village and for its evacuation. But the village chief is not a dictator, and he acts with the advice of the other household heads. If a family feels abused, it is free to establish residence in another area.

When a village contains households from more than one clan, disputes are more common. Apparently the government recognizes only one chief for such a village, while the local population generally recognizes the eldest household head of *each* clan to be a chief. There appears to be harmony in most local affairs, but difficulty arises and tensions develop when outside or upper-level authorities attempt to enforce measures through only one of the chiefs. Strong feelings may result in the loss of cooperation between the clans. In one case the author observed, the minority clan group moved to a new site only a five-minute walk away. Subsequently the two groups regained friendly relationships,

[279]

which were cemented by intermarriage, but the settlements remained apart.

The district chief (*tasseng*) may have as many as forty villages under his supervision. It is at this level that resemblance to traditional Meo political structure may break down. At the time of the author's field work, the district chiefs were appointed by the paramount Meo chief (for Xieng Khouang), Touby Lyfong, acting in conjunction with the Lao province governor. Touby seems to have attempted to conform to what may have been the traditional pattern by selecting as district chiefs men who were village chiefs and who were members of the predominant clan in the district. The district chief is the primary channel of communication between the villages and high government officials. He is often called upon to settle disputes between villages or members of different villages (e.g. the marriage dispute mentioned above).

The Meo hope to settle disputes at the lowest level of authority: intra-family disputes should be settled within the household; inter-household disputes within the village; inter-village disputes within the district; and inter-district disputes should be settled within the sphere of Touby's authority. Such disputes are not necessarily between massed groups at the different levels, but might be between individuals from these different levels. Disputes between Xieng Khouang Meo are seldom allowed to go beyond Touby. In cases involving the Meo with members of other ethnic groups, Touby has served as counsel for the Meo. In this role he has proved himself very influential among French and Lao officials.

Touby Lyfong, Paramount Chief. Touby Lyfong's relation to the Governor of Xieng Khouang has already been mentioned. His position was recognized by the French, and he has continued to receive recognition from the Royal Lao Government in Vientiane. For a short time in 1960 he was a member of the cabinet (as Minister of Justice and Minister of Health and Welfare). He also ran successfully for election as a deputy when it became evident that if he did not do so a follower of Faydang would be elected. At the present time (1965) he is an appointed member of the King's Council, representing the Meo. He has consistently championed the Meo people. While holding positions of influence within the government administration, he has retained the respect, confidence, and support of the Meo people. He is known throughout the whole area, and the Meo are quick to respond to requests made by him. The government has given him a house in Vientiane, but he makes frequent trips to the Meo area and has moved his family back to Xieng Khouang Province to maintain his contact with the Meo there.

During the early 1950's Touby lived in Xieng Khouang next to the Lao governor, and he maintained a Meo militia. During World War II and again during the Communist invasion of 1953–1954 he was given a field command beside the French and Lao commanders and through his Meo militia furnished the government forces with intelligence and guerrilla support.

His military role was probably important in establishing his present position of influence, though he no longer has a military command. He helped to bring about the cooperation of the Meo and central government forces in resisting the Japanese and later the Communist invaders.

Today the government sees Touby as the representative of the Meo and the communicator between the Meo people and the administration. The Meo see Touby as one who can communicate their thoughts to the government and can influence the government. Thus Touby acts as the connecting link between the Lao government and the Meo's indigenous political system. The various Meo districts are now brought together under an office which they have not instituted but in which Touby has been installed with power from the central government. Thus he seems to warrant the title "paramount chief" of the Meo, at least in Xieng Khouang. Meo in other provinces are *not* represented in the same way. Touby is generally well received by the Meo in other provinces, but the degree of his influence among them is uncertain.

Rewards of Political Leadership. The economic returns of political office are significant, but not sufficient to support a man and his family. Neither village chief nor district chief receives a regular salary, though both may be in a position to benefit from control of trade. The village chief receives gifts from his villagers, but these are essentially to assist him in the hospitality he is expected to show to visitors, including Chinese traders, who always stay in the chief's house when they visit the village.

Both the village chief and the district chief are supposed to receive a small commission on all taxes and fees they collect. Fees and taxes for such things as birth and marriage certificates have been collected from the Meo only in recent years.

The writer considers the village to be the level at which the indigenous Meo political system operates today. The district level seems to be a transition from traditional Meo villages to the central government's bureaucracy, and Touby has been a major factor in the maintenance of this relationship. The extended family household has not yet been directly affected by central government administration, and it continues to be the basic unit of Meo social and political structure.

Laotian Policy toward Tribesmen. The declared Laotian policy has been to consider all individuals born in Laos to be Laotian citizens and to incorporate all ethnic groups into the national policy. As citizens, all are supposed to be responsible for taxes, military service, and conformance to Lao law, although enforcement of these provisions has been difficult because of the civil war. Nonetheless, the various ethnic groups are gradually being introduced to the national political system, and contact with representatives of the national government has sometimes been very intensive, as in the refugee programs described in Ward's paper. The Meo of Xieng Khouang have twice sent representatives to the national assembly (Touby and his brother Toulya). But it is still difficult to say whether this has been an honest attempt to have these peoples fully represented in the federal government or whether it is merely a stopgap measure to stem the apparent nationalism of the Meo. The honor and prestige given to Touby and other Meo leaders, the educational facilities being offered to the Meo on an increasing scale, and other benefits now available to the Meo would indicate the former motive. The government's ruling against using the Meo language in a written form might indicate the latter motive.

MEO ECONOMY

The role of the household in the Meo social and political structure is reflected as well in Meo economy. The division of labor, pattern of subsistence, land tenure, property rights, inheritance, and the economic factors relating to marriage and religious rites are all tied into socio-political aspects of the household.

Rice. Upland rice is the basic food staple of the Meo population in Xieng Khouang. Its production, which is supervised by the household head, requires the full cooperation of the entire household. A regular annual cycle of activities similar to those of other upland peoples in Southeast Asia is followed.

Planting is carried out at the beginning of the rainy season in late April and May. The work may be done by any member of the family. Late in October when the rainy season closes, the grain ripens quickly, and everyone joins in the harvest. Temporary shelters are erected on the field, which must be watched until the harvest is completed and the rice is safely stored in the village. The rice stalks are cut by hand and gathered into large stacks on the field. This work must be done quickly so that overripe grain will not be lost.

The women and girls flail the stalks to remove the rice, which is then carried as much as one day's walk to the village, where it is stored in granaries the men have built. The entire household is involved in the harvest.

A rice field may be used for three or four successive years. Ideally, some new ground is cleared each year, and poorer soil is allowed to lie fallow. Clearing starts as soon as it is certain that the harvest can be successfully completed. Some of the stronger men begin the clearing, and others join them as soon as the harvest is finished. The heavy vegetation of the new fields is cut and allowed to dry until March, when it is burned. The field is then cleared for planting, which takes place after the first few rainy days allow the soil to be loosened.

Other Crops. Potatoes, corn, squash, and other minor food crops are grown, but play a minor role in the Meo diet. Potatoes are sometimes sold to Westerners, but are most commonly used as fertilizer in the opium fields. (This example of the sophisticated upland agriculture seems quite different from the methods employed by Meo in Thailand, described in Geddes' paper.) Corn and squash are fed to livestock unless the rice harvest is light.

Opium. It appears that every household has its opium field, a fenced plot near the village. The soil must be carefully prepared, and fertilized with potatoes. Most of the opium cultivation, including the harvest (which requires great skill), is done by women.

Opium has been the main source of cash income for the Meo and often serves as a medium of exchange. The first missionaries in the area were quite shocked to find carefully wrapped lumps of opium in the offerings at church. The use of opium as a standard of exchange in Xieng Khouang markets could be observed openly during the early 1950's. The French authorities were supposed to control opium production, but even during the colonial period much illicit trade in opium took place. Undoubtedly, some of the opium went into Thailand in exchange for foreign manufactured goods (Embree 1949:155), and this pattern persists.

The French had an inspector in the field during the harvest season, who visited the villages and was supposed to purchase all the opium. No opium was supposed to be shipped out of the province except by the French. Though the same law still applies under the Lao government, the Lao government does not have a program to purchase opium and is unable to control its shipment. Production in Xieng Khouang is now greatly reduced because of the war and resulting difficulties in maintaining opium fields and arranging transport and marketing.

At the time of the writer's field work (early 1950's) Xieng Khouang was the only province in all of Indochina where the government officially permitted cultivation of the opium poppy. The French administrator told the writer that an estimated 60 percent of the men of the province were users of opium.

Its great worth and the ease of transport made opium of unique value. At the time of the field work one kilo was worth one-half ton of rice. It was used for barter in the Xieng Khouang market, in district markets, and in the villages.

Other Products. Flax is less important today than in earlier periods since Chinese merchants trade cloth for opium.[8] But women still spin flax and make their elaborately dyed and embroidered skirts out of heavy linen.

Livestock. Livestock play a very important part in Meo economy. Poultry, goats, pigs, buffalo, and cattle are found in most villages. They are used for meat and for cash sales in the market.

[8] Trading in the villages was done by Chinese merchants who had settled in the valley towns. This pattern was beginning to break down in the 1950's, by which time Meo were coming to valley-town markets themselves. Caravans of Chinese traders from North Vietnam used to come into the valley towns, but these traders did not ordinarily venture into the mountain villages for trade.

The reputation of Meo as careful animal husbandmen is confirmed by comparing their livestock with those of other ethnic groups. Poultry is used for meat and as the most common sacrifice in case of illness. Eggs are eaten only occasionally. Larger animals are used for sacrifice only for severe illnesses.

Meo horses are well groomed and fed and splendidly trained as pack and saddle animals. They are very important in extending the speed and range of Meo transport and travel. Every household has at least one horse, which is under the supervision of the household head. Although another member of the household may consider the horse to be his, it is his only to use and care for—actual ownership resides in the household, and care of the animal is supervised by the household head.

Land Ownership. Land is owned and used by the people who have cleared it. Usually a Meo household will have three or four rice fields and one opium field in production. This varies with the size of the household, number of nuclear families, wives, and children. A married man may start work on a field of his own if he can do so without upsetting the distribution of labor in the household's interests.

Division of Labor. The division of labor in agriculture has already been described. In addition, it should be noted that women are responsible for the preparation and serving of food, including pounding or grinding grain, winnowing, and cooking. Women carry all the water.

Firewood is brought in by the boys, but older men assist them from time to time in felling trees and cutting the wood into lengths for carrying. Men build and repair fences and buildings and care for the livestock. Part-time specialists serve as silversmiths and gunsmiths, but they must supplement their income with rice production.

MEO MATERIAL CULTURE—HOUSEHOLD POSSESSIONS

The Meo house is made entirely of wood. Unlike the houses of the Laotians, it is built directly on the ground, with a dirt floor. Two fireplaces are found in every house—one is used for cooking, and the other is used as the center for all social gatherings. One area of the wall is reserved for a shrine or altar for the spirits, or *Tlan.*

Every household has at least one rice pounder for husking rice. One rotating stone corn mill is also the common property of the household. This item is not found among other ethnic groups in Laos. Tools, saddles, crossbows, Meo-made flintlock guns, musical instruments, and the various items needed for food preparation make up most of the material goods which one finds in all Meo households. Wealth is tied up in livestock, opium, and silver. Solid silver bars are used in trade, and other pieces are used for ornament. Silver or opium, not paper money, is the medium of exchange in the hills.

Inheritance and Property Distribution. Household property, including livestock, is under the supervision of the household head. Upon his death the property is not really inherited, since it continues to belong to the household. The property now comes under the supervision of the new household head, who may be a younger brother or the eldest son of the deceased. In the event of the death of a husband in the household, the widow continues to have the use of the materials which he "possessed." Unless she is quite elderly, she is likely to become a second wife of her husband's brother. Upon her death the material she had from her first husband is redistributed within the household. Once an individual has moved out of the household (by marriage or fission of the household), he or she no longer shares in this distribution.

The contributions of the household in marriage ceremonies have already been mentioned. The entire household also contributes to the financial burdens of religious rites, taxes, and funerals of household members.

MEO FOLKLORE AND BELIEFS

Meo folklore, which contains the "History of the Meo," is in a vocabulary little used in current speech. The forms either have passed out of use or reflect contact with the Chinese. The lore is told in couplet form and can be recited for days by the few old men who remember it. Their history refers to ancestral heroes who supposedly took on spirit-like qualities and continue to aid the Meo today. Other ancestral figures became jealous and continue today to attempt to thwart the benevolent ancestors. Both varieties of these spirit-like beings are referred to as *Tlan* (see Graham 1954; Savina 1930).

The folklore tells of a first creation, followed by a great flood, with two survivors in a barrel, and a great series of conflicts and exploits before the time of the clan "fathers." These "fathers" are vaguely identified with the present-day clans.

It appears that the Meo clan system is tied in with the folklore both as a myth of its origin and as a description of its internal organization. The relationships between folklore personages are consistent with behavior in the household and clans described in this paper.

The Meo are predominantly animistic and believe in many *Tlan*, which they classify according to their functions. There are *Tlan* of the water, of fertility, of the trail, of the hearth, of the sleeping quarters, of the rice field, for hunting, and numerous other categories. The Meo also have a concept of a supreme being, whom they call *Fua Tai*. In Meo thinking, Fua Tai created all things and originally had close communication with man. He became dismayed with man and left him in the charge of the world of the *Tlan*. Fua Tai still exists, but is no longer concerned with man's affairs. Some Meo believe that a person's spirit goes to live in the land of the *Tlan* after his funeral; others say his spirit returns to live in his old house. Differences of opinion or interpretation of this kind are common; Meo belief is not a unified or universally accepted body of doctrine (cf. Morechand 1955, who indicates similar variations in beliefs among the Meo of North Vietnam).

The Meo observe an annual visit with their household *Tlan*, which some believe to represent their ancestors. The doors are shut, and no one is allowed to enter or leave until the visit is over. Informants have reported that they never saw or heard anything during this period, but knew that they should all be gathered in one house so the *Tlan* would find them.

Religious Practitioners. The *Tu-ua-neng* (religious practitioner) has a very important role in a Meo village. There may be more than one in a sizable village. The position may be taken by males or females. Certain powers and responsibilities are believed to be given to the *Tu-ua-neng* by the *Tlan*. A "power," possibly a *Tlan* which dwells in him, enables the *Tu-ua-neng* to cure the sick, determine the meaning of signs and dreams, give security to a new infant, predict the future through ordeals, and in general communicate between the living Meo and the *Tlan* worlds. He may achieve increased status depending on his effectiveness in dealing with the *Tlan* world. This is reflected in his success at curing, driving away malevolent *Tlan,* and influencing the *Tlan* world for the welfare of Meo society.

The *Tu-ua-neng* is called in to divine the cause of illness, cure the sick, protect the village from epidemics, officiate at funerals, make all fetishes, and erect shrines and altars in homes, along trails, and in rice fields. Small fees are paid to him for his services, but he is not a full-time specialist and must supplement his income with rice farming. The office is not directly inherited; the *Tu-ua-neng* is appointed and given his powers by the *Tlan.* Such appointment is tested pragmatically.

The *Tu-ua-neng* are not in competition with secular village chiefs—their realms are in different areas of behavior. But the *Tu-ua-neng* are not necessarily conservative. In fact, they may be among the first in a village to accept religious change and conversion to Christianity.

Meo are generally aware of their association with the *Tlan* and of their obligations toward them in order to cultivate their goodwill and secure their assistance. The Meo show their deference by numerous taboos and ceremonies. But individuals vary in their attitudes toward *Tlan*. Some seem deeply confident of the effectiveness of the varied observances. Others appear to continue in their belief because of tradition and the hope that it will do them some good. It appears to this writer that the Meo he observed may have been involved in much more specific attempts to control the *Tlan* world than would be indicated by Bernatzik (1947) and other investigators whom he quotes. At the same time it appears that the Meo of Xieng Khouang are not united in any pattern of beliefs.

One may ask whether this disparity in beliefs may not indicate an attitude of insecurity among the Meo. Although the clan and household remain tightly integrated, there appear to be changes taking place in traditional patterns of Meo life, especially in the matter of belief. This may be the first evidence of a breakdown in Meo culture.

RECENT CHANGES IN MEO CULTURE

The years since 1940 have brought many changes to the Meo of Laos. These people had been drifting southward from China for about three generations. They entered an area where they were more accessible to Western influence and to contacts with other ethnic groups. Their geographic position in the mountains which lie across major routes of transportation, and their capacity for military organization, have made them of great strategic importance. They have been engulfed in a series of wars and political upheavals. After 1940 control of Laos passed from the French to the Japanese, to the Lao, back to the French, and back again to the Lao, who became embroiled in a conflict with the Vietnamese Communists and a lingering civil war (with the Pathet Lao). During these times of stress the various ethnic groups were placed under common dangers and hardships. In some cases such conditions resulted in closer communication and cooperation between them. Thus the Meo were under severe external pressure, in addition to the constant change that takes place within any culture. In recent years their entire environment has been drastically altered—the hills have become the scene of almost continuous warfare, most of the Meo have been relocated into refugee camps, and their traditional economic patterns can no longer be followed.

But even between 1940 and 1950, when external pressures were not so great, there were startling changes. A market scene after 1950 would reveal a large number of Meo both buying and selling. A decade earlier they were rarely seen in town. In the 1950's many Meo were engaged in wage work, albeit still primarily as a supplement to the livelihood derived from horticulture.

After 1950 a few Meo actually had changed their economic patterns completely.[9] A few had leased terraced fields for irrigated-rice farming; some of these were encouraged and under-

---

[9] Some of these changes may have been due to conversion to Christianity. Meo Christians were no longer subject to taboos which made animist Meo reluctant to engage in lowland occupations.

written by Touby. Still other Meo had become mechanics, trained medical practitioners, and specialists in other types of work.

Although most Meo maintained a basic mountain rice-opium economy, a trend toward a modified cash economy was evident. The Meo were anxious to possess Western goods, including saddles, knives, saws, and other tools, bicycles, guns, medicine, sunglasses, clothing, and flashlights; and those living near town had even begun to buy motor bikes and jeeps. The Meo displayed an avid interest in new items of material technology, being quick to adopt new tools such as sewing machines. Such purchases required cash, which was obtained largely through sale of opium, wage labor, and sale of surplus agricultural products.

There were also changes in the political sphere. The district-level bridge between Meo and the national government has already been indicated. However, intelligent interest in this larger political configuration was only beginning to emerge as the Meo came to be considered citizens of Laos and were represented in the National Assembly. The Meo interest in such things was stimulated by increased enforcement of taxation and licensing. The interest was augmented by increased literacy, more frequent contact with town, and Meo candidates for provincial and national office.

The changes had not yet affected Meo village political structure because the traditional links between district and village continued to be used. But the increasing participation in government taxation, legislation, and military programs indicated a definite change in the basic Meo attitude toward authority.

Meo began to receive, and to make, their own opportunities for medical care and various civil functions, especially education. In many Meo villages schools were set up by the village householders themselves. Often the villages were able to pay a higher salary to the Lao schoolteacher than the government paid in the official public schools (the normal fee was one bar of silver per pupil per semester). The rate of literacy had been extremely low among the Meo, but was increasing rapidly. Even the public school in Xieng Khouang, basically for the Lao, admitted Meo children. Those with consistently high scholarship were permitted to complete their elementary education, and some were sent on to *lycées* at Vientiane and Saigon. Others received specialized training in various trades and professions.

Of course, there were points of stress in this pattern of modernization. A child who attended school for many months in Xieng Khouang was not subject to the direct social sanctions of his household. He was intellectually superior to his elders when he returned home, and might wish to dominate the household, or to move away to become a specialist in some new line of work. Although some returned to their households to participate as much as possible in traditional affairs, those who forgot their household's claim on them were subject to general criticism from the Meo population.

Wage labor was another source of stress. Traditionally, the household met its needs for cash through endeavors in which the entire household participated, e.g. opium production, the raising and selling of livestock, and so forth. The communal endeavors reinforced the traditional social pattern of the Meo, but wage labor and individual specialization put a strain on traditional patterns of cooperation.

Political change has not yet caused severe strains in the household, but ultimately it stands as a threat to household stability. If free elections led an individual to place confidence and respect in people who were not traditional-style leaders, some instability might also develop within the household, upon which the traditional political system has been modeled.

Despite the changes in Meo culture, there is still little intermarriage between the Meo and other ethnic groups. The Meo appear to want to maintain recognition and distinction as a group, and this desire seems to continue even in the changing conditions of the 1960's. The cultural horizons of the Meo seem to have widened as a result of recent experiences, but the basic orientations do not seem to have changed. The Meo appear to be ready to adopt new techniques and methods if by doing so they think that Meo society can benefit and gain prominence.

One example of this is religion. Here again it is instructive to look at the reaction of Touby Lyfong. The Protestant missionaries (mostly Americans) have continued to work with the Meo through the troubled years since the end of the French Indochina War.

They have offered a form of identification with a religion clearly distinct from the Buddhist religion of the lowland Lao. Touby has not declared himself to be a Christian, but he has allowed one of his wives and several of his children to become Christian.[10] He has also advised the Meo people to listen sympathetically to the message of the missionaries, and on ceremonial occasions, in the presence of Laotian and American officials, he has asked for Christian prayers to be said. I do not mean to imply that all Meo Christianity is simply expedient, but I do want to indicate that, though it was never intended as such, identification with Christianity also can serve as a means of symbolic distinction from the Buddhist Lao.

Perhaps the Meo are undergoing a revitalization movement as Wallace defines it (1956:265): "a deliberate, organized, conscious effort by members of a society to construct a more satisfying culture." The Meo appear to be competing consciously in the Lao national society for recognition in many phases of life—political, economic, occupational, educational, and religious.

Obviously the Lao government recognizes the loyalty of the Meo to their own group. The government views the Meo attitude with some apprehension—admittedly, this is why the government has prohibited the printing of any material in the Meo language.[11] It has feared that the possession of their own written

[10] Given the nature of Meo family structure, "allowed" is probably a misleading verb; his relatives must have had his explicit permission, if not his orders, to become Christian.

The pattern of conversion within Touby's family is not typical. In most Meo villages the decision to convert to Christianity is discussed within the community by the household heads. A vote is taken, and if there is a substantial minority opposed to Christianity, none will become Christian. If there is no substantial opposition, those household heads who voted to become Christian inform their families that thenceforth they will be Christians. But, unlike the Yao (see Kandre's paper), there is no need for Christian and non-Christian Meo to split into separate villages.

Touby's stand and the position of other high-ranking Meo have, no doubt, been important in influencing the high rate of conversion to Christianity among the Meo. There are now at least 5,000 Meo Christians out of 8,500 Christians in all of Laos. Protestant missionaries have worked in northern Laos for about fifty years, and although they entered Xieng Khouang Province for a short period before World War II, they have been continually active there only since 1949. The conversions of Meo have all been made in the past fifteen years.

[11] This prohibition has not been enforced in recent years. A Meo Cultural Committee has been formed, under a Catholic priest, with Catholic Meo and Protestant Meo members. They publish a newspaper in a Meo phonetic script, which does not reflect any particular religious persuasion.

language might be the capstone to the already strong in-group feeling of the Meo, thus destroying all hope of forming a national unity which crosses ethnic barriers.

Several features of the refugee program (which is outlined in Ward's paper) are relevant in concluding our discussion of recent changes. The traditional economy of the Meo has been totally disrupted as a result of the almost continuous warfare. Today most of them are living in refugee centers with far larger concentrations of population than ever were attained under normal conditions (roughly fourteen thousand Meo in one refugee center). Although some resettlement has taken place in areas which have been secured by the central government, the Meo in the larger refugee camps and in areas not securely controlled are dependent for subsistence on airlifted rice, and of course can not produce or transport opium to markets. Many men have become members of the Royal Lao army, and their extended families have followed them to the army camps. The army has found that the Meo do not make dependable soldiers when separated from their families for long periods, and the Meo have found that rice drops are more dependable when they are near an army camp.

Finally, it is indicative of the resilience of Meo social structure that household, village, and even district groupings have been maintained within the refugee camps. The houses have been regrouped according to the villages they were in before they were forced to flee their homes, and the traditional patterns of leadership in household, village, and district have been maintained.

BIBLIOGRAPHY

BERNATZIK, HUGO
    1947 Akha und Meau: Probleme der angewandten Völkerkunde in Hinterindien. Innsbruck, Wagner, 2 vols.

EMBREE, JOHN FEE
    1949 A visit to Laos, French Indochina. Journal of the Washington Academy of Science 39.

EMBREE, JOHN FEE and LILLIAN DOTSON
    1950 Bibliography of the peoples and cultures of Mainland Southeast Asia. New Haven, Yale University, Southeast Asia Studies.

GRAHAM, DAVID CROCKETT

1954   Songs and stories of the Ch'uan Miao. Washington, D.C., Smithsonian Institution Miscellaneous Collections Vol. 123, no. 1.

MATHIEU, A. R.

1959   Chronological table of the history of Laos. *In* Kingdom of Laos. Saigon, France-Asie, English edn.

MORECHAND, GUY

1955   Principaux traits du chamanisme Meo Blanc en Indochine. Bulletin de l'Ecole Française d'Extrême-Orient 47:509–542.

ROUX, HENRI and TRAN VAN CHU

1954   Quelques minorités ethniques du Nord Indo-Chine. France-Asie 10:135–419.

SAVINA, F. M.

1916   Dictionnaire Miao-Tseu-Français. Bulletin de l'Ecole Française d'Extrême-Orient 16(2). Hanoi.

1930   Histoire des Miao. Hongkong, Imprimerie de la Société des Missions-Etrangères de Paris, 2d. edn.

SMALLEY, WILLIAM A.

1956   The gospel and the cultures of Laos. Practical Anthropology 3:47–57.

WARNER, DENIS

1965   A cautionary report on Laos. The Reporter, 33 (10):35–38 (December 2).

CHAPTER 8

U.S. Aid to Hill Tribe Refugees in Laos

JAMES THOMAS WARD

INTRODUCTION

Although this paper provides a general description of the United States Agency for International Development (USAID) Refugee Relief Program, conducted in cooperation with the Royal Laotian Government (RLG), its main emphasis is on a particular phase of the program: assistance to Meo hill tribe refugees in Xieng Khouang Province from 1963 to 1965. The opinions expressed in this paper are those of the author and entirely his responsibility.

BACKGROUND

The Kingdom of Laos attained independence in 1954 as a result of the Geneva Conference. This conference, which marked the end of French domination in the Indochinese peninsula, also created the independent states of Cambodia and Vietnam. During the colonial period the French had set the boundaries of Laos for their administrative purposes. French administration in Laos followed the pattern of indirect rule; extensive exploitation or development of the economy was not attempted, and little modernization was achieved. The problems of building a modern nation that confronted the RLG were as formidable as those facing any of the new nations. The creation of a sense of unity among the diverse ethnic, linguistic, and cultural groups was paramount. On top of all this was a civil war that is still in progress. The 1962 fourteen-nation Geneva Conference was an attempt to resolve the problems of internal discord that had escalated into a great power confrontation. The resulting treaty provided for a neutral, independent, and unified Laos, ruled by a Government of National Union composed of the Conservative, Neutral, and Communist-oriented Pathet Lao factions.

The Kingdom consists of approximately two million citizens, who are spread over an area of 91,000 square miles. The ethnic Lao, comprising only half of the total population, are generally found in the lowlands, especially in the Mekong River Valley. The elite ethnic Lao live in the cities, and they dominate the political, economic, and social life of the country; whereas the peasant masses live in rural villages and practice subsistence paddy-rice cultivation.

The other half of the population are hill tribes, who usually live in remote upland areas and practice swidden or shifting rice cultivation. The Lao Theng or "Kha," including the Khmu?, are Mon-Khmer-speaking groups that may antedate all the other inhabitants; they comprise about 25 percent of the total population and are distributed throughout Laos, generally in the lower hill elevations. The remaining 25 percent are the Meo (Miao), Yao (Man), Upland Tai (Black, White, Red, and Lue groups), Akha (Ekaw), and Lahu (Mussuh). These groups are found in northern and central Laos, areas of widespread Pathet Lao insurgency. As a consequence, the large majority of refugees in Laos are tribal peoples who inhabit these areas.

USAID REFUGEE RELIEF

The widespread refugee problem is caused by the protracted "revolutionary warfare" being waged by the Pathet Lao with support from the Democratic Republic of Vietnam. Much of the area of Xieng Khouang, Sam Neua, and Nam Tha provinces has been occupied by Pathet Lao fighting units, and, as a consequence, thousands of mountain people have been dislocated from their homes and rice fields. Most have sought refuge in the more remote mountain areas and have defended themselves against the aggressors. Many refugees have lost all of their household goods except those items which they could carry away on their backs. As a humanitarian gesture, and in response to a request from the Prime Minister of the Lao government, USAID has undertaken an emergency assistance program in cooperation with the RLG Ministry of Social Welfare.

By the end of 1964 over 150,000 refugees were receiving assistance, primarily rice, and also other basic necessities, such as clothing, blankets, cooking-pots, tools, and seed. Because roads in these remote mountain areas are almost nonexistent, 90 percent of the refugee supplies are delivered by air drop. This amounts to a daily drop of about fifty tons.

Of the approximately 141,500 refugees in the north, there are an estimated 88,000 Meo tribesmen located primarily in Xieng Khouang and Sam Neua provinces. Sizable numbers of Lao Theng refugees (26,500) are found in the northern provinces. There are an estimated 19,000 ethnic Lao refugees, mainly in Sam Neua, with others in Luang Prabang and Xieng Khouang. In Nam Tha Province there are approximately 6,000 Yao and 2,000 Lue, with smaller numbers of other tribes represented. The remaining refugees are Lao and Lao Theng refugees who have gone to Vientiane or to the southern provinces of Khamoune, Sedone, and Attopeu.

The total number of refugees fluctuates greatly. As fighting increases, the people are forced to leave their homes; they may be new refugees, or old refugees who had previously received assistance and had possibly become self-sufficient in food production. As a result of the Pathet Lao 1964 spring offensive, 30,000 new refugees were added to the rolls, offsetting approximately the same number who became self-sufficient because of a good harvest in other areas. Under the most ideal conditions (good security and a good rice crop), the 30,000 new refugees displaced after spring planting were expected to require support for the remainder of 1964 and until November 1965, when their new crop was harvested.

The amount of need varies greatly from place to place. In locations near the fighting areas, the dependence on relief is much greater than in relatively secure areas. Of the total number of refugees at the beginning of 1965, it was estimated that by the end of the year probably one-third would become self-sufficient, one-third partially self-sufficient (grow enough rice for maybe six months), and one-third completely dependent because of the fighting, crop failure, etc. While the immediate aim of the relief program has been to provide basic sustenance to hard-pressed refugees, the long-range aim is permanent resettlement in secure, productive areas, in a manner that will be acceptable to the tribal peoples. Since the military situation in the northern areas does not offer much encouragement at present, extensive resettlement has not been attempted there.

AID TO MEO REFUGEES IN XIENG KHOUANG PROVINCE

The largest number of refugees is to be found in Xieng Khouang Province among the Meo tribe. The Meo are relative newcomers to Laos. Most immigrated in the past century from China and North Vietnam. It has been estimated that there are between two and one-half and three million Meo people living in Thailand, Laos, North Vietnam, and the Chinese provinces of Kweichow, Kwangsi, and Yunnan. In Laos the Lao language is the lingua franca, and most Meo village leaders, even in the most remote areas, know some Lao in addition to their own language.

Traditionally, the Meo have preferred mountain living. Most build homes in the higher elevations, explaining that they find it difficult to become acclimatized to valley living and paddy-rice cultivation. In any case, their isolation has helped preserve their cultural identity. Although Meo history has been characterized by centuries of oppression and disruption (first in China, later in Vietnam and Laos), the Meo have maintained a strong feeling of independence and a fierce resistance to their oppressors. They have often demonstrated that no matter how difficult their plight as refugees may be, they are able to overcome these disadvantages. Generally speaking, the Meo have unusual initiative, adaptability, and an ability to organize themselves. This latter trait is probably based on their strong clan system.

The Meo practice an animistic type of religion rather than the Buddhism that predominates among the Lao. Their Meo ancestors are venerated; village shamans communicate with spirits, disperse evil spirits, and practice medicine (see Barney's paper).

The agriculture of the Meo depends on shifting cultivation. The cycle of dry-rice culture begins in February when the forest area of a mountainside is cleared. After the trees have been cut and dried, they are burned. In April or May the soil of the swidden is loosened and rice seeds planted. Then comes the rainy season, and afterwards the rice is harvested, usually in November. Maize is an important crop among the Meo, who also raise

cabbage, green beans, squash, cucumbers, turnips, sweet potatoes, eggplant, etc. Opium cultivation is traditional and has in
the past served as a cash crop. Its importance has declined, however, in the past several years as good production areas have
been lost and access to markets has been limited. In some cases
non-refugee tribesmen who grow opium and who have a way
of getting it to lowland market areas will trade it for consumer
commodities—cloth, sugar, sweetened canned milk, flashlight
batteries, etc.—either for their own consumption or for marketing
in their own locale. Some authorities believe that in a period
of military security, after transportation facilities make markets
more accessible, increased vegetable production could replace
opium in importance as a cash crop. The Meo are enthusiastic
about livestock production and raise cattle, pigs, horses, and
water buffalo. In addition to animal husbandry, the Meo excel
as blacksmiths. Most villages have at least one blacksmith, who
is usually quite competent in making agricultural implements,
axes, knives, and muskets.

The center of refugee activities in Xieng Khouang Province
is the Meo village of Sam Thong, situated in a mountain valley
south of the Plain of Jars at an elevation of 4,000 feet. Approximately one-half of the province, particularly the lower elevations
including the Plain of Jars, the old provincial capital, and the
main road which connects the Plain of Jars with Vinh on the
Gulf of Tonkin, is under Pathet Lao control. The Meo refugee
villages are located in the mountains, which range up to 9,000
feet. While rice is delivered by air drop, other relief requirements
are delivered by short take-off and landing (STOL) aircraft designed for landing on short, rough air strips. These air strips
have been built by the refugees. Use of aircraft is essential to
the operation of the relief program because it is the only way
of getting to the refugees. Relief commodities are landed at Sam
Thong by larger aircraft, usually Caribous, and shuttled to refugee locations via smaller aircraft, usually Helio Couriers.

The USAID refugee coordinator for Xieng Khouang is Edgar
Buell, a man with vast experience with tribal peoples in general,
and the Meo in particular. Perhaps the secrets of Buell's success
have been his empathy and tirelessness. His language facility
and agricultural background have helped his understanding of

local problems, and in five years with the hill people he has developed numerous personal contacts. He probably knows most of the leaders in the larger villages in the area, and he visits them regularly. He always travels with a Laotian counterpart, bringing the message of the greater community of Laos. Buell's efforts at assisting refugees on the village level have gained for him the admiration of both the tribal people and the Lao government.

When reports of new refugees are received at Sam Thong, Buell or one of his two American assistants, with a native counterpart, visit the displaced people. At this time relocation sites are discussed, and the headman compiles a list of the families and numbers of people involved. The villagers are encouraged to reestablish themselves quickly, to build their homes, and to select areas for rice cultivation. They are told that they will receive rice from the sky only temporarily, until they are able to harvest their own. The most pressing needs of the villagers are determined and commodities quickly provided. Most common needs are blankets, cooking-pots, clothing, and tools. Meo refugees receive steel bars to fashion their own tools, which are superior to "ready-made" tools. If they need clothing, they are furnished with black cloth to make their own. Villagers receive vegetable seeds to plant gardens as a means of varying their diets.

Refugees are encouraged to build a school for their children, and they are provided with school supplies and a teacher to help the children to learn Lao as a second language. The larger village schools may have several classes for several grades. The highest school is a *groupe scholaire* located at Sam Thong. This school accepts advanced students from a number of villages and is supervised by the Ministry of Education. Some of the tribal graduates have been accepted for further study at the Lycée and Teacher Training Center in Vientiane. Mass education for hill people, never attempted in the past, has been enthusiastically received by the villagers.

A Meo medic will visit the new refugees and treat their numerous ailments with modern medication. The medic supervises the construction of a small dispensary, and the village elders are asked to select a young man to go to Sam Thong for medic training. The training program consists of classroom and on-the-job training for four months. After the medic completes the course, he returns to his village with medicines to care for his own people. The USAID Public Health Division supports an eighty-bed hospital at Sam Thong with personnel and medicines. Equipment for the hospital was provided by USAID and the Colombo Plan. Most of the hospital beds are filled with casualties of war or victims of malaria, malnutrition, and other ailments.

VILLAGE CLUSTER PROGRAM

A common problem among new nations with traditional societies is the great gap between dominant urban elites and the rural masses; in Laos the latter probably constitutes 95 percent of the population. The Pathet Lao movement is attempting to mobilize the rural population with the technique of "revolutionary warfare" that was successfully applied in North Vietnam. The Royal Lao Government with USAID assistance is attempting to influence rural areas through the Village Cluster Program (Khet Phatanakhane) and the Refugee Relief Program.

The Cluster Program is a pilot rural development program for the lowland areas where the ethnic Lao are predominant. It concentrates assistance for the improvement of education, health, agriculture, and transportation in a complex of existing villages. While the location of clusters is determined by need for economic improvement, strategic considerations are important, as some clusters are located on the perimeters of RLG influence. Lao provincial officials and their USAID counterparts meet with district or village leaders to determine the most urgent community needs—whether they are wells, schools, access roads, small irrigation dams, dispensaries, or agricultural or livestock improvements. The multi-purpose village-level workers assisting the villagers are the U.N.-trained Lao Fundamental Educators and the young American volunteers of the International Voluntary Services. There is no relocation of villagers involved. Usually a market town is selected as cluster headquarters, the center for development work. In the center, depending on the villagers' desires, an improved school is built, a demonstration garden is established, and a dispensary to serve all the villages in the cluster is constructed. The cluster center serves the surrounding villages, which may number anywhere from a half-dozen to two dozen. This is a self-help program: the villagers contribute their labor, land, and local materials, while the government and USAID furnish advice, equipment, and other materials. The degree of village cooperation and the success of the cluster depend on the caliber of the local leadership. It is felt that the cluster program has been moderately successful, and the six original cluster areas started in September 1963 have been expanded to twelve. Villagers' attitudes toward the program are not easy to determine, and additional research should be conducted here. Changed attitudes are much more important than the number of projects completed.

CENTRAL GOVERNMENT AND TRIBES

In the northern tribal areas the authority of the central government has been virtually nonexistent; however, this non-involvement with the tribes is changing (but see Barney's chapter regarding Meo-Lao relationships in Xieng Khouang). The problem of the tribes has been one of informal discrimination by the lowland Lao, perhaps because of cultural and economic differences. This has been intensified by lack of communication and transportation facilities. While the ethnic Lao feel superior to the tribesmen, they do not view them with the same contempt reputedly held by the Vietnamese toward the *montagnards*. Two Meos hold high government positions in Laos. The RLG has closely cooperated with Touby Lyfong, formerly a government minister and vice-chairman of the National Assembly, and General Vang Pao, Commander of the Second Military Region. Visits to the tribal areas by the King, the Crown Price, Prime Minister Souvanna Phouma, and other government leaders have been important. The return to Xieng Khouang Province of the civilian Lao Provincial Governor from exile in Vientiane is most significant.

The Civil War has itensified the fragmentation of the tribes. The Pathet Lao movement with its "War of National Liberation" has, in the past, successfully recruited many tribal peoples, especially among the Lao Theng, the most deprived group. Their propaganda appeal promises equality and an end to oppression from colonialists and neo-colonialists. The Pathet Lao has emphasized a popular united front of all peoples rather than the autonomous regions for tribal groups found in China and the Democratic Republic of Vietnam. The Meo have proven effective guerrilla fighters on both sides; in their native environs, they are often superior to lowland troops. While a dissident Meo leader named Faydang joined Prince Souphanavong in the early days of the Pathet Lao movement, the majority of Meo have remained loyal to the central government in Vientiane, probably because of the leadership of Touby Lyfong and General Vang Pao. The Refugee Relief Program has provided a vehicle for the central government to become directly involved with the tribal peoples. The central government is now in a strong position to assess their needs and to offer relief and services to the victims of the fighting. Although the program has been limited in scope, it is hoped that the returns will be promising among not only Meo, but also Lao Theng, Yao, and ethnic Lao refugees. It is only through village-level contacts such as these that the Royal Lao Government will be able to present to the tribes a clear image of itself—an image that will be respected and supported.

PART VI: MALAYSIA

MALAYSIA, including the states of Sarawak and Sabah (North Borneo) on Borneo, Singapore, and the Malay states, was founded in September 1963. Previously these states had been administered by the British under a variety of administrative devices, though the Federation of Malaya (the Malay states) had achieved independence in 1957. In August 1965 Singapore was separated from the other members of Malaysia. The papers in this volume deal with Sarawak and Sabah, but some background on the rest of Malaysia is also relevant.

The pre-colonial inhabitants of Malaysia were almost all speakers of Malayo-Polynesian languages, but they were not culturally uniform, nor were they politically unified (see Gullick 1958 for a description of indigenous political structure). There was the usual split between the sophisticated, literate, aristocratic families and the rural masses, and there was also a difference between the coastal people, who had been converted to Islam as a result of contacts with Arab and Indian traders, and the peoples of the interior of the Malayan peninsula and Borneo, most of whom retained their traditional animistic religions. The population of the interior of the Malayan peninsula has evidently always been quite small, consisting of shifting cultivators and hunters and gatherers (most of these people—Senoi and Semang—are non-Malay in speech). But, as Harrisson tells us, the interior population of Borneo was, and still is, relatively large, and has enjoyed a high standard of living and a fairly sophisticated culture without, however, having direct contact with one of the world's major centers of civilization.

The present ethnic composition is even more diverse since it now contains very substantial numbers of Chinese and Indians in addition to the Malays and "indigenous minority" (i.e., non-Islamic) peoples.

What is now Malaysia was not politically unified or centrally controlled under native rule when the British began to take over the area in 1824. There had already been three centuries of European contact by this time. Coastal sultanates had waxed and waned. Their orientation, like that of the early Europeans, was toward the sea and control of trade, rather than consolidation of the hinterlands. The control by coastal sultanates over the inland areas was based on control of rivers, and thus over the only practical routes to the interior. Early Malay settlements were on the coast and at river mouths, where they could control the overseas exchanges of prestige goods such as hornbill ivory from the interior of Borneo and jars from China.

After the British, in one guise or another, had gained control over what was to become Malaysia, interest in the hinterlands as sources of raw materials increased, especially in tin and rubber on the Malayan peninsula and pepper and gold on Borneo.

Ordinarily ethnic Malays were not used as workers on plantations or in mines. Instead, workers were imported, first from southeastern China and later, especially in Malaya, from southern India and Ceylon. Apparently the Indians were imported in a deliberate attempt to weaken the potential control the Chinese would have over the economy. Thus long before independence problems of balancing ethnic minorities were recognized, and attempts were made to deal with them. Until it became evident that the constituent parts of Malaysia would become independent, the policy was one of divide and rule. Indian and Chinese participation in politics was not encouraged, and the Malays were recognized as having a "special position" in spite of the fact that the economy was largely in non-Malay hands.

The "indigenous minority" people in Malaya are relatively few, but they form the majority of the populations of Sabah and Sarawak. In Malaya where the aborigines have been under the administration of a Protector of Aborigines, the official policy is that they should be integrated with the Malay population (Carey 1961; Federation of Malaya 1961). However, relatively few attempts have been made to integrate them into the national economy and society. On Borneo, especially in Sarawak, the situation has evidently been quite different, since the indigenous peoples have been given education for a number of years under British administration. Some of these educated Borneans fear that they may come to be treated as a "protected" and isolated minority along the same lines as the Malayan aborigines. So far their window to the civilized world has been through the British, using the English language, and thus they may fear the Malaysianization of the educational system and the replacement of English by Malay as the language of civilization. This is a situation analogous to the one found in Burma. But at least the fiscal problems are not comparable to those in Burma, since Malaysia is investing more in the Borneo states than it receives in the form of taxes in attempts to raise the Borneans to the levels of literacy and health already achieved in Malaya. The problems of minorities continue to be among the knottiest with which Malaysia must deal.

The British took control over Malaysia in a series of steps recognizing or creating many different sorts of political entities in the process. The result has been a complex legal picture, which persists under the Malaysian constitution, including the recognition of the political and religious positions of the heirs to the ancient sultanates. Such laws have implications to the almost uniformly non-Moslem minorities, since they clearly imply a national religion (Islam) with its implied social and political features. Harrisson has indicated some of the anxieties felt by some of the people of Sarawak as a result of this—anxieties which are quite similar to those reported by Lehman among the minorities in Burma after the passage of the State Religion Act.

The danger which this raises for the construction and maintenance of national unity is particularly clear because of the very different ethnic composition of the several states. Sabah and Sarawak are predominantly non-Malay and non-Moslem. Singapore, which is approximately 75 percent Chinese, evidently left the Federation of Malaysia at least in part because of the economic and political disadvantages given to Singapore, which were designed into the constitution in order to protect the position of the Malays in the Federation as a whole. But resistance to federation is not only ethnically based. Brunei, which is the most "Malay" of all the Borneo states, apparently declined to join the Federation because of conflicts over the position of the Sultan of Brunei vis-à-vis the sultans of the Malay states (a dispute going back to pre-colonial history), and also because of the oil-based affluence of Brunei as compared with the other states.

The ethnic differences are reflected in differences in settlement pattern and occupation as well as religion. The Malays have been primarily rice cultivators, small-holding rubber growers, or fishermen. They are generally found in ethnically homogeneous communities, in the coastal areas. The Chinese and Indians have usually been economically and geographically distinct.

They are often found inland, in plantations or mines. The Chinese have become laborers, traders, and shopkeepers. Many have become well educated and are involved in the professions, and they have attained a dominant place in commerce. The Indians and Ceylonese have become plantation and railroad workers and, as in Burma, have become involved in money-lending and banking. Both the Chinese and the Indians have traditionally sent remittances to their overseas relatives, and both have been responsive to political events affecting their homelands.

The minorities were involved in the Second World War and its aftermath in a variety of significant ways which have affected the internal cohesion of the nation. The indigenous minorities in Borneo were quite active and effective as guerrillas against the Japanese (Harrisson 1959). The Japanese were at least partially successful in inciting anti-British sentiment among the Indians of Malaya by promising to liberate India from British colonial rule. The Chinese, largely with Communist organization but also with British backing, carried out organized and effective resistance after the Japanese invasion. Especially after the Communist take-over in China, the Chinese Communists in Malaya organized resistance to the British, who had returned to reclaim their colony and found economic chaos left by the Japanese. In this rebellion, the so-called Malayan Emergency, the Chinese were quite unsuccessful in developing large-scale support among the Malays or among the other minorities.[1]

Today the problems of nation-building are complicated for Malaysia by the Philippine claims in Sabah (based on claims of the old Sulu sultanate) and Indonesia's policy of "Confrontation." The "Confrontation" policy has involved the Indonesians in a pledge to "crush Malaysia," and it seems to have two rationales which hold implications for minorities. First, it appeals to pan-Malay sentiment, and second, it appeals against neo-colonialism. These appeals have evidently fallen quite flat in Borneo, where the confrontation has involved the greatest amount of military action. Here the indigenous population does not view itself as being ethnically Malay, and has regarded the British

[1] The aborigines of the Malay peninsula were less effective than the Borneo natives against the Japanese (Slimming 1958). However, they played a major role during the Malayan Emergency because the guerrillas were operating out of the interior, which was occupied almost exclusively by aborigines (Madoc 1961; Stacey 1953; Westwood 1962).

[310]

as its protectors against armed invasion.[2] As Harrisson and Ley tell us, the indigenous peoples of Borneo have continued to be loyal to Malaysia and her British advisers, and have strongly resisted the Indonesian invasions. Like most borders in Southeast Asia, the boundary between Malaysian and Indonesian Borneo cuts across ethnic distributions. But the Indonesians do not seem to have been successful in persuading the indigenous people on either side of the border to join the Indonesian cause. In fact, "Confrontation," and the special military and economic aid which it produced in Sabah and Sarawak, may have resulted in greater loyalty of the indigenous minorities to Malaysia than would have been the case if there had been no outside threat.

BIBLIOGRAPHY

For bibliographic information on the ethnic groups of Malaysia see Kennedy (1962). For general ethnological background see Cole (1945) and Skeat and Blagden (1906). For two excellent studies of groups in Malaysian Borneo see Freeman (1955) and Geddes (1954). For a shorter account of the Dusun see Williams (1965). See Firth (1946) and Swift (1964) for studies of Malayan peasant communities. For studies of the Malayan "Emergency" see Pye (1956), Purcell (1954), Short (1964), and Osborne (1965:9–19). For a discussion of the role of the Malayan aborigines in this struggle see Federation of Malaya (1960, Appendix F), Holman (1958), and Williams-Hunt (1952). For general treatments of Malaysia see Wang (1964), Gullick (1964), and Parmer (1964). For a discussion of relations between Singapore and Malaysia see Osborne (1964). For some aspects of the Indonesian view on "Confrontation" see Willner (1965). For some aspects of problems of development of national loyalties among the diverse peoples in Indonesia see Skinner (1959).

REFERENCES CITED

CAREY, I. Y.
    1961   Ranchangan lima tahun. Five year plan. Kuala Lumpur.

  [2] Certainly the pan-Malay rationale would have no appeal to the Chinese; however, the Indonesians seem to have had considerable success among the Chinese of Sarawak in appeals for anti-Malaysia action, including political assassinations (*New York Times*, July 4, 1965; see also Harrisson's paper, n. 1). The question of the Sarawak Chinese response to "Confrontation" may actually be much more complicated, since it apparently involves direct ties with the Communists of mainland China (Topping 1966) as well as with Chinese Communists in Indonesia. Evidence for the latter suggestion is found in the fact that *armed* confrontation has been abandoned by Indonesia since the Communist coup failed in Indonesia in September 1965. This coup attempt was followed by anti-Chinese measures coupled with bloody suppression of the Indonesian Communists (Lewis 1966).

COLE, F. C.
1945   The peoples of Malaysia. New York, D. Van Nostrand.
FEDERATION OF MALAYA, MINISTRY OF INFORMATION
1960   End of the Emergency. Kuala Lumpur.
1961   Statement of policy regarding the administration of the aborig-
        ine people of the Federation of Malaya. Kuala Lumpur.
FIRTH, RAYMOND
1946   Malay fishermen: their peasant economy. London, Kegan Paul,
        Trench, Trubner and Co., Ltd.
FREEMAN, J. D.
1955   Iban agriculture. London, British Colonial Office, Colonial Re-
        search Studies.
GEDDES, W. R.
1954   The Land Dyaks of Sarawak. London, British Colonial Office,
        Colonial Research Studies.
GULLICK, J. M.
1958   Indigenous political systems of western Malaya. London, Uni-
        versity of London, The Athlone Press. London School of
        Economics Monographs on Social Anthropology 17.
1964   Malaya. New York and Washington, Frederick A. Praeger, re-
        vised edn.
HARRISSON, T.
1961   World within: a Borneo story. London, Cresset Press.
HOLMAN, DENNIS
1958   Noone of the Ulu. London, Heinemann.
KENNEDY, RAYMOND
1962   Bibliography of Indonesian peoples and cultures. Revised and
        edited by Thomas W. Maretzki and H. Th. Fischer. New
        Haven, Yale University, Southeast Asia Studies, by arrangement
        with Human Relations Area Files, 2d revised edn.
LEWIS, ANTHONY
1966   Indonesia purge: 100,000 said to die. Reds and pro-Reds re-
        ported slain since coup attempt. The New York Times, January
        13, pp. 1–2, story datelined London.
MADOC, G. C.
1959   Jungle fort. In Straits Times Annual for 1961, pp. 70–73.
        Singapore, Straits Times Press.
OSBORNE, MILTON E.
1964   Singapore and Malaysia. Ithaca, New York, Cornell University,
        Department of Asian Studies, Southeast Asia Program, Data
        Paper 53.
1965   Strategic hamlets in South Vietnam: a survey and a comparison.
        Ithaca, New York, Cornell University, Department of Asian
        Studies, Southeast Asia Program, Data Paper 55.
PARMER, J. NORMAN
1964   Malaysia. In Governments and politics of Southeast Asia,
        George McTurnan Kahin, ed. Ithaca, New York, Cornell Uni-
        versity Press, 2d edn., pp. 279–371.

PURCELL, VICTOR
1954 Malaya: communist or free. Stanford, Stanford University Press.

PYE, LUCIAN
1956 Guerrilla communism in Malaya: its social and political meaning. Princeton, N.J., Princeton University Press.

SHORT, ANTHONY
1964 Communism and the Emergency. *In* Malaysia: a survey, Wang Gungwu, ed. New York, Washington, and London, Frederick A. Praeger.

SKEAT, W. W., and C. O. BLAGDEN
1906 Pagan races of the Malay peninsula. 2 vols. London, Macmillan.

SKINNER, G. WILLIAM (ed.)
1959 Local, ethnic, and national loyalties in village Indonesia: a symposium. New Haven, Conn., Yale University, Southeast Asia Studies, Cultural Report Series. Distributed in cooperation with the Institute of Pacific Relations, New York.

SLIMMING, J.
1958 Temiar jungle; a Malayan journey. London, J. Murray.

STACEY, T.
1953 The hostile sun; a Malayan journey. London, Duckworth.

SWIFT, M. G.
1964 Capital, saving and credit in a Malay peasant economy. *In* Capital, saving and credit in peasant societies, Raymond Firth and B. S. Yamey, eds. Chicago, Aldine Publishing Co., pp. 133–156.

TOPPING, SEYMOUR
1966 Red China helps Malaysia rebels. Welcomes leader of group formed to topple regime. The New York Times, January 14, story datelined Hong Kong.

WANG GUNGWU (ed.)
1964 Malaysia: a survey. New York, Washington, and London, Frederick A. Praeger.

WESTWOOD, T.
1962 The face of the beloved. London, G. Allen.

WILLIAMS, THOMAS RHYS
1965 The Dusun: a North Borneo society. New York, Holt, Rinehart and Winston, Inc.

WILLIAMS-HUNT, P. D. R.
1952 An introduction to the Malayan Aborigines. Kuala Lumpur, The Government Printer.

WILLNER, ANN R.
1965 The view from Jakarta. The New Leader, March 15, pp. 12–15.

Periodicals

THE NEW YORK TIMES. New York.

TABLE 11
DISTRIBUTION OF ETHNIC GROUPS IN BRUNEI, SABAH, AND SARAWAK (1960 CENSUS)[a]

| Group[b] | BRUNEI | MALAYSIA | |
		Sabah	Sarawak
Bajau (indigenous population) [Bahau group?]		59,710	
Bajau		55,779	
Illanun		3,931	
Bisaya (indigenous population) [Klamantan group]	7,000	10,053	2,803
Brunei (indigenous population)		23,450	
Ceylonese (includes Indian and Pakistani)	2,900[c]	3,180	2,355
Chinese	21,800	104,542	229,154
Cantonese		15,251	17,432
Foochow			70,125
Hailam (Hainanese)		5,270	5,717
Hakka		57,338	70,221
Henghua			8,278
Hokkien		11,924	28,304
Teochew		5,991	21,952
Other		8,768	7,125
Cocos Islander		1,909	
Eurasian		772	538
European		1,124	1,093
Indonesian	300	24,784	3,241
Kadazan (Dusun) (indigenous population) [Klamantan group]		145,229	
Kayan (indigenous population) [Bahau group]			7,899
Kedayan (Kadayan) (indigenous population) [Klamantan group]	13,000	7,871	7,207
Kelabit (indigenous population) [Klamantan group]			2,040
Kenyah (indigenous population) [Bahau group]			8,093
Land Dayak [Land Dayak group]			57,619
Malay	33,500	1,645	129,300
Melanau (Milanau) [Klamantan group]	400		44,661
Murut (indigenous population) [Klamantan group]		22,138	5,214
Orang Sungei		15,112	
Philippine native		7,473	
Punan (indigenous population) [Punan group]	100		4,669
Sarawak native		1,911	
Sea Dayak (Iban)			237,741

(continued)

[314]

TABLE 11
(continued)

Group[b]	BRUNEI	MALAYSIA Sabah	Sarawak
Sino-native (indigenous population)		7,438	
Sulu (indigenous population)		11,080	
Tidong (indigenous population)		4,417	
Other		583	902
Other indigenous Muslims	400		
Total all communities	83,300	454,421	744,529

[a] Sources for population figures: Jones (1962A, 1962B).

[b] For meaning of "indigenous population" see Harrisson's paper (pp. 320–343 ff.). Classification of the groups [in square brackets] is from Kennedy 1962). The basis for classification of Borneo populations is quite unclear, and inconsistent among the several censuses and other sources.

[c] This figure includes European population.

REFERENCES CITED

Jones, L. W.

   1962A   North Borneo, a report on the census of population 1960. Kuching.

   1962B   Sarawak, a report on the census of population 1960. Kuching.

Kennedy, Raymond

   1962   Bibliography of Indonesian peoples and cultures. Revised and edited by Thomas W. Maretzki and H. Th. Fischer. New Haven, Yale University, Southeast Asian Studies, by arrangement with the Human Relations Area Files, 2d revised edn.

TABLE 12
POPULATION AND LINGUISTIC AFFILIATION OF ETHNIC
GROUPS OF THE FEDERATION OF MALAYA[a]

Group	Est. Population	Language
Chinese total (1957 census)	2,333,756	Chinese
Hokien	740,600	
Hakka	508,800	
Cantonese	505,200	
Tiechieu	283,100	
Hainanese	123,000	
Kwongsai	69,100	
Hengkwa	46,100	
Hokchia	11,900	
Other	34,300	
Indian (including Pakistani)	696,186	Indo-European
"Malaysian" total	3,125,474	—
Malay	2,802,900	Malayo-Polynesian: Malay
Indonesian	281,200	Malayo-Polynesian: Malay
"Aborigines"	41,360	—
Jakun (aboriginal Malays)	4,213–14,000+	Malayo-Polynesian: Malay
Negrito (Semang)	841– 3,000	Senoi-Semang
Senoi	20,480–26,900	Senoi-Semang
Semai	12,451–15,000	
Temiar	9,408–10,000	
Jah Hut	1,300– 1,700	
Che Wong	180– 200	
Semelai (= Jakun?)	2,821	?
Other	11,626	—
Buddhist Thai	15,000[b]	Tai: Southwestern
Total (1957 census)	6,278,758	

[a] Population figures are from *Census of the Federation of Malaya, 1957* (Fell 1959); linguistic classifications and underlined population figures are from LeBar *et al.* 1964. Because population figures are taken from several sources, the total of this table does not equal the census total.

[b] Figure from Thompson and Adloff (1955:160).

REFERENCES CITED

FELL, H.
    1959   1957 population census of Malaya, Report No. 14. Kuala Lumpur.
LEBAR, FRANK M., GERALD C. HICKEY, and JOHN K. MUSGRAVE
    1964   Ethnic groups of mainland Southeast Asia. New Haven, Human Relations Area Files Press.
THOMPSON, VIRGINIA, and RICHARD ADLOFF
    1955   Minority problems in Southeast Asia. Stanford, Stanford University Press.

CHAPTER 9

Tribes, Minorities, and the Central Government in Sarawak, Malaysia

TOM HARRISSON

I. INTRODUCTION

THE HISTORICAL AND GEOGRAPHICAL BACKGROUND OF
CONFRONTATION

The first general consideration with regard to Sarawak is that, although it is only one state in the Federation of Malaysia, it is much the largest. It is one of the newest and has many features in common with Sabah, the other Malaysian state on Borneo, and not so much in common with the much older and more homogeneous political units of the old Malay Federation. The old Federation of Malaya on the peninsula is now the central nexus of the new Federation of Malaysia, formed of old British-administered territories in 1963. This now includes Sabah, and Sarawak, but not Brunei, which was previously also British territory in western Borneo, nor Singapore, which left the Federation in August 1965.

Second, while politically, psychologically, and now also militarily we have to think of Sarawak in the context of Malaysia, it is also unavoidable to think of it in the context of Borneo. This context of Borneo is in many respects the main one in which Sarawak has developed the characteristics of the interior and of the minorities and hill peoples with which this book is concerned. On the whole, the direct influence from Malaya, and indeed from much of the mainland, has been rather small until very recent times. Contacts within the great island of Borneo, and between Borneo and the surrounding islands which are now part of Indonesia or the Republic of the Philippines have been great indeed over thousands and perhaps even tens of thousands of years. Intra-island contact, evolution, and independent development have also taken place within Borneo. While Sarawak is an integral, geographically large, and indeed enthusiastic segment of Malaysia, it is comparatively unimportant economically and numerically as regards the vote. On the other hand, it is also a large part of the island of Borneo, of which more than two-thirds is in the hands of, under the control of, and to some extent, historically connected with the Republic of Indonesia (under the previous Dutch regime).

These aspects come into all that follows, because thinking within the island can often greatly influence the thinking outward or the thinking from outside about any part of the island, and it is in this pattern that we have to put the present Confrontation situation between Malaysia and Indonesia. Confrontation is to some extent a continuation of, and also a contradiction of, a very ancient historical process. There has been a generally northwestward movement through the island of Borneo over many centuries which has involved many of the interior tribes. This movement has led large elements of groups such as the Kelabits, Kenyahs, Kayans, Iban (Sea Dayaks), and Land Dayaks to the west side of the island, which is now a part of Malaysia. Much larger sections of the same groups still remain on the east and southern sides (now a part of Indonesia).

Confrontation generally follows the geographical watershed between the rivers that flow west and the rivers that flow east in Borneo. This line was adopted as the political boundary between the Dutch and the British in the last century. Confrontation is recognized as a geographical fact of life which greatly influenced the people long before any white-skins ever came to this part of the world and, at the same time, as a contradiction of geographical realities. The people themselves are intimately intermixed on both sides of the border. They are the same ethnically and culturally and have a common aristocracy and elaborate trade and other associations—cultural, religious, and so on—which were never broken until the Indonesians forcibly exercised the policy of Confrontation in 1963.

THE CHINESE MINORITY

It is also necessary to add a third, rather different and in some ways lesser, consideration. Lesser, that is, from the point of view of a special attention to minorities and hill tribes of the interior borders and those other related matters which particularly concern this book. This third element is the Chinese presence in Sarawak (as indeed in Malaysia generally). Once more we find both a continuation of an ancient tradition and an interruption. Chinese influence in trade and Chinese cultural contact (and to a small extent physical and genetical contacts) have continued. They began at the start of the Christian era, long before the advent of Islam in west Borneo and into Sarawak particularly.

The great China trade which came down before the beginning of the T'ang dynasty in the seventh century brought iron, porcelain, beads, silks, and the many other things which were of the highest value to the people. These were traded right into the interior of Borneo, where you still find very ancient Chinese beads and T'ang jars as the high-value objects of the upland Kelabits, Kenyahs, and Kayans. This continuity of Chinese outside influence was then largely submerged by a multiplicity of factors, including the growing influence from the West, and of Islam from Arabia through Malaya and Java, and so on. These reached Sarawak and west Borneo only in the fourteenth century, at the beginning of the Ming dynasty. By that time the China trade in this area was already much reduced, but the Chinese cultural background, though subsequently very much submerged, has some relevance to the other main conflict situation inside Sarawak: Confrontation and the hill and other minority questions.

With the coming of Islam, we have the loss of Chinese influence through trade, then the return of the Chinese as gold miners and as workers in the pepper groves, and then their advent to political and economic power over a large part of Sarawak only during this century. I do not propose in the rest of this paper to pursue this matter of the Chinese, but it is essential to recognize it, because it is these Chinese who pose the other great problem inside Sarawak and Malaysia—that of Communism. Very few people in Sarawak, other than the Chinese, are involved in Communism. On the other hand, many of the attitudes of the large Chinese population in Sarawak which are attributed to Communism are in part actually due to their feelings of ancient pride and cultural continuity and to the fact of a complete lack of any continuity inside Sarawak itself.

There are about 250,000 Chinese in Sarawak at present, almost the same number as in the other racial "minority," the Sea Dayaks, and both of them outnumber the Malays in Sarawak by almost two to one. The Chinese population is increasing fastest of all. Of these Sarawak Chinese, about 80 percent were born in Sarawak, but less than 1 percent are in the third or fourth generations of native born. (See "Definition of Citizenship," on pp. 344 ff. below.) It is here, entirely in the lowlands, away from the Indonesian border (except where the border comes very close to the coast in the southwest), that the CCO (Chinese Communist Organization) situation is serious.[1] Though the Chinese are now almost a numerical majority in Sarawak and are indeed dominant economically, they are adopting all the attitudes of a minority group. Thus a great many of the attitudes which are described in other chapters in this book as characteristic of hill and inland minorities are in fact taken by the much more educated, sophisticated, and economically well-off Chinese in the lowlands and mainly in the towns—the big towns like Kuching, Sibu, and Miri in Sarawak. We cannot pursue this here, but I think it should be noted for consideration in the future: "minority" attitudes can be expressed, very strongly indeed and in more sophisticated terms, by majority groups if there is no long cultural tradition *in situ* or if there is any feeling of instability, lack of tenure, and so on.

Although these Chinese are all fully recognized as citizens of Sarawak, they are distinguished from what are called the "indigenous" people who are citizens but are also classed as "natives." "Natives" have certain additional rights, for instance in land, which are not possessed by the non-natives, that is the Chinese, nor by the English, nor of course by others like the Indians, who are only a very small number in Sarawak.

---

[1] Since this chapter was written, events have moved to within a few miles of the capital, Kuching. On June 27, 1965, there was a raid on the police station at the eighteenth mile, in which two police officers (one the brother of Sarawak's Iban Chief Minister) were murdered, as were several Chinese civilians, including women and children. The background of this incident is not clear concerning the degree of direct Indonesian influence. Extensive resettlement, along the lines followed during the Malayan Emergency, has now been put into effect in this area. Some 8,000 Chinese have been regrouped. The "native" peoples of the area have been allowed to remain in their own homes and holdings (as of July 20, 1965).

THE CULTURAL BACKGROUND OF NATIVE MINORITIES

Cultural background and cultural continuity are the most important things in the Borneo context. In fact, it is very difficult to understand any of the attitudes of the people today—whether in central government or in state government on the coast, in Kuching, or among the very remote peoples like the nomadic Punans in the interior of the Rajang Delta or the upland Kelabits in the remote highlands of the Fourth and Fifth Divisions—if we do not recognize the traditional backgrounds and associations of the people themselves. In connection with this cultural background, three things require emphasis. First, there is today a great deal of cultural diversity within Sarawak in particular and Borneo generally. There are a number of distinct linguistic and cultural groups, and even though these people are rapidly learning Malay (the national language), new ethics and outlooks, and even though they are very loyal Malaysians (many are in fact fighting or running great risks for Malaysia along the border right now), they are, besides being Malaysians, very decidedly Kelabits, Kenyahs, Kayans, Muruts, Bisayas, Ibans, or Dayaks. There is at present no indication that this attitude is diminishing. On the contrary, there are strong indications that the very act of becoming nationally conscious as Malaysians is also accentuating their local group, traditional group, and ancestral group consciousness as Kelabits or Ibans or even nomadic Punans. This is a familiar pattern all through Southeast Asia, perhaps becoming accentuated in Sarawak. Because Malaysia is an entirely new concept, whose operation has affected Sarawak for only two years, there is no traditional pattern to facilitate the acceptance of a national outlook, as there is for instance in Thailand, which has been an entity for hundreds of years, or even in Laos, which was an administrative entity within the French Indochinese state for quite a long time.

In Sarawak, although there are only quite small numbers of people like Kelabits, they nevertheless are very strongly Kelabits. Even if they are cutting their hair, or going to school, or being Christians (which they increasingly are), or possibly later on becoming Mohammedans, the strength of their tribal identification is likely not only to remain, but possibly to increase. This is, of course, not necessarily unhealthy or contradictory within Malaysia, because these people have got to have a very strong feeling of identification, especially when they are being asked to suffer considerably under Confrontation.

The second implication of cultural background is that this diversity and identity of small and often remote groups is tied up with the geography of Sarawak in Borneo. This geography is somewhat distinct from that of most of mainland Southeast Asia, and indeed from most of the islands too, except New Guinea. Like New Guinea, the interior of Borneo is extremely difficult to get into, and the terrain itself is enormously complicated. One is well aware that although the more remote parts of Thailand and Laos and the Malaya Peninsula are mountainous and difficult country, nonetheless, on the whole like Burma, they have an order and a symmetry and an explorability which is lacking in Borneo as in New Guinea. In the interior of these islands we have a great mass of chaotic, confused mountainous terrain intersected by rivers which, although in Borneo they generally run west and east, nevertheless have all kinds of diversifications and crisscrosses, so that at any one moment in the interior, unless you have a compass, you cannot possibly tell where you are merely from the direction of rivers or mountains.

This terrain means that it takes literally months to walk across the island of Borneo (and until very recently walking had been the only way to travel). Indeed many of the Indonesian activities connected with Confrontation in the interior—confronting northern Sarawak and also southern Sabah—are still conducted on foot, with immense supply problems and long journeys from the east coast of Indonesian Kalimantan. Terrain has of course greatly complicated the population and inhabitation of interior Borneo. It has meant, briefly, that large areas of Borneo are still uninhabited. There is probably more uninhabited, unused country in Borneo than almost anywhere else in the world except in the Amazon Basin.

Second, the terrain has meant that where a group settles in and becomes locally successful, as for instance the Kelabits in the uplands above 3,000 feet in north Sarawak and northwestern Kalimantan, it is possible for them to live in considerable immunity and isolation and to develop a very successful way of life and a fairly high standard of living even by modern standards. This is something that they are most reluctant to give up or give away to anybody outside for any reason.

OUTSIDE INFLUENCES AND INTERNAL DEVELOPMENT

Third, this terrain and this background of diversity link up with a very long tradition of biologically modern man (*Homo sapiens*) within Borneo itself. Kelabits in the middle of Borneo or Sea Dayaks a little nearer the coast have very advanced cultures, beautiful arts, and high craftsmanship, good standards of living, highly developed philosophies and theologies, personal courage, immediate intelligence, and adaptability: these are all genuine characteristics of most of the people I am talking about. Outsiders all too often assume that these things must have been acquired elsewhere. All sorts of writings and most of the contemporary standard works on this area attribute the highly developed culture and personal integrity of these peoples to all sorts of migrations from the north and the west, or to the interpolation of Buddhism, or to some other outside influence. I do not think this is a valid historical reconstruction for the interior of Borneo.

Our own Sarawak Museum excavations of the Great Cave at Niah in western Sarawak, running continuously since 1954, have now identified *Homo sapiens* material at a depth in stratified deposit which has been dated by Carbon 14 from over 35,000 years ago. This evidence is now widely accepted as showing that biologically modern man was present in west Borneo, in Sarawak, at least 35,000 years ago. Similar evidence is coming from Palawan in the southern Philippines, and I have no doubt that more will be found elsewhere in Southeast Asia.

This means that we have to look at these cultures, and the minorities among them, as things that have developed over a very long period of time. Further, my own researches during the last twenty years that I have spent in Sarawak do not indicate that outside influences have been the main ones, although they have been an important factor. There has been a tremendous ancient, indigenous growth of these local cultures, which have, of course, diversified, as all human and all animal activities do; but they have a high degree of indigenous and endemic characteristics.

[323]

The really striking impression gained from all the archeological work we have done in Sarawak since 1947 and in the Niah Cave since 1954, taken in correlation with other work that has been done in Indonesia, in Malaya, and especially in the Philippines, is the picture of a very highly advanced culture achieved by the late Stone Age all through this area.[2] Before any of the modern theological or intellectual impacts such as Christianity, Buddhism, Hinduism and Mohammedism, there was a high degree of organized civilization (in the broad sense) in many of these places. In fact, of course, this is continued in a rather crude form by over a million people in central New Guinea, who were isolated from the outside world until less than ten years ago. Again, there were great geographical barriers which prevented outside penetration.

By the late neolithic Stone Age, say about 2,000 years before Christ, there were already beautifully made objects and highly organized societies in western Borneo. The people had an elaboration of jewelry, artistry, and craftsmanship, and they showed what could be fairly described as a love of the dead that was obviously connected with a deep intellectual and spiritual feeling. This was displayed not only in exquisitely laid-out primary burials of the dead, but also in loving, detailed, and expensive treatments of the bones by secondary burials and cremation, especially of babies and of mothers who died in childbirth. This sort of thing long pre-dated the Hindu influences to which customs like cremation have usually been attributed by authors writing from a Southeast Asian perspective. These people had a dynamic culture (which we know intimately because of the caves) which extended even into the remotest uplands that are inhabited today, where we find the stone tools *in situ* in irrigated root-crop situations. Offshore, they penetrated in boats even to the tiniest islands and tiny caves on these islands, which were used for burials. In fact, Borneo generally, and particularly Sarawak, has an astonishingly rich cultural background, which is expressed in its life today.

Of course, this background has been influenced by many out-

---

[2] This material is detailed in a paper I gave to the Royal Society of Arts, published by the Smithsonian Institution in 1965.

side sources; I am stressing endemic native aspects because they are most relevant for the present book.

Outside influences from China, from India, and especially along the coast from Arabia by way of India, Malaya, and Java in the form of Islam in later times, also have been important. But they have not shifted the basic pattern of what one might call Borneo-ness, except where access from the coast is easy. The areas which are of easy access to the coast are, relative to the whole of Borneo, small, and in the case of Sarawak, particularly so. On the other hand, the influences which have brought people into contact with more recent outside civilization such as Mohammedan, and still more recent European or Western civilization, are, and have been, at work to bring people down toward the coast. This sort of centrifugal effect is evidently not an ancient one, or at least not an overwhelmingly powerful ancient one, in western Borneo. The evidence is strong that there were so many attractions and advantages of living inland among the mountains and in the cooler climates with more easily controlled vegetations at the slightly higher altitudes which were more secure from interference, that a very large population (running to millions of people) lived mainly in what we now consider to be the "minority tribal border areas." There is overwhelming evidence that many of these areas which now have small populations once had much larger ones, as they still do in similar conditions in central New Guinea. Moreover, there is absolute evidence from archeology, folklore, and proto-history that large areas which are now only inhabited by nomadic Punans (e.g. in the central Third Division of Sarawak) were once densely inhabited. For instance, it is now possible to walk for ten days in what appears to be virgin jungle in the upper Rajang area in Sarawak and yet on analysis and detailed exploration to discover that in one quite small area of a few miles there are the remains of big prehistorical longhouses, more than fourteen in one specific area.

RELATIONS BETWEEN INTERIOR AND COAST

This is also important in a way for our present theme, since many lowlanders today cling to their upland and inland origins.

There is no longer a tendency to move downward and outward; and, on the contrary, some thinking in favor of a reverse move is now developing. Indeed, some younger leaders and thinkers are perhaps coming to the conclusion that their fairly recent ancestors made a mistake in moving so far northwest and west and coming out on the coast. The people of the coastal plains, whose population is developing rapidly, now face a land shortage and the problems of the very poor soil characteristic of the lowlands of Sarawak.[3]

In the past the outward movement was conditioned by the advent of trade goods and new demands introduced from the outside. There is archeological evidence that in the past there were changes of fashion and what one might call consumer unrest. The idea that there has been a rigidly stable, conservative outlook among these hill tribes in Borneo is unfounded even in short terms; there is change in the values of, and interests in, old objects, even jars and glass beads. There is no reason whatever to think that there ever has been any complete conservatism. In fact, conservatism is maladaptive for survival under the pressures of equatorial tropical rain forest. Borneo living is extremely difficult and requires constant experiment, innovation, and initiative. The advent of iron on the coast was tremendously important. It effected just as great a technological revolution as the advent of malaria control, or schoolbooks, or anything else from the West today; in fact the resultant revolution was probably much greater.

In addition to the introduction of new material wants, another important factor in reducing the interior population for a time was the advent of the Europeans in the sixteenth century; the introduction of new diseases and epidemics had a decimating effect on the previously isolated inland populations. Again, in folklore and genealogies there is abundant evidence of the terrible impact of new diseases such as smallpox, influenza, measles, and even whooping-cough, which sometimes devastated upland

[3] I should add here that the poverty of the lowland sandstone soil is a very important factor in Sarawak and west Borneo. This is not the case in Sabah, where there is a rich volcanic soil on the coast, and is seldom true on the mainland, where there are alluvial deposits and other good soils which are generally lacking on the Sarawak coast.

valleys in a single stroke. Only recently has there been any medical control.

BORNEO AS A PART OF SOUTHEAST ASIA

An adequate explanation of human behavior in Sarawak must be quite complicated. The longer one stays, and the more one travels (and I think I have traveled to almost every corner, valley, and tribal group in Sarawak), the more one becomes aware of the country's extreme complexity and diversity. We cannot ignore these complications, but we must not overemphasize them. Indeed, after reading about, and traveling to some extent in other parts of Southeast Asia, I am convinced that while the Kelabits of the central uplands of Borneo, for instance, are a highly specialized people, there are a great many major parallels not only between them and the people in Malaya, but also between them and the Kachins and Karens in Burma, the tribes in the Chiengmai area of Thailand and the peoples in the extreme north of Laos, and elsewhere. Therefore any emphasis on differences includes the conviction that there is a distinct sort of Southeast Asian person.

We have to face, therefore, this seeming contradiction, which is probably largely a matter of communications and time. A Kelabit in central Borneo is probably prepared in the ultimate analysis to sacrifice his life rather than stop being a Kelabit; on the other hand, he would probably settle down in a year if you put him in the Karen hills of Burma. We have actually had in the last two years an experimental situation of this kind which has not been adequately studied: a large element in the British forces invoked to assist in east Malaysia under treaty with Malaya are Ghurkas from Nepal, and the Ghurkas have been extensively used to protect the border areas in Sarawak. This is the first time that outsiders of any kind have suddenly appeared in the remotest hinterland minority-group situations. Usually within just a day the Ghurkas have become integrated with the local communities, and quite a number of them are thinking of settling down in Sarawak; some have actually already settled down in retirement in the hinterlands of Sabah. This development is being welcomed by the local people.

In sum, the minority groups feel like a "minority," and yet, at the same time, they feel a oneness with a much wider group of people. And there is some real cultural validity in that feeling of oneness.

SARAWAK AS A PART OF BORNEO

As I have already explained, the gradual pattern of migration through Borneo over the last 10,000 years and more has been from the southeast to the northwest. Many of the peoples in the Malaysian part of Borneo, as also in the state of Brunei, which is not a part of Malaysia, still have the most intimate and self-recognized cultural affinities and even kinship affinities with the people to the east in Indonesian Kalimantan. These are not just the feelings of common experiences at meetings, such as those that occur when a Ghurka meets a Kayan, but actual associations and known folklore genealogies showing common origins at points on the eastern side of Borneo.

If we start from the extreme north of the Sarawak border where it joins Sabah, behind Long Pasia in the headwaters of the Padas, and continue southward, we come upon a succession of people to whom this applies. The Muruts of the Trusan River in the Fifth Division of Sarawak know that they have all migrated northwestward from Kalimantan. The Kelabits a little further south in the top of the Fourth Division of Sarawak, though they have been there probably longer than any other people in Sarawak, have a much larger segment of their own people across the border in Kalimantan, and the Sarawak element is only a small minority. There are at least ten times as many Kelabits on the other side of the watershed. Coming further south again, we have the Kayans and the Kenyahs in the Fourth and Third Divisions, who have all their old cultural stories and origin stories centered in Kalimantan. There are only a few thousand of these people, though they occupy a huge area in central Sarawak, but there are nearly a hundred thousand of them over in Kalimantan. Moving south again, we come to the Sea Dayaks (the Ibans), the most numerous racial group in Sarawak, but they are also more numerous in Kalimantan, and their genealogies show that in fact most of them migrated westward into present-day Sarawak, approximately eighteen to twenty generations ago, from the Kapuas River in Kalimantan. The same applies to various people now called Land Dayaks. So, for about five hundred miles of border, along which we are now confronted with Indonesian troops, there is an absolutely common heritage, and in every case for each person in Sarawak there are between five and fifty people of the same linguistic, cultural, ethnic, and self-conscious entities on the Indonesian side of the border.

This has great implications, of course. One of them is that the Indonesians are proving unable to use any local, indigenous native people of the interior in these Confrontation activities. They have to be carried out almost entirely by Javanese. And secondly, of course, the Javanese are intensely unpopular in their whole activity along that border, where everything they do is disturbing a previously completely satisfactory relationship over the watersheds along a border which was never recognized except in purely national or international political terms. So we have to think of the middle of Borneo as a huge area, larger than the state of Laos or Vietnam, where there are many hill tribes. Though the statistics for Sarawak or for Sabah show few of them, and there is no proper census of Kalimantan, if the three are taken together, the center of Borneo has an overwhelming majority of such people for the whole island of Borneo. They outnumber the Chinese or any other group in the lowland. And here I should add, of course, that the Chinese and the Malays only live in the lowlands, though they occasionally go inland, e.g. for Confrontation purposes. In normal times, and until 1963, in the whole interior of Sarawak there were no Chinese living, and only one or two very small communities of rather atypical Malays at places like Belaga in the middle Rajang, and none permanently in the interior proper.

II. DEMOGRAPHIC AND ECONOMIC CONSIDERATIONS

POLITICAL VS. ETHNIC BOUNDARIES

The first consideration with respect to the statistics of population is that the boundaries of the states bear little or no relation to the realities of ethnic, cultural, or religious distribution. Sarawak is a political creation of the Brookes, and most of it is well under a century old, as indeed is the case also with Sabah. Of course, this situation is similar over much of Southeast Asia.

RELIGION

We are fortunate, in the former British territories of Borneo (Sarawak, Sabah, and Brunei), in having an accurate census undertaken in 1960, from which we derive the following information for the religion of the population.

TABLE 13
RELIGION IN BRUNEI, SABAH, AND SARAWAK

	STATE					
	Brunei		*Sabah*		*Sarawak*	
RELIGION	Number	Percent	Number	Percent	Number	Percent
Muslim	50,516	60.2	172,324	37.9	174,123	23.4
Christian	6,796	8.1	75,247	16.6	117,755	15.8
Animist	26,565	31.7	206,850	45.5	452,651	60.8
Total	83,877	100.0	454,421	100.0	744,529	100.0

In Brunei, the only one of the three territories where the Muslims are in the majority, the population did not support the "Malaysian solution"—that is, they did not join with the other two British-administered Borneo states, together with Singapore and the Malay States, in forming the Federation of Malaysia. In Sarawak and Sabah, Malay Muslims are now exercising increased influence (though they form a minority of the population) through the federal legal system operating from Malaya proper.

Table 11 (on pp. 314–315 of the Malaysia section of this book) shows a detailed breakdown of the ethnic groups in these territories. The animists mentioned in Table 13 are predominantly Dayaks, plus "minority" or tribal people, although some of these peoples, notably among the Muruts, have recently been converted to Christianity.

"MINORITY" AND "MAJORITY" POPULATIONS

The term "minority" has to be applied with care for several reasons. Firstly, some smaller groups "own" such vast areas, within which they are the exclusive residents, that they have not, until very recently, felt themselves to be minorities. They live in a basically localized cultural context. Secondly, as already mentioned, although the Kelabits, for instance, number only a few thousand in Malaysian Borneo, their linguistic, cultural, and kin associates number in the tens of thousands in Kalimantan. Thirdly, attitudes within the group and attitudes of those outside of it do not necessarily depend on a consideration of numerical majority or minority position. The situation of the Chinese in this regard has already been referred to.

With these qualifications in mind, we can consider the following peoples as "minority": Murut, Kelabit, Kenyah, Kayan, and Punan. These groups are found primarily inland in remote areas, along the approximately five-hundred-mile-long common border with northern Kalimantan. Working from north to south, these groups are arranged as in Table 14.

TABLE 14
LOCATION OF "MINORITY" POPULATIONS IN SARAWAK

Ethnic Group	"Inland" Number (approximate)	Sarawak Administrative Division
Murut	3,000	Fifth
Kelabit	2,000	Fourth
Kenyah	8,100	Fourth and some Third
Kayan	6,000	Mostly Third
Punan (nomads)	4,700	Third and Fourth

These groups, plus a few tiny ones numbering under 100 each (Ukit, Bukitan, Ba Mali, etc.), give a total of about 25,000 who are minority peoples in the sense that they are small, isolated groups.

Sea and Land Dayaks live near the border only as it comes closer to the coastal plain in the Lower Third Division and down to the First. Here remoteness is no longer a factor, and the communications and other criteria discussed below (under "Legal Relationships") do not operate to keep these people exclusive, "undeveloped," etc., although other factors may have similar effects. About 10,000 of the Land Dayaks live in the interior, and a small fraction of the Sea Dayaks (Iban) also live in remote areas. When these are added to the groups enumerated above, we get far less than 50,000, or about 7 percent of the total Sarawak population of 750,000, who inhabit about one-half of the total area.

These inlanders and uplanders therefore control, even if only by custom and knowledge, a huge land area which is still primitive in communications. It is this area which is now the crucial one for some security and related operations under direct Confrontation (as contrasted with the most accessible lowland areas, mainly in the southwest, where internal pressures, which have not affected the interior, continue to loom largest).

The northern section is, in these and all other respects, the truly "tribal" one in the sense used in the rest of this book. The 25,000 people involved can be broken down in two dimensions: location of settlement and type of community. Nine thousand live in the mountainous regions which cannot be reached by water, and this includes most of the actual "border," while sixteen thousand live on the river lines. Twenty-one thousand live in longhouse communities of from one hundred to eight hundred people, while four thousand are nomads, though many of these are now at least temporarily "semi-settled." A small, fully nomadic element (in about ten bands) covers a vast area otherwise uninhabited.

ECONOMIC RELATIONS OF "HILL TRIBES"

The economy of the hill areas is characterized by relatively primitive methods of production and distribution accentuated by remoteness and the physical difficulty in reaching the area. Several points deserve emphasis here. First, no trade of any kind can be carried out by these hill minorities except through the coastal centers and the Chinese, though cooperatives are now beginning to gain strength. On the whole, the previous government had taken very little part in inland trade matters, for reasons made clear below.

The total contribution of the "inside half" of Sarawak to the national economy is almost insignificant. I would estimate it at less than 1 percent of the "export economy" (probably far less), and not more than 2 percent (probably less than 1 percent) of the "import economy" in consumer goods, etc. Of the imports, a large part had gone over to Kalimantan for many decades until 1963. Confrontation has now completely cut off that trade. Principal "exports" of the past were rattan, damar-gum, wild rubber, rhino horn, hornbill ivory, bezoar stones, and deer's antlers. These have either much less value now, or are in short supply due to earlier "overproduction" inland. Buffaloes (live) remain a Murut specialty. They are walked to the coast for sale, which takes up to fifteen days.

The basis of the inland economy was one of making their own subsistence by rice and (wild) protein, a pattern which is dependent for its success on a great expanse of land and jungle. There was also barter-trade between groups, valleys, and across the border. For example, Punan mats for Kenyah knives; Kelabit spring salt (very important) for Kayan beads; hill tobacco for lowland cook-pots. Small-scale periodic "export" trips were made to lowlands for cash goods, such as cloth.

The presence, for the first time, of large outside groups began in 1945 (parachutists under the author's command), and reappeared in 1963 (British and Malaysian forces), both times due to military necessity. In some areas this has introduced much more cash and demand for labor, which was previously nil; but the impact has been very uneven and so far without lasting influence on the basic economy discussed above.

The small sums needed for taxes, shotgun cartridges, etc., until now have been met by the means of occasional trading trips to the coast. However, owing to the decline in supply of some items (because of earlier overintensive hunting) and to the decline in demand for other products, increasingly this "export" has been of inland *men,* who come down and work for periods of some months, usually in the Chinese sawmills or on the Brunei oilfields in order to get cash. Until the recent increase in demand for consumer goods, often a man would do this in one stretch to provide for a lifetime, making all his cash needs in one operation. This is changing too, with education and the new consumer tastes of the young.

GOVERNMENT PROGRAMS FOR THE INTERIOR

Before the formation of Malaysia there were few government programs directed at the interior, nor was the situation under the rule of the Brookes resented. The advantages of being "left in undisturbed possession and peace," and an end to all head-hunting, after all, were great. Once Sarawak became a Crown colony, the pace increased. But distances are great, and population vastly scattered. The big impacts came in the following order of succession and eventual importance. I have arranged them by the 1964 scale in the interior, though they are not necessarily still the same in importance.

Service	Scale	Order of appearance	Present importance
Law	Uneven (see below)	1	5
Police, etc.	Slight	2	4
Education	Rapidly accelerated, large now	3	2
Medical, including WHO	Steady development	4	1
Airways, subsidy	Local and somewhat erratic	5	Locally very important
Agriculture	Local advice and aid	6	3

There have also been expensive new government operations arising from border and Confrontation repercussions. For example, in April 1965 a new scheme to supply fire extinguishers to longhouses was announced at a cost of one million dollars.

The expenditure by government far exceeds any form of revenue or service received from the area. Great effort and devotion has been shown by some sections of the government, notably individual district officers, schoolteachers, doctors, and others (mostly British, Chinese, Malay, and Indians) in these services. Such work can be dangerous and is often thankless.

The cooperative movement has got a small but strengthening hold in the interior lately, but will present considerable difficulties of administration, audit, etc., until communications improve.

No inland community has yet succeeded in producing a "cash crop" that can be economically exported to the coast, which would help to solve the economic imbalance. This imbalance is of course one factor which has encouraged a "let-alone" attitude once the responsibilities of the government, i.e., health, education, security, have been fulfilled.

This is not for want of trying. Some expensive inland experiments made within my own knowledge since 1950 have included cocoa, coffee, turkeys, Brahmin cattle, ponies (for transport), oranges, cabbages, potatoes. All have failed primarily because of supervisory and transport difficulties directly due to distances, terrain, and the long periods of rain and "permanent cloud" in the interior.

No valuable minerals have been found inland in workable amounts. There is one big coal deposit, but it is in an uninhabited valley at an elevation of 4,000 feet.

III. SOME SPECIFIC ISSUES

GEOGRAPHICAL THINKING

As I have tried to indicate in the preliminary parts of this paper, geography is one of the most complicated and complicating things for human beings in Sarawak, and in Borneo generally. The geographical factors which led to the political boundaries now dividing Malaysia and Indonesia are realistic in physical terms, but bear little relation to human realities. On the other hand, there is another type of structure within Borneo which has a much greater antiquity and remains of underlying significance to many of the native peoples. This is the old conception of the sultanate, which was based on a natural geography. The sultanate operated from the coastal outflow center of one or more river systems and their hinterlands. This pattern goes back long before the Mohammedan sultanates; there is ample evidence that the native (pagan) sultanates existed as early as the eighth century, some six centuries before the advent of Islam in west Borneo.

One of the reasons why the sultanate of Brunei was so weak that it lost much of its territory to the Brookes in Sarawak, and to the chartered company in Sabah, was that it was extended to the point of geographical unreality. It had tried to control the whole west coast of Brunei instead of the outflows into Brunei Bay itself, which formed the natural entity. The other sultanates of Borneo did not get involved in such territorial complexities and in fact have remained important right through the Dutch occupation and into Indonesian occupation today. I only mention this because not only are the other present political boundaries complicated for human beings, though perfectly adequate for geography and politics, but the subdivisions of the country itself are sometimes complicated.

CENTRALIZATION AND DECENTRALIZATION OF THE STATE

One of the great difficulties for any central government is knowing how far to entrust major responsibilities to remote and little-known minorities. This has become particularly important very recently in Confrontation and affects such problems as the arming of the border people, and particularly the degree of arms and independence which may or may not be given to such organizations as the Border Scouts. The difficulties of regular soldiers and regular military units in controlling hundreds of miles of border through extremely difficult and often uninhabited country, as in much of the Third Division in Sarawak, where a great area of the border is nowhere near any human settlement, puts a premium on giving big responsibilities to the local people. This, of course, is always limited by the fear that they might become irresponsible at some later date.

LOCAL ATTITUDES AND REPRESENTATION FROM THE INTERIOR

There is, in Sarawak, an active tradition of internal leadership expressed outward to the coast which was built up by the Brookes from the middle of the last century. This contrasts with the situation in most countries of Southeast Asia and even with Sabah within Malaysia. Administrative contact with the coast was accentuated by the second postwar governor under the colonial system, Sir Charles Arden Clarke, who introduced local elections. These local elections and local authorities were strongly developed in Sarawak within the last decade preceding the Federation of Malaysia. Even in the remotest areas in the interior, the people have conducted one man-one vote elections and have elected representatives democratically to district councils, from there to divisional councils, and from there to the Council Negeri (national council). From this national council at present a very generous quota of members of parliament and senators go through to the Malaysian Parliament in Kuala Lumpur. This recent tradition of local government is extremely important in Sarawak and does not seem to find any parallel, for instance, in Thailand or Laos or Cambodia. The people have got this idea very clearly in mind now and are extremely keen on it. It means that the Muruts, Kelabits, the Kenyahs, the Kayans, and such people, minorities everywhere, are represented in the very center of government. For example, Temonggong Oyau Lawai Jau, a member of the Government Alliance Party, who is the head of the Kenyahs and Kayans in the Fourth Division of Sarawak, is also on all the following councils: district, divisional, and Council Negeri; and is also in the Senate in Kuala Lumpur. Moreover, the Sarawak State government and the Malaysian government have shown great common sense in not restricting politics to a one-party system or any other kind. To take an example, Temong-gong Oyau Lawai Jau's own first cousin is in the opposition party, the SUPP (Sarawak United People's Party), which is very critical of the Alliance government, though not anti-Malaysian, and he also has been elected through these channels to the Parliament in Kuala Lumpur, where he sits in opposition to his cousin.

This means that the people in the remote areas are not really placid and directed from the center. If they are not being adequately considered, they are still in a strong position to express their opinions. If they do not think that sufficient measures are being taken to protect them, for instance, or they are not being sufficiently allowed to protect themselves against Confrontation, they are in a position to say so. And, of course, this affects all sorts of other things: education, medical facilities, veterinary services, communications, and so on. Therefore, we have in Sarawak something which appears to be lacking in many of the countries under discussion in this book, that is that the minorities are able to communicate directly to the central government, and they do so. There have been a number of cases where they have raised issues which have been sympathetically and immediately considered by the central government, and their requests have been met. This is, perhaps, one of the healthiest features of the whole situation as far as the minorities are concerned.

It is quite clear that in certain countries in Southeast Asia, the hill tribes have been significantly neglected or underrated, as in Laos and probably Vietnam. In Sarawak this has never really been entirely so even under the Brookes, as I have described earlier in this section, and it is definitely not so today. Indeed, priorities are being given by the Malaysian government to anything that concerns these remoter peoples, priorities even more out of proportion to their economic and numerical contribution than was the case in the past. This is a vital distinction which I must emphasize.

THE QUESTION OF LANGUAGE

The issue of language is extremely complicated throughout Southeast Asia. Perhaps it is not so complicated in Sarawak as elsewhere because Malay is now widely used as the lingua franca among these diverse groups of people, though, of course, this is only spoken Malay. On the other hand, English had previously been adopted under the colonial regime as the language of teaching. Considerable confusion developed between 1946 and the formation of Malaysia in 1963 over this requirement and the new and very natural requirement of Malay as a national language. This is a problem that has to be thrashed out further. Fundamentally, it appears that anybody in Sarawak is prepared to learn Malay, and to speak Malay and adopt Malay fully. But again we come back to the underlying feeling of fear that too much pressure on this issue may accentuate the feeling of local tribalism and minority anxiety which I referred to at the very beginning of these observations.

THE EFFECT OF RELIGION: ISLAM AND ANIMISM

It is perhaps relevant to mention that there is a difference between the outlook of Islam and Buddhism in regard to other peoples. It is implicit in true Mohammedan belief that it is desirable, if not necessary, to convert others. There is also a much more forceful element in Mohammedan missionizing and proseletyzing, which is absent in much of Buddhist thinking, and it is Buddhist thinking which affects so many of the countries of Southeast Asia and most of those represented in this book. This is not to make any distinction of major importance between the common Asian outlook of the two, but only to say that the broad atmosphere of Malaysia is perhaps less gentle and less negative in a religious sense than it would be, say, in Laos, where Buddhism is very mild, where Christianity is almost negligible, and where animism is extremely diffuse. In Sarawak we have a situation where there is a very active Islam on the coast, an increasingly active Christian minority, and a large and very complicated form of animism inland, which is now under pressure.

This is all tied up with the past traditions of headhunting and aggression and warlikeness which were very much a part of pagan animism among the hill peoples of Sarawak and the rest of Borneo. This aggressiveness has found its expression also in the enthusiastic response that these inland people made to British parachute units organized against the Japanese. The internal tribes retook a very large part of Borneo even right down to Brunei Bay, killing Japanese in the ratio of about three hundred Japanese for every one of themselves killed in their guerrilla warfare. Again, in the rebellion in the state of Brunei in December 1962, the hill tribes rallied and blocked the whole area, the hinterland behind Brunei, so that it was impossible for the rebellion to spread inland or for the rebels themselves to get back to Indonesia.

This sort of male dynamism and aggressiveness is extremely important in Borneo. It is a part of the thinking not only of the hill people but also, in a different way, of the Malays on the coast who have part of the same sort of Borneo tradition which I mentioned earlier. The outlook is therefore different for anyone trying to dominate the area. Although there is violence in a country like Vietnam, it seems to have fewer and shallower cultural roots as compared with Borneo where, in Sarawak, standing up for yourself and not being pushed around is a tremendously important part of thinking. For the same reason, people have taken actively to politics, as mentioned above, because politics is a way of self-expression and self-assertion. There is no hesitation in saying exactly what you think and giving your opinion in Sarawak, whereas one is immediately struck, as I have been, when traveling in Thailand or Laos, with the quietness, gentility—gentleness, almost negativeness—of the people. The people in Sarawak are generous, hospitable, nice and polite, but they will not hesitate to stand up for themselves, speak up for themselves, and, if necessary, shoot for themselves, which is exactly what they are doing against Indonesia.

CONFRONTATION WITH INDONESIA

Finally, it ought to be made clear that there is no sympathy among the interior peoples for the Indonesian attitudes of Confrontation. There has been no case of disaffection and movement *across* the border from the Malaysian side. On the contrary, there has been considerable movement from the Kalimantan side toward Sarawak, and if we allowed it to be so, there would probably be a massive one. The Indonesian Confrontation, as far as it concerns the interior and the hill peoples is a contradiction of all their own feelings and there is evidence that the people on the Indonesian side of the border are even more fed up with it than anybody on the Sarawak side of the border.

COMPARISONS WITH FOUR ADJACENT COUNTRIES

The State of Sabah. Although the Sarawak position compares fairly closely to that in Sabah, with a basically common tradition, three factors are importantly different there:

(1) Sabah (as North Borneo) was developed by British businessmen and directed by a Board of Directors in London; there was no local white hierarchy and not always a very visible continuity of control. The primary concern was not inherited family principles, albeit vague, as in Sarawak, but dividends, in a decent way. Therefore, less attention was paid to small groups and their rights than in Sarawak. If these ever came into conflict with such outside thrusts as *development,* land use, etc., they had to take second place (n.b. the great differences in timber and rubber land use in Sabah compared with Sarawak). A different attitude toward government and authority resulted. In Sarawak outsiders, money, missions, and so on were largely excluded until 1946.

(2) For associated reasons, Sabah gave more attention to the extension of communications and at least minimal administration than the Brookes, whose *laissez-faire* was extreme, but in native terms "positive" in that it was based on a wide knowledge of, sympathy for, and support of, the minority native ideas and institutions.

(3) Ethnologically, almost the whole of the Sabah British-Dutch (now Malaysian-Indonesian) border hinterland was inhabited by one group, the (Tagal) Muruts, except for a small group of "Lun Daye" (Kelabits) at Long Pasia and the Mohammedan Tedongs toward the east coast.

Kalimantan (Indonesian Borneo). The Dutch attitude in the

eastern two-thirds of Borneo was determined, even more than in Sarawak, by the great distances and terrain difficulties involved. It is still a major expedition to get from Tarekan to the border. To walk along the border requires extraordinary heroism.

Broadly, the Dutch, with many economic opportunities in the other easier and more fertile-soiled zones of their great archipelagic empire, left the Borneo hinterland to itself almost as the Brookes did. The Dutch also looked at it with a hard and practical view, rather different from the intellectual approach of the Brookes.

The Netherlands administration exercised, from outside and a few inland stations like Long Nawang, much more legalistic, paper control. Although, in fact, this was largely nominal and did not operate at the longhouse level, it reflected an attitude of *dominance* which they constantly made felt in other ways in dealings with native chiefs and customs.

Within this system they showed close responsibility and paternalism. (They did more with education than the British or the Brookes.) This was appreciably affected by the nearness of Sarawak. The existence of benevolent feudalism and liberal *laissez-faire* over the border posed a challenge to the Dutch then exactly as it has done to the Indonesians since—and it is indeed a direct reason for Confrontation now that the discrepancy in conditions on the other side of the border among people of intimately interrelated (and often intermarried) groups is so acute. Despite differences in theory, interior Kalimantan has therefore developed in practice closely to resemble interior Sarawak.

Malaya (the Pre-Malaysian Federation of Malaya). In Malaya proper, for various reasons (including the demography of the late Stone Age and the geography of the peninsula), Islam came to dominate the whole country from its inception in the fourteenth century to the establishment of full outside government in the nineteenth century, this latter tending to crystalize the theological *status quo* in all these countries, except in regard to Christianity. This is important to Malaysia, because central government thinking on Borneo has been insistently conditioned by the peninsula experience.

Islam only holds the coastal plain (and by no means all of that) in Sarawak, Sabah, and Kalimantan. In Malaya only a small and weakened fragment of "pagans" remains inland in fragmental groups and with extensive deculturalization over five centuries.

They have no "hinterland retreat," as there is a coast within a few days' walk on either side; and the interior terrain, though tough, does not compare in complexity with that of Sarawak-Kalimantan, where the common border runs for five hundred miles, of which over half is really rugged. Thus retreat from the coastal pressures, which built up dense upland populations in Borneo (reduced by a reverse movement since white government), was seldom possible en masse in Malaya. Those who resisted the outer world usually ended up somewhat adrift (semi-nomadic, nothing like the richer settled cultures of Kelabit or Kayan) and in smallish "pockets" rather than great, though distant, valleys (Bario, Kalalan, Usun Apau, Usun Lenau, Baloi; cf. Bawang, Bahau, Apo Kayan, Kapuas in Kalimantan).

The position of these pagan peoples in Malaya was much as among the aboriginal peoples of Australia—and very different from that in Borneo as a whole. This is a fundamental point that was not properly understood by some of the interested Malaya parties before the implementation of Malaysia as a new nation.

As in Australia, these peoples have long been officially classed as "aborigines" and treated not only as a minority, but also, by implication, as somewhat inferior. This attitude was largely set up by the British and was inherited by Malaysia. Now understandable pressures are developing to de-aboriginize the rather feeble Sakai, etc., broadly termed as *orang asli* ("the early men"). This is well known among the residents of Borneo.

It must be emphasized that the inland people of Borneo generally, and of Sarawak especially (for reasons outlined above), do not even begin to feel that they are inferior. For historical reasons of war, etc., they may even feel a bit superior to some. Their culture dates back thousands of years. They feel it to be as rich and as deep as any that has come since, at least until Western technocracy. But they are not conservative and seldom "backward" in attitude toward modern times.

The idea that these *outsiders*, however many times more numerous, should dominate the inland by process of law, even if it is "democratic," is fundamentally intolerable to them. And this is one of the basic problems, perhaps the basic problem in the context of this volume, in this particular field for the years almost immediately ahead in Malaysia, in Indonesia, and in other areas.

New Guinea: A Borneo Parallel? Though perhaps New Guinea is out of the main area of consideration, I draw attention to the appreciable parallels between the human situations there, in an even tougher terrain of similar size, divided into territories now on the fringes of a confrontation, but with an even higher degree of "internal isolation" until recently.

The situation in central New Guinea (with which the author is familiar) today approximates that in central Borneo some centuries ago. There was then a much greater inland population in Borneo, centered on a series of great plateaus (only one of which is populated today), cultivating root crops before rice was known there, with Stone Age techniques.

The impacts of (a) iron tools, (b) gunpowder, (c) communications and technology, in that order, have followed a closely similar course. But New Guinea has been saved on enormous parallel effect in the early stages: the decimating epidemics of smallpox, cholera, etc., which stripped whole river systems of human life from about 1600 to 1890 A.D. Medical techniques, a fourth item of change, have been introduced in phase with diseases in this generation. The effect of a fifth factor, Christian missionaries, is too complex for concise comparison.

I indicated briefly some of these "old plateaus" of population and depopulation problems in the Dickson Asia lecture to the Royal Geographical Society (published in their *Geographical Journal* 1964). The question suggested by these comparisons is: Does New Guinea face in the future a more intricate version of what we are facing now in Borneo?

APPENDIX

LEGAL RELATIONSHIPS BETWEEN TRIBAL AND MINORITY PEOPLES AND CENTRAL GOVERNMENTS: SARAWAK

LEGAL STATUS OF MINORITY PEOPLES: SUMMARY

Much of the legal status of the "minority" or "tribal population" is undefined and based primarily on tradition and "mutual respect." It is therefore rather vulnerable to new, outside, formal litigation or codification by the "majority." These people are deeply aware of that. They trusted the British so much because they were an even smaller, indeed a microcosmic, *minority* in their midst and even in the capital. It is worth emphasizing here that although outside legislation could alter remote status and upset minority rights, (a) there is no sign of any intention to do so on any significant scale at present (but a new order must involve some changes, to bring about that order); (b) the lack of intention to make major changes is partly because everyone is well aware of the fact that, at least as things were in 1965, it would be impracticable to carry through sudden changes of any kind in this terrain and cultural climate without the goodwill of the inland people; (c) to lose that goodwill could have serious repercussions, on the border, for example. Once more, in fact, geography operates in Borneo politics.

DEFINITION OF CITIZENSHIP

Citizenship is defined basically by birth. All Sarawak-born hold, theoretically, proof of citizenship in the form of a simple identity card. In fact, several thousand inland folk have no papers, though they are fully recognized as citizens. Even the pure nomads are full citizens in this sense. In Brooke times, up to 1946, no papers were needed. The fact of paying tax meant citizenship. This was usually one dollar (Straits) per male or, in the case of nomads, payment in kind, mats for example.

There is an important distinction between "natives" and "non-natives," mostly verbal, but significant. This began in the late 1950's and was directed at control of Chinese dominance. "Natives" continue to enjoy special privileges under the Malaysian constitution. These natives are, in effect, all the Sarawakians except for the Chinese. No present Chinese are more than sixth generation here, and few more than even four. Actually, many Kenyahs and Land Dayaks in border areas are also recent immigrants, but from across the Kalimantan border, not from overseas.

All hill tribal people are therefore "citizens." They have never been bothered in detail with lowland governmental regulations involving liberties, and, until the Indonesians made it impossible, they literally ignored national boundaries.

Special efforts have been made for the hill people, particularly since 1946, in the spheres of medical services ("the ulu dresser system") and education. I started the first upland school as early as 1946, and much priority has been given to remote schools if and when the local people have become enthusiastic. An important result is that the go-ahead tribes have been able to advance themselves considerably in the past decade. A Baram Kenyah recently got a First Honours degree in Law at Cambridge, England, and a Kelabit represented Sarawak at a Colombo Plan meeting, where his English dazzled the "Indians."

In general, the old policy of "kindness to the remote" has been continued, but slowly reduced in balance (notably leniency before the new law). However, at no time have the most "primitive" Punan nomads been treated as a separate class of person. They are just inland citizens, with allowances made for the facts of remoteness. The nearest thing to any special attitude to them is the priority given in the author's official appointment to the post of "Government Ethnologist and Curator." But this appointment only gives a vague advisory or interventionary role to this officer if some aspect is being seriously neglected, for example, real motives for a tribal killing. In fact, curating has proved to take up 95 percent of this job, unlike the situation in Malaya, where under the British "aborigines" and "museums" were often conjoined, to the 95 percent neglect of the latter prior to 1960.

CUSTOMARY LAW AND LOCAL AUTONOMY

Variations in customary law were accepted as implicit in the whole Brooke method of government for a century. This was to some extent dictated by extremely difficult terrain, very poor communications, the great area to be covered, low population density, and the multiplicity of sub-groups (at least fifteen languages).

Many of the tribal groups in the hinterland had a very strong hereditary class structure, based on mythological culture heroes, carefully kept genealogies, and a long-established way of life. This provided rather easy controls; the chiefs were "appointed" on a traditional basis and paid, until recently, by a share of fines, etc.

Only serious crime was dealt with downriver, by white or

Malay magistrates (administrative officers in court). The Kenyah-Kayan-Kelabit peoples especially lent themselves to this process. This situation continues, and all their elected representatives since 1963 have been the same class leaders, in truly free elections. (See also pp. 347–48 below.)

The Ibans (Sea Dayaks) and Land Dayaks have less hereditary political structure, and leadership was formerly largely based on war and headhunting. The suppression of these activities by the government led to control problems with many complications (e.g. "rebellions" by local "live-wires") right up to 1940. Here the new electoral system since 1950 has met a real need and produced quite new sorts of leaders—including the Chief Minister and others, Ibans previously not known.

Judges and other officials, therefore, were for a long time all locally supplied, for any but most serious offenses. However, better communications and the "orderly mind" of post-Brooke government have gradually reduced legal powers at this level. This has been compensated for, however, by an increase in all sorts of duties, such as looking after visiting WHO personnel, agricultural advisers, and other persons only seen since new financing and communications have been available—outboard motors on rivers, planes, and now helicopters overland.

It should be noted, however, that in practice a good deal more has always been settled at the local level than authorized officially—and this is still the case. The unity of the longhouse, still dominant everywhere in the interior, lends itself to such arrangements so long as the issue is not between two communities. The worst cases are those of land disputes and, sometimes, disputes between adjacent longhouses over individual durian and other fruit trees. Some of these have continued for decades—and are tried out on every new district officer, for example, the Bidayuh case on the Serian-Kalimantan border.

Until very recently, ethnological overlap was slight, and no Malays or Chinese lived inland except at a few trading points (Belaga, Long Akar). This is changing now, and even remote areas are being drawn into possible clashes of group interest, notably over timber rights (see p. 349 below).

It will be clear from the above that the "villages" have full rights of self-organization. One major tension point here has been a tendency to fragmentation with population growth or because of secondary disputes within a longhouse, for example when two upper-class brothers fall out. The Brookes made it illegal to split up longhouses for trivial reasons such as this, and discouraged opposition to the headman or to communal decisions reached in the proper traditional way. Legislation was used to support communal leaders, and big penalties were imposed at points where individual decisions could affect the whole of a longhouse community.

Prior to Brooke rule the people had to get on together, because the whole headhunting pattern made for tight longhouse unity, as the lone individual could not survive. Any decision was acted upon by the community as a whole. With the suppression of headhunting, it became possible for the first time for people to be "selfish" and individualistic. Had this tendency been allowed to go unchecked, no further authority would have been possible in the interior, and the situation in regard to land tenure would have become chaotic as communities fragmented. The Brookes, therefore, continued the old tradition of longhouse solidarity in a new setting. But, of course, by mutual consent or even on administrative decision, a longhouse could split up if necessary, for example because of growth of population and pressure on the land.

This outside influence has been increased since 1946, but to a very large extent the basic attitudes are still decided locally and not seriously affected from outside. The more remote the area, the more this is so, of course; for instance, some Punans have still never seen a film or heard a radio.

LOCAL ORGANIZATION AND CENTRAL GOVERNMENT

The system of local government representation up to the central government, started by Sir Arden Clarke and much developed by Sir Anthony Abell, gives each group of longhouses an elected representative (often a man younger than the older chiefly type, and usually the son or nephew of one of these— never females). Through district councils this pyramids to Council Negeri, where in 1965 the remoter minorities are quite powerfully represented by a Murut English-speaking Baptist, aged 42; the paramount chief of the Kayan-Kenyahs, aged 65, and his

English-educated Roman Catholic son; and a Lahahan Kayan, ex-teacher, aged 40, a full minister in the state government (as of June 1965).

The old tradition of direct access to the governor from remote peoples continues. The present governor is a beloved Malay with many years of Brooke and then colonial service. The remoter peoples are jealous of their very considerable rights, and there is always concern lest these be lost by change of regime or control from afar. One of the worst mistakes the Japanese made was to ignore this in 1942; and the Indonesians made similar mistakes after the Republic took over a wide area of Kalimantan, but they are now going almost to the other extreme, insofar as conditions allow them to do so.

There have been no thoughts of semi-autonomous states. The nature of the terrain has made each area—not necessarily "tribe"—in effect semi-autonomous in all matters of concern to them until very recently.

The big new problems of the state now are to a considerable extent connected with population increase and pressures (Sarawak was formerly widely underpopulated, enabling "extravagant" agriculture and jungle use) and with the new overlaps of race resulting from this, from new communications, and also from new and less traditional outside attitudes.

LAND AND RESOURCE LAW

Title to land is simply secured by hereditary occupation, and there are no real land titles for the interior other than "custom and agreement." However, an important new land study, based on careful research before the formation of the Federation of Malaysia, produced new legislation originally scheduled to come up at Council Negeri in March 1965. Some immediate reactions to the "realism" of the bills were so sharp that the meeting was, in an unusual step, deferred until May for further consideration.[4]

[4] When these land laws were due to come up in Council Negeri in May 1965, they precipitated a political crisis which nearly split the Alliance Party along the lines of "native" and "non-native" interests. Two Malay-Melanau ministers temporarily withdrew from the state government, which has since been reformed to include them, plus one more leading Malay, one more Iban, and one Kayan (see pp. 347–348). The land matter has been shelved for detailed re-examination.

Until now the longhouse has been the normal landholding unit. But within this there are a multiplicity of individual rights, both temporary and hereditary, arrived at by "custom and agreement," as well as by status.

Native government reserves are formulated by law to cover the above and apply equally over large coastal areas inhabited by Malays and Melanaus. The situation is therefore extremely complex, in terms of future *development* and administrative *logic*.

ECOLOGICAL DIFFERENCES AND LAND LAWS

Upland areas are not specially differentiated in law from lowlands, but by definition (since access until very recently has been only on foot and infrequent) have been totally under traditional native controls. Now both Ibans and Chinese have, under need for land, begun to push at even some of the remote places—Usun Apau, Long Seridan, for example.

Inland irrigation has until very recently been confined to two small groups and has never been legally differentiated.

Forests, which still cover 75 percent of Sarawak, have been the subject of extensive legislation and massive control since the thirties. The government holds all but "own use" rights over vast areas. It is here that race and population pressures are building up strongly. Sarawak is not a rich country, and timber is a major asset—it is far and away the number one resource in more developed Sabah.

Broadly then, forest resources are considered government property. But, whatever the map says, the peoples of the area feel that deep local rights are involved, especially when, as is happening now, any question of development by outsiders arises. The government may take one view, and the Dayak another in this.

As a result of the above situation, felling jungle is now not allowed over wide areas. In practice, it has proved extremely difficult to enforce the law, and large-scale intrusions have been made, especially by Ibans and Land Dayaks, in the now crowded, poor-soil areas of the southwest. In some districts, attempting to control what is called the Kasar system is about the biggest administrative headache (even up to Niah in the Fourth Division and middle Limbang in the Fifth Division).

Shifting cultivation is the only system used over most of the interior, and there is no law of any kind, customary or written, against it unless it intrudes on the interests of another group or, latterly, of government itself.

No laws control specific crops. Rubber and coconuts have been under assisted schemes during various regimes: Brooke, colonial, and Malaysian. Opium, and the smoking of it, are illegal. Tobacco is grown for its own use—but one Christian mission has prohibited its growth since 1950 with damaging effects on the barter economy in that area.

REQUIREMENTS FOR LAND TITLES

Fencing is unknown in the interior, except temporarily, for example, around rice fields against deer and pig. Survey is now required for all title in the lowlands, but not in the areas at present under discussion. Despite heroic efforts by one of the most competent departments, title registration is slow due to terrain troubles and so on. It is noteworthy that a large slice of the interior is still not properly surveyed, including the old Dutch border. Therefore, "use-right" is the effective determinant of land title in practice in the interior. Cadastral survey has been attempted but not completed. Military and naval units are now giving priority to final survey inland, as are Russian-aided surveyors in Kalimantan.

Streams and river courses fall within the traditional land patterns and are not excluded from use. They are often determinant boundaries, as they are easily recognized and little changing.

WATER RESOURCES

There is so much rain and water that water *rights* have never been of concern except on the saline coast. However, the tiny upland-irrigation sector has known difficulties and one very serious dispute between individuals over an irrigation ditch (in the Bario Valley, 1951). Recently increased population concentrations, as well as the spread of irrigation techniques into new interior areas, under government encouragement since 1950, may increase the tendency toward disputes.

GAME RESOURCES

Hunting rights fall within the same pattern, naturally; but it is often impracticable to define mountainous jungle sectors as between adjacent longhouses, and the use of jungle for hunting is more elastic than use for "potential felling" and other exploitation. Moreover, the requirements of certain sorts of hunting, for example, rhino, wild ox, or pig migration pursuit, may take parties over long journeys (for example, the author was out for one of these for twenty-six days in 1946).

NOMADS AND SETTLEMENT

The still fully nomadic Punan groups in the Third Division, who live entirely on wild-jungle produce, have a separate network of inter-group relationships connected with their special niche in Borneo ecology.

Again, new conditions and pressures are working to accelerate a long (prehistoric) process leading toward the settling of these nomads. Powerful incentives to roam remain, involving only a few hundred people but thousands of square miles.

TAXATION

Taxation is still simply on a capitation basis in the interior and is very low. All moneys go first to the state, not to the central government, and most are returned, visibly, to the local authority.

There is no tax on land, property, income, house, livestock, or slaughtering. There are taxes payable on: shotguns, school fees (often waived and likely to be wholly so before long as in Malaya; it was a current political issue in Sarawak in 1965), wireless receivers (often only one per longhouse needed), alcohol if purchased (most is still homemade and therefore not taxable), and on a wide range of previously rare and now common commodities such as cloth, tinned foods, and cartridges, by customs revenue.

No sort of *corvée* labor has ever been required except for the following:

(1) In Brooke times, free porterage of duty officers from one house to the next (this is now paid for).

(2) Since late 1964 there has been national registration with a potential for compulsory service in defense by the young. (No inland people are as yet affected, nor are they likely to be immediately.)

There is no recognized system of intra-group taxation, but there are extensive systems of cooperation and group duty in the many aspects of life in the interior which can only be done on that basis; for example, felling jungle for rice fields, or building a longhouse.

CHAPTER 10

Muruts of Sabah (North Borneo)

C. H. LEY

INTRODUCTION

Sabah. Sabah, until 1963 known as British North Borneo, forms the northern extremity of the island of Borneo, being bordered to the south by Sarawak and Kalimantan (Indonesian Borneo). There are approximately 850 miles of coast and about 280 miles of border—the border with Indonesian Kalimantan being approximately 200 miles long. This territory lies roughly equidistant from Manila, Saigon, and Singapore.

Sabah's total territorial area is now 29,500 square miles and consists of fertile coastal and central plain areas with large undeveloped mountainous jungles, mainly to the south. Mount Kinabalu, 13,455 feet, is the highest mountain in the north, much of the remainder of the high ground being on the southern border, where three- to four-thousand-foot ridges and mountains make communications and administrative work very difficult.

Although the coastal areas are relatively well developed, the urban areas in the interior are inadequately serviced by dust roads subject to flooding, and the majority of rivers on the west side are unsuitable for transporting anything larger than small perahus powered by outboard motors. Except on the east side near Tawau no road as yet reaches nearer than within forty miles of the southern border, thus leaving communications in this border area reliant on air travel. Borneo Airways and commercial charter services supply a regular passenger and freight service to the larger centers, but most of the border-area air travel is now made possible by the presence of Security Forces whose military operations demand the construction of airfields and helicopter landing zones.

Population of Sabah. The total population of Sabah is approximately 455,000 (see Table 15). The indigenous people of Sabah can be divided into three main groups, totaling about 306,500. (See pp. 320, 344 for definition of "native" and "indigenous" populations.)

TABLE 15
DISTRIBUTION OF ETHNIC GROUPS IN SABAH
(1960 CENSUS)

Ethnic Group	Number
Indigenous	306,498
Dusun (Kadazan)	145,229
Bajau	59,710
Murut	22,138
Other indigenous	79,421
Non-Indigenous	147,923
Chinese	104,542
Other non-indigenous	43,381
All communities	454,421

The Kadazans (or Dusun) are the largest single tribe and are divided into "coastal" and "hill" peoples; their cultivations cover the central plains of Sabah and large coastal areas. Many have been influenced by outside societies and have accepted Chinese and European methods of cultivation.

The Bajau (horsemen) are one of the Malay or para-Malay groups, which also include the Brunei Malay, Dayak, Sulu, Il-lanun, and Tidong.

The Murut are the smallest and most backward indigenous group and fall far behind those mentioned above in nearly all aspects of economic progress, health, and education. As they inhabit the border areas, this paper deals only with them.

The Chinese are the largest immigrant group and, as in most places in Southeast Asia, control general commerce in all towns. Their number and influence is constantly expanding. In 1912 they formed 12.5 percent of the population and now number over 23 percent of the population.

Historical Background. The whole of this area, including the Malay Peninsula, Borneo, and Celebes, was plagued by anarchy and piracy for many years until Western trading companies began to take an interest in the area in the nineteenth century. One of the first contacts was made by the East India Company, to whom Sultan Amir of Sulu ceded his possession (the north and east of Sabah) in 1763. A trading base was made in the northern island of Balembangan, but it did not flourish.

Meanwhile, Rajah Brooke had created his astonishing administrative paradise in Kuching, and the British were ceded the island of Labuan by the sultan of Brunei in 1847. Brunei, through years of rebellion, corruption, and strife, was in a state of decay, and the other territories then controlled by the Sultan were in the same condition.

Strangely enough, one of the first contacts was made by an American in 1865, when the Sultan of Brunei ceded the west coast of Sabah to the American Trading Company, led by Joseph Torrey of Massachusetts. Torrey set up a trading post at Kimanis and imported some of the first Chinese workers from Hong Kong. However, lack of experience and finance led him to hand over the enterprise to Baron Overbeck, Austrian Consul in Hong Kong, in 1875. Overbeck in turn was superseded by Alfred Dent, a British businessman, in 1877.

Dent acquired possessions covering nearly all Sabah (ceded by the Sultans of Brunei and Sulu), produced the first semblance of law and order, and initiated organized trade. This venture was supported by the smooth-running Rajah Brooke administration in Kuching, Sarawak, and, of course, by the presence of the British navy on the island of Labuan, from which they controlled piracy and protected the main trade line to Japan and China.

Dent's administration led to the granting of the Royal Charter forming the North Borneo Charter Company, which administered the country from 1881 until 1941, when the Japanese invaded.

Although the territories were made a British protectorate in 1888, finance for the administration came from London business houses; and it was only in 1946, after the devastating Japanese war, that North Borneo was taken on as a British colony.

In 1963 North Borneo gained self-government and was renamed Sabah. Also in 1963 Sabah joined the Federation of Malaysia, an act which was directly followed by protests from the Philippines and Indonesia and their attempts to reassert claims to this territory. Indonesia's subsequent Confrontation policy (with actual armed incursions) has necessitated the strengthening of border control.

It should be noted that while recruiting, training, and administering the Sabah Border Scouts, we have been greatly hampered by the fact that there are very few natural leaders to be found who are sufficiently educated to be able to carry out elementary administrative duties. This can possibly be attributed to the fact that the North Borneo Charter Company (in contrast to the Rajah Brooke regime in Sarawak) did little to further the advanced education of its subjects. The ravages and slaughter during the Japanese occupation were also contributory factors.

The Muruts. The Muruts are a proto-Malay people originating from Asia and are closely related to the Kelabits of Sarawak. The present-day Muruts live inland, and the area they occupy lies south of the line which joins Bukit Trus Madi and the north of Brunei Bay.

They are divided into two groups: those who cultivate hill paddy; and those cultivating wet paddy.

The Murut sub-tribes are as follows:

(1) Timogun		(5) Tagal		Mostly hill-
(2) Nabai	Wet-	(6) Kolur		paddy/tapioca
(3) Boakan	paddy	(7) Lundaya		cultivators
(4) Peluan	cultivators			

In this paper we are dealing with the second group almost exclusively, as the Muruts of the border areas are reliant entirely on hill-paddy and/or tapioca (shifting) cultivation, with the usual supporting crops.

Except in areas where the Borneo Evangelical Missionaries have influence, the Muruts are pagan, their attitude and approach to life being comparable to the Semai Senoi of Malay and the Jarai of central Vietnam.

The present-day Murut villages consist of several bamboo or jungle hewn-plank huts with attap or zinc roofing, and seldom exceed one hundred people. This total would have been housed in one large longhouse some years ago when headhunting was prevalent. The suppression of headhunting has had several detrimental side effects, the most important being the causing of a vacuum in the religious aspect of the Murut life and the subsequent increased state of apathy. Headhunting and the awareness of being hunted by another group bonded each longhouse into a purposeful unit led by the headman, who arranged the communal ceremonies which virtually generated their way of life.

The denial of headhunting also possibly caused the following:

(1) Increase in cases of violence within the community (usually psychotic seizures—amok), which were unheard of when headhunting provided the outlet for violence.

(2) The greater spread of disease through increased friendly contact between villages

(3) The undermining of traditional group leadership

Although strictly banned, headhunting is still thought about in the backward areas, and one can discuss the merits of cannibalism with some of the older men. The method of decapitation, processing, and preserving the skull has been described to the writer—the essential ceremonial tasting of the victim's flesh (sweet like monkey) sounding particularly repugnant to non-Murut ears. This, of course, is one of the most striking of the cultural differences setting these people apart from lowland administrators.

Diet. The Muruts plant hill paddy and tapioca as their staple crops, great ceremonial importance being attached to harvest. Cultivation generally follows the standard pattern where the jungle is cleared in April, burnt off in August—the women planting the seeds in the holes made by the men's planting sticks. Field houses are constructed, and these are used as guard posts and eventual storage points for the crops.

The harvest is celebrated with much festival, markets, and the consumption of large quantities of a potent local wine called *tapai,* processed either from rice or tapioca. The supplementary crops include sweet potatoes, maize, local spinach, edible fungi, bananas, and jungle fruit.

Male hunters supply protein in the form of wild fowl, deer, pig, and fish. Fishing methods include net, line, traps, or the stupefying of the fish with tuber juice. Fish (and meat) is often salted and stored in bamboo containers with rice and herbs for six to nine months. The result is a dish, particularly unappetizing to the foreign tongue, called Jaruk in the Pensiangan area. It is usually presented on festive occasions with the *tapai* wine, when all-night singing parties and dancing to gong music last for several days.

Resources. Although Sabah has large timber concessions and deposits of chromite, copper, coal, and peat, none of these are workable in the Murut hill area. There are no rubber estates in the southern border region, and consequently the Murut economy in this area has no chance of development by these means.

Trade, Barter, and Exchange. The prize possessions in a Murut household are *tapai* jars, brass gongs, water buffaloes, beads, blowpipes, spears, and, more recently, shotguns and paper money.

An idea of the value of these material possessions can be gained from the following account of the marriage procedure among the Tagal group of Muruts. The suitor initially informs his parents or guardian that he is interested in his prospective bride, and, following family discussions, his parents visit the house of the girl and in further discussions determine whether the girl herself is interested and also whether her parents have any objections to the proposed marriage. If the girl agrees, the mother of the suitor takes the prospective bride home to her house, the father of the girl having decided when the marriage feast will be held at his house. The suitor and the betrothed then live as man and wife until such time as the feast is arranged and the dowry established and collected. This period is generally between a month and six weeks. The dowry usually consists of cash, buffaloes, jars, and gongs, and is adjusted to conform with the financial status of the suitor and the status of the bride's parents. Nowadays, cash takes precedence, followed by buffaloes and jars, although previously the latter two were predominant. Jars are divided into four categories, and although the difference is difficult to describe, the evaluation is made according to type (old Chinese), material (glazed or otherwise), and age. The four types of jars are:

Tiluan, worth about $600 (Malaysian dollar = U.S. $0.33)
Binikul, worth about $200
Balayong, worth about $150
Mandalalair, worth about $150

The dowry is paid at the wedding festival, but if the bridegroom is unable to pay it in full at that time, another festival is held the following year, when the balance of payment is made. The father of the bride is, however, permitted to visit the house of the newly-married couple at any time in later years and claim any article which he chooses as an additional dowry payment. Although this practice is not vigorously enforced, I have known recently a squabble over a brand-new transistor radio set which was asked for in this context.

The *Orang Tua* ("headman") witnesses the festival and dowry payment, and the marriage is finalized. The couple commence their married life by living in the groom's parents' house.

The requirement of the dowry as one of the powerful forces pushing the Muruts into the labor market is clearly seen from the preceding example. Part of their income is now obtained by men who work as casual labor on rubber estates to the north or who are directly employed under the Police as Border Scouts or in other government labor activities. The barter trade continues, and frequent Tamus (or markets) provide the opportunity to trade jungle produce for the "shining essentials" supplied by the Chinese shopkeepers.

It should be noted that until Confrontation closed the borders between Kalimantan and Sabah, all trade goods were brought into the area by the few Chinese shopkeepers in the Pensiangan and Sapulut by way of the main rivers, whose outlets are in Kalimantan. The closing of the border has necessitated the supply of goods by air from the trade center in Sabah. Some means of price control has been achieved by the fact that military aircraft assist in supplying essential goods (iodized salt, etc.) by airdrop.

The Administration. Although the Murut follow their own regulations and customs concerning hereditary laws (Pesaka and Pencharian), marriages, burials, etc., the day-to-day structure is based on the Sabah government's administrative law, which covers all groups in the territory.

The chain of administration is passed from the elected Legislative Assembly in the capital to the residents, who in turn control the district officers. Both government-appointed and hereditary headmen work from this level and have direct and continual contact with the native population. (Central government representation has not, as yet, been decentralized to the extent of allowing local elections, as in Sarawak.)

All Sabah's population is served in the same way, and with the present confrontation several emergency war committees are also operative, which allow military and operational matters to be brought into the normal pattern of administration.

Legal Status. All tribal people resident in Sabah are citizens of Sabah and receive the same benefits of citizenship, being permitted to take part in any occupation and to own land or property of any sort.

Immigration laws apply to all, but the small amount of local cross-border traffic is not controlled, as it would be impracticable to do so with limited staff and poor communications.

Native Law. Native law is recognized by the central government, each district having its own native court, which deals with breaches of native custom subject to the approval of the district officer. Crimes of violence are a State Police matter and are dealt with accordingly.

Native chiefs, appointed by the government, are leaders of these courts and with the district officer's sanction pass judgments and sentences (usually fines but sometimes imprisonment) for cases which infringe on the religious, inheritance, matrimonial, sexual, or day-to-day customs of the group. Local laws vary slightly from area to area.

The native court has jurisdiction over anybody, but can only apply local laws pertaining to marriage, etc., if one of the parties is a native. If the parties are of different sex and race, then the native court will rule according to the local laws and customs of the female's group. The district officer is always referred to and his sanction is required before the native court can operate.

Villages are organized with *Orang Tuas* (lit. "Old Men") as appointed leaders reporting to district officers, who in turn report to residents. They are not permitted to organize themselves and are not organized into autonomous groups. No special representatives on the ministerial level exist, as certain members of ministries are in fact natives. Anyone can have quick and direct access to the central government by bypassing the local administration and writing directly to a minister.

Government Programs. It is the long-term policy of the Sabah government to encourage the change-over from cultivation of hill paddy to that of wet paddy. This might entail the resettlement of Murut groups from border areas to plains areas further to the north. Here they could settle and benefit from improved crops (including wet paddy) and the many aids from government agencies, including medicines, education, and agricultural assistance. This action would definitely be of material benefit to many of the Murut groups, provided they moved of their own free will. However, at present there is a traditonal fear and distrust of being resettled, and it is unlikely that they will agree to move in the foreseeable future. If they are ever to be moved, advice from an anthropologist will be essential.

While they still live in their present inaccessible areas, they do inadvertently receive tax concessions, but these concessions are due to the administration's physical inability to levy rather than to a deliberate relief.

Native Land Titles are, however, subject to tax relief as follows:

Native	*Other*
No premiums	Premiums $5 up to $50
1st–6th year nil rent	1st–6th year $1 per acre/year
6th year onwards 50 cents per acre/year	6th–10th year $4 per acre/year
	Thereafter $6 per acre/year

Special schools, education schemes in general, and Health Centre schemes are all being organized to cover the wet-paddy areas; hill areas are being dealt with more on an *ad hoc* and temporary basis.

In the Keningau and other accessible areas schooling is free, as is medicine, although hospitals charge nominal fees when the patient is able to pay.

Present Land Settlement Schemes provide free roads, irrigation, drainage, planting materials, fertilizers, and occasionally buffaloes and housing assistance. When the time comes to resettle the Muruts of the hill border areas, these schemes will be specially adjusted to attract the people and initiate a voluntary change of cultivation methods.

Land and Resources Law. Title to land is secured through the district officer on application. Groups can have areas gazetted to them as native reserves or grazing reserves. Alienation is only possible after the land is regazetted and no longer used for its original purpose.

No fencing is required for titles to be recognized, but land must be officially surveyed to be titled. Use-right to land is recognized. There has been no official cadastral survey made. Upland areas are often not gazetted owing to lack of administrative facilities, but in theory there should be no difference from the lowland areas. Irrigated areas are the same as non-irrigated areas.

Forest land is differentiated from other land where timber concessions exist. This comes under the "Major Scheme," and teak and other timber extraction is subject to royalties paid eventually to the State Development Fund. Forest resources are government property, and only secondary jungle can be cut for cultivation.

There are no laws against shifting cultivation, but encouragement is, and will be, given to eventual resettlement in lowland areas. There are no laws against cultivation, although there is a law against the possession of opium ($2,000 fine) and this is therefore not cultivated.

The central government owns streams and river courses, also the water rights. There are no hunting rights except by mutual group agreement, which is entirely local and varies in different areas. Licenses must be obtained to shoot pigeons, deer, and elephants, and firearm permits are necessary for shotgun owners.

Taxation. Taxation applies to all groups, although certain areas escape because of their remote location. Land tax has been mentioned above. Cattle tax ($1 per buffalo/year) is payable to the local district council. Cattle- and pig-removal tax ($10 for cattle and $2 for pig) is also payable to the district council. Dwelling-house tax is $1.50 per house/year. Income tax is on state scales but generally not applicable.

There is also a land tax or education tax on land, payable to the central government, which provides funds for school staff wages ($1 per acre/year). There is no tax on the local *tapai* (rice wine), although it is an offence to distill it. Groups are no longer subject to call for casual labor, although this was so under Charter Company rule. Groups do not have the right to tax themselves.

Confrontation. Following Indonesia's policy of Confrontation of Malaysia and physical cross-border attacks in Sarawak and Sabah in 1963, Malaysian Security Forces (including Gurkha and Commonwealth troops) were deployed to contain this offensive.

In Sabah the border with Kalimantan (Indonesia) stretches from Long Pa Sia to Tawau on the east coast—a large part of this border being unexplored and totally uninhabited.

Naturally, it was necessary that the indigenous population should be invited to assist in the defense of the territory and, as a result, the Sabah Border Scouts were recruited from the resident Murut population in the border areas.

It is interesting to note that in this area Confrontation has done a great deal in uniting the Muruts. Although the idea of "Malaysia" is somewhat remote to them, the influx of various Security Forces has involved them in a united defense scheme for Malaysia.

It is greatly to the advantage of Malaysia that there is no need to "win over" these tribes; their allegiance to the administration is firm as a result of years of sympathetic treatment under the British. Some of the Indonesian soldiers, in garrison on the Kalimantan side of the border, have antagonized Murut groups, thus convincing the Muruts in Sabah that Indonesian rule would not benefit them. Several parties of discontented Murut refugees have arrived in Sabah from across the border, supporting this idea, despite the fact that no attempt has been made to encourage such migration and no special inducements have been offered to the refugees.

Plan of Action. The threats from Indonesia can be listed as follows:

(1) A direct invasion using airborne and land troops

(2) Small incursion operations, ambushes, sneak attacks

(3) Subversion in all areas, particularly those known to be pro-Indonesia (there are approximately 13,000 people in Sabah who originate from Kalimantan) or who are politically ripe for revolt

The first threat would be an almost purely military commitment. The third one is a Police Special Branch task, which is currently being dealt with successfully. The second threat represents what has actually happened in the border areas to date, and our Plan of Action is therefore based on this. It is regretted that owing to security reasons I am not permitted to give any detailed description of the current Plan of Action in this area. However, broadly speaking, the policy is to activate the local population so that they form a forward screen of national loyalty reporting on sightings of people and aircraft, and incidents, and where possible defending their land against attack and taking an active part in apprehending intruders. This entails improvements in communications, new roads, better river services, and assistance from military Security Forces in the area in the form of air travel.

Several government/military welfare campaigns are constantly in progress, and these are aimed at maintaining the population's cooperation and awareness of the political situation and constantly reminding them of the central government's support.

The plan is proving successful, and the general excitement of Confrontation supplies a satisfying outlet for the Murut's natural aggressiveness. It is, however, a scheme which needs continual moral support in all forms. It would not take much mismanagement or lack of support to start a decay which, once established, would cause the whole scheme to deteriorate.

It is vital that Malaysia keep the initiative with the border population and maintain a progressive enlightened policy.

CONCLUSIONS

As stated above, our Action Program is progressing well, but the following suggestions are put forward, as their implementation would do a great deal to assist in administrative work in this area. Often too much emphasis is put on National Aid and assistance in the form of military assistance. In this area an enormous amount of good could be done with the following:

(1) Additional health aid (the Government Health Centre scheme does not cover remote border areas adequately) in the form of a "helicopter dispensary," possibly manned by Malayan personnel, thus providing an important and direct service to the hill tribesman as well as fostering "Malaysia" and nationhood.

(2) Increase and improvement of radio programs in Murut language (allowing for various dialects). Mount Kinabalu in the north of Sabah now has an FM transmitter in operation,

and it should not be difficult to supply FM receivers to the tribal population in remote areas. A well-organized program would provide an invaluable service both educationally and politically. The present fifteen-minutes-a-day Murut program put out by Radio Sabah is inadequate and sometimes inaudible.

(3) This area requires facilities for additional training in the following fields:

(a) Local leadership courses such as obtained at an Outward Bound School ("Outward Bound Schools" are leadership-training establishments which have been formed for young people who, on completion of the course, return to their industrial or administrative employment in Britain or the Commonwealth territories—they combine instruction in self-reliance and initiative with physical conditioning and instruction in techniques for working with other nationalities). These should incorporate as many tribes and nationalities as possible, thus fostering enterprise and promoting international understanding.

(b) Special civic courses for established local leaders, to encourage their understanding of similar adjacent societies in direct relationship to bolstering nationalism.

(c) Facilities to train central government officers in dealing with minority-group problems, with the object of their working into the administrative network at local government level.

All these courses would benefit if they were conducted on an international footing, thereby increasing national pride as well as aiding international tolerance.

PART VII: THAILAND

IN THAILAND, as elsewhere in Southeast Asia, it is difficult to arrive at a satisfactory and consistent definition or characterization of tribal and minority populations. Neither language, nor literacy, nor ecology is completely effective in predicting the sort of life the people lead or their relationship with the central government. The papers on Thailand which follow deal with a series of populations, some of whom, like the Lua?, conform fairly well to the classic definition of tribes as somewhat isolated groups with distinctive cultures. But in general the picture we get is a variable one. For example, the Iu Mien (Yao), described by Kandre, are quite worldly in their outlook and individualistic in their orientation, in marked contrast to the stereotype of tribesmen as communalistic.

The criterion of literacy is sometimes used to distinguish tribes from minorities, but here also the difference is blurred, as many of the Yao and Meo are literate in Chinese, and the Karen have used a missionary-invented script for over a hundred years. Likewise, criteria based on ecology or economy do not serve to distinguish tribal from other populations. Thai peoples in some areas of Thailand live in the hills and practice swidden (slash-and-burn) agriculture, rather than irrigated agriculture (e.g. around Nan, see Judd 1964, in Kanchanaburi Province, see Stern 1965:7). Religion serves us no better—the worship of spirits (*phi*) in some of the more isolated Thai communities may be more important than Buddhism, and "tribal" people like the Lua? claim to have been Buddhists for centuries.

The dominant majority may not be *economically* dominant in the nation (witness the numerous charges against the Chinese minority); and in fact the Central Thais (defined linguistically) are not even a plurality of the nation's population.

Minority and Tribal Populations. Thailand, according to census figures, is one of the most homogeneous nations in Southeast Asia, in terms of language (the people are predominantly Thai speakers), ethnic or "national" origin (predominantly Thai), and religion (predominantly Buddhist) (see Table 16). A breakdown of census figures on each of these dimensions will allow us to sort out most of the important minorities and some of the tribes,

TABLE 16

LANGUAGE, RELIGION, AND NATIONALITY IN THAILAND[a]

	REGION											
	Whole Kingdom (Number)	(Per-cent)	Northeast[b] (Number)	(Per-cent)	Southern[c] (Number)	(Per-cent)	Eastern[d] (Number)	(Per-cent)	Western[e] (Number)	(Per-cent)	Urban[f] (Number)	(Per-cent)
Language												
Population over five years able to speak Thai	21,256,766	97.0	7,408,663	98.7	691,487	63.5	915,917	92.1	934,463	87.7	1,741,689	96.4
Population over five years unable to speak Thai	661,779	3.0	99,502	1.2	396,630	36.5	73,255	7.9	131,126	12.3	64,682	3.6
Total	22,018,545		7,508,165		1,088,117		1,994,172		1,065,589		1,806,371	
Religion												
Buddhism	24,563,523	93.5	8,938,025	99.4	560,662	44.2	1,180,520	99.3	1,235,493	96.5	1,711,117	80.1
Islam	1,025,569	3.9	973	+	669,011	52.8	68	+	3,078	.2	104,105	4.9
Christianity	150,053	.6	40,044	.4	1,242	.1	1,706	.1	15,964	1.2	30,092	1.4
Hinduism	3,483	+	231	+	117	+	19	+	536	+	2,169	.1
Confucianism	461,317	1.8	10,056	.1	34,695	2.7	694	+	2,183	.2	281,205	13.2
Others	35,238	.1	969	+	265	+	23	+	16,074	1.3	4,277	.2
None	13,979	+	232	+	350	+	9	+	6,402	.5	989	+
Unknown	4,754	+	1,013	+	552	+	40	+	193	+	1,381	.1
Total	26,257,916		8,991,543		1,267,194		1,183,088		1,280,623		2,136,435	

(continued)

[370]

Nationality

Thailand	25,737,180	98.2	8,930,187	99.3	1,240,456	97.2	1,180,518	99.3	1,271,173	99.3	1,921,500	89.9
Chinese	409,508	1.6	21,010	.3	24,213	1.9	2,305	.2	6,938	.5	204,301	9.6
Burmese, Lao, Cambodian, Vietnamese	45,002	.2	29,139	.3	984	.1	188	+	1,502	.1	347	+
Indian, Pakistani, Ceylon	6,694	+	555	+	596	+	45	+	585	+	3,452	.2
European	5,043	+	154	+	270	+	5	+	207	+	3,644	.2
Other	2,830	+	51	+	227	+	1	+	63	+	1,838	.1
Unknown	1,603	+	497	+	148	+	26	+	55	+	296	+
Total	26,257,860		8,991,543		1,276,434		1,183,088		1,280,623		2,136,379	

+ = Less than 1/10%

[a] Source: *Thailand Population Census, 1960, Changwad Series* (Bangkok).

[b] The northeast region, included in this table for comparative purposes, is more "typically Thai" according to these demographic measures than the rest of Thailand. The census definition of the northeast area includes Buri-ram, Chayaphum, Kalasin, Khon-kaen, Loei, Mahasarakham, Nakhonphanom, Nakhornratchsima, Nongkhai, Roi-et, Sakonnakhorn, Srisaket, Surin, Ubonratch-thani, and Udornthani provinces.

[c] The southern area for purposes of this table includes the provinces of Nara-thiwat, Pattani, Satun, Songkhla, and Yala, which contain the greatest proportion of Malays. The other southern provinces of Krabi, Phang-nga, Phuket, Ranong, and Trang have a total of 98,928 Moslems; Phranakhorn Province (Bangkok), Phranakhornsri-ayuthaya and Thonburi add another 123,011, most of whom are probably Malays.

[d] The eastern area for purposes of this table includes the provinces of Srisaket and Surin, which contain the highest proportion of Cambodians in Thailand.

[e] The western and northern border area for purposes of this table includes the provinces of Chiengmai, Kanchanaburi, Maehongson, and Tak, which contain the highest proportion of tribal people *as measured by this census.*

[f] Urban area includes only Phranakhorn and Thonburi provinces (which include the metropolitan area of Bangkok), an area of Chinese concentration. Urban vs. rural breakdowns by ability to speak Thai, religion, and nationality are not available in published census materials. Census figures yield an underestimate of total *ethnic* Chinese population since many ethnic Chinese were born in Thailand, are able to speak Thai, and are Buddhists, and thus are indistinguishable from ethnic Thais in the census.

but for reasons detailed below these census figures should not be thought of as anything but crude *minimal* estimates for tribal and minority populations.[1]

Despite the overall appearance of homogeneity, there are important regional and cultural differences. Even within regions that give the outward appearance of uniformity, there may be historical differences which are important in the minds of the people involved. There is now, and has been for many years, considerable internal migration in Thailand. Some of this has been spontaneous as individuals, families, or segments of communities have moved primarily in response to economic opportunities. There has also been deliberate policy for movement of communities or sections of communities following warfare or as a form of tribute. Thus many communities in the north trace their origins to other geographical locations, sometimes in Burma or Laos, from where they were moved as a result of wars between the various Northern Thai principalities. Such groups as the Thai Yawng and Thai-Lue are not distinguishable from other Thai peoples in census records.

The Malay minority, located primarily in the southern provinces of Nara-thiwat, Yala, Pattani, Songkhla, and Satun, appears most clearly when census figures for language (inability to speak Thai) and religion (Islam, rather than Buddhism) are examined.[2] There was a total of 1,025,569 Moslems in 1960, with 670,000 of them in the five southernmost provinces.

The Cambodian (or Khmer) minority, located in the eastern provinces of Surin and Srisaket, emerges from an examination of census figures on language (almost 80,000 non-Thai speakers). They are nominally Thai citizens and are Buddhists.

Because they are Thai nationals and speakers of a dialect of

[1] *Thailand Population Census, 1960,* is the source for all population figures unless otherwise specified.

[2] There are also many Malays (as indicated by the number of Moslems) around Bangkok (Phranakorn and Thonburi provinces) and Ayuthaya (Phranakhornsri-ayuthaya Province), primarily due to the deliberate policy of moving Malays out of the South during the nineteenth century. Blanchard's assertions that "seven-eighths of all the Moslems are concentrated in the area directly adjacent to the Federation of Malay" and that "they account for about 80 percent of the population in the four southernmost provinces" are not confirmed by the 1960 census. Cf. Wendell Blanchard *et al.* (1957:60) and the *Thailand Population Census, 1960.*

Thai, the large population of Northeastern Thais, who have a somewhat distinctive culture and economy, do not appear in census breakdowns. The Northeastern Thais discussed by Huff are isolated by lack of communication and transportation facilities. Though they speak a dialect of Thai, it is at best barely understandable to officials from central Thailand. The same may be true of other Thai dialect groups, such as the Lue (see Moerman's paper in this volume and Moerman 1965) and the Shan in northern Thailand.

The Chinese are concentrated in central Thailand, along railways and major transportation routes and in urban areas, and are found predominantly in business and commercial occupations (see Skinner, 1957). They appear in the census figures as Chinese nationals (409,508) and also as practitioners of Confucianism (461,317). These are gross underestimates of the total *ethnic* Chinese, who may number as many as 2,600,000 (Skinner 1965) or even 3,799,000 (*Overseas Chinese Economy Yearbook* 1964). These urban Chinese are quite different from the rural Yunnanese described by Mote.

People identified ethnically as Indians, who may also be Pakistani by nationality, show up in census figures under Indian and Pakistan nationalities (only 6,694) and as Hindus (3,483) and Moslems. It is impossible to distinguish Thai-speaking Malays from Thai-speaking "Indians" by means of those rough breakdowns of census figures. Although no studies have been done of the "Indians," they seem even more concentrated in urban areas and marketing occupations than are the Chinese.

Still other minority groups cannot be detected by these crude methods of analysis of the population figures from the 1960 census. These include such groups as the Soai or Kui, living near the Cambodian border, with estimated population of 150,000 (Smalley 1964:85), former tribal people who have become Thai-ized or Khmer-ized. The Mon, most of whom live in Ratburi Province, west of Bangkok, "are descendants of prisoners of war or of refugees from Burmese oppression who migrated in 1600, 1660, 1774, and finally in 1814 . . . . Estimates of their population range from 60,000 to 100,000" (Blanchard 1957:63–64). More have moved to Thailand since the Union of Burma failed to establish a Mon state (Stern 1965:3). Various Thai-speaking

groups, such as the Phu Thai, living in the Northeast, with estimated population between 70,000 and 100,000, and the Shan,
who live between Chiengmai and the Burma border, with estimated population of 30,000 (Blanchard 1957:63–64), are fairly
similar to other Thais in culture and are at least nominally
Buddhist, Thai-speaking, and Thai nationals, thus indistinguishable from other Thais in the census.

The tribal people do not form a homogeneous group. They
are concentrated mainly in the north and west (there are also
about three hundred very primitive Negrito peoples in the extreme south).[3] The tribes can be divided into at least three major
linguistic groups: Tibeto-Burman (including Karen, Akha, Lahu,
Lisu); Miao-Yao; and Mon-Khmer (including Tʔin, Luaʔ,
Khmuʔ, Phi Thong Luang, and Mrabri).[4] (See Table 17.) The
tribal peoples have several distinct economies: wet rice, dry rice;
opium-corn-livestock; truck-gardening; hunting and gathering;
wage labor. They also have numerous varieties of culture, social
organization, and religion.

Estimation of total tribal population is difficult. "Nomadic
hill tribes" were not counted in the 1960 census. Some of the
settled tribesmen show up in the northern provinces as people
who are unable to speak Thai, or as people with religion listed
as "Others" or "None." Examination of census figures along
these lines reveals a high proportion of tribal people in Maehongson Province (about 40 percent non-Thai-speaking), who are
probably primarily Karens living in the Khun Yuam Valley. Use
of census materials in this way gives only a minimal estimate
of tribal people, since the nomadic hill tribes were not counted,
and since many of the hill people are bilingual and may call
themselves Buddhists for census purposes.

[3] Brandt (1961:128–137) estimates that there are three hundred Negritos in
several different bands in Trang, Phatalung, Nara-thiwat, and Yala provinces.
They are speakers of Mon-Khmer languages and exhibit varying degrees of
acculturation.

[4] Language groupings here do not necessarily conform to ultimate historical
relationships. Karen and Akha-Lahu-Lisu are evidently representatives of quite
distinct groups of Tibeto-Burman languages, though they are probably ultimately
related; affiliation of Miao-Yao is uncertain, but may be Sino-Tibetan and thus
ultimately related to the above languages; the Mon-Khmer languages evidently
belong to several distinct groups of that family. See notes accompanying the
Burma population and linguistic affiliation table for further discussion of the
problems involved in linguistic classification.

This brief review of the census materials indicates the inadequacy of census materials for all but the most general guesses with regard to numbers and distributions of tribal and minority peoples, and suggests that a special effort must be made to get accurate census material if the true extent of the tribal and minority population and their problems is to be known.

Laws Regarding Minorities and Tribes. Until recent years, when the special problems of hill tribes have begun to be recognized by government officials, the legislation with respect to minorities has been directed primarily at the Chinese. The policy has vacillated between encouraging immigration and discouraging it, and between allowing or encouraging assimilation or making it difficult or impossible to "become Thai" even for people born in Thailand, with one Thai parent. Variations in policy have been clearly related to internal economic conditions (needs for labor, desires to encourage Thai participation in, or control of, certain industries or occupations, desires to control balance of payments) and internal or external political conditions (use of anti-minority-group action to promote national solidarity; response to threats from Japan during the Second World War, and from Communist China since the 1950's). The primary legal means used to implement government policies have been laws respecting immigration and naturalization, restrictions on employment in government service, restrictions on certain occupations and nationalization of industries in which minorities were predominant, restrictions on the leasing and holding of property, and restrictions on schooling and use of non-Thai-language textbooks (see Skinner 1957:219–20, 368–70, 374).

The implications of all of these laws for tribal and non-Chinese minority groups have not been clearly worked out. However, it is clear that definition of citizenship is one of the crucial laws. The laws seem to have had virtually no effect on the Thai-speaking minorities who are simply assumed to be full citizens. There seems to be no clear policy as to whether hill peoples are or are not citizens. The Lua? seem to be, but some Meo groups (because they are assumed to be recent immigrants) apparently are not. It is vital that this question be clarified since citizenship determines legal treatment in so many facets of life. For example, from many standpoints it would be desirable for hill tribe members to serve in the Border Patrol Police. They know tribal languages and customs and are familiar with the territory; membership in the Border Patrol would be a method by which they could participate on a more or less equal level in Thai government agencies and learn about Thailand and Thai culture in the process. Unfortunately, however, if tribesmen are considered as aliens, they cannot serve in the Border Patrol. Likewise, there may be doubt as to whether they are legally eligible for benefits received from the Hill Tribes Division of the Department of Public Welfare.

Another problem for aliens is the ownership of land. If landholding laws are enforced on the "alien" tribesmen (or on alien minorities such as the Yunnanese "Haw"), they will have no security in their agricultural land, and it will be useless for the government to try to stabilize their settlements.[5]

Restrictions on occupations are not yet a problem, since virtually all of the hill people are self-employed agriculturalists, but if any attempt is made to bring "alien" tribesmen into the lowland economy, inhibiting laws would have to be removed.

Laws with respect to foreign-language schools and textbooks have become a problem only in a few special instances, because in general there are no schools for the hill peoples, and the people are illiterate. The government has, however, shown concern with the possibility of schooling for Haw hill people (Yunnanese Chinese), and some use of foreign (i.e., tribal) language in hill schools is now being considered (see p. 386 below). With the exception of the Karen and possibly some Meo and Yao (who are literate in Chinese), there is no long tradition of education and literacy among tribal people.

The Karen script, a modification of the Burmese script, was developed in Burma by missionaries over a hundred years ago. A considerable literature exists in this script, and an unknown number of Karens in Thailand, primarily Christian, are literate in their own language. This is taught to them by missionaries, both Karen and foreign.

Government policy, as far as it has manifested itself with re-

---

[5] In fact the problem of land ownership by hill tribesmen is more complicated than this because of the general question of legality or illegality of upland swidden cultivation.

gard to hill tribe languages, has been to teach tribal students (both in Border Patrol and public schools) to speak and become literate in Central Thai. Attempts have been made in recent years to convert missionary scripts of tribal languages from a Roman-style phonetic script to a phonetic script based on Thai characters (Schlatter 1963; Smalley 1964:80 ff.). Examples of some of the problems which develop once there is a vested interest in a particular script are as follows. Some Yao tribesmen do not wish to give up a Yao script making use of Chinese characters, since they value the Chinese cultural tradition and consider Roman or Thai characters to have lower prestige. The Lua?, who have been using a missionary phonetic script only since the late 1950's, consider the script to be their own (they are surprised to see English written with the same kind of letters), and are reluctant to change over to a Thai-character phonetic script which was developed in 1961.

In spite of their ambiguous status as citizens, hill tribesmen are evidently subject, as residents of Thailand, to taxes and to the criminal laws of Thailand.[6] In practice, since most hill tribesmen live remote from police or courts, their daily activities are probably not controlled by Thai law, though apparently no study has been made of this subject (see Kunstadter's paper below for illustration in the case of the Lua?). Customary family patterns, inheritance laws, and property and religious customs[7] of the tribal peoples conflict at a number of points with Thai law, but since these matters are rarely, if ever, brought into Thai courts at the present time, the issue is not as yet an important one.

As already mentioned, the question of tribal property is not at all clear. I have not been able to find a written reference to the law which is supposed to claim for the Thai government all land over 2,500 feet (800 meters) elevation. Presumably house sites, gardens, and irrigated fields could be excepted from this if title were registered, but there is little evidence that hill tribesmen

[6] The law in this repect seems unambiguous. "Whoever commits an offense within the Kingdom shall be punished according to the law." The Penal Code of Thailand and Its Amendment, Section 4.

[7] For example, Section 381 of the Penal Code of Thailand: "Whoever cruelly illtreats, or kills any animal with unnecessary sufferings shall be punished with imprisonment not exceeding one month or fine not exceeding one thousand baht, or both." The effect of this law, if it were enforced, could be to prohibit buffalo sacrifices, an essential part of many tribal rituals.

have availed themselves of the opportunity to file claims for title, though tribesmen living in the lowlands often do register their land (e.g. Stern 1965:8). As mentioned above, hill tribesmen's ambiguous citizenship status makes such registration problematical. Since the cutting of swidden fields (*rai*) is illegal (though taxed), and since forest resources are claimed by the government, it is doubtful if hill tribesmen could lay claim to most of the land which they actually use. There is apparently no legal recognition even of use-right to swidden areas.

There are apparently no laws recognizing, or protecting from alienation, land held communally by tribal villages (apparently villages could own land if they were formally organized as corporations, partnerships, or some other legally constituted body). Water rights seem assured to hill tribesmen under Thai law, again dependent on the question of land ownership.[8]

Second to the law of land ownership, the law which potentially would have the greatest economic effect on some hill tribes if it were enforced is that prohibiting sale of opium.[9] For practical and political reasons this law has been enforced only sporadically. Most opium fields and opium growers are in areas remote from police posts. Also, governmental officials have come to realize that unless an adequate substitute were found for opium production, the actual prohibition of opium sales would be economically disastrous for the several tribes dependent on opium for a living (see, e.g., Patya Saihoo 1963; and papers by Geddes and Manndorff in this volume). The Border Patrol Police, who visit opium-growing tribes and now the location of opium fields, are under (informal?) orders not to interfere with opium-growing at this time, and to the best of my knowledge have not interfered. There have been accusations by tribesmen that Provincial Police have threatened destruction of their opium fields as a means of extortion, but I have no direct evidence of this from personal observation. Nonetheless, the fact that the tribesmen are practic-

[8] The Civil and Commercial Code (Thailand), Section 1339: "The owner of a piece of land is bound to take the water that flows naturally onto it from higher land. Water that flows naturally onto lower land and is necessary to such land may be retained by the owner of the higher land only to such extent as it is indispensable to his land."

[9] Proclamation of the Revolutionary Party, No. 37, December 9, 1958.

ing an illegal occupation would make them easy targets for extortion.

Hill tribe populations are subject to various forms of taxation, but enforcement of these taxes apparently varies with distance from administrative centers (see Kunstadter's paper below for taxation among the Lua?).

THAI ORGANIZATIONS CONCERNED WITH HILL TRIBES

There is a surprising number of fingers in the pie of tribal programs. Despite the fact that some hill tribe villages are integrated into the Thai governmental system through official recognition of village headmen, the ordinary services (police, schools, public health, and medical care) have been brought into the hills only infrequently. Instead, a series of special programs has been developed for hill tribes and other more or less isolated minority peoples. Some of these will be mentioned here only briefly, since they are dealt with at greater length in the papers which follow (for an earlier review of these programs see Patya Saihoo 1962).

Local Administration. Thailand is divided into seventy-one provinces (*changwad*), which are further divided into districts (*amphur*), which are in turn divided into communes (*tambon*), each composed of several villages (*muban*).[10] Officials at the provincial and district level are civil servants, appointed by the central government. Assistants to the district officers are often drawn from the locality in which they serve and more often, therefore, have firsthand knowledge of the district and its minority and remote rural populations than do the district officers, who are regularly transferred from one district to another. The selection of commune headman (*kamnan*) is made, or approved, by the district officer, as is selection of village headmen (*pu jai ban* or *kae ban*). Judges, police, welfare, and health workers have their local offices in district towns or sub-district towns,

[10] A higher level of administration groups the provinces into regions or circles (*phak*). For example, Region Five consists of Maehongson, Chiengmai, Chiengrai, Lamphun, Lampang, and Phrae provinces. Military and religious organizational levels are also grouped into parallel regions, e.g. for the Buddhist church and for the army.

and confine most of their activities to these immediate regions—they do not often tour the more remote sections of the districts.

The general pattern of Thai local administration has been imposed on some tribal villages—most of the larger tribal villages have headmen nominated by the villagers and recognized by the district officer (*nai amphur*). At present only rarely do hill tribesmen occupy as high a position as that of commune headman (*kamnan*).[11] This seems to represent a change from the older days when the government (or principalities) used more of a system of indirect rule and gave official recognition to higher-level tribal leaders. Few tribal groups in Thailand are politically organized at more than a village or related-village level,[12] although there are, of course, kinship and economic connections between villages, and recognition of cultural identity.

Provincial Police. The Provincial Police are responsible for law enforcement throughout the country, but have relatively little to do with law enforcement in remote tribal villages. However, there have been numerous stories of abuse of their powers for extortion in hill villages. Provincial Police are available on call by the village headman in the event of a serious crime. Provincial Police may take the initiative in coming up to the hills if they believe a crime has been committed in the valley by a hill dweller. Provincial Police are charged with enforcing laws with regard to opium and liquor-brewing, which are frequently violated by hill tribesmen. They have no special program for enforcement of laws in the hills.

Border Patrol Police (BPP). The Border Patrol Police is an elite, specially trained para-military organization distinct from Provincial Police and the armed forces, which was founded about ten years ago (see USOM 1963 for a general description of this

[11] I do know of a *valley* Lua꜒ village whose headman is the *kamnan* of a series of Thai villages. He and his village are so Thai-ized as to make them indistinguishable in language, dress, economy, and religion from other Thai villages. Smalley (1965) reports that there are many Kui and Cambodian *kamnans* in the Northeast. Stern reports that there have been valley Karen district officers in the region of Sangkhlaburi. This was a hereditary office granted by the provincial governor and passed on for several generations until 1924. At present the higher-level officers in this area are Thai civil servants (Stern 1965:2).

[12] Kandre's paper in this volume indicates a grouping of a series of Yao villages under a single headman, and evidently this grouping is not determined by kinship. Several Karen "daughter" villages may be grouped under the headman of the "parent" village (see below).

program). The primary mission of the BPP is to maintain the security of the border and to gather intelligence in border and remote regions. The BPP is supplied and trained with the assistance of U.S. funds, advice, and equipment, channeled through the United States Operations Mission (USOM).

In order to carry out its missions, the BPP has tried deliberately to befriend local populations. Since its geographical area of responsibility includes the areas where tribal populations are concentrated (border and internal hill areas), it has come to assume certain responsibilities with regard to tribal people. Recruitment policies for the BPP have favored men who know tribal language, and these men have been stationed in the localities with which they are already familiar. Training stresses respect for tribal people and their customs. The BPP defers to Provincial Police for actual law enforcement.

A number of programs with specific application to tribal people have been designed and carried out by the BPP. In remote areas the general procedure is as follows. A patrol walks into the area, sites are selected, and tribesmen are persuaded to build airstrips. They are rewarded for their time by being given tools (which they would ordinarily purchase), food, and incidental medical attention. When the airstrip is completed, a plane is landed, often with medical and technical personnel. Seeds and animal breeding stock are distributed. Complaints with regard to local administration are listened to, and attempts are made, by relaying these complaints directly to Bangkok, to straighten out problems at the highest level (e.g. complaints with regard to abuses of Provincial Police may go directly to Border Patrol headquarters in Bangkok, then to Provincial Police national headquarters, whence orders for action are issued to the local Provincial Police post). Border Patrol Police have orders *not* to interfere with administration at the local tribal village level (e.g. they will not make decisions with regard to choice of village headman). They are not supposed to interfere with such illegal activities as opium culture, unlicensed brewing of liquor, sacrifice of animals, possession of unlicensed guns, etc. and apparently are under no obligation to interfere, nor do they report these activities to Provincial Police. Neither do they interfere with local customs with regard to marriage, religion, and so forth, though these customs may conflict with Thai law. The Patrols return to the villages once a month. Informally, throughout their stay, they talk to the people about Thailand and its government and distribute pictures of the King and Queen and the Emerald Buddha, which serve as symbols of national unity.

In another program, started early in 1964, about a hundred hill tribesmen from several different tribes were selected for training by the BPP. Two or three young leaders from each of thirty or forty villages were taken to Chiengmai and trained in first aid, agriculture, sanitation, and so forth, as well as being given political indoctrination. They were then returned to their villages to establish aid stations and distribution points for technical information.

For at least five years the Border Police have been establishing schools in some tribal villages where there are concentrations of school-age children, and staffing them with BPP teachers. Classes, up through the fourth primary grade, are conducted in which the children are taught to speak, read, and write Central Thai. There are now 144 of these schools, with a total of 6,000 students (Young 1965:11). The general pattern of the curriculum is that of the Thai public schools. School buildings are built with the assistance of villagers, using materials gathered in the forest or supplied by the BPP. School supplies are provided, as are uniforms for the children. The program has not expanded as rapidly as tribes-people have desired, apparently because of lack of teachers. As of late 1964, plans were underway to send tribal students who had finished the four years to the public schools nearest their villages, or to establish an advanced tribal school in Chiengmai or Chiengrai.

On the whole, the BPP program with tribal people seems to work quite well, but there are some problems. The difficulty of enlisting "alien" tribesmen into the BPP has already been mentioned. The potential conflict between the BPP and Provincial Police has also been suggested. The BPP is a potential rival of the Provincial Police, or even the army, and is perhaps deliberately being kept in a weakened condition to prevent this. As indicated, the BPP has a direct line to communicate tales of misconduct (blackmail, abuse of tribal women, etc.) to Bangkok. Another source of friction is that BPP men on patrol are supposed to get per diem allowances, while Provincial Police do not. However, per diem payments have been withheld from BPP men (at least in the area with which I am familiar), forcing the patrols to pay for their own food and carriers, or to take food from the villages they visit and impress local people to carry them for nothing—a procedure which defeats the BPP's effectiveness.

The Ministry of Education. A hill tribes program has been set up in the Ministry of Education to oversee programs of hill tribe education. The woman in charge of this program was formerly assigned to one of the schools in Maesariang, Changwad Maehongson, a border province which has a high proportion of tribal population. She cooperated with and gave moral support to missionary education programs. Special encouragement was offered to tribal students (primarily sympathetic treatment)— but no special programs had been established for them as of 1964. Meetings were held in Chiengmai in June 1965 at which curricula for hill tribes schools were worked out, and an attempt was made to define a policy on use of tribal languages in these schools. Both Ministry of Education and Border Patrol personnel cooperated in this effort (Smalley 1965). Further work on this project will be financed, in part, by the Asia Foundation.

An offer was made by the Asia Foundation to give scholarships to hill tribe students. Implementation of the project was delayed when questions were raised about the amounts of the scholarships (they were felt to be inappropriately large, since they were equal to about double the average cash income in that part of Thailand) and about the place where the scholarships should be given (the provincial seat vs. the district where most of the tribal students were concentrated). These problems have apparently been successfully resolved.

Department of Public Welfare, Hill Tribes Division. The Department of Public Welfare, Hill Tribes Division, has a program (complete with anthropological adviser) which is especially concerned with the economic development of hill tribes. This program is discussed at length in Dr. Manndorff's paper.

Activities of the Tribal Research Centre, also under the Department of Public Welfare, are described in Dr. Geddes' paper.

The Ministry of Defense. The Ministry of Defense is responsible for the Mobile Development Unit (MDU) program, which was originally a Thai idea, strongly backed by the late Prime Minister Sarit. Teams of agricultural, medical, economic, and propaganda experts go out into the rural countryside to try to determine and to satisfy felt needs and to spread the word that the government is benevolent and interested in rural areas. The program was originally designed to combat subversion and infiltration in the Northeast of Thailand, but is now (or is about to be) applied in hill tribe country in the North. (This program is dealt with at length in Dr. Huff's paper.) The Ministry of Defense has also become active in encouraging research on the problems of people in the remote areas of Thailand.

The Ministry of Health. The Ministry of Health, in cooperation with the World Health Organization and USOM, has a malaria control and eradication program, which attempts to reach all villages in Thailand. Malaria has been eradicated in most of lowland Thailand but remains a major problem in most of the hill areas. The program operates in two stages. Activity in the first ("control") phase attempts to reduce the mosquito population by use of insecticide sprays in all houses in the nation. The second ("eradication") phase attempts to eliminate the malaria organism by treating all human "carriers" with drugs. The malaria control people are supposed to take a census of each house and, in the eradication phase, treat "fevers" and give medicine to close contacts of persons suspected of having malaria. So far the problems in the tribal villages are so great that they have not gone beyond the spraying phase in the more accessible areas. No pattern of economic development or birth control is geared in with the malaria program in spite of its tremendous efficiency, even at the "control" phase, in reducing the death rate.[13]

The Ministry of Health is also supposed to provide free medical care to those who need it. So far there has been no attempt to extend this service to the hills (probably because of shortages of money and trained personnel even in the more heavily popu-

---

[13] "The malaria control program successfully reduced the malaria death rate from an average of 250 deaths per 100,000 population to 35 deaths per 100,000 population." United States Operation Mission to Thailand (USOM) 1962:P.D. 39.

lated lowland areas). Tribesmen are eligible (apparently) for this service, but there have been complaints that they have been charged excessively for it.

Department of Forestry. The Thai government has taken a monopoly on teak and thus "owns" all teak trees and other valuable lumber trees. Since many of these trees grow in hill areas, and since these trees were customarily used for construction by hill peoples, there is an inevitable source of conflict over this resource. At the minimum, this condition leads to the possibility of extortion by the forestry officials. Another conflict possibility exists because of the practice of swidden (slash-and-burn) agriculture. Forestry officials claim that this method of agriculture destroys forest resources, but tribal people claim that teak forests do not make good rice land, so they do not cut there anyway, and if they ceased making swidden fields entirely, as the foresters might desire, they would starve.[14]

Postwar expansion of the lumber industry has offered some wage labor (e.g. elephant-driving) to tribesmen, but the jobs available to tribal people decrease as work and transportation become more mechanized.

INTERESTS OF FOREIGN GOVERNMENTS AND
INTERNATIONAL ORGANIZATIONS

United States Information Service (USIS). The United States Information Service (USIS) has two sorts of interests with regard to hill tribes and rural minorities, both of which fall under the general classification of increasing popular support for the Royal Thai Government and strengthening national integration.

USIS attempts to strengthen ties between tribal groups and the nation through broadcasts in tribal and regional dialects. This project has not been very active recently for two reasons. First, the central government policy is to promote the use of Central Thai language and script, so as to discourage regionalism; the government therefore restricts broadcasts in regional dialects, except, apparently, in use of regional song styles, such as the

[14] These statements are based on my observations in northwestern Thailand. Stern, in western Thailand, confirms the generalization that swidden agriculture is not destructive to existing forest resources (1965:8). He also indicates that swidden agriculture may be considerably more productive than irrigated agriculture (1965:7).

molam of the Northeast. Second, USIS does not have sufficient technical staff to monitor tribal-language broadcasts, so that, although it is possible, for example, to get someone to translate from Thai into Meo and to make Meo-language broadcasts, it has not proved possible to get an independent translation back into Thai and English, and so check on what is actually being said.

There is at present no precise knowledge of the numbers of radio sets in tribal villages. Apparently this is quite variable, with the richer tribes (opium-growing groups) much more likely to have radios than the other groups. There are plans underway to expand the capacity for broadcasting, in part in response to the fact that Radio Peking regularly broadcasts in such languages as Meo.

Another approach aimed at increasing national integration is to educate the Thai population on the subject of tribal and regional minorities in Thailand. A series of films with Thai sound tracks has been made by USIS, showing tribal and minority groups and emphasizing their human-ness as well as showing cultural differences. USIS has also put on exhibitions for Thais, showing examples of tribal arts and crafts.

United States Operations Mission (USOM). Activities of USOM with regard to tribes are primarily directed to giving support to the Border Patrol Police (q.v.), principally by furnishing advisory and training personnel and equipment. With regard to rural minorities, activities include the normal range of community development and other services, with concentration on the Northeast because of its relative economic underdevelopment and strategic importance, not because of its regional minority characteristics.

USOM has assisted the Thai Ministry of Health (q.v.), the malaria control and eradication program, and other health programs. USOM has also given financial support and some supplies and equipment for the Rehabilitation Villages and New Life Foundation run by Mr. Robert Wulff. Two of these villages, located in Chieng Dao and Hot districts of Chiengmai Province, are in tribal areas and involve tribal people.

U.S. Department of Defense. The Department of Defense is involved in minority and tribal affairs primarily through assistance in terms of equipment for the MDU program of the Thai Ministry of Defense (q.v.). It is also actively promoting research on hill and minority peoples in cooperation with the Thai Ministry of Defense.

Southeast Asia Treaty Organization (SEATO). SEATO has shown its interests in hill tribes through provision of fellowships for study of hill tribe groups (see Dr. Geddes' paper in this volume). As a result of experiences in Malaya and South Vietnam, SEATO is well aware of the strategic importance of these groups.

UNESCO Division of Narcotic Drugs and the Opium Trade. The opium trade has many international implications since the drug is often transported illegally across national borders. In the case of Thailand, the problem is one of control of flow of opium from Burma and Laos as well as control of production in the export from Thailand. The UNESCO Division of Narcotic Drugs is concerned to assist the countries involved to stop this traffic, and to eliminate opium production. In Thailand tribal people are the chief, if not the only, producers of opium and are also said to be involved in the early stages of opium transportation. The extent of the problem can be judged from the estimate of 75 to 100 tons annual production of raw opium (figures cited by Patya Saihoo 1963).

Some of the problems of opium production by tribal people in Thailand are discussed in the papers of Dr. Geddes and Dr. Manndorff.

International Interests—Nationalist Political Movements. Thailand has borders with Burma and Laos where nationalistic, separatist, and other political movements are taking place among segments of populations which are also present in Thailand. Therefore Thailand might be used as a "neutral land base" from which Karen, Shan, Lao, or Chinese Nationalists could operate, much as the Viet Cong have used North Vietnam to operate against South Vietnam. The minority and tribal populations in Thailand might also be targets for infiltration from the outside, e.g. by the Pathet Lao.

As regards the Burma border, there is a clear possibility of such an occurrence, because there are Chinese, Shan, and Karen minorities in Thailand, and because there are, or have been, a series of uprisings of Chinese, Shan, and Karen minorities in Burma.

With regard to Karens, it is Thai government policy to reduce this possibility by patrolling the border area and restricting the flow of arms and supplies across the border. The Thai Karens with whom I am familiar have relatively little or no "nationalistic" sentiment except for a general feeling of fellowship with other Karens (see Lehman's paper regarding Karen "nationalism" in Burma). There is no agitation or overt organization of Karens in Thailand for political purposes. While there may be passive support for the movement in Burma in terms of friendship and hospitality, there is little active support in terms of providing money, supplies, equipment, or men. Aid to the Karen revolt in Burma, such as it is, seems motivated by profit, not patriotism.

Communist Activities. There is no evidence of successful Communist activity among the hill peoples in the northwest. Broadcasts from Chinese stations can be received quite easily, but there are few if any radios owned by Lua? or Karen. There is no evidence of direct subversion, such as the politically motivated assassinations which have been reported in the Northeast.

PRIVATE ORGANIZATIONS

Missionary Activity. Christian missionaries have been active among tribal and minority peoples in Thailand longer than any other organizations. The first Catholic priests in Thailand accompanied the Duke of Albuquerque in 1511. Two Dominicans, who arrived in 1555, were the first resident missionaries. Both were put to death within fifteen years. Three French missionaries arrived in 1662—they were imprisoned or driven out of the country in 1688 in a reaction against the French following the death of King Narai in Ayuthaya. Most of the early work of the Catholic missionaries was directed toward foreigners (Annamites and Cambodians as well as Europeans) after initial attempts with the Thais failed (Jesuit Fathers 1963:B-12–B-14). A few Catholic churches remained at the time the first Protestant missionaries arrived in 1828. Work was started by the Protestants among the Chinese and Mon minorities almost immediately in the area around Bangkok. Medical work was started in the 1830's and has remained an important aspect of mission activity up to the present day (Wells 1958:5).

The first Protestant missionary to go to the North was the Reverend Daniel McGilvary, who went to Chiengmai in 1867 for the purpose of teaching religion, establishing schools, and caring for the sick (McGilvary 1912:Ch. IV; Wells 1958:53). His activities soon brought him into conflict with the Prince of Chiengmai, Chao Kawilorot. Appeals for assistance from the Thai government in Bangkok by McGilvary as well as by British lumber interests resulted in the sending of a Siamese High Commissioner to Chiengmai in 1869, along with two American missionaries, one of whom, the Reverend N. A. McDonald, was acting American Consul. The Prince died in 1870 on the way home from a trip to pay tribute to the King in Bangkok. In 1878 his successor Chao Intanon yielded to pressure from King Chulalongkorn and the Siamese High Commissioner in Chiengmai to accept a proclamation of religious toleration which allowed freedom of religion in Thailand.

Much of the early work and early success of missionaries in the North was among tribal people and former slaves. McGilvary had started work among the Karens the first year he was in Chiengmai (Wells 1958:54), and he continued to visit among the hill tribes throughout his career. He visited a "Mū-sô" (Lahu) group in 1891–1892, where he had considerable success in converting one whole village, but no success with individuals or other villages (McGilvary 1912:326 ff., 344 ff.). The Lahu at that time were already cultivating opium in the hills between the Mae Kok and Fang, and in some cases were addicted to it. The original cause of addiction, according to McGilvary, was medicinal use of opium for dysentery (McGilvary 1912:346 ff.). McGilvary visited among the Khmu? and Lamet in Laos in 1898, but permission for Protestants to missionize in Laos was denied by the French.

An American Baptist missionary accompanied Karen Christians from Burma to Chiengmai as early as 1872. Karen Christians from Burma have continued missionary activity, sometimes independently and sometimes with American Baptist help, since that time (Truxton 1958:56).

Chiengmai has continued to be a center for missionary work

in Northern Thailand and the adjacent parts of Laos and Burma.

The following list will give an idea of the extent and variety of work by foreign Protestant groups among minority and tribal groups in Thailand.

(1) American Bible Society—work with northern peoples including the Lao, Meo, Yao, Thai-Lue, and Thai-Yuan. Portions of the Bible published in northern languages and distributed as early as the 1890's (Wells 1958:195). Work of the American Bible Society continues at the present time with Dr. William Smalley, an anthropological linguist resident in Thailand, giving professional linguistic advice on transcription of tribal dialects.

(2) The United Christian Missionary Society—work with Mon and Chinese minorities (Wells 1958:198).

(3) The Worldwide Evangelization Crusade—work with the Karens (Wells 1958:198), and with Khmuʔ in Nan Province (Judd 1966).

(4) The Southern Baptist Mission—work with Chinese (Wells 1958:205).

(5) American Churches of Christ (or Christian Churches) Mission—work with Yao and Meo in Chiengrai and Nan provinces, and with the Thai-Lue in Chiengrai (Wells 1958:205).

(6) The Overseas Missionary Fellowship of the China Inland Mission in Thailand—came into Thailand after being forced out of China after the Communist revolution. They work with tribal groups such as Lisu, Meo, Lahu, and Yao, which are also found in China (Wells 1958:205–206). They have also begun work with Pwo Karens.

(7) The American Baptist Mission—work with the Karens, especially Skaw Karens, and with Swatow-speaking Chinese (Fridell 1956:20–27; Truxton 1958:56–59; Wells 1958:208–209).

(8) New Tribes Mission—work with the Luaʔ (Lawa), Karens, and Northern Thais (Wells 1958:209; Schlatter 1963).

(9) The Christian Brethren Mission—an English group working primarily in Malaya, but also among the Malay and Chinese Christians in Thailand.

(10) The Bible Societies in Southeast Asia—work with various missionary groups on problems of translation of tribal and minority languages.

(11) The Church of Christ in Thailand (see below, n. 17).

A meeting of Protestant missionaries was held in the 1950's at which territorial and tribal assignments of missionary groups were made to avoid, where possible, duplication of efforts and conflicts of interest.

There are several orders of Roman Catholics who have been active among tribal and minority groups. As with some of the Protestant groups in the North, many of the Catholics were originally working in China and moved to Thailand after the Communist take-over. Both Catholic and Protestant missionaries work among some of the same groups, e.g. the Karens. (See Kunstadter's paper below for details of some of the missionary programs.)

The effectiveness of Christian missionaries in converting the population of Thailand has not been great. They have had their greatest success with tribal, minority, and economically depressed groups (e.g. former slaves). There are only about 150,000 Christians in Thailand[15] out of a population of 26,000,000—about .6 percent (*Thailand Population Census, 1960*)—but missionaries have done important work in medicine and, paradoxically, secular education, introducing these to areas where they did not previously exist in Thailand. In general it can be stated that the missionaries have not fostered separatism or tribal nationalism to the extent that they have been accused of doing, for example in Burma or India.[16] This is probably because of the greater degree of religious toleration among the dominant population (as compared with India), the relative remoteness and small number of tribal people as compared with the main part of the Thai population (and their consequent lack of conflict), the relative ease of assimilation into Thai society at the same level as other peasants, and to the fact that missionaries have not been so directly identified with a single colonial power (as they were in India, Burma, or Vietnam). Laws

[15] The *Catholic Directory of Thailand* (Jesuit Fathers 1963:B-28) states that there were 109,133 Catholics in Thailand in 1959, almost half of whom were in the Bangkok area. These figures are not necessarily comparable to census figures for Christians.

[16] But see Maran La Raw's paper in this volume for an example of the nation-*building* effects of missionaries in Burma.

with respect to property ownership and education have required religious organizations to develop, at the minimum, parallel Thai-national and foreign missionary structures. For example, the Presbyterian missionary activity, which was once largely American dominated, has become Thai-ized as the Church of Christ in Thailand, with Thai officers and title to land and property in the names of Thai nationals.[17]

Other Private Organizations—the Asia Foundation. Activities of the Asia Foundation with respect to tribes and minorities are summarized in Mr. Pierson's paper in this volume.

FINGERS IN THE TRIBAL PIE—SUMMARY AND CONCLUSIONS

It is clear from the preceding paragraphs that there are many different interests impinging from the outside onto the tribal and rural minority peoples. These include the interests of the Royal Thai Government and of governments of other nations as well as of international organizations. Some of the other interests in tribal and rural minorities have not yet been specified—such as interests in the land, lumber, game, and agricultural resources

[17] The Presbyterians started work in Thailand in 1840, and a Thai national Protestant church, the Church of Christ in Thailand, was established in 1934. Until the Japanese occupation fored the suspension of American missionary work in 1941, most of the reponsibility for the program and institutions of this church remained in the hands of the Presbyterian Mission. Thai leadership kept some institutions and most local churches operating during the Second World War. After the war the work was carried on by joint committees, half appointed by the Thai national church, and half by the cooperating missions. Since 1957, when the Presbyterian Mission in Thailand was dissolved, all policy and programs have been the full responsibility of the national church. Individual missionaries are still serving under the Church of Christ as "fraternal workers," but they come only upon specific request of the national church. A similar arrangement has existed between the national church and the Disciples of Christ since 1961. The Church of South India, the United Church of Christ in the Philippines, the Church of Christ in Japan, the Korean Presbyterian Church, and the Chinese Church of Indonesia have also sent fraternal workers to Thailand.

The American Baptists and the Marburger Mission (a German group, primarily Lutheran) work under the national church, but maintain their own missionary organizations in Thailand.

The regional organizations (*phak*) of the Church of Christ in Thailand are structured in part along ethnic lines which are not parallel with the government's regions (n. 10, above). *Phak* XII of the national church, around Bangkok, is Chinese. *Phak* X is Karen (American Baptists work with all Protestant Karens in Thailand, but three of the four Karen "associations" of Baptist churches are still related to the Burma Baptist Convention). The northern districts of the national church (*phaks* I-V) have churches with Lue, Tʔin, and Khmuʔ members, but all of these churches now use the Northern Thai dialect (Judd 1966).

of the areas occupied by these peoples. Tribal people have been deprived of their land resources when, as in the example of the Phumibol Dam, parts of the area flooded happen to be occupied by tribal people, though of course this condition is not confined to tribal people alone. Lumber resources in areas traditionally occupied by tribal people have been lost to these people as the Royal Thai Government has taken a monopoly on them and has granted rights to large corporations for exploitation of these resources. Access to game in tribal areas is not restricted, and game is hunted in increasing amounts by lowland peoples. There are also economic interests of lowland people in the tribal peoples, both as markets for manufactured goods and as producers of agricultural produce, rice, vegetable, livestock, opium, and certain craft products (woven mats, shoulder bags, basketry, etc.), and some forest products. In general the upland people are at the mercy of the lowlanders to set the conditions of trade: itinerant traders are able to set their own prices, since there is little competition. Lowland buyers of hill products ordinarily have the advantage in setting prices, because the burden of transportation to market is placed on the producers, who are naturally reluctant to return their produce to the hills and who have no way to store their goods near the market in order to wait for favorable prices.

In general it can be said that the hill and rural minority peoples have no channels of communication to the agencies or persons whose decisions affect their lives. The only possible exception to this is the system which exists in some of the Border Patrol programs. On the side of the administration of programs affecting hill tribes and rural minorities there is little evidence of coordination of efforts either in planning or in carrying out programs. This situation will become increasingly troublesome as more and more programs move from the planning and pilot project stage into full-scale action.

In comparison with many Southeast Asian nations Thailand is fortunate in enjoying a relatively homogeneous population, a long tradition of independence, boundaries which correspond reasonably well with ethnic distributions (except for Lao and Shan populations in the Northeast and Northwest), a common set of symbols of national unity (the monarchy and Buddhism), and dialects which, though they may not always be mutually intelligible, at least can be transcribed with a common writing system and offer relatively simple problems of cross-dialect teaching. In view of the common background, it should be relatively easy to blur the boundaries between the various minority groups. It remains to be seen whether or not the Royal Thai Government can capitalize on these advantages and can use the existing rural community structures (as discussed in Moerman's paper) to bind the rural masses into a national structure.

Although the papers which follow indicate that there is a great deal of variation among the tribal peoples, there are many reasons to be hopeful that some form of cultural pluralism can be worked out. In general the Thais have been quite tolerant of cultural and religious differences, and thus they can start the attempt to draw tribes-people into the national structure with much less of a residue of ill will than is the case in other countries. But under the present circumstances of rapid expansion of the lowland Thai population into previously remote areas contact and conflicts are bound to take place; the tribesmen are no longer remote, and simple abstract toleration will no longer be a satisfactory basis for national integration.

REFERENCES CITED

BLANCHARD, WENDELL, *et al.*
    1957   Thailand: its people, its society, its culture. New Haven, Human Relations Area Files Press.
BRANDT, JOHN
    1961   The Negrito of Peninsular Thailand, Journal of the Siam Society 49 (2):123–158.
FRIDELL, ELMER A.
    1956   Baptists in Thailand and the Philippines. Philadelphia, The Judson Press.
JESUIT FATHERS (eds.)
    1963   The Catholic directory of Thailand 1963. Bangkok, Thai Inc.
JUDD, LAURENCE C.
    1964   Dry rice agriculture in Northern Thailand. Ithaca, Southeast Asia Program, Department of Asian Studies, Cornell University, Data Paper No. 52. (This is a portion of a doctoral dissertation entitled "Chao Rai: dry rice farmers in Northern Thailand," Cornell University 1961, which contains additional information

on tribal peoples who are "becoming Thai" and on attitudes of the peoples toward the government.)
1966　Personal communication.

McGILVARY, DANIEL
1912　A half century among the Siamese and the Lao: an autobiography. New York, Fleming H. Revell Company.

MOERMAN, MICHAEL
1965　Ethnic identification in a complex civilization: who are the Lue? American Anthropologist 67 (5):1215–1230.

OVERSEAS CHINESE ECONOMY YEARBOOK
1964　Overseas Chinese economy yearbook of 1964. Taipeh.

PATYA SAIHOO
1962　Report on the hill tribes of Northern Thailand. [Bangkok] mimeographed.
1963　The hill tribes of Northern Thailand and the opium problem. Bulletin on Narcotics 15 (2): 35–45.

PRASOBCHAI YAMALI and WATANA RATANAWICHIT
1962　The civil and commercial code (of Thailand), Books I–IV. Bangkok, Wichit Nilapaichit.

SCHLATTER, DONALD
1963　Personal communication.

SKINNER, G. WILLIAM
1957　Chinese Society in Thailand. Ithaca, Cornell University Press.
1965　Personal communication.

SMALLEY, WILLIAM A., et al.
1964　Orthography studies: articles on new writing systems. London, United Bible Societies.
1965　Personal communication.

STERN, THEODORE
1965　Research upon Karen in village and town; Upper Khwae Noi, Western Thailand [Bangkok], mimeographed.

THAILAND
N.D.　The penal code of Thailand and its amendment. Translated by Luang Dulya Sathya Patived, Bangkok.

THAILAND, CENTRAL STATICAL OFFICE, NATIONAL ECONOMIC DEVELOPMENT BOARD
1962　Thailand population census, 1960, Changwad Series.

TRUXTON, ADDISON STRONG
1958　The integration of the Karen peoples of Burma and Thailand into their respective national cultures: a study in the dynamics of culture contact. Ithaca, Cornell University, Master's thesis.

UNITED STATES OPERATION MISSION TO THAILAND (USOM)
1962　Thai-American economic and technical cooperation. November 1962, Bangkok, United States Operations Mission.

1963 The civic action program of the Border Patrol Police and the USOM Public Safety Division. Bangkok, USOM Communications Media Division.

WELLS, KENNETH E.

1958 History of Protestant work in Thailand: 1828–1958. Bangkok, Church of Christ in Thailand.

YOUNG, GORDON

1962 The hill tribes of Northern Thailand. Bangkok, the Siam Society, Monograph 1, 2d edn.

1965 A light in the jungle. Sawaddi 3(4):10–11, 26. Bangkok.

TABLE 17
POPULATION AND LINGUISTIC AFFILIATION
OF ETHNIC GROUPS OF THAILAND[a]

Group [Sub-groups (Synonyms in Parentheses)]	Est. Population in Thailand[b]	Location (in Order of Size of Population)	Language
Central Thai [(Siamese)]	10,000,000[c]	Thailand, Malaya, Laos	Tai: Southwestern
Lao-Thai [(Northeastern Thai, Thai Isan)]	9,000,000[c]	Thailand, Laos	Tai: Southwestern
Chinese	2,600,000[d]	China, Southeast Asia	Chinese
Northern Thai [(Khon Muang, Yuan)]	2,000,000[c]	Thailand	Tai: Southwestern
Southern Thai	2,000,000[c,e]	Thailand, Malaya	Tai: Southwestern
Thai-Malay	1,025,000[f]	Malaya, Thailand	Malayo-Polynesian: Malay
Kui	150,000[g]	Thailand, Cambodia	Mon-Khmer: Khmeric
Phu Thai [(Phoutai)]	100,000[h]	Laos, North Vietnam, Thailand	Tai: Southwestern
Thai-Lue [(Lü)]	71,600	Yunnan, Burma, Thailand, Laos, North Vietnam	Tai: Southwestern
Karen [(Yang, Kaliong), Sgaw (Sʔkaw), Pwo, Bʔghwe (Kayah), Taungthu]	71,400[i]	Burma, Thailand	Sino-Tibetan: probably Tibeto-Burman, Karen
Mon	60,000	Burma, Thailand	Mon-Khmer: Mon
Meo [(Miao), several dialects]	45,800[j]	Kweichow, Hunan, Szechwan, Kwangsi, Yunnan, North Vietnam, Laos, Thailand	Miao-Yao: Miao
Akha [(Ekaw, Ikaw)]	25,000[j]	Yunnan, Burma, Thailand, Laos	Tibeto-Burman: Burmese-Lolo, Lolo group
Tʔin [(Kha Tin)]	18,900[j,k]	Thailand, Laos	Mon-Khmer: N. Laos
Lisu [(Lasaw, Lishaw, Lisaw)]	17,300[j]	Yunnan, Burma, Thailand	Tibeto-Burman: Burmese-Lolo, Lolo group
Lahu [(Musser), several dialects]	15,050[j]	Yunnan, Burma, Thailand, Laos	Tibeto-Burman: Burmese-Lolo, Lolo group

(continued)

TABLE 17
(continued)

Group [Sub-groups (Synonyms in Parentheses)]	Est. Population in Thailand[b]	Location (in Order of Size of Population)	Language
Yao [(Iu Mien, Man)]	10,200[j]	Kwangsi, Kwangtung, Hainan, North Vietnam, Laos, Thailand	Miao-Yao: Yao
Lawa [(Lua?)]	9,000[j,l]	Thailand	Mon-Khmer: Palaungic
Khmu? [(Khamu, Mou)]	7,600[j,m]	Laos, Thailand	Mon-Khmer: N. Laos
Haw [(Ho, Hor, Yunnanese)]	6,617+[n]	Yunnan, Burma, Thailand, Laos	Chinese: Yunnanese
Chaobon [("Lawa")]	2,000	Thailand	Mon-Khmer: Palaungic
Negrito [(Tonga)]	300[o]	Malaya, Thailand	Senoi-Semang: Senoi
Phi Tong Luang [(Yumbri)]	100[j]	Thailand	Mon-Khmer: N. Laos?
Mrabri	40+[p]	Thailand	Mon-Khmer: N. Laos?
Brao [(Lave, Love)]	[unavailable]	Laos, Thailand, Cambodia, South Vietnam	Mon-Khmer: ?Bahnaric, N. Bahnaric
Jinghpaw [(Kachin)]	[unavailable][q]	Burma, Yunnan, Thailand	Tibeto-Burman: close to Bodo group
Khmer [(Cambodian)]	[unavailable]	Cambodia, South Vietnam, Thailand	Mon-Khmer: Khmeric
Khorat Thai	[unavailable]	Thailand	Tai: Southwestern
Moken	[unavailable]	Burma, Thailand, Malaya	Malayo-Polynesian: Malay
Phuan	[unavailable][r]	Laos, Thailand	Tai: Southwestern
Saek [(Sek)]	[unavailable]	Laos, Thailand	Tai: Northern[s]
Shan [(Ngio, Tai Yai)]	[unavailable]	Burma, Yunnan, Thailand	Tai: Southwestern
So	[unavailable]	Laos, Thailand	Mon-Khmer: ?
Thailand total (1960 census)	26,257,916		

(continued)

[a] See notes accompanying Burma population table for sources of linguistic classification. Information on population distribution is from LeBar *et al.* (1964), except where noted.

[b] Groups whose populations are unknown are listed alphabetically.

[c] Source for estimates of speakers of various Thai dialects in Thailand is Brown (1965).

TABLE 17

(continued)

^d The *Thailand Population Census, 1960* (Thailand 1962A) lists 409,508 as citizens of China; Skinner (1965) gives 2,600,000 as the number of ethnic Chinese in Thailand; the *Overseas Chinese Economy Yearbook of 1964* gives 3,799,000 as the number of Chinese in Thailand.

^e LeBar *et al.* (1964:205) gives 1,500,000 as the estimated population for the "Pak Tai," who are said to be speakers of a patois called *dambrö*, and who live in Chumpon and Nakhornsrithammarat Provinces. Brown (1965) discusses a Southern Thai dialect called Tak Bai, but does not mention Pak Tai or *dambrö*. He states that speakers of Southern Thai dialects live in the southern provinces from Chumphorn to Nara–thiwat.

^f Figure for Thai-Malay population is derived from the 1960 census; the estimate is based on the number of Moslems. This religious grouping is not strictly comparable with the estimates for linguistic groupings elsewhere in this table.

^g Kui population figure from Smalley (1964:85).

^h LeBar *et al.* (1964:228) give 70,000 to 100,000 as the estimated Phu Thai population in Thailand. Brown (1965:14) gives no population estimate, but states that Phu Thai "is spoken in the villages of Sakon Nakhon and Nakhon Phanom Provinces." The combined "agriculture" population of these two provinces in the 1960 census was over 750,000, but we have no way of telling how many of these rural people were Phu Thai speakers.

ⁱ Figure for Karen includes Sgaw (S?kaw), Pwo, B?ghwe, and Taungthu Karen. The figure quoted is from Young (1964:85), but on the basis of experience in Maehongson Province I feel that this is a minimal estimate.

^j Estimates of these tribal populations are from Young (1964:85).

^k LeBar *et al.* (1964:128) state that the estimated T?in population in Thailand is between 12,000 and 35,000.

^l Young's estimate for Lawa population is for mountain villages only. There are uncounted thousands of Lawa in the valleys in various stages of becoming Thai.

^m Young's estimate of the number of Khmu? living in mountain villages is 3,300 (Young 1962:85). LeBar (1965) estimates that there are at least 5,000 to 7,600 Khmu? in Thailand. His figures refer to ethnic Khmu?, born in Laos or Thailand of Khmu? parents. Because there are many Khmu? individuals living all over Thailand in various stages of "becoming Thai," it is very difficult to arrive at an accurate figure. Smalley (in LeBar *et al.* 1964:113) considers the Khmu? language to be closer to the Mon-Khmer languages of South Vietnam, although it is usually classified with Palaung and Wa. We have followed Thomas (1965) in assigning Khmu? to the N. Laos group.

ⁿ Population estimate for the rural Yunnanese "Haw" is from Mote (in this volume).

^o Estimate of Negrito (Tonga) population in Thailand is from Brandt (1961:133); the same people are called Semang by LeBar *et al.* (1964:182), citing a 1958 publication of Seidenfaden.

^p Population figure for Mrabri is from Boeles (1963:154), who states that there are probably forty individuals in one of the two groups visited. We follow Smalley (1963:191) in distinguishing Mrabri from the Yumbri on linguistic

(continued)

TABLE 17
(continued)

grounds. Smalley states that neither Yumbri nor Mrabri is closely related to Khmu? or T?in, but Thomas (1965) lumps all of these in his N. Laos group.

q Maran La Raw (personal communication) reports having met a Jinghpaw Kachin whose family was originally from Kengtung (Shan State, Burma). This man's family, along with a number of others including some Atzi Kachin, have lived in Thailand for about two generations. Quite a few Jinghpaw are reported to have come into Chiengrai Province, Thailand, following the military take-over in Burma in 1962.

r Brown states that there are "relatively few" Phuan in Thailand (1965:13).

s Linguistic identification of the Saek is from Gedney (1965).

REFERENCES CITED

BOELES, J. J.
  1963 Second expedition to the Mrabri of North Thailand ("Khon Pa"). Journal of the Siam Society 51(2):133–160.
BRANDT, JOHN H.
  1961 The Negrito of peninsular Thailand. Journal of the Siam Society 49(2):123–158.
BROWN, J. MARVIN
  1965 From ancient Thai to modern dialects. Bangkok, Social Science Association Press.
GEDNEY, WILLIAM J.
  1965 Personal communications.
LeBAR, FRANK M., GERALD C. HICKEY, and JOHN K. MUSGRAVE
  1964 Ethnic groups of mainland Southeast Asia. New Haven, Human Relations Area Files Press.
MARAN LA RAW
  1965 Personal communication.
OVERSEAS CHINESE ECONOMY YEARBOOK
  1964 Overseas Chinese economy yearbook of 1964. Taipeh.
SKINNER, G. WILLIAM
  1965 Personal communication.
SMALLEY, WILLIAM A.
  1963 Notes on Kraisri's and Bernatzik's word lists. Journal of the Siam Society 51(2):189–201.
  1964 The use of non-Roman script for new languages. In Orthography studies: articles on new writing systems, William A. Smalley et al. London, The United Bible Societies.
THAILAND, CENTRAL STATISTICAL OFFICE
  1962 Thailand population census, 1960: whole kingdom. Bangkok, Central Statistical Office, National Economic Development Board.
THOMAS, DAVID D.
  1965 Personal communications.

CHAPTER 11

A Minority and Its Government: The Thai-Lue of Northern Thailand

MICHAEL MOERMAN

This paper argues that concern with hill peoples should not blind us to the importance of settled rural minorities. After briefly suggesting why work among Thai lowlanders is feasible and important, I will describe a Thai-Lue village.[1] Then I will relate in some detail how that village reacted to the announcement of an impending Communist attack. This episode will permit me to suggest some general strategies for improving the relationship between Northern Thai minorities and their government.

THE SETTING

The Lue are not a "tribe," since that term is best reserved for peoples whose basic means of production is shifting cultivation or foraging and who therefore usually live in the hills. Such tribal peoples comprise about 1 percent of Thailand's population.[2] Aside from them, and from the Chinese and Indians, Thailand is relatively homogeneous. Yet in this Buddhist nation there are more than one million Muslim lowlanders. Although Central Thai is the national language, at least half of the population speaks

[1] Ban Ping is a Thai-Lue village of about 120 households in Chiengrai Province, where my wife and I lived for fourteen months from 1959 to 1961. I am pleased to be able to thank the Foreign Area Training Fellowship Program of the Ford Foundation for generously sponsoring my research. Some of the observations upon which this paper is based were made in the summers of 1964 and 1965 while I was in Thailand as a consultant to USOM. In 1965 grants from the Center for International Studies at Berkeley and from the Academic Senate of UCLA permitted me to return to Ban Ping for three weeks. This paper, however, is based almost entirely on observations made during 1960. My institutional affiliations have absolutely no implication that opinions are shared by the Ford Foundation, the University of California, AID, or USOM.
[2] Population percentages come from *Census for Thailand*, 1960, and Young, 1962. (See Introduction: Thailand, and Table 17 for further details of numbers of minority populations.)

other Thai dialects. Their linguistic diversity need not concern us here, were it not often associated with divergencies of ethnic identification (Moerman 1965). Like the hill tribes, many of these people live near borders. Thai minorities are far more numerous than the hill peoples and located quite as strategically. Lue villagers in Chiengkham and Chiengkhawng, and probably other minority Thai as well, ridicule and resent military and economic aid directed solely at the hill peoples, whom they generally regard as odd or foreign and whom they often think inferior.

There is concern about the hill peoples because they live in small communities, isolated from one another, and without much supra-village political organization. The minority Thai, on the other hand, are usually under the surveillance and control of the Royal Thai Government and are comparatively accessible by road. There is concern about some hill peoples because they grow an annual three million dollars worth of opium (Thailand 1962:63), a crop for which we have no profitable legal alternative. The Thai grow rice and other crops of which we approve and have some knowledge. Compared with our abysmal ignorance of the hill peoples, we know rather a lot about the land tenure systems and agricultural technology of minority Thai. Moreover, many government officials know their language, their aspirations, and their way of life.

In sum, the lowland minorities are numerous, strategically located, and amenable to present knowledge and administrative resources. There are also pressing political reasons why they should be given our attention. Newspaper reports, rumors, policy statements, and current development programs suggest that some of us are alerted to the possibilities of danger from the Thai-Lao of the Northeast and from the Malays of the South. Similar dangers are possible in the North.

In 1960, when I was living in Ban Ping, a Thai-Lue village in the extreme north of Thailand, a messenger brought a note on official paper to the headman's house. Since the headman had gone fishing, his wife had their twenty-three-year-old son read the note to her. Its text:

Fieldnote No. 1. This is to inform the headman that Meo [Communists from Laos] will enter Tambon Yuan, Amphur Chiengkham today [3 December 1960]. Tell your people to be ready. If your see them, rush immediately to the district office, or to the border police or local police stations. They will be able to help you. [Signature]

This message, once read, was sent along to the next village.

As might be expected, the note caused anxiety and confusion—so much so that its author later denied having sent it. As might further be expected, the peasants of Ban Ping did not immediately form an efficient citizens' army. What one might not expect, and certainly would not expect in central Thailand, is the following sentiment, which was widely repeated by the villagers.

Fieldnote No. 2. About 60 years ago we were conquered by the Central Thai. We offered them candles and flowers [signs of respect and loyalty]. They became our *caw naj* ["officials" or "rulers"] and we pay them taxes. When the Communists come, they may conquer the Central Thai. Then we will offer them flowers and candles and call them *caw naj*. We will pay them taxes and all will be as before. We are the common people; what happens to officials does not concern us. If there is war, we must leave for a while in order to avoid vandals and stray bullets. Whatever side wins, we will return and call them our leaders.[3]

I have written elsewhere (Moerman 1961:8) of my reluctant belief that such sentiments would probably be found in many villages which are significantly similar to Ban Ping. It is also my hopeful belief that in such villages similar sentiments might be made as harmless as they were in Ban Ping. Let us try then to discover which of Ban Ping's specifications are both relevant to its reaction and likely to be found in other, similar, communities.

Communality. Ban Ping is a physically and administratively demarcated community of kinsmen who all have the same family name. Fields, river, forest, ceremonial gates, and village pride separate Ban Ping from neighboring villages. All village children

[3] Many villagers told versions of this tale. The three men whom my notes mention specifically have all traveled and traded widely. One is literate in Northern Thai, and another, a former headman, literate in both Northern and Central Thai scripts. This man completed the third grade of elementary school. My previous report (1961:6) that no one expressed these sentiments "who had completed their four years of elementary education" is thus technically correct, but quite misleading.

attend the same school; all villagers attend and support the same temple. Once each year Ban Ping is sealed off from outsiders for the ceremony at which the village spirit is propitiated.

In central Thailand administrative jurisdictions, local names, topographic borders, and school zones often fail to coincide. There the "village community" is frequently the analytic creation of the social scientist, just as the "administrative hamlet" (*mu ban*) is frequently the artificial creation of the Ministry of the Interior. I do not claim that clearly demarcated strong natural communities are either restricted to the North or universal there. But such communities seem to be characteristic of the region, and this is probably based on general similarities of history and geography which distinguish northern from central Thailand.

Much of central Thailand consists of broad flood plain crisscrossed with navigable canals. The North is composed of relatively narrow river valleys united by a few poor roads and separated by difficult terrain which is unsuitable for Thai methods of irrigated agriculture. These environmental features may underlie the relative compactness and isolation of northern villages. The irrigation systems and the pre-modern states of the North were local and limited. Trade was in the hands of Thai peoples (and Yunnanese Moslems or "Haw"), for only after the Siamese[4] began direct administration of the North did settled Chinese merchants become conspicuous there. In Chiengkham, and probably throughout the North, religious organization was also acephalous. Priests with seniority and spiritual attainments were highly respected, but they exerted little authority over temples other than their own. Compared to central Thailand, the regions and states of the North were politically, culturally, economically, and ecclesiastically isolated, independent, and self-sufficient. The North not only shares this heritage with Chiengkham, it shares the Central Thai conquest which abruptly altered it.

The Siamese Conquest. The internal history of Thailand is largely the history of the gradual expansion of Siamese control over other Thai rulers. The power of Bangkok increased rapidly toward the close of the nineteenth century, perhaps in defense

[4] For convenience, this paper sometimes uses the word "Siamese" to mean Central Thai.

against the European colonial powers in Burma and Laos who were threatening the loosely governed principalities of the North. A Royal Commissioner was sent from Bangkok to Chiengmai in 1869 (McGilvary 1912:121), and a governor in 1873 (Kingshill 1960:12). In 1904 Chiengkham received its first district officer. The Shan rebellion of 1901–1902 was the immediate stimulus for enforcing the direct administration of Lampang, Chiengrai, Nan, and perhaps other northern provinces also. The rebellion,

> trivial enough in itself, had far-reaching effects, for it revealed to the Siamese the weakness of their hold on the [Northern Thai] States, the poverty of their rural administration, and the inadequacy of their military administration, which triple revelation was the direct instigation of some of the most important reforms of the administration of the last twenty years. (Graham 1924:172)

The inception of direct Siamese administration was a sudden and recent event for much of North Thailand. I have shown the importance of that event for Ban Ping's attitudes toward the nation and toward the Communist invasion with which it was threatened (see *Fieldnote No. 2*, above). Since I have found no detailed accounts of the Siamese conquest of the North in the historical literature (*vide* Curtis 1903: Appendix), it is worthwhile to quote an elderly villager's report of the Shan rebellion and of the first appearance of Central Thai officials. In the many northern communities where they presumably exist, it is such reports and memories which help to form villagers' attitudes toward their government.

Fieldnote No. 3. The Siamese came in the following way. They had taken Phrae and sat there. In Chiengkham, Chiengrai, Chiengsaen and other places the Shan were making a lot of trouble. They refused to pay the head tax. They roamed about in small bands and pillaged, just as the Meo presently do in Laos. The local Shan merchants of Chiengkham and other places joined with the Shan bandits. The Lord of Life of Nan [who ruled Chiengkham] either did not know or could not do anything about it. Then, when I had left the temple [*ca.* 1901], the Siamese came from Phrae to put down the Shan. The Shan conscripted Grandfather Naw [another old villager, not liked by my informant] along with people from other villages to carry and clean for them. The conscripts went with Shan army as far as Ban Oj [30 kilometers away] where they met the Siamese. After the Siamese twice fired their cannon, Naw and the others ran away. Naw ran all the way home. The Siamese then entered Chiengkham. . . . They entered on horseback, elephant, and on foot. The Caw Muang Chiengkham came out to meet them with an offering tray of candles covered with gold leaf and with branches to which gold and silver were tied. He welcomed them to Chiengkham and they called him "*kamnan.*" They built a fort where the distillery is now, and began to appoint officials until this day. They began to call the village chief "headman" [*phu jaj ban*].

With this and similar events the North became part of Thailand: suddenly, forcefully, and completely.

Insularity. Ban Ping, like some other villages in the districts of Chiengkham, Chiengkhawng, Therng, Pua, Lae, Maesai, and Chiengsaen, is a Thai-Lue village. Although there are comparatively few Lue in Thailand, it should be remembered that almost all northern villagers can be recognized as, and often identify themselves as, some *variety* of Thai: Khon Muang (Yuan), Shan, Lao, Lue, Yawng, Khyn, etc. The divergent ethnic identification of Ban Ping, although unusually strong, is not unique (Moerman 1965). Ethnic identification as a minority Thai people can sometimes impede national identification. If it persists, it might, in extreme situations, make a group sympathetic to irredentist propaganda. The Lue of Ban Ping often speak nostalgically of the "Old Country" in Yunnan. They listen regularly to folk-song broadcasts from China.

The life of the villagers of Ban Ping is based on growing, eating, and selling inundated rice. Like other Thai who inhabit North and Northeast Thailand, Laos, and Yunnan, they eat only glutinous rice, and most of the rice they grow is glutinous. Since officials eat non-glutinous rice, this preference symbolizes the differences of culture and of class which separate the northern villager from his government.[5] Further cultural differences involve villagers' pride in their self-sufficiency. Although Ban

---

[5] I was impressed by a Mobile Development Unit team in Northeast Thailand eating glutinous rice for the one meal I observed during the summer of 1964. Although the kind of rice eaten may seem a minor matter, it is frequently alluded to when northern villagers talk about officials. (See paper by Lee Huff in this book for further discussion of Mobile Development Units.)

Ping's retention of weaving is atypical, the contrast between the Western-style khaki uniforms of officials and the loose-fitting indigo garments of northern villagers is nearly universal. The official, of course, also speaks in Central Thai, a dialect which many villagers understand with difficulty and most speak with diffidence. Probably throughout the North, invidious differences of diet, dialect, and dress distinguish officials—"people who eat monthly money"—from "our kind of Thai who work for a living."

Ban Ping is but a long day's walk from the mountains which separate Chiengkham from the Muang Khawp District of northern Laos. Sixty kilometers of rutted track and washed-out bridges connect it with the nearest paved road. The thick dust of the dry season conceals holes and ridges from the rice-truck drivers, who need eight hours to reach the paved road at Phayao. In the rainy season, men and ox-carts slog through a knee-deep porridge of heavy mud, and the trip takes three, or even ten, days. The path to Chiengkham, although said to be one of the worst in Thailand (Blofeld 1960:54), is not unrepresentative of the North and is better than many in Maehongson and isolated parts of Nan.[6]

Harassing Regulations. In Ban Ping, as in most isolated villages, the farmer's main contacts with the government are the taxes and fees collected and the orders given by its representatives. This gives him a view of officials which I think it quite imperative for Thai national leaders to be aware of. My attempt to depict that viewpoint does not necessarily mean that I agree with it. The villager's attitude toward his government depends neither on my view of his situation nor even on his "actual" situation; it depends on what he thinks his situation ought to be.

The villager fears the police, sends and gets no mail, is given few health services, has never heard of agricultural extension, and sometimes sees little use in compulsory education.[7] Most

---

[6] A road currently being constructed with American help will probably reduce rainy-season travel time to Chiengrai from three days to three hours.

[7] Although they sometimes complain that compulsory primary education deprives them of young boys to care for the cattle, villagers are glad that they and their children are literate. In their realistic view, however, there is no point to education beyond the fourth grade unless one is assured of government employment.

villagers are usually quite unaware of receiving any valuable services whatsoever from the government. Officials, in addition to demanding labor and passing on unsolicited and often confusing advice, seem to be mainly concerned with collecting license fees for gambling, distilling, tree-felling, and butchering. The villager, however, thinks these latter activities perfectly legitimate and explains their official proscription as being motivated only by a desire to raise revenue. In Ban Ping villagers assume that these fees and taxes, these exactions for which nothing is returned, become the officials' salaries. Since the Thai use reciprocity as the rhetoric for social relations, it seems especially unjust for officials to harass and control while providing no palpable beneficial services.

An occasional official may be admired; a rare villager may form a short-lived profitable friendship with a low-ranking civil servant; perhaps there is a general expectation that the government could be asked to ameliorate calamities. Far more typically, villagers fear officials and try to avoid them; officials are ignorant of villagers and treat them condescendingly. When officials, and the government they stand for, can no longer guarantee order and protection, one no longer owes them taxes and obedience. So it was toward the Prince of Nan when the Shan held Chiengkham, so it was toward the Shan when the Siamese took Chiengkham from them, so it would be toward the Royal Thai Government should they, in turn, fail as protectors. The term "political loyalty" would be difficult to translate into the Thai-Lue dialect; the concept has no relevance to the traditional relationship between peasant and official, between village and nation, between state and state. I rather suspect that the concept is ephemeral even for modern Thailand. Perhaps the most that can be expected from peasants is passive acceptance of government and faith that officials know, care about, and are competent to accomplish the well-being of common people. Not affection, but a willingness to defer defection is a reasonable goal for "national loyalty" programs. When force fails, legitimacy, not love, is the strength of governments.

THE MEO PANIC OF 1960

The insularity, isolation, ethnic pecularity, social and cultural disadvantages, hostility toward officials, and history of conquest with which I have described Ban Ping are quite widespread among minority Thai. Although Ban Ping is perhaps unusual in the extent to which it shows these characteristics, its farmers neither welcomed the Meo nor fled their village. The reasons for this resoluteness, or indifference, can help us to understand and to develop the strength of Northern Thai communities.

The villagers expected an attack from Meo Communist invaders. As invaders from Laos, they were, for the old men at least, probably no more foreign nor objectionable than were the Shan who conquered the Yuan of Nan, or the Siamese who conquered the Shan of Chiengkham. I specify the old men, because the young, largely as a result of their schooling (Moerman 1964:43–47), identify themselves with Thailand more generally than do the old and have also ceased to practice some distinctively Lue customs. I suspect, however, that even the young failed to support "the enemy," not because they came from across the border, but because they were Communists, attackers, and Meo.

The expected invaders were Communists, a word which means "wicked person" and little more—although some in Chiengkham, especially in the market town, know and claim to object to the Communist policy of taking from the rich to give to the poor. There are no influential villagers who know that "Communism" threatens such valued things as the practice of Buddhism, leisure and respect for the aged, national independence, and family privacy.[8]

For over four months before the announcement of the impending attack, villagers had been hearing reports that Meo tribesmen, who wanted to assert their control over the lowland people, were sacking and burning villages in the contiguous part of Laos. Ban Ping, then, expected armed, violent, and destructive people with hostile interests. The expected invaders, moreover, were hill peoples of whom lowland villagers are often fearful and comtemptuous. The villagers' reaction to political agents able to mobilize their grievances, or even to invaders who were fellow Lue, might have been quite different.

It is comforting that Ban Ping did not welcome the Meo invaders. It is striking that Ban Ping, unlike some nearby villages,

---

[8] In 1965 villagers seemed more knowledgeable about Communism than they were in 1960.

did not flee the feared attack. It is remarkable that Ban Ping, without any outside leadership or inspiration, reacted in the ideal manner: by forming a village sentry force. Since an anthropologist rarely has the opportunity—although he always has the obligation—of presenting his readers with the information upon which his analysis is based, I should like to quote at some length from my fieldnotes.[9] For the privilege of doing this I incur the duty of pointing out how Ban Ping's unique reaction to a particular event suggests how similar communities might be expected to react to similar events.

Fieldnote No. 4 i. 3 December 1960. The headman's son, wife
     and the messenger interpret the notice [see *Fieldnote No.*
     1, above] to mean that the Meo may enter at some indefinite
     time in the future.

The headman's son has completed school and is one of the more "citified" youths. The young messenger is also literate and currently in school. Their miscomprehension of a simple announcement does not stem from stupidity or ignorance. We who board planes, extinguish cigarettes, take medicines, select detergents, and attend conferences all on the basis of written instructions, have learned to read closely, seriously, and attentively, as if our lives depended—as indeed they often do—upon the word-for-word correctness with which we interpret written messages. Information officers and government officials often make the fundamental error of assuming that villagers assign the same, or even greater, reality to written words as they do to spoken words and to observed phenomena. Reading is largely irrelevant to village life, and messages conveyed in writing are usually fanciful or approximate.[10]

Fieldnote No. 4 ii. When the headman returns, his opinion is
     quite different. Before calling a meeting, he walks quickly
     down the road delivering verbal messages to *M* and others.
     The headman rings the bamboo gong which summons a
     group of men, young and old, very quickly. Much excited

[9] These are the unedited fieldnotes typed while the events they describe were occurring. The only changes made for this presentation are deletions of proper names, translations of native words, and the additions enclosed in brackets.

[10] Some of the very few types of written messages upon which actions are based are usually phrased with false precision. An invitation to attend an ordination at "12:00 hours" means "Come after breakfast, at any time between 10:00 A.M. and 3:00 P.M."

talk because they all already know the issue. An old man says rumor had it that the Meo had reached the headman's house. The headman tells them that the district office says the Meo are coming today. They should gather their valuables and prepare to flee. M says that if the soldiers were here, there would be nothing to fear.

M is a wealthy former headman. Although quite unpopular, he is often influential.

In other situations, as in this one, villagers show rather high regard for the army, which they consider efficient and relatively free from corruption. On another occasion, when an old woman wandered off into the forest, I was quite impressed by the way in which two common soldiers who happened to be in the village took charge of the search party, leading the villagers respectfully and politely.

Fieldnote No. 4 iii. M and then P suggest that a *mu kot* [group of young men to patrol the paths] be formed. After first objecting that all are in the fields, the headman agrees.

A *mu kot* (Thai: *mu truad*), "inspection group," of bachelors and young married men is sometimes formed to patrol the village when fire, cattle theft, or violence are feared. We can also see how M and even P, a trader, have begun to exert more leadership than the headman, whose authority is nonetheless still necessary if M's suggestions are to be carried out.

Fieldnote No. 4 iv. M. says loudly, and all agree, that the night is the time of danger. A, an aggressive young man, suggests as a joke that all flee into town right now. Some suggest a forest village to flee to when the time comes. Headman says we need merely to go to some secluded fields near the village. A former policeman suggests that the village do whatever I do. "If he flees, we flee." Another man says that I cannot flee because I have too many possessions to carry. An older man seems quite pleased and relieved at my plan to question the district officer and police chief tomorrow in order to find the truth. He says that rural people are easily fooled. Perhaps the note from [. . .] was just a device to have us leave our homes so they can be looted. He will ask me tomorrow what the truth is in order to know the best thing to do.

After excited discussion of many points, including the rumor that a large contingent of Thai soldiers has already reached a village about 20 kilometers distant, the group disperses.

This discussion suggests, as many subsequent events confirm, the villagers' reasonableness, their pathetic desire for accurate information, and their mistrust of its official channels. They realize that the presumably knowledgeable stranger is an inappropriate model, but hope to make use of his superior contacts with the outside world.

Fieldnote No. 4 v. Almost immediately afterwards, people begin to carry . . . valuables from their houses to those of relatives with carts. Long lines of women form to mill rice against any possible trip.

Villagers of both sexes and various ages, all with "troubled hearts," come to our house in order to learn whether we know more than they do. An elderly man says what many others will: We won't really flee the village, but just take the children away from the danger of stray bullets and leave the older people to watch the possessions.

After the meeting, many say they are afraid. Headman draws up a list of two guard groups, each of twelve men who are not in the fields. Shortly before dark, the almost continuous group before the headman's house grows larger.

K joins the group and, after some war stories, suggests that a military-style watch be formed, with each group to stand watch half the night; the second group should sleep all together and be awakened by the first group when it wants relief. After some short discussion, this suggestion is accepted, M being the loudest supporter. Headman accepts it as a *fait accompli.*

K suggests, M quickly seconding, that the second group sleep on our porch. Headman suggests we give the group our alarm-clock.

Constructive leadership has now passed to K, whose possible role in rural development programs will be discussed in the concluding section of this paper. However, if the headman could not salvage his appearance of leadership (by making lists, nodding approval, requisitioning the alarm clock) pride might make

him an active and effective opponent of the plans developed
by *K* and *M*.

Fieldnote No. 4 vi. The villagers intercept a few travelers from
town who say that all is quiet there. A cyclist from town
reports: many have closed up their houses, civilian watch-
men have been posted at a number of places; *K* later tells
me that it was this news which spurred him to suggest the
military-style posting of the guard. He said that it was what
they used to do in the army.

4 December 1960. I go to town to find out whether there
is any basis for all the anxiety. Other Ping people who go
for the same purpose: *K* and five young household heads,
all of whom have had rather extensive experience working
and trading outside the village.

A answers those who ask where he is going that he wants
to see the helicopter. To me and *P* he says a few times
that he wants to find out the truth. He is ill at ease because
living in the country one never knows what is happening
and he wants to hear the market news . . . .

Honest and intelligible information about the world beyond their
village is one of the basic services which an anthropologist provides for the people upon whose hospitality his research depends.
This is clearly a service which Thai officials could easily and
casually perform for isolated villagers. Back in America, I receive
occasional letters from Ban Ping. It is pathetic, but indicative
of the state of communication in this area, that men who can
hear shooting from across the mountains feel that they must
ask a foreigner who lives half a world away for accurate information about events in Laos.

Fieldnote No. 4 vii. The twelve-man *mu kot* is on duty and the
night is quiet until 11:00. Then three carts pass through
bringing the district officer to the tobacco plant [he had
been at the provincial capital for a few days] and, from
there, to town. Their noise causes some excitement. Two
of the carters, upon returning, tell our *mu kot* that the Meo
have entered and that the townsmen are fleeing. After this,
people begin to mill about on the brightly moon-lit road.
The headman, though shouting for calm, tells his family
to steam rice and pack the cart. As evidence of real cause

for fear, villagers shout that the district officer's wife has fled to the tobacco plant.

Ban Ping's anxiety is illustrated by the turmoil caused by the rumor-mongering carters. Since the district officer's wife is better informed than they, what she does to protect herself is a better guide to villagers than what officials tell them to do. Actually, the district officer's wife and some other prominent townswomen spent the previous night as well at the tobacco plant. It was unfortunate that the Meo scare coincided with a provincial meeting which Chiengkham's experienced district officer was required to attend. Had he been present in Chiengkham, I am sure that the attack rumor would have caused less anxiety and confusion.

Fieldnote No. 4 viii. K becomes the leader, as he did last night.

He tells the *mu kot* group to go back to their posts, shouts over and over again that there have been no shots, suggests that a few people bicycle toward the town to see if there really is any trouble. He has no takers, even after making the final suggestion that he and the headman do it together. The headman divides his time between shouting that the *kot* group should go to alert an isolated section of the village and making sure that his own cart is ready for a getaway.

Of the many strangers going both ways on the road, the most exciting, after the rumor-mongers, were two carts of old women, children and mattresses fleeing a Lue village near town. One of the fleeing women spoke of having seen Meo: "They have entered. I know of 10 of them, one a woman." After talking with the headman, whom they excited greatly with their story, the refugees request permission to sleep here.

N says that if other villages are fleeing here, then we have nothing to worry about.

K is now extremely anxious to find the truth. While headman talks with refugees, K harangues the young men: Are they really men? are they afraid to fight? will they merely flee and welcome those who have come to take their property and houses? He speaks quite fiercely and with little self-consciousness. The youths shift about uneasily.

Those acquainted with village Thailand will find this scene of determined and aggressive leadership as striking and surprising as I did.

[414]

Fieldnote No. 4 ix. Thamacaj, the village sage, tells the old women refugees to be calm, there is no reason to flee. They should return and care for the sick old man they have left behind.

Thamacaj then tells that when the Siamese first came to take Chiengkham, it was also the Lue villagers closest to town who fled. People from other villages and the stay-at-homes from their village looted their houses. At that time, Thamacaj's elder brother was very sick. His father pleaded with the village not to leave, for there would be no one to comfort the boy, or bury him if he died. Ban Ping and a neighboring village stayed behind and so lost nothing. Everything was taken from the abandoned villages.

Thamacaj suggests the following course of action: Hear a lot of shooting from the market, take valuables and supplies and send the women and children away. Leave one person to guard each house. When the guards see the soldiers, they can leave. Soldiers do not loot because they do not have either place or use for household stuffs.

Headman and *K* speak to a group of people at the edge of the village. Some of them walking from villages near town, some from tobacco plant. They say that many people have fled the neighboring village and that its animals have been let loose by their owners.

At least one other village was completely abandoned. No one fled Ban Ping.

Fieldnote No. 5. 5 December 1960. *C* reports that the isolated part of Ban Ping where he lives was far less excited than the main village. Just a few households with parents or children in the main village wanted to go and stay with their relatives. After all, if one's parents flee and one doesn't, what's the use?

Later in the day, *P* visits: his job is to repair the *kot* shelter opposite the shop. He attempts to get some children to go from house to house and request spare thatch to reroof the shelter. Children refuse to go because they are "shy." They say that people will refuse them and tell them they don't have any thatch.

The emergency over, Ban Ping's ability to cooperate becomes dormant.

RECOMMENDATIONS

Having enticed the reader this far, I can confess that the recommendations which follow from my lengthy narrative neither follow from the incident described nor are meant as recommendations for action programs. Instead, they are merely intended to stimulate the thinking of those in the Thai and U.S. governments who are more competent and responsible than I to devise programs. They do not follow from the narrative, in the sense that they are suggested not by "The Great Meo Panic" itself, but by the causes which I think underlie "The Panic." To the Lue, as to the Forsythes, "danger is . . . indispensable in bringing out the fundamental quality of any society, group, or individual," and a uniquely stressful event may reveal important features which are always present, but normally unobservable.

In addition to comments made during the course of the narrative, there are three general features of Ban Ping's reaction which have implications for the development of stability and resistance to subversion among Northern Thai minorities. The villagers had little faith in officials; under appropriate leadership they were able to organize for community protection and benefit.

Harassing Regulations and Faith in Officials. Throughout this essay I have emphasized, perhaps even exaggerated, the components of indifference, ambivalence, suspicion, and hostility in the villager's attitude toward officials. Although these are not his only feelings toward officials, government, and nation, these feelings are nonetheless often present and always potentially important. I have attempted to trace them to insularity, isolation, ethnicity, relative deprivation, and to the memory of conquest. These factors Ban Ping shares with much of the North. Economic development, education, enhanced social opportunities, road construction, improved local administration, and the death of the elders will probably alter all of these specifications and diminish their consequences. But is there nothing swifter and cheaper than the many years of elaborate programs which such developments require?

Along with some forms of "voluntary" labor—especially on roads outside the village—there are probably no government regulations which antagonize villagers more than those concerning

gambling, distilling, butchering, and forestry. It is less the regulations themselves than their apparent motive and the seeming
injustice in their enforcement that the villagers find so objectionable. In discussing these regulations, I shall be talking of trivialities. The villager's world is composed of such trivialities, which
to him, and to his national loyalty, sometimes loom much larger
than millions of dollars worth of construction equipment in the
hands, and on the roads, of government officials.

To the villager, the police appear unable, or unwilling to prevent or even investigate cattle thefts, the crime most thought
of and feared. During their periodic inspection trips, the police,
instead, ask only about gamblers, moonshiners, butchers and
trouble-makers (*phu-raj*). The police are pleased when the headman, who protects his villagers, reports none, but the villagers
think that they are willing to accept bribes for the release of
any whom they find or accuse.

At their monthly audience with the district officer, headmen
are officially told, as all villagers know, that the purpose of out-
lawing homemade spirits is to increase the sales of the licensed
distillery from which the government collects a substantial fee.
Since villagers do not think that moneys collected by the government are ever used for their benefit, this justification hardly
elicits their active support.

Regulations against unlicensed gambling antagonize few villagers in Chiengkham because the district officer intelligently
waives the regulations for wakes, at which local custom requires
card games. Villagers, however, are disturbed when the police
seem unable to control (and sometimes even participate in) the
large-scale gambling which semi-professionals, often townsmen,
conduct in the countryside during the rainy season. In addition,
villagers, for whom national lottery tickets are usually too expensive, see no reason other than revenue and bribe collection for
proscribing the cheap "three number lottery" on which they
place their bets.

With rare exceptions, the villagers butcher animals, usually
pigs, only for feasts or to eat in the fields at harvest time, or
to exchange for rice. Since their purposes are not commercial,
they find it quite objectionable to pay a fee, the motives for
which, once again, they regard as purely fiscal. To save the fee

and avoid confronting an official, they butcher secretly, but in fear of informers or detection.

Villagers fell trees in order to build their houses and granaries. When the species of timber used requires a government stamp, they find that some officials may be willing to pocket a smaller payment than the listed fee. When a new species is put on the restricted list, they complain that the officials will next collect fees for permission to cut bamboo or even grass. Like the regulation of animal slaughter, felling fees are seen by the villager to interfere with his livelihood.

Taxation and Licensing. If trivial regulations are of crucial importance to villagers, perhaps these regulations would be easy to modify. I suggest the following:

1. Encourage district officials, and especially low-ranking ones, *to report honestly whether villagers resent the collection of these fees.*

2. The Royal Thai Government should consider the extent to which revenue collection is the main purpose of these regulations. *The amount of revenue collected should be compared to the administrative costs.* Far more importantly, but of far greater difficulty, *the social and political costs of antagonism toward officials should be considered.*

3. The Royal Thai Government should consider whether the regulations properly serve their non-fiscal purposes. Does paying fees to butcher an uninspected animal which will be eaten at home maintain public health? Does proscribing petty gambling while supporting a national lottery discourage villagers from squandering their savings? Would unrestricted village construction destroy silvicultural resources? I do not assume that the answer to these and similar questions is "No." I merely suggest: (a) that the questions be asked about the effects of these regulations; (b) that the non-fiscal benefits be compared with the non-fiscal costs; (c) that the regulations be enforced so as to maximize their non-fiscal benefits; (d) that their non-fiscal purposes be explained to villagers honestly and intelligibly.

Northern villagers, like middle-class Americans, would rather not pay fees to their government. Some fees, however much the villagers try to avoid them, are not resented. Villagers are convinced that registering their cattle will help them recover stolen animals. Although most complain of the inconvenience of registration, and some accuse low-ranking officials of charging more than they report to provincial officers, villagers value the registration service and thus do not feel that its fee is unjustified. It would be worth the effort of trying to explain to villagers how other fees and regulations are intended to protect natural resources or public health and welfare.

4. Greater attention should be given to *showing villagers the ways in which they benefit from government expenditures.* Since these "nuisance fees" are probably a very small fraction of government revenues, it might well prove possible to *retain fee revenues for use in the district (or tambon) where they were collected.* If villagers knew that a particular school, or well, or health station, or pesticide had been provided by means of their license fees (or even fines), they would, I expect, object far less than they now do to fees which appear to serve no purpose other than paying the "monthly money eaten" by officials. The next stage of such a program would be to *have village representatives choose the projects for which the fees could be used.* The selection of such projects might well be assigned to the *tambon* councils which the Thai government hopes to revitalize. The only way to make these councils, or any government agency, meaningful is to give them budget and authority.

Community Organization. Those for whom rural Thailand means only the central plains are likely to be surprised at Ban Ping's reaction to the attack announcement. The native organization of a sentry force, appeals to village history and to village pride, the feeling that the village should act as a unit, the fact that no single individual or household took solitary refuge, the mutual concern of kinsmen and neighbors—all this seems foreign to the alleged "loose structure" of Thai society (Embree 1950). The fact of Ban Ping's communality challenges accepted notions of Thai rural society. It was, in part, to document this challenge that I quoted at such length from my fieldnotes. The fact that what I have seen in Ban Ping is different from what one hears and reads about Bang Chan (Sharp *et al.* 1953)—the village upon which most scholarly ideas about rural Thailand are based—has interesting implications for ethnography. That northern minority Thai villages may differ from Central Thai villages

[419]

in precisely those ways in which Ban Ping differs from Bang Chan has intriguing implications for development programs.

Perhaps one reason why community development (CD) has often been ineffective in Thailand is that CD workers have rarely tried to develop a community: a natural social unit whose residents think of themselves as members, a unit with some degree of organization, leadership, and pride. To the extent that such community units exist in the North, CD and similar community-based programs should prove more effective there than elsewhere. But the community must not merely exist, it must also be officially recognized. The natural community rarely and only accidentally coincides with the *mu-ban* and *tambon,* the "hamlets" and "communes," into which Thailand is divided for administrative purposes. The units recognized by government agencies are usually irrelevant to the rural community and sometimes weaken the rural community. Village names and the ways in which villagers use them are probably the best indices of community boundaries (Moerman 1965). For rapidly surveying a large area, it would be a fairly accurate procedure to assume that temple congregations, especially when they coincide with school districts, constitute a natural community. I suggest:

(1) *that this procedure, or more intensive ones, be used to locate and delimit natural northern villages;*

(2) *that only such natural villages or,* when villages are too small in resources or population redistricted *tambons* composed of such villages and never violating their boundaries *be used for programs intended to develop or revitalize rural communities;*

(3) that the failure of CD where these demarcating procedures have not been used is insufficient proof that CD and similar programs will not work when they are used.

Appropriate Leadership. Some critics of rural programs have suggested that insufficient use has been made of the Buddhist clergy. It would always be a mistake to antagonize village priests and always desirable to solicit their cooperation. It is impossible to make regular use of them as leaders, however, since in many villages their very prestige depends on dissociation from secular concerns. Moreover, in Ban Ping, in Chiengkham, and, I think, rather generally in the North, the youth of the rural clergy diminishes their capacity for leadership. In much of North Thailand, the normal clerical career consists of ordination as a novice (when about fourteen), remaining in the temple only until shortly before or just after one is old enough (twenty) to become a priest, and then leaving to resume the secular life by courting and starting a family (cf. Moerman 1966). Ban Ping's temple has never had a priest older than thirty. The wide distribution of this clerical career—with its young, and therefore powerless, priests—is suggested by the regional ratio of novices to priests (see Table 18), and by the age distribution of "priests" (including novices) as shown in the census (see Table 19).

TABLE 18*
CLERGY IN NORTH AND CENTRAL THAILAND, 1960

Region	Priests	Novices	Ratio of Priests to Novices
Central	85,955	19,010	5:1
North	7,591	20,935	1:3
Chiengkham	183	608	1:3

* Source: Personal communication, Department of Religion, Bangkok.

TABLE 19*
PERCENTAGE OF "PRIESTS" AT DIFFERENT AGES

Region	Age of "Priests"		
	13–19	20–29	30+
Central	17	45	39
North	48	36	10
Chiengrai Province	71	20	9

* Source: Derived from *Thailand Population Census 1960, Changwad Series*, tables of marital status. Census definition of "priests" includes novices.

Ban Ping's encouraging reaction to the threatened invasion required and received effective secular leadership. Since I knew the villagers well, I might have been able to predict that men like *K* and *M*, and *S*, *N*, *Kk*, and *Ss*, would make effective leaders. But predictions, like community demarcations, which require a year of intensive field work to be accurate for a single village have no large-scale practical value. Is there not some more general procedure which would permit us to locate effective leaders with approximate accuracy?

The effective emergency leaders of Ban Ping were former headmen, ex-policemen, traders, former teachers, and in the crucial instance of K, army veterans. Such men are all acquainted with the world outside the village. Veterans, especially, have learned to take and to give commands and have experienced one of the most modern and modernizing institutions available to rural Thais.[11] It is such men whom the headman has appointed to the "development committee" that is supposed to improve the village. It is such men who in their agricultural and commercial practices, as in the ambitions they have for their children's education, are most receptive to innovation. Perhaps the most important characteristic of these persons is that despite the stimulus and training they have received in towns and camps and cities, they have returned to Ban Ping and are full members of the village community. These men have gained, and use, knowledge from their extra-village experiences. They are often influenced by the expectations and judgments which they think that townsmen and officials make, yet think of themselves, and have chosen to live, as villagers.[12]

From the above, it is reasonable to conclude that *former headmen, ex-civil servants, and especially veterans are worth training.* How, and in what should they be trained? I suggest that anything we want the villagers to know and do can be taught and done through such men.

Much of the effort, and money, and hope invested in developing national loyalty in Thai villages goes into programs which consist in part of increasing the contact between peasant and official by bringing officials into villages. In North, Northeast, and Central Thailand, I have witnessed and closely observed very many confrontations between villagers and officials. These observations, admittedly casual and imprecise, lead me to feel that with the general exceptions of schoolteachers and of high-

[11] It should also be noted that veterans know how to take orders and how to use arms, training which I presume is not ignored by subversives. Were I trying to subvert villages, I would concentrate on veterans, underemployed, aggressive young men, and *nakleng* ("ruffians").

[12] In more technical terms, their extra-village experiences and training have changed their reference groups but not their identification group.

ranking officials who meet villagers infrequently, and with the special exception of some extraordinary individuals, officials rarely show understanding, knowledge, or interest in the villager's point of view. Although I hope that my observations are unrepresentative and my analysis false, it is presently my conviction that the ways in which officials typically comport themselves in villages and the actions which they often demand (unrequited feasting, road-widening, house-moving, toilet construction) often have the consequence of increasing the resentment and hostility which villagers feel toward them.

In all agrarian countries, villager and official have long lived in different worlds, so that each has a somewhat distorted view of the other. Thai leaders are aware of this and are commited to doing something about it. In order to increase the unity and mutual understanding of peasant and official, I suggest that programs which inject civil servants into villages be complemented by programs which remove villagers for training. The Mexican government, especially in Chiapas, has had rich experience and some success at training promising villagers who then return to their communities to teach and encourage literacy, sanitation, agricultural improvement. The programs of the Instituto Nacional Indigenista should be examined in order to discover whether they could profitably be modified for Thai conditions.

I would think it quite desirable to train selected northern minority Thai villagers in the rudiments of village sanitation, first aid, midwifery, pest control, home crafts, poultry-breeding, etc. The trained villagers then could teach and lead their fellows. Such knowledge is better taught, and its relevance to rural conditions occasionally better understood (cf. Moerman 1964:36–37) by villagers than by officials. The great danger of such training is that those who receive it may be unwilling to return to their villages. This danger would be minimized by offering the training to those, like veterans and former civil servants, who have ready shown that they find village life more rewarding than its alternatives. It would be further minimized, and other advantages derived, by encouraging those who have been trained to make reasonable charges for the (medical, veterinary, etc.) services they perform for their neighbors. Moreover, instruction conducted and exemplified by fellow villagers might well encourage the creativity and self-reliance which development programs directed by socially distant officials preclude.

REFERENCES CITED

BLOFELD, J.
    1960   People of the sun: encounters in Siam. London, Hutchinson.

CURTIS, L. J.
    1903   The Laos of North Siam. Philadelphia, The Westminster Press.

EMBREE, J. F.
    1950   Thailand: a loosely structured social system. American Anthropologist 52:181–193.

GRAHAM, W. A.
    1924   Siam. Two vols.: Vol. II. London, Alexander Moring, Ltd., The De La More Press.

KINGSHILL, K.
    1960   Ku Daeng—the Red Tomb: a village study in Northern Thailand. Chiengmai (Thailand), Prince Royal's College.

McGILVARY, D.
    1912   A half century among the Siamese and the Lao. New York, Fleming H. Revell Company.

MOERMAN, M.
    1961   A Northern Thai village. Bangkok, USIS. Southeast Asia Survey, Regional Research Report 8.
    1964   Western culture and the Thai way of life. Asia, 1:31–50.
    1965   Ethnic identification in a complex civilization: who are the Lue? American Anthropologist 67(5):1215–1230.
    1966   Bang Ping's temple: the center of a "loosely structured" society. In Anthropological Studies in Theravada Buddhism. New Haven, Yale University, Southeast Asia Studies. Cultural Report Series 13, pp. 137–174.

SHARP, L., et al.
    1953   Siamese rice village: a preliminary study of Bang Chan, 1948–1949. Bangkok, Cornell Research Center.

THAILAND, CENTRAL STATISTICAL OFFICE
    1961   Thailand population census, 1960, changwad series. Bangkok, National Economic Development Board, Central Statistical office.

THAILAND, DEPARTMENT OF PUBLIC WELFARE
    1962   Report on the socio-economic survey of the hill tribes in Northern Thailand. Bangkok, Ministry of the Interior, Department of Public Welfare.

YOUNG, G.
    1962   The hill tribes of Northern Thailand. Bangkok, The Siam Society, Monograph 1, 2d edn.

CHAPTER 12

The Thai Mobile Development Unit Program

LEE W. HUFF

INTRODUCTION

The principal Thai government effort devoted to development of the country's generally remote areas is called the Mobile Development Unit, or MDU program. "Remote," as used here, refers to all territory outside Bangkok and the central plains area. MDU was not specifically designed as a "minority" program, but it has or will affect many minority groups. Furthermore, in the sense that for decades Bangkok has been Thailand—a reference to the centralization of authority, wealth, religion, and culture in the capital city and the relative isolation and neglect of the provinces (*changwad*)—one is not remiss in considering all the residents of outlying areas as minorities of a sort.

Background. The Royal Thai Government (RTG) gave birth to the mobile development concept in 1962. The obvious political and military instabilities of its neighbors in Southeast Asia, often Communist-inspired, led to a little stock-taking within Thailand. The widespread use and success of insurgency suggested that the same technique might be applied there, and an assessment of this danger was made. It was concluded that in the remote sections of the country there were conditions which could conceivably be exploited by skilled insurgents, unless corrected:

> The establishment of Mobile Development Units is the result of the initiation of His Excellency the Prime Minister after seeing the impoverished living conditions of the people in various rural places. They live their lives now in the same way as that of their forefathers. They are needy, lack education, proper houses and have not enough food nor clothing. When they are sick there is no doctor to attend them. It is necessary to help these sorrowful people immediately so that they may be moderately happier (sic). (Anon. 1963A:20)[1]

[1] *Mobile Development* is an official publication of the National Security Command, Ministry of Defense, Bangkok, Thailand. Its purpose is to keep the public informed of the varied activities of the Mobile Development Unit Program.

[425]

The RTG very wisely saw the problem in terms of preventing the growth of conditions conducive to insurgency; hence the action response has been framed largely in terms of prevention rather than suppression.

There were several nation-wide development programs already in existence at the time MDU was started. As a rule, however, they functioned more or less independently, and they were not strongly in evidence in the remotest areas. It makes sense, of course, to plan and base development efforts in areas with reasonable concentrations of population, local resources, etc. But looked at in a security context, these perfectly sensible programs are likely to reach last the areas that need them most. MDU was to fill this gap and, hopefully, form a bridge between the present and a future when more conventional programs could take their place. Its primary rationale was to extend a meaningful government presence to the remote areas, often for the first time. Thus MDU is a development program motivated by the RTG's concern for a potential security problem. Americans call it preventive counter-insurgency. Clearly, it does not involve combat, and it goes well beyond normally understood versions of short-term military civic action. The RTG simply discerned the close connection between underdevelopment and national security and defined the work of helping the people to develop themselves as "one facet of the national security problem" (*ibid*.:11).

The Thai judgment to go to the remote areas, well in advance of formulating detailed plans for large-scale economic development and with no plans for a dramatic social revolution, shows an understanding of the past insurgency experience in nearby Malaya and the Philippines:

> What was successfully accomplished in both countries and contributed perhaps more to the control of insurgency was the reestablishment of the authority of the government. This was achieved by implementing firm policies and also by reawakening the people's confidence and hope through convincing evidence that the Government did care about their welfare. (Pauker 1962:12)

This frame of reference catches the spirit of MDU.

"Development" in Thailand, whether economic, social, or political, contains an element of paradox. The country is in no sense impoverished. By and large, there is enough food to eat. Most farmers own their land, and there has been no shortage of it. The climate is mild, thereby minimizing requirements for shelter and clothing. Although minorities exist, relatively speaking, the population is considered ethnically homogeneous. Language difficulties are minimal. Perhaps 90 percent of the people are Buddhist, and this group appears to be generally free of factionalism. Toleration of religious minorities, particularly Moslems and Christians, is remarkably "pure." Most city people can find a job, and, at the worst, underemployment or seasonal unemployment may occur. Violence is regarded unfavorably as a means of settling disputes. A young and beloved royal family serves as a real symbol of national unity. Historically, governments, whatever their form, have been paternalistic. Of singular significance, Thailand's success in avoiding colonial conquest has protected the nation against the psychological scars which have so preoccupied the rest of Asia since 1945. The Thai have been a self-governing nation for as long as they can remember, without interruption. The economy has never been seriously strained.

Many Thai people are aware of this abundance and are grateful for it. It has been succinctly summarized by one of them:

> Peoples of other countries die of famine. We Thais die of overeating. Even though most of us do not go about in motorcars, nearly all have, at least, a loin-cloth to wear around our middle. Since we are high in our standard of contentment, living and eating simply as our forefathers in the past, most of us consider this country good enough for continued existence. (Seni Pramoj 1965)

Why, then, be concerned about potential insurgency? And how does one resolve the above contradictory statements about poverty and wealth?

In point of fact, both are correct, the second as a general conclusion, the first when applied to particular areas of the country, especially in the Northeast. All advantages are relative, and within Thailand they are unevenly spread. The deficiencies which do occur are found in the most inaccessible parts of the kingdom, far from Bangkok. In view of the ease with which Thailand's strengths can be viewed from the perspective of Bangkok's charm and affluence, the Thai government has been unusually perceptive in recognizing and assessing realistically the problem areas which do exist.

Several "remote areas" fail to share fully in the national endowment. In the mountainous North the major problems are geographic and ethnic, and are discussed in detail in other papers in this volume. In the South problems sometimes recur with respect to the remnants of the Malayan Communist Terrorist movement, who hide out in jungles on both sides of the Thai-Malaysian border; an Islamic minority is concentrated in a few of the southern provinces, and there are occasional Malay separatist groups. In the sparsely populated western provinces robber bands flourish. But it is the Northeast which presents the greatest worry.

The Environment. Northeast Thailand is a high, semi-arid plateau area covering fifteen provinces, or about one-third of the total land area of the country. According to the 1960 census, its population was almost nine million (see Table 20). With a growth rate of about 3 percent annually, the figure must be about ten million in 1965. It is the poorest region in Thailand. The land is not good, largely due to the presence of sandy and lateritic soils and poor drainage; nevertheless, 95 percent of the heads of village families reportedly own their own land, and

TABLE 20
POPULATION OF THE NORTHEAST*

Province	Population
Buriram	583,585
Chayaphum	486,472
Kalasin	426,795
Khon-Kaen	844,075
Loei	210,535
Mahasarakham	499,373
Nakhornphanom	436,482
Nakornratchsima (Korat)	1,094,774
Nongkhai	256,530
Roi-et	668,193
Sakonnakhorn	426,755
Srisaket	601,356
Surin	581,732
Ubonratch-thani (Ubon)	1,130,712
Udornthani (Udorn)	744,174
Total	8,991,543

* Source: *Thailand Population Census, 1960.*

in many areas soils are "poor" only in the sense that they are used improperly to grow rice when they are better suited to other crops (*Bangkok World,* October 28, 1964). Diets are unbalanced, and undernutrition is widespread. The principal crop and staple foodstuff is glutinous rice; in fact, about 75 percent of the rice consumed in Northeast villages is of this "sticky" variety (*ibid.*). The area is subject to flooding in the four- or five-month rainy season, although mean average rainfall is less than in the south and central plains. Daytime temperatures are especially hot. Water is in short supply much of the rest of the year due to a combination of geologic, climatic, and human factors, e.g. rapid runoff, high evapo-transpiration, and inadequate catchment facilities. Ground water is often brackish, and soils are so saline in some places that villagers readily produce salt by running water through handfuls of dirt and boiling the runoff. Villagers may have to walk four kilometers to find drinking water at the peak of the dry season. It has been estimated that only about 4,000 of 14,000 villages in the area have an adequate water supply.[2]

Underemployment tends to be high, but few farmers are in debt. The average monthly cash income of a Northeast village family is 249 baht (U.S. $12.45). Average annual income per capita throughout the region is 910 baht ($45.50), with the figure being 2,503 baht in towns and 801 baht in villages. The town figure is comparable to that found in other towns in the country, except in Bangkok, but it has been estimated that Northeast village incomes are only about 65 percent of those in other Thai villages (see Thailand 1964; Long 1964:8; *Bangkok World,* October 28, 1964). MDU often operates in the poorest of those, for instance, in Ban Fa Huan, Changwat Ubol, where cash income per family is estimated at only 200 baht ($10.00) annually.

Education has also lagged in the Northeast. Most villages have to share a poorly-equipped school; and good teachers are not attracted by austere village living. As of 1962, 95 percent of the heads of village families in the Northeast had had less than four years of education or none at all.

Traditionally, relations between farmers and officials have been

[2] Figures attributed to Mr. Bunchana Arthakorn, Deputy Minister of National Development, *Bangkok World,* June 29, 1963.

indifferent or worse, in large part because men sent to posts in the provinces have characteristically taken the assignment as a mark of failure. Careers were made in the capital, not in the hinterland, reflecting the old tradition that "the only advantage an official saw in a distant post was the greater freedom it gave to use an official position to gain wealth by dubious means or perhaps, if the official were governor in an important distant province, the opportunity to glory in heading a regime that represented a miniature Bangkok" (Vella 1955:325). On the other hand, officials have had to work within a highly centralized bureaucratic system: "Tight control over their operations is exercised from Bangkok, with initiative discouraged and little discretion permitted" (Thomas 1962:17–18). The further one is from Bangkok, the less responsive the system tends to be. There are also, or can be, serious "discontinuities" between the official and the villager—socially, politically, and culturally—and these lead to feelings among villagers of apartness from the government and its representatives (for excellent examples, analysis, and summary see Moerman 1961:4–7). These are often exacerbated in the remote areas, and one finds the white-collar workers and farmers living in highly compartmentalized, separate local worlds.

During periods of parliamentary government, the Northeast was frequently represented by parties and groups given generally to opposing the government in power, formulating "leftist" programs, demanding alleviation of regional economic distress, and supporting a neutralist foreign policy (Wilson 1961:13; 1962:31, 241).

A group of about 60,000 North Vietnamese refugees settled on the Thai side of the Mekong River after fleeing the French Indochina War in the mid-1950's. They now live together in large groups, mostly in or near towns. They have not been assimilated into Thai society, and their allegiance to Ho Chi Minh, who they revere and remember as a great nationalist figure, is cause for concern.[3] Periodic repatriations to North Vietnam are arranged under Red Cross auspices, but the migration tends

[3] Ho worked as an organizer in Thailand in the late 1920's. I have visited Ban Nong On, Changwat Udon, where he allegedly lived. Several very old Vietnamese families are still there today.

to be offset by the birthrate. Finally, there is the troublesome question of the ethnic significance of the population of the Northeast, which has ties with people across the river in Laos. On the basis of this catalogue of considerations, it became obvious that conditions did exist which a skilled dissident might be able to exploit to his own advantage. Accordingly, seven of the first nine MDU operations areas were placed in Northeast Thailand.[4]

The Population. The people of the Northeast comprise about 30 percent of the population of the entire country. About 90 percent of them live in villages and farm to earn their living. There is some confusion over the proper ethnic designation or designations for them, and one can cite evidence to support either homogeneity or heterogeneity. In my experience, most villagers in the Northeast usually describe themselves and their language in one of three ways: *Thai Isan* (Northeast Thai), *Thai-Lao,* or *Lao.* The official census does not distinguish between them and Thai, or Cambodian Thai. Anthropologists usually lump Thai and Lao together in a single "Thai" or "Greater Thai" ethnolinguistic classification.

Seidenfaden has said that the "Laos of the Mekhong valley . . . form the bulk of the population in the former circles of Udorn and Roi-et in Northeast Thailand and in the former circle of Prachin" (1958:10), but he further asserts that "It has been argued that the people of Laos including those of Northeast Thailand, never called themselves anything else than Laos. To this it may be said that in the census, taken by the King of Lan Chang (Laos) in the year 1376, the inhabitants were called Thai" (*ibid:* 90). Another explanation or interpretation is more dogmatic: "The Lao differ but little from the Thai, and are in reality as much Thai as are the Thai (Siamese). The name Lao having been bestowed on them by the Thai and may be due to the fact that the Lao occupied land formerly peopled by Lawa. Their language has some dialectical variations and contains fewer imported Sanscrit and Pali words than Thai" (Ninth Pacific Science Congress 1957:26). The recent HRAF study of ethnic groups in Southeast Asia sheds very little light on this question, noting simply that "the Siamese at times refer to the

[4] For a contemporary Thai account of events leading to establishment of the MDU program see Theh Chongkhadikij, 1963.

Tai-speaking glutinous-rice eaters living in the plains and low-land river valleys to the north and northeast of central Thailand as Lao" (LeBar *et al.* 1964:215).

I am inclined to agree with the "conservative estimate" by Keyes that about seven and one-half million of the nine million people in the Northeast are Thai-Lao and consider themselves as such (Keyes 1964A:2). This is all the more interesting because there are only about a million Lao people in Laos itself (about one-half of the population) (*ibid.*; LeBar *et al.* 1964:215). The Thai-Lao of the Northeast are distinguished mainly by their dialect, their taste for glutinous rice, and their folk music, all of which may be less significant in their minds than the general differentiation of themselves as "country hicks" and their Bangkok and vicinity cousins as educated, wealthy, "city slickers."[5] It is all rather difficult to judge, but on the basis of visits to dozens of villages in Northeast Thailand, particularly throughout Udorn, Sakonnakhorn, and Nakhon Panom, it is my impression that the "Lao-ness" displayed by villagers tends to be a matter of family feeling or kinship rather than any particular association with governments or states, i.e., it is something they take for granted. It is noteworthy, however, that the Thai Isan (and most other Thai) is quick to consider a Vietnamese, Chinese, or Indian as an alien even if he has citizenship; he is not likely to so classify a visitor from Laos. Nevertheless, the government's concern is with "potential," and it is at least possible that this ethnic differentiation in the Northeast could be played upon, perhaps in combination with problems of economic depression, social inertia, and administrative laxity.

It should be said that the national system of compulsory four-year schooling, in force since 1932 and recently increased to seven years, has begun to affect citizens living outside the central plains area. Moerman, for instance, reached a very unambiguous conclusion while living in a Northern Thai village:

[5] In this connection I have been struck by Professor Amyot's account of the relationship between a small market town in Srisaket Province and the even smaller villages around it. He say there is a strict "town and country difference" between the town and its satellites: "Its people easily take superior attitudes and poke fun at the country yokels. The peasants . . . are ill-at-ease with them and by preference seek out people of their own condition . . . elsewhere" (Amyot 1964:4).

> It is our strong impression that in areas . . . where officials are estranged, the draft widely scattered, official radio broadcasts largely irrelevant to village life, and government services almost non-existent, the local elementary school is overwhelmingly the main source of national consciousness and loyalty. Lessons in the national language, in Thai history, religion, and geography—however superficial and imperfectly remembered—have a profound effect on village life. . . . It is one of the foundations of national consciousness and thus of national security. (Moerman 1961:8)

Keyes has expressed similar views after lengthy personal observation of Northeast villages (Keyes 1964A:3).

MDU teams occasionally encounter another type of ethnic or religious minority problem in the Northeast, on a much smaller scale. These are very widely scattered villages composed of people who take pride in distinguishing themselves from both their Thai and Lao neighbors. For instance, I have been in So, Kha, Phu Thai, and Catholic villages. One sees few significant identifying physical characteristics in people, dress, agriculture, or buildings, but language and custom may differ.

Perhaps the greatest problem in the Northeast is the possible disastrous consequences of rapid population growth, a serious shortage of land, inefficient land use, and falling incomes throughout the region. As the World Bank Report noted in 1963: "Considering the North-East as a whole, population pressure has not yet become an acute problem, but the decreasing fertility of the land in combination with a rapid increase in population could cause the North-East to become a truly depressed area within a decade"[6] (Platenius 1963:2).

THE MDU CONCEPT

The exact sources of the MDU concept are difficult to pin down. Some believe that it grew out of discussions among students at the Thai National Defense College, an institution analagous to the American National War College. Certain mobile team activities are close relatives of those performed first by the Mobile Information Teams (MIT) organized by the Ministry of Interior and put in the field in February 1962 with the advice and assistance of the United States Information Service. Thai

[6] Platenius was advisor to the Committee on the Development of the Northeast and represented the World Bank Advisory Group. See also Long (1964:25–28).

military officers and their American colleagues at the Joint
United States Military Assistance Advisory Group (JUSMAAG)
also discussed the insurgency issue and the problems involved in
planning to meet it. It is probably fair to say that all these factors
had some influence on the formulation of the program and organization which were subsequently created. In essence, however, the MDU program has been Thai created, Thai initiated,
and Thai operated.[7]

Although program, not organization, is the focus of this paper,
one organizational decision merits brief attention. In accordance
with the above-mentioned linkage of underdevelopment with insurgency and development with counter-insurgency, the RTG
decided to integrate civil, police, and military resources within
a single command structure. In this fashion each contribution
would be made in coordination with the others, and the disadvantages of separate programs with particular vested bureaucratic interests and goals would be minimized. This directing
authority was established in a National Security Central Command by cabinet decision on April 10, 1962 (Anon. 1963B:12).
The new command has functioned as part of the Office of the
Prime Minister and the Supreme Command, Ministry of Defense.

Following policy guidance developed by a twenty-one-man
Policy Committee, composed primarily of the ministers of participating ministries, this central office has authority to develop com-
prehensive development programs in the areas in which MDU
operates and to call upon civil, police, and military departments
for the material and personnel required to do the job (*ibid.*:13).
In brief, the problem is defined and analyzed at a single source,
a single set of objectives and an action program are formulated
there, and the resources required for execution are acquired by
it and applied through it. The positions in the central headquarters are filled primarily by military officers from the army, navy,
and air force. They provide the analytical, planning, and operational skills, but especially leadership. The civil ministries supply
technical knowledge and experience.

[7] There is some popular misconception on this point. Press accounts frequently
call MDU an American assistance program, e.g. Methvin (1964:121–122). Although the United States has purchased some expensive equipment items for
MDU and has begun to focus certain conventional development programs in
MDU areas, the MDU program has not been dependent on outside advice
and assistance.

The underlying themes of the MDU program are essentially "nation-belonging" and "nation-building." The government wishes to tell the people in remote areas that they are valued citizens of the country, that they have a stake in the nation, and that they can assist in improving the nation so as to benefit it and themselves. Considerable effort is expended to show that the government does care about the welfare of all its people and wishes to help them; however, MDU is very careful to avoid making promises which it cannot fulfill. It also tries to emphasize the self-help concept, in which the villagers must show some evidence of wishing to help themselves.

Slogans such as "Thai helps Thai to develop Thailand," "The people are the heart of the nation," and "Everyone must work against time to develop the Thai nation" are characteristic of the MDU message to rural citizens. Thousands upon thousands of photographs of the King and Queen, the Emerald Buddha, and the Prime Minister are distributed and often accompanied with short explanatory talks to dramatize the three pillars of stability in the nation—crown, religion, and government. It is not uncommon for MDU teams to find people living in remote areas who do not know who their King and Queen or Prime Minister are.[8]

This campaign to encourage "nation-belonging" and "nation-building" appears to have a great deal of resemblance to King Wachirawut's efforts to introduce the concept of nationalism into Thailand at the turn of this century. Vella has written that although the Thai had long demonstrated a sense of patriotism, they had taken their cultural identity very much for granted. Wachirawut, worried that his people might overindulge their acceptance of Western ideas, exalted "the Thai country, the Thai nation, the Thai people, the Thai virtues," and underscored the significance of Thai Buddhism as a national asset (Vella 1955:352).[9] Some fifty years later, the Thai are making much the same appeal to countrymen who very likely missed the first one.

[8] Nor is this phenomenon unique to Thailand. (Cf. Schramm 1964:69–72.)

[9] It is revealing in this context that Thai administrators list "nationalistic" as one of several traits with a "distinct modern, non-traditional connotation" to which they aspire but may not possess. The other traits mentioned in this category are ambition, efficiency, group-mindedness, and ability to plan. See Mosel (1964:4).

The most telling example of the government's sincerity, however, is the willingness of officials to go into the rural areas and to behave in accordance with the messages they bring. The RTG believes that if it acts in this fashion while the Communists only talk, the latter will gather no following and indeed will be discredited. Prime Minister Thanom Kittikachorn stated this position clearly, after a field inspection of MDU areas, when he remarked that Communist propaganda was "only a lot of talk with no action to benefit the people so the people can now see the difference between the Communist talk and what the government is actually accomplishing" (*Bangkok World,* February 18, 1965).

MDU operations areas are selected on the basis of their remoteness, the relative absence of long-term development programs and other government services, and a judgment concerning their potential as sources of future insurgency activity. Extensive surveys of each area are made in advance, and a centrally located village is picked to be the site of a field headquarters. Note that province capitals and district towns are not chosen. This has the effect of emphasizing both the "people-to-people" character of the program and the fact that it is not intended to be an assistance program brought by one set of officials solely to benefit another.

As of May 1965, MDU programs had been initiated in the following provinces: Kalasin, Sakonnakhorn, Nakhonphanom, Nongkhai, Udornthani, Loei, and Ubonratch-thani in the Northeast and Yala and Nara-thiwat in the South. The next two MDU's are scheduled for Uttradit and Nan in North Thailand. Size varies widely, e.g. from the single small district in Kalasin, which launched an MDU in the summer of 1962, to a 9,900-square-kilometer area in Ubon involving about 55,000 families. Terrain factors affecting ease of movement frequently control this decision.

In Bangkok personnel for each new MDU field group are drawn from various contributing ministries and placed in a rigorous training program. They are briefed on the MDU mission, the specific tasks to be performed, and the performance expected from each man and the group to which he belongs. As a result of accumulated experience, training in "face-to-face" contact with village people has been increased from thirty minutes to about ten hours. Map exercises and field trials are also held in order to improve the efficiency of the group and to reduce the learning time required when actual operations begin. The MDU program is divided into three phases, the last two of which are only vaguely separable. The body of this paper is devoted to discussion of them.

Phase I: Impact. The primary purpose of the first phase of an MDU operation is psychological impact. Very little "development" in any formal sense is achieved. Three mobile teams of seventeen men each are sent out from the headquarters to visit a pre-selected number of villages in the area for forty to forty-five days. They stay in each village for one to three days, stop briefly in others along the way, and encourage residents of neighboring villages to "drop in" at those places scheduled for a visit.[10]

Each mobile team is led by a young military officer, many of whom have been trained in American military schools. His deputy is frequently the deputy district officer or local education officer. A doctor is provided by the Ministry of Public Health, and he is assisted by the local Public Health Officer if there is one. There are representatives from the Department of Public Welfare and the Ministry of Cooperatives. Public Relations Department personnel operate audiovisual equipment. Service men are used as drivers, mechanics, cooks, and communications specialists.[11]

All team members are dressed in civilian clothes, and no weapons are carried; indeed, many of the teams buy caps or shirts distinctive for the areas they work in and wear them proudly as a team badge of membership. A typical team travels in a small caravan of about four vehicles, one of which is equipped as a sound truck. They are as self-sufficient as possible, including providing their own bedding and food supplies, so as to minimize demands on the village. Even "gifts" are turned down because it is known that this traditional form of appeasing

[10] For a detailed account of a typical Phase-I MDU operation see Huff (1963).

[11] It is important to note that the mobile teams are composed of Thai members only. They are not accompanied by foreign advisory personnel. Methvin's remark (1964:121) that MDU groups "are staffed by personnel from several Thai and U.S. government branches" is completely incorrect. Individual Americans have been permitted to accompany mobile teams for brief periods as observers, but only on an occasional basis.

visiting dignitaries is accomplished at the villagers' expense. Some food may be purchased locally if surplus items are available. Village youngsters are asked to draw water for the team, but the water is carefully rationed by the team leader if the village supply is low (and often it is).

The team's camp is made as public as possible so that the villagers will come to it to watch and talk. Part of the team's mission is to talk about the importance of public health and sanitation, and the villagers are given plenty of opportunity to observe team members eating well-cooked food, taking baths with soap and water, Thai style, in open-air surroundings, and using crude temporary latrines. The purpose of these demonstrations is not to transform Thai rural villages into spotless model towns, but merely to inspire the people to remove the worst excesses which contribute to the incredible variety and amount of enteric disease which beset people of all ages. One sample of five hundred schoolchildren, for example, was found to be completely infested with stomach parasites, and 90 percent of them had two or more varieties.

The team doctor is extremely popular. He may treat 150–200 patients per day. Serious illnesses are not common, but enteric diseases, malaria-induced diseases, and vitamin deficiencies are found everywhere. Interestingly, kidney stones are quite evident, perhaps due to the high mineral content of the water, and respiratory ailments are abundant. Some MDU teams have also undertaken special vaccination campaigns to thwart epidemics. It should be noted that villagers in the Northeast are not afraid of the doctor or his medicine. Pills, and especially injections, are real status symbols—everybody wants one. This does not necessarily reduce the influence of local herb doctors, because people are inclined to feel that the new and the old medicine each has its place and can be expected to be worthwhile in different situations.[12] Mobile teams that encounter extremely serious

[12] Keyes (1964B:8–9) has defined the various kinds of local "doctor" who have the ability to prevent or cure sickness or ward off evil influences: he may be a practitioner of traditional medicine, trained in giving shots, an exorciser and appeaser of spirits, a medium who can communicate with discontented ancestor spirits, or "he can have the power to destroy spirits which possess an individual and 'eat' his soul." See also Lux (1962:38, 51).

cases of illness try to arrange evacuation of patients by land vehicle or helicopter to a provincial hospital.

The public welfare official asks the headman or schoolteacher to draw up a list of needy families. The list is then verified by the team, using such techniques as looking at the rice in the prospective recipient's storage building and counting his buffalo. This is done to insure that village officials do not pack the list with friends, relatives, and creditors, and it in turn underscores the sincerity of the government's " people-to-people" message.

Welfare assistance takes the form of clothing for school-age children—shorts and shirts for the boys, skirts and blouses for the girls—and T-shirts and blankets for old folks. These are usually presented at large outdoor assemblies, with adults invited, where a public address system is set up, names are called, presentations are made, and senior team members give short talks on public health, education, cooperatives, and other general themes associated with the MDU mission. Westerners sometimes feel that these assemblies cause embarrassment to the aid recipients, who allegedly do not like to parade before their peers, and cause resentment among those who receive nothing. My own opinion, after observing these ceremonies in countless villages, is that the recipients are pleased and most of the rest are delighted that somebody got something. Nearly all the schoolchildren receive a pencil, eraser, piece of candy, or other token gift. Occasionally very old people are sent to a national home for the aged; blind boys are offered a chance to attend a special school; or a new house is provided to old people without families who are existing on village charity alone.

Evenings are devoted to a long program of movies and shorts. At least once between reels the team leader gives a talk and repeats the general purpose of the MDU operation. This procedure is used partly because of the knowledge that repetition of themes helps people remember and partly because the village in question is jam-packed with new people who have walked or arrived by ox-cart from other locations to take part in the occasion. For most of the villages affected, the MDU movies are the first (some have been visited by small drug trucks showing movies about their patent medicine cure-alls). The films range from newsreel-type coverage of the royal family's periodic visits around the country to shorts about Buddhism and Bangkok, Thai railways, and considerably edited "full-length" epics about the American West and Tarzan. The use of local-dialect sound tracks maximizes audience comprehension, but entertainment value is high regardless of language, at least the first time around. To achieve real substantive effect, however, movies should be in the local dialect, attuned to the educational level of the audience, amply illustrated with shots of things familiar to the villager, very simple in photographic technique, and reasonably sensitive to the cultural frame of reference of the audience (for more detailed discussion see Huff 1964:46–51; Moerman 1961:Appendix). It is easy to excite and visibly impress the village audience, but much more difficult to determine exactly what interpretation they put on what they see.

Team leaders also seek out the best musicians and singers in the village and invite them to perform over the public address system before the home-town audience. Invariably this is an outstanding "crowd pleaser." I recall being present during a friendly, impromptu, but real competition between two village headmen who excelled in singing *moh lam,* the local folk music. The large audience was thrilled with the duel and was more than just a little pleased with the interest the team took in the proceedings.

The use of local music has been developed in three ways. The first is achieved by making tape recordings "on the scene" and replaying them over the sound system. Some mobile team leaders have this music playing at their headquarters much of the day. A second method is to use professional *moh lam* troupes to give performances. This involves a sort of sung narrative about events in the history of the village, the immediately surrounding area, and the region. Some of the songs resemble historical epic stories, but many involve recent happenings, and a high premium is placed on the performer who is able to innovate and cleverly ad lib on the spot. Jokes, often a few shades off color, are woven into the story to provide comic relief, and in the case of *moh lam* groups accompanying MDU teams, appropriate MDU themes are included. The third use of the music, not necessarily related to MDU specifically, is on radio programs beamed into the region. Radios are no longer a luxury, thanks to the advent of the transistor. Approximately 5 percent of the families in Northeast villages own one, and growth in sales in recent years has been phenomenal. In a study of forty villages I directed in a relatively remote section of Udorn Province, villagers had about seven hundred transistor radios of varied size and make. Shortwave is received from all over the world, but even on regular broadcast bands it is possible to pick up a variety of Thai stations and broadcasts from Laos, China, Burma, Cambodia, and the Phillippines. *Moh lam* is the overwhelming program favorite with villagers. The government radio station at Khon Kaen is especially popular because it caters to its audience accordingly.[13] In short, this simple demonstration of sensitivity to local culture appears to have great appeal to people of all ages in the Northeast.[14]

MDU does not make an issue of "Communism" or subversion unless villagers have been exposed to propaganda or have questions. Then they discuss it frankly; in particular they move quickly to expose and discredit the usually inept broadcasts of the clandestine "Voice of the Thai People" radio which occasionally are directed against a specific MDU. For instance, the radio reported that MDU personnel in Ubon were indoctrinating the children with imperialist ideas and giving them poisoned candy. The MDU commander called the youngsters and their parents to an assembly with alacrity, poked fun at the broadcasts, conducted a question and answer game about Thai national heroes, and passed out candy all around. He made his point.

The key to success of MDU work clearly is not the various functions which are performed per se—e.g. health or public welfare—but the manner in which they are executed. The team leader sets the tone for his group, and if he succeeds in communicating convincingly with villagers, the operation is likely to be productive. Good team leaders spend a great deal of time

---

[13] The station's effectiveness in competing for listeners may spark some unethical counter-measures. Prime Minister Thanom reported earlier this year that he had been warned of Communist plans to sabotage the station, and he ordered the Army to provide security accordingly. (*Bangkok Post*, January 24, 1965.)

[14] See *Bangkok World*, October 28, 1964; Keyes (1964A:3); USIS/Thailand (1964:20, 24–33). The effects of mass media on the information levels in rural villages are discussed in Schramm (1964:73–76).

just talking—to headmen, farmers, housewives, teachers, village priests, shopkeepers, and schoolchildren.[15] The strong and favorable impact of a Bangkok official inquiring and talking about local problems on a low-pressure, informal basis, often in the local dialect, cannot be overestimated. His willingness to eat sticky rice without making wisecracks, to drink local water without fear, to observe such customs as removing one's shoes in a villager's house or the *wat* (Buddhist temple), and to deal with local people without condescension is equally important in enhancing the credibility of the government's message. It may very well outlast the pills, clothing, movies, and other material aspects of the team's visit in the minds of the village people.

Moerman's analysis of the cultural discontinuity which can exist between district officials and villagers includes the following succinct description:

> An official dressed in his western-style khaki uniform goes to address the wide-trousered, home-spun clad residents of a village. He speaks in Central Thai, which many understand only with difficulty and all speak with diffidence. The address over, he is fed a meal of boiled rice which he eats with a fork and spoon. The villagers eat steamed glutinous rice with their fingers. These seemingly superficial distinctions are emblems of real differences in identification. (Moerman 1961:6)

MDU behavior, by and large, aims at elimination of this stereotype.

Perhaps I should underscore the fact that my faith in the value of this behavior is not based on a Western background and normative bias. The facts are that on the basis of numerous observations, it became clear that this informal, open sort of behavior produced more effective responses among village people than did behavior which was more formal or "official," or relied heavily on a relationship of superior to inferior. Village people already recognize the official's status. They do not, therefore, expect him to act contrary to it, either by undue self-effacement or by an unnecessary show of power. They respect those who can and will explain the reasons why a particular course of action is or

---

[15] The number of shops in villages throughout the Northeast is startling, and the rising power and status of the merchant is forcing realignment of the traditional village status system. See Keyes (1964B:7–8).

is not desirable; their enthusiasm and response are often noticeably reduced when explanations are not forthcoming. As Amyot (1964:14) has noted cogently: "Learning (and conviction) require the continuing presence of a teacher, who teaches preferably by doing, over an extended period, so that all may have an opportunity to convince themselves of the utility of the innovation." In a similar vein, one of the difficulties facing the Ministry of Cooperatives representative on a mobile team is the short amount of time available to explain the intricacies of a farmer's cooperative. This idea is not grasped easily in a one-hour talk, and cooperatives' organizers soon learned that their proselytizing required a longer-term effort than mobile teams could accommodate.

One significant aspect of mobile team operations is the self-help project, and it is significant by either its presence or its absence in any particular village. The self-help concept is basic in the philosophy of community development. It has been described as the "fundamental tenet" of successful military civic-action programs, and Secretary of State Dean Rusk has said that "self-help is the most important single factor in the development process as a whole" (Walterhouse 1964:17).[16] It may likewise be one of the most delicate of issues to handle at the village level.

MDU has received two kinds of advice about self-help. Some said that the people in the Northeast had received so little attention for such a long time and had so commonly associated requests to do village work with sterile road-building exercises in lieu of taxes or to impress visiting officials that it would be dangerous to ask them to do anything. In short, this view was a compound of belief that the government "owed" the people something plus some fear that a totally negative or cynical response would be forthcoming to any self-help work request, i.e., a compound of the normative and the practical. The second type of advice counseled that the entire effort must be based on the self-help principle lest the MDU program encourage farmers to believe that the government existed solely to do things for them and that "development" or "progress" was entirely somebody

[16] The Rusk quotation is cited from U.S. House of Representatives, *Hearings before the Committee on Foreign Affairs on HR 5490* (April 1963), p. 5.

else's responsibility, not their own.[17] Thus MDU was damned if it did and damned if it did not rely on self-help.

In fact, MDU has followed a pragmatic path between these positions that emerges in word and deed as a sort of principle of "joint help." It tends to believe, as I do, that "the villager expects the government to do things for him, but given some help and organization, he is willing to go along with government projects," and it operates on this assumption (Moerman 1961:7). It is recognized that Thai villagers do not have a strong tradition of undertaking public or community projects, excepting collective concern for the *wat* and certain religious celebrations[18] and, in my opinion, concern when cattle thieves harrass their cattle and buffalo. This is not to say villagers are absolutely selfish, rather that cooperation tends to be extended within families or among close friends for readily identifiable mutual gain.[19] The bases of social relationships tend to be kinship ties, marriage, and friendship. In this scheme "doing something for the village" is not always a self-evident "good." In its general themes MDU constantly emphasizes the fact that the government can and will help some to improve village life, but that basic improvement is greatly dependent on the villagers' own efforts. During the Phase I period of an MDU, self-help is used with restraint. There is a feeling that "make work" is worse than "no work," and team leaders tend to err on the side of caution. Wisely used, however, self-help brings a very high payoff.

[17] It is noteworthy that one of the mobile teams with MDU-2 reported a few instances in which agitators allegedly told villagers before the team arrived that the team had been instructed to do everything *for* the villagers and had been given money to distribute to them, when in fact the team was told to encourage villager participation in self-help projects and had no cash handouts. The reports were considered rather suspect because of certain weaknesses in this mobile team, but taken at face value they suggest the kind of "counter-measure" which can be used against a legitimate development program, playing on old experiences with, or attitudes about, malpractice in government administration. For details see Huff (1963:55–56).

[18] For examples of self-initiated cooperative effort within villages and between neighboring villages which have affinal and consanguineal ties see Lux (1962:92–93, 110).

[19] The following thesis is relevant in this context: "A peasant family can function with less outside cooperation than any other social form. . . . One reason, then, that peasants are not very cooperative is that they do not have to be. Paradoxical as it may sound, their technology permits them a degree of independence denied members of more primitive and more advanced societies" (Foster 1959:178).

[444]

The difficulties are apparent. It is hard to identify a meaningful work project that can be completed during a one- or two-day stay. MDU teams tend to shy away from the traditional desultory display of road repair work, which is likely to recall old and unpleasant associations with the government. They have learned that simple projects such as erecting village bulletin boards or installing a water-seal latrine at the *wat* have a limited effect and may require a great deal of explanation. Bulletin boards, for example, are often thought to be the government's property, not the village's, and a demonstration of "public" ownership and use is needed. Similarly, latrines at the *wat* are thought to be the exclusive property of the monks and not a village asset (there is a clear belief held and sometimes expressed concurrently by villagers that the latrine is not likely to be a village asset under any circumstance). Nor do small projects involve enough people of the village. Ideally, one wants widespread participation in the doing and widespread sharing in the final product.

But when a good project can be identified, a competent team leader can exploit it, in the best sense of the word, to advantage. A "good project" tends to be one related to a village problem that for one reason or another has meaning for the villagers. Amyot has suggested that public works projects "seem to dominate the cooperative efforts of the villagers, being both more often undertaken and more often successful" (Amyot 1964:14–15). Likewise, projects that failed were those requiring a change in the villagers' pattern of living, e.g. "raising chickens." He notes, not surprisingly, that the villagers always do best on projects they have initiated themselves. On occasion one finds a village where there is unanimous concern about a problem and people are ready to act, but need, or think they need, leadership, equipment, special skills, or some other missing ingredient. In other places village opinion may be split between a large majority and a small but relatively powerful minority. A wise team leader may seek to mediate this controversy. In one fairly large village in Sakonnakhorn Province, for example, the main streets were so filled with trees that carts could not go through and had to make inconvenient detours. There was

[445]

widespread agreement that the streets should be cleared; however, each tree had an owner, and no one would be the first to remove his trees. Some of the owners were village leaders, well liked and respected, and it was hard to pressure them. One of them was also an exceedingly influential schoolmaster, who inspired a certain amount of awe and fear because of his obvious wealth, education, a prosperous shop, and a reported twenty-seven wives. The team leader negotiated with the owner of each tree and gradually obtained consent to cut the trees down. A cash payment was given to a widow who would lose a few productive coconut trees, and some other tree-owners agreed to cut down specified fruit trees after harvesting the next crop. The bargaining was spirited, friendly, and engaged the attention of the entire village. The villagers all pitched in to cut down the trees and to move two kitchen porches that protruded into the street. The project was handled so as to reflect honor and esteem on those who sacrificed most, including a special meeting for them at which the final arrangements were made. The village priest advised that they were exemplifying the best in the Buddhist precept of "right conduct," the foreigner present noted the similarity of this method of problem-solving with that used in developing rural areas in the United States, a drink was shared, and cigars were passed around. These men, not the government, emerged as the village heroes.

Another setting for a useful self-help project is that in which a real problem exists, but has never been defined or discussed seriously. The team leader, especially one who goes around continuously chatting with village people, is often able to relate what he picks up in conversation with visual observations of the village and perceive, if you will, a significant but unarticulated "felt need." The best example of this was a village divided in two by a deep stream spanned only by a log. Villagers were afraid of this "bridge." Children and others carrying water had slipped off. Yet there had never been an attempt made by residents on either side to do anything about it. The team leader in question gauged the depth of this feeling and gambled on a community bridge-building effort. The team provided leadership, organization (although none of them had ever built a bridge before), tools, and key items, like nuts, bolts, and nails.

Both halves of the village joined in the labor to cut the wood and erect it. There was great pride taken in this accomplishment.

Team leaders also find that villagers are interested in repairing or adding to the *wat* complex of buildings and fences, shoring up wells and small reservoirs, and improving the school building, again tending to support Amyot's observations. In cases of doubt, though, team leaders may waive the whole idea of a project and emphasize the services the government has brought. They are likely to send their staff out to talk with villagers informally—something called the "saturation technique"—for much of the visit, explaining the government's plans, inquiring about local conditions, and engaging in the small talk which helps eliminate "social distance," and the like. The crucial factor in this *modus operandi* is analysis of each situation rather than any concern with a specific type of project. Unlike so many handbooks on civic action and community development, MDU is problem- or situation-oriented, not project-oriented; hence it behooves those who seek to copy MDU techniques to teach sensitivity to local situations first and project skills second.

It is particularly important to note that the use of coercion in MDU activities has been conspicuous by its absence. Obviously, coercive action would completely defeat the purpose of MDU and, indeed, be downright counter-productive. With respect to self-help work, it can be argued that the Thai farmer will take any "suggestion" from someone in authority as a command and do it, i.e., surface behavior may be the epitome of sweetness and light, but in reality a very polite or subtle coercive pressure is exerted. Similarly, one hears often that villagers sit docilely in meetings, never debate or argue, and always do what they are told. It is impossible to say categorically that these phenomena never occur in MDU activities. What can be said, on the basis of observation and participation, is that they are remarkably reduced from the customary norm. One can discern between the suggestion carried out enthusiastically and that carried out *pro forma,* and the significant feature is the increasing frequency of the former. The restraint shown by MDU officials in not pursuing activities which do not command some popular support is equally observable. And I have seen too many vocal, argumentative farmers in meetings to support as sacrosanct principle the notion that they are always subservient.[20] In conditions where participation is encouraged, many will participate.[21]

It is also important to note that local officials, especially those at the district level, get their first hints of the "New Look" in governmental style. They take their cues from Bangkok, and they begin to see Bangkok as represented by MDU developing an entirely new relationship with individuals at the "rice roots" level.

In summary, Phase I activities are designed to inform and to influence. The government's intentions are made known, and a small down payment to support them is made in the form of services and entertainment. The role envisaged for the people and their government in the future is outlined, but no rash promises for a soon-to-be-delivered Utopia are made. Emphasis is placed on the ability of both parties to achieve progress jointly, and the government's actions and behavior are intended to convey the conviction that it will do its share.

Phases II and III: The Follow-up. Intentions, convictions, and an impact operation lasting all of one or two days are hardly sufficient to transform a village population into "true believers," especially if they have customarily seen their district officer only once every third year. Obviously, an impact operation can backfire if it succeeds in inciting new expectations which remain unfulfilled. Therefore impact in and of itself is meaningless; some worthwhile follow-up activity is needed to validate it, although nobody yet knows how much is enough. The "meaningful government presence" noted above must be retained.

The MDU approach to follow-up has centered on the field headquarters. During Phase I, teams of experts based at the head-

---

[20] Gordon Murchie (N.D.:4) had similar experiences: "Surprisingly enough, the villagers in the area covered by the team were not in any way shy in asking pointed and direct questions." Cf. Amyot (1964:14–15), who notes that in the conventional village situation he studied, villagers discussed but never openly opposed projects proposed by their headman or abbot.

[21] It has been the experience of community development (CD) workers that villagers show little initiative and are cowed by officials. I would speculate that villagers feel the views of the CD workers are not backed by sufficient power and influence among the officials who really govern the areas in which they live. MDU people, however, possess considerable power in their own right. They represent Bangkok directly. Local officials defer to them; hence, if they encourage village-level participation and expression of views, it is much easier for villagers to comply.

quarters roam the area surveying possibilities for small development projects. Many of them, for example, are versed in various phases of agriculture and animal husbandry, water and soils management, and education. Out of their survey recommendations the MDU field commander coordinates the preparation of a development plan. In addition, several villages are selected to be "model villages," and a Highway Department road-construction crew is at work constructing or improving roads that will last longer than those built by men with shovels. Whenever possible, road work is started before the main MDU team reaches the field in order to maximize the latter's mobility. Much of the time, however, the mobile teams active in Phase I operate in essentially "roadless" terrain.

Initially, Phases II and III were intended to be quite distinct. It was believed that Phase II would last about six to eight months, encompassing completion of a number of small projects involving dams, schools, gardens, and the like. Phase III was to be marked by a turnover of authority from MDU officials to local officials (district officers and/or the province governor). The latter would then direct the long-term follow-up operation in conjunction with representatives of the traditional functional ministries, and MDU personnel would withdraw. In fact, experience during the first two years of the program demonstrated that this planned arrangement was not practicable, in part because local authorities were inadequately equipped or motivated to assume the responsibility, but largely because the contribution of MDU personnel grew to be both successful and unique. The nature of this contribution is discussed more fully below. Suffice it to say that the two phases have merged in practice into a single "follow-up" period, and MDU personnel have remained in the field to serve as the catalyst for development activity.

The list of individual follow-up activities is very impressive and almost unending. Apparently there is no hesitation to innovate, and this is a healthy sign. There is no MDU "field manual" on what to do in every instance in rural areas, and it is probably a good idea not to have one; otherwise, there would be latrines, tin roofs, and foot bridges in every village in the Northeast whether or not they were desired or needed. Foreigners often fail to appreciate that "cultural conditions" vary not only between nations, but also within them, and not only between a nation's obvious geographic regions, but within them as well. This seriously limits the validity of highly generalized operational field manuals. The closest approach to the "field manual" mentality in MDU is the much-debated "model village" concept, and even this varies a little, depending upon the field commander's point of view. Roads, of course, are significant. Their impact on rural communities over a period of years is very impressive. It should be underscored, however, that no detailed research to measure the consequent economic and social changes has yet been done. Therefore nobody really knows how much new roadway is "enough," nor what the long-run implications of road-building on rural life are likely to be.

Personal "before and after" observations do confirm the fact of change, however, and several factors stand out. Bus and truck traffic begins immediately on almost any new road or improved "track." There is a substantial amount of this traffic anyhow in the dry season when temporary routes are established across dry rice fields. Decent roads lead to regularization of this traffic, all-year service, and reduced fares. What is more important, villagers use them.

It is said from time to time that villagers, if asked, say they do not want roads or are indifferent to the idea; however, where they have been put in, there seem to be few with regrets. The economic advantages become quickly evident. The news about market prices arrives sooner via road, and villagers can arrange to ship their rice and other products by truck or bus when prices are high. Previously, this had to be done by ox-cart. Buyers in the market towns knew most farmers would not take their loads back home and used this competitive power in bargaining to their own advantage. In some cases farmers have been able to double their income from rice sales by waiting for a good market and shipping by truck.[22]

Roads also facilitate movement of people, and are used for that purpose, e.g. to visit friends, look for work, visit *wats* and

---

[22] Incidents of this kind are very encouraging and not hard to find. What remains to be established by research is the extent to which this intelligent economic behavior is shared and practiced among farmers.

large towns previously inaccessible, and attend to business in the *amphur* town. They also bring medical facilities, schools, model villages, and the like within the reach of many more people. In theory, at least, utilization of limited government resources of this type can be greatly increased by establishing them in conjunction with a road network. It may be less expensive and more realistic to worry about transporting people to special schools, clinics, and agricultural demonstration centers than to wait until there is one of each of these in every rural village.

As a matter of record, there were about five hundred kilometers of laterite-surfaced new road and track constructed in the first three MDU areas as of September 1964.[23] Maintenance was very good. As a rule of thumb, MDU field commanders try to put in about ninety kilometers of road per year in the larger MDU areas, at least for the first two years. Initially, MDU was totally dependent on the Highway Department for road-building equipment and crews; however, in 1964 the Thai and American governments signed an agreement under which the United States agreed to provide three construction units for direct use by MDU and six units for assignment to the governors of six key Northeast border provinces. It is intended that all will be used for road construction and repair and other public works projects. The MDU units will permit timely advance work before MDU groups move into new field areas and rapid commitment to unique or special emergency situations, should they arise. The provincial units should encourage and greatly enhance the independent capability of governors to provide systematic follow-up work within their jurisdictions.

MDU follow-up activities in the field of medicine take two forms: establishment of permanent clinics at MDU field headquarters villages and the periodic dispatch of mobile medical teams throughout the area serviced by that headquarters. These clinics are staffed by doctors (one at a time per clinic) from the Ministry of Public Health in Bangkok and are rotated about once a month. It is hoped that permanent health officers will eventually be assigned; however, fully aware of the possible neg-

[23] Figures supplied by Mobile Development Unit headquarters, Ministry of Defense, Bangkok.

ative consequences if the initially established level of service is not maintained, the Ministry has developed the present temporary-duty arrangement. Medical officials are especially alert to the problem of epidemics and can react quickly because of their firsthand knowledge of the area. The headquarter's clinic doctor makes periodic mobile visits. Occasionally a very special program is undertaken, as in the case of an experimental project to cure opium addicts in Kalasin Province. This is "medical" in the sense that it is addressed to a medical problem; the treatment regime, however, is administered by a priest in a remote section of Saraburi Province (for details see Huff 1964:23). Results in the first four months of the pilot project were very encouraging, and it will doubtless be expanded if continuing success is achieved. Volunteers have flocked to attend the course. Ministry of Public Health efforts to train more medical personnel, build more health stations, and put a trained midwife in as many villages as possible all contribute to the follow-up.

Two health problems are noteworthy and are likely to be encountered elsewhere. Health education seriously lags behind the availability of rudimentary medical care. In particular, clearing up enteric and skin diseases is a profitless exercise because the villager returns immediately to a home and field environment where he contracts the disease or ailment all over again. Doctors see this very clearly with babies who are born fat and healthy, but gradually succumb to an environment over which they have little control. It is also frustrating because the medical man can easily persuade villagers to take pills, shots, medicines, and certain treatments, but he has almost no success in getting them to clean and cook food properly, wash properly (despite a genuine fondness for baths), and follow minimal community hygiene practices. This seems to be a task requiring joint application of the skills of the psychologist, the specialist in communication and education, and the health expert. There has been a little improvement in keeping clean the areas beneath the familiar raised houses where livestock is kept, but the motivation for this seems more often due to the fact that villagers "like the look of it" then to an appreciation of health benefits.

The second and more operationally oriented issue is that of introducing some system of payment for health services consistent with ability to pay. This is less difficult than one would expect, at least in Thailand, because villagers are used to paying something for the help they get from the traditional herb doctor, or midwife, or even health officer. The question is not whether to pay, but how much. First steps by MDU personnel to encourage payment by those who can afford it have not backfired. It is expected that a system of partial payment of costs will be experimented with in the oldest MDU areas.

Work in education has been concentrated on the village schoolhouse and experimentation with adult education courses. New schools are being built and many others susbstantially renovated. Villages quite often share in the costs of construction. Desks, teaching aids, books, and even paper are in very short supply, and MDU is trying to remedy these deficiencies (especially in textbooks). One district with 15,000 students, for example, has less than 500 desks. Fabrication of desks and basic furnishings for the school could be a reasonable self-help task, even for Phase I mobile teams, but it has not been exploited. The increased number of graduates from the country's expanded teachers colleges has already begun to have an impact on areas where the customary four-year compulsory education has been taught mostly by teachers with little or no formal training beyond the same four years.

Experimentation in adult education has been inconclusive. Courses in reading and writing tend to fail in the sense that adults lose interest quickly. Success with vocational training courses varies by subject and sometimes by area. Some MDU officials believe that the best results may come from combining popular vocational courses with reading and writing. Two of the most successful courses to date have been barbering for young men (a haircut may yield two baht, or about ten cents), and beautician and sewing courses for women.[24] There have been other attempts with pottery, carpentry, weaving, brick-making, and woodworking and painting.

In a very real sense, of course, "community development, agricultural extension, and a host of other projects that go by differ-

---

[24] Dr. G. C. Hickey, presently doing field research in South Vietnam, has told me that barbering courses are also very popular with young men from certain hill tribes located in Vietnam.

ent names are basically programs in adult education for villagers"
(Long 1964:17). Clearly, we do not know what techniques are
most effective in achieving the education, persuasion, and motivation desired in village populations. Whether it be by resident
general instructors, specialists in each subject, mixed teams,
audiovisual means, or whatever, systematic evaluation of each
is a significant unfilled gap in our knowledge.

Agriculture is of paramount interest in a section of the country
commonly thought to have 85–95 percent of its population employed in farming. Clearly then, progress in this field seems likely
to influence favorably the largest number of people. Indeed, this
logic has led Long to conclude that "to fight insurgency in the
Northeast our first concern must be agriculture" (Long 1964:12).
MDU started slowly in its approach to agriculture, but by
MDU-3 (Nakhornphanom) it began to move to the forefront
in follow-up activity. This was doubtless due in large measure
to the fact that Nakhornphanom, while no garden paradise, tends
to be better endowed naturally for farming than many of its
neighbors in the Northeast. Nevertheless, agricultural activities
receive emphasis in MDU follow-up activities everywhere.

The phrase "agricultural extension" seems to best blanket
these activities. The "demonstration plot," in particular, is becoming a formidable tool in convincing the farmer that modern
technology can influence him directly and put money in his
pocket. To the extent that it succeeds in doing so, the government receives credit for introducing the new techniques and
showing an interest in helping farmers in terms which they can
understand. Success is dependent, of course, on the extent to
which the farmers in question are sensitive to changes in income
and will accept new techniques in order to achieve it. In my
opinion the farmer in the Northeast has this sensitivity and will
innovate, if shown convincingly.[25]

Demonstration plots at key locations do part of the selling
job. Perhaps more effective is the technique of inducing the most
progressive farmers in a village to "try" a new crop or farming

---

[25] Long (1964:14–15, 20) points to the rapid growth in recent years of production of new crops such as kenaf, corn, and cassava as evidence in support
of this contention. For a somewhat negative view of the Central Thai villager's
ability to modernize see Piker (1964:10).

method by offering them free seed, fertilizer, pesticide, marketing assistance, etc., to get started. It has been said that "probably the most effective educational tool with Thai farmers is seeing their neighbors do successfully something new" (Long 1964:19). MDU leans heavily on this technique in its agricultural pursuits, looking in every village for "the most diligent farmers." It may also prove useful in achieving progress in the health education field, although the difficulties are admittedly greater. Quite often the demonstration plots are located on land donated for the purpose by a *kamnan,* headman, schoolteacher, or a well-to-do villager in hopes that their "good example" will motivate other villagers. A display of confidence in the government's recommendations by a respected village personality is a definite asset; on the other hand, it may be necessary then to emphasize that utilization of the new crop or technique is not dependent on being as wealthy as the donor.

Very often the central issue in achieving innovation in agriculture among a large number of farmers, most of whom do not have spare or idle land, is fear of total failure. "Innovation" often means switching from rice to a crop which cannot be eaten if the market is bad, e.g. a fiber such as cotton or kenaf, or one which is not a popular dinnertime favorite, e.g. corn. The strongly independent farmer simply dislikes the notion of utter dependence on a possibly fickle market. Whatever the market, he can eat his rice.

The number of individual agricultural tasks and projects tried out under MDU auspices is staggering (for examples see Huff 1964:26–30). They may be as small as giving ten farmers samples of American hay, or as large as distributing fruit trees to an entire village or fertilizer throughout an entire district. Field crops, gardens, animal husbandry, agriculture, fish, soils management, and use of tractors and modern equipment, indeed, "the works," have received some attention. All of this effort contributes to the fact of "follow-up," but it also makes evaluation very difficult. Research is needed to determine the most effective projects or types of projects so that in the future resources can be concentrated on the most productive activities. Field trial with crops and techniques is useful, up to a point, but it should not be extended indefinitely. The observer can collect many examples of success. There are reports of excellent new crop yields and increases in income, success in marketing new crops, and in cooperative ventures in which villagers combine resources to rent a vehicle in order to ship products to more attractive, distant markets. But close analysis of cause and effect has yet to be done.

One of the most interesting features of the agricultural work has been the way in which progress has been achieved. Initially, at least, it was accomplished with almost no increase in agricultural extension personnel (although a large number of newly trained men began work in the Northeast in 1965, a step which should sustain the early momentum). Individual rice, or agriculture, or livestock officers already working in areas selected for MDU activity merely joined forces with MDU when it arrived. But these men, and others representing the regular functional ministries, found that association with MDU was or could be a blessing. The MDU field commanders insist on good work and take an interest in promoting it. Furthermore, some of their own resources—vehicles, communications, audiovisual equipment, or occasionally small budgetary assistance—are made available to assist the local officer. MDU often pays this man's per diem, and this is an excellent incentive. The MDU staff can also solve related problems which are beyond his capability, for example, arrange transportation of agricultural products to appropriate markets.

Long has complained that one of the major difficulties with agricultural extension in Thailand is the plethora of agencies engaged in doing pieces of it. He has also noted that it would probably be easier to coordinate or integrate them at the field or working level than at the seat of government in Bangkok (Long 1964:17–19). In effect, MDU has been providing such coordination in the field (and to some extent in Bangkok) and in so doing has provided a demonstration of the value of applying developmental resources in this fashion. Whether MDU is the ideal organizational choice for this function, either now or in the future, is perhaps irrelevant, in view of the practical and factual contribution it has been able to make to date.

Students of the Northeast usually have their own favorite candidate or candidates for the most pressing village "need" or "want."[26] I have two: (1) protection against cattle thieves, which is discussed more fully below, and (2) water. Alleviation of these two problems would, in my judgment, result in the greatest favorable psychological impact among the village population we are considering. It was noted above that only about 30 percent of the villages in the Northeast have adequate water supplies, and it has been estimated that it will be approximately the year 2013 before one can expect a drilled well in every village, with continued drilling at the present rate (*Bangkok World,* June 29, 1963; Platenius 1963:11).

In severe shortage areas, MDU has tried desperately to drill from the first day of Phase I; indeed, I have been with drilling teams provided by the Department of Mines who stuck to a twenty-four-hour schedule in the hottest days of the dry season. They have not had much success, and the historical record suggests that this was to be expected. MDU headquarters survey teams have managed to recommend sites for small dams, reservoirs, and fish ponds, many of which have been built. And even when a well with brackish water is brought in, the water can be used for bathing, gardens, and livestock purposes. However, this is not the place to discuss the water issue at length (for details see Plantenius 1963:9–13; Huff 1963:33–35; 1964:31–33). Suffice it to say that the MDU program has not been able to make serious inroads on this problem as yet. In my opinion, significant progress must await the development of an integrated water-resource management approach which takes account of all the special factors which so complicate the water supply problem.

For purposes of comparison with other development programs,

---

[26] In the village Amyot studied, residents listed their preferences, in order, as more land, protection from drought and flooding, livestock, better housing, and better roads. He is correct in stating that "felt and real needs do not necessarily coincide. In many instances, people are not aware of what they need to solve their problems out of lack of experience of sophistication." In another sample survey of five villages in Nakhornphanom, villagers listed money, land (although 92 percent already owned land, prompting the investigator to comment, "as other statistical studies have also demonstrated, landless farmers are scarce in Thailand"), elimination of flooding and rice pests, increasing farm income, and better roads (Yatsushiro 1963:4–5).

and to avoid misunderstanding, I should like to restate explicitly that the bulk of the work accomplished in the follow-up period is done by specialists from the regular civil ministries, most of whom already operate in the area in question. As developed in the discussion of agriculture above, MDU personnel merely guide, motivate, and coordinate the work of others, and occasionally contribute liberal doses of imagination and their own resources to spark a project or program. The reasons they succeed in this amorphous, catalytic role are explained more fully below.

Model Villages and Self-Help. Most of the follow-up activities mentioned thus far are heavily dependent on other ministries for manpower and financing. In the earliest days of MDU, when the follow-up response of these ministries was an unknown quantity, MDU headquarters sought means to ensure at least some modest follow-up directly under its own control. The "sample village" or "model village" was selected as the most likely candidate, and in this context it emerged as a cornerstone of the follow-up program. It provides two practical advantages: (1) a guarantee of some follow-up regardless of support from other quarters, and (2) an opportunity for MDU to set the pace for work by others.

In each large MDU area approximately four villages are selected to be model villages. They are usually widely separated. In physical terms this means that a good road will be constructed to the village to connect it with the nearest provincial road of any consequence, and it will receive a large number of relatively expensive assets. Radio comunications are installed; and a radio operator and perhaps a community development worker or health officer will be placed in residence. Indeed, commencing with MDU-8, the model villages have been assigned ten-man staffs and designated as sub-headquarters. The staff is headed by a military officer and includes a deputy district officer and officers drawn from Public Health, Welfare, Education, Agriculture and Community Development. The MDU field headquarters begins work on these villages during Phase I and continues to develop them well into the follow-up. The model villages generally receive a new school, meeting house, TV receiver and fancy aerial, a children's playground, health station, electric street lights, public address system, water-seal latrines, straight streets and fences, new streets, wells and pumps, and water-tank storage and distribution systems.

The model village is probably the most controversial element of the MDU program. Foreign observers, especially, are likely to criticize it. Opposition is usually based on the belief that giving special attention to four or five villages in an operation that might involve two hundred villages will only create ill will and jealousy among the unfavored majority. The many improvements incorporated into the most favored few are felt to be unduly lavish frills, and it is argued that the money would be better spent in bringing less ostentatious benefits to a much larger number of villages. Some consider the model villages as no more than showplaces intended to impress visitors from Bangkok. It is also argued that such free-spending behavior by the government will tend to stifle the very self-help spirit which the government wishes to promote among the people. There is merit in these criticisms.

There is also something to be said for the position taken by MDU. Too often the constructive aspects of the model village technique are lost in the emotional blur in the mind of the critic caused by the sight of a TV set and electric lights in a remote rural village. Officially, the explanation given for model villages is to provide a convincing demonstration of what the government and the people can do when they work together, and to show what the "good life" will be like in the future. Government spokesmen do not promise to transform every other village in the country into exact replicas of the model village overnight. Among other things, they realize that villagers are not quite that gullible. One cannot say with certainty that residents of other villages which do not get the special treatment are not jealous or envious. On the other hand, it cannot be stated categorically that they all violently disapprove, either. The fact that this smacks of favoritism and unequal treatment when viewed through some (especially Western) eyes, does not necessarily make it so. It is at least plausible that people in areas which have not known government services (and have experienced favoritism in application whenever they did appear), or have been mistreated by government, will view the appearance of any reasonable demonstration of RTG effort and concern with some favor, and take some pride in the fact that it is occurring in "their" district, if not in their village.[27] And for once it is occurring in a village, instead of in the back yard of the *nai amphur* (district officer), where past experience suggests it would logically be placed. The Thai villager is sufficiently intelligent to realize that when resources are limited, distribution becomes a problem. He may even concede that one television set in the district is better than none at all. And it is at least debatable whether the government would achieve a greater impact if it substituted garden seeds for the TV set and gave each family in a given large village one package.

One especially effective MDU field commander has encountered villagers who questioned the government's choice of a village in his area as a model village. He takes pains to explain the government's objectives to them, and he uses an analogy with considerable effect. He explains first that Thailand has only one great capital city and that it took hundreds of years to develop it. He also points out that there is only one province capital, and closer to home, he calls on their own experience to remember how long it took to establish and develop their own *amphur* (district headquarters) town. From this base he leads into the RTG's dependence on citizen taxes, the necessity to progress slowly, and the fact that the model village is a first step in a long development process. Villagers can understand this logic. By and large, MDU commanders do not count villager envy about not being selected as a model village as one of their major problems.

Another official reason given for establishing model villages is that they will stimulate others to try and help themselves, i.e., they will give others an idea of what can be done to change and presumably improve village life. Now, the criticism that what they see is totally beyond their own capability to provide must be discussed in this context. First, there is probably more self-help or villager participation involved in model village development then is commonly realized. This is especially true in model villages which are not also an MDU headquarters with

[27] The lack of village and district loyalties or identification in the central plains area should not be permitted to obscure the fact that such loyalties do exist in the Northeast. For some plausible explanations see Lux (1962:99–100).

a large resident staff of experts on hand for a considerable time.[28] When the electric generator is offered, villagers often have to agree to cut the poles for the lines. I am aware of a model village whose residents were cool to this proposal. When the governor then offered to recommend the MDU take the generator elsewhere, they changed their minds; now an ever increasing number are signing up for electricity in their homes. The street lighting is free, but there is a charge for power in the home. There is also a charge for water in the larger villages with pumping and distribution systems. Villagers in model villages often contribute labor for schools, meeting houses, and other projects, and sometimes donate land for the new facilities. People from other villages who come in with proposals to repair their schools often get MDU aid, especially tin roofing. Some even get new schools. They see demonstration garden and field plots and can get MDU assistance to start some in their own village. They also see cleaner houses, new streets, straight streets and fences, and small ponds, all of which they can copy if they wish.

MDU officials are candid about the effect of model villages in stimulating self-help improvements in other villages. The stimulation occurs "sometimes." Some of the MDU commanders have brought headmen and other village leaders to see the model villages, and in some instances they have taken villagers from the model villages out to talk to their neighbors in other villages. In instances where there has been a successful project, credit is usually given to the headman or *kamnan* for providing energetic leadership. MDU headquarters have a good record of responding to villagers who do come up with sensible village projects.

MDU field officials and local *nai amphur* (district officer) generally approve the use of model villages as a focus for local development programming, although differences of opinion exist. A few flatly prefer to "spread the wealth" rather than concentrate on model villages. Of two particularly good *nai amphur,* one felt model villages had a place in development work if they were built close to a main road where many people could see them;

[28] The combined model village-MDU headquarters villages of Ban Na Khu (Kalasin), Ban Kut Rua Kham (Sakonnakhorn), and Ban Phon Thum (Nakhornphanom) are well known and frequently visited. The other model villages in these MDU areas are seen far less frequently by outsiders.

the other official argued that they were far more valuable in a remote location because a road was built to them, thereby encouraging heavier traffic all along the route and a wider impact throughout a much larger area. Outside villagers do come to associate the model village with advantages for themselves. If it has a health station, it may be the only one for miles, and a good road leads to it.

Undeniably, different villages have different reactions. A whole new series of streets was cleared out of the bush adjacent to one large village, where they remain in majestic isolation because nobody will move onto them. In contrast, residents of another village requested the MDU commander to assist in cutting a new street for them because they felt too crowded, and the young people had nowhere to go. I was present when the street was cut by the villagers in 1963, with minimal help from MDU. When I returned over a year later (April 1964), a dozen new houses were on the new street. By the time another visit was paid in August 1964, a second smaller street had been cleared on village initiative as a community project. MDU merely loaned some equipment. These villagers also recently decided to give three days' labor each month to village improvement work (on the tenth, twentieth, and thirtieth). This is noteworthy in that the MDU staff in residence had been reduced to half a dozen, all its major projects had long been completed, and no pressure was being applied.

In the MDU-1 headquarters village, villagers became so accustomed to the rudimentary underground water distribution system, a pipe leading from the water tank to two or three tap outlets in the village, that they took it upon themselves to extend it. They put in cement pipe made in the village with MDU help in the planting season. This is one of the very few times I have seen village men anywhere engaged in community work at this busy time of year. Two villages in Sakonnakhorn, blessed with aggressive Community Development (CD) workers, reported that 100 percent of the houses have water-seal latrines, for which each household paid twenty-five baht ($1.25). Phon Thum model village also has close to 100 percent coverage.

I have revisited villages which had participated in successful self-help projects during the mobile team visits in Phase I. In just about every instance the improvement made has been maintained, and pride is taken in it; in a few instances, there is evidence of additional self-help work in the village; in most of them almost nothing new has been started, and a reason frequently given by villagers is their inability to organize themselves for the purpose. Thus one sees some signs of hope, but many indications that the traditional forces continue to dominate. The ever present model village which these people will see periodically may very well be of much greater importance than a fleet of transitory mobile teams in stimulating the "improvement habit."

MDU officials also report that villagers who see the fencing in model villages are sometimes motivated to copy it. They are not particularly excited about straightening old streets, especially if houses have to be moved; however, fences are different. Most villages in the Northeast have a great deal of fencing to begin with. Fences are popular because they can be used to mark personal property boundaries and to keep animals either in or out. MDU officials have also said that villagers simply like the "look of them," and some consider them to be a "mark of progress."[29] In any event, there is no evidence of strong-arm methods to force fence-building, and it continues to occur.

We must also be careful not to underestimate the villager's capacity to change his way of life. Arguments that he does not need, does not want, and cannot get TV, electric power, machinery, and other luxuries may turn out to be shortsighted, in which case the MDU's instinct in establishing and supporting the model village concept will look somewhat better in retrospect. Some statistics from a 125-square-mile area in Changwat Udorn, part of which is now included in MDU-6, are enlightening (data which follow are from Blakeslee *et al.* 1965). This was the area, mentioned above, in which forty villages had about seven hundred transistor radios. Twelve of the villages (a respectable 30 percent of the total) have their own electric generators. These are communally owned in every case and are used to power strings of lights and loudspeakers at *wat* fairs. They may be used fifteen times a year in a single village and are avail-

[29] I have encountered villages that have had no contact whatsoever with MDU or Community Development, with quite extensive village fencing networks. Some villagers point to their value in keeping cattle from thieves; often they will indicate that fences around homes or the *wat* have an aesthetic appeal.

able on loan to other villages. There are also eleven villages with pumps, all privately owned, which can be rented for about twenty baht ($1.00) an hour. They are used to pump water for irrigation and to drain fish ponds. A few years ago the suggestion that rural villages should have their own rice mills was considered foolish. There are now sixty-two mills in the forty villages in this area. These examples are given to suggest that the willingness and ability of Northeast villagers to "progress" may be greater than heretofore realized. Radios, electric generators, pumps, and rice-milling equipment are not far behind TV and elementary water-supply systems. Indeed, I suspect that there would already be a small commercial demand for TV sets in many parts of the Northeast today if reception and good programming were guaranteed. In this regard, one very remote model village that gets good TV reception draws three hundred to four hundred people a night to watch, many of whom walk in from other villages.

The demand for electricity in the model villages has been quite surprising. The government-provided generator is used to produce street-lighting free of charge from about seven to nine P.M. Villagers have the option of bringing the electricity into their homes if they pay for it. Several of the villages have waiting lists for connection, and villagers pay four to six baht (twenty to thirty cents) per month for light in the evening. Some install fluorescent lights at twice the cost.

An additional factor in the use of the model village is its flexibility in serving a variety of objectives. Field commanders vary in their own use of it, some being far more elaborate than others. In MDU-1 and the two sections of MDU-4, there are only about one or two each, including the MDU headquarters villages. In Nakornphanom they have been selected, doubtless with some forethought, so that each is an ethnic minority village. For example, Ban Don Luang is a So village, and in Ban Lao the people are Kha. Rebuilding a badly rundown old *wat* at Ban Kut Rua Kham, which was revered throughout the area, had a very favorable widespread impact on the Buddhist population, and it reinforced the religious image of the government. The large village of Ban Akas, Sakonnakhorn, has been treated virtually as a model village in order to achieve a psychological and political objective.

Prior to the arrival of the MDU the village had experienced several arrests of its citizens as suspected Communists, lost its official status as a sub-*amphur* office, and in general looked upon the government rather sullenly. The government promised to up-grade the village to a sub-*amphur*, build thirty-five kilometers of road to connect the village with the main Sakonnakhorn-Udorn highway at Amphur Phannanikom, put in a water-supply system, and add all the usual features associated with a model village. Through MDU the government has made good on all these promises and also included a personal visit from the Prime Minister for good measure. The authorities report that there no longer is unrest in Ban Akas. Of parenthetical interest, the bus and truck traffic increased so much on the Akas-Phannanikom road that fares dropped from ten baht (fifty cents) to seven baht (thirty-five cents).

In Nakhornphanom and Sakonnakhorn most model villages are assigned a CD worker and a radio operator, and they become the main agricultural demonstration location in their area. In brief, they are to be the focal point of long-term development work in the area. The decision to strengthen the staffs at model villages underscores the government's determination on this point. It is felt that stretching out manpower and resources so that every village receives a little bit of something would be self-defeating in such large areas, and impact would be negligible at best. In concentrating many things in a few villages, the latter become magnets drawing many visitors, each of whom receives maximum exposure on the basis of a single trip.

This lengthy discussion of model villages is intended to bring to light as much information as possible about them. It is not expected that it will suffice to make "believers" of those whose experience with model villages elsewhere has been to the contrary; however, it may make the Thai position on this subject more understandable and explain why MDU is not prepared to accept as definitive statements to the effect that "the model village has failed in every country in which it has been tried."

Community development programs are often found in the rural areas of the developing nations, although they are not necessarily associated with problems peculiar to minorities. In the context of MDU, Community Development (CD) workers have played a relatively minor role, usually limited to participation in some model village efforts. With a few notable exceptions, their performance has not been very satisfactory. One difficulty has been the serious problem of finding and training properly motivated young people to fulfill the very demanding responsibilities of CD workers in the complex socio-cultural setting found in Northeast Thai villages. This is intensified by ambiguities in defining precisely what the function of CD workers and the CD program as a whole is and ought to be. As an example, the following conclusion in a very frank study by a Thai observer is quoted at length:

> Community development implies the implantation of democracy and it is explicitly recognized as the goal of the Thai Community Development Program. One of the important questions to consider is whether or not the workers, who are the key personnel, have a clear vision of their work goals. This study furnished data which contradicts any assumption of congruence between the ideas of the workers' and organization's goals. The following table describes the workers' vision of what community development is aiming toward. Surprisingly enough, they tend to place heavy emphasis on economic development or on irrelevant points, rather than implantation of democracy and cultivation of local leadership. It is obvious that they do not have a clear conception of what community development is seeking. This table [below] is a synopsis of the worker's own replies in answer to the open-ended request for a summary of the core ideas of community development. (Titaya Suvanajata 1964:42)

THAI COMMUNITY DEVELOPMENT WORKERS' CONCEPTIONS OF THE AIMS OF COMMUNITY DEVELOPMENT WORK THAILAND: 1962

Items	Percentage (N = 102)
Implantation of democracy	1
Cultivation of local leadership for self-help activity	2
Improvement of villagers' wealth	13
Change in villagers' attitude toward self-help	13
Improvement in local government	7
General improvement in rural economy	34
General improvement in rural education	15
No information and irrelevant answers	56
	100

[466]

Obviously, if there is any relationship between the goals of the CD workers and their effectiveness, the contribution of the CD program to MDU in these unsettled conditions is not likely to be a major one. Ideally, men trained to encourage the development of rural villages and to imbue villagers with the spirit of self-help could be extremely significant in underwriting the success of long-term follow-up efforts. It should be noted that as a rule MDU does not operate in rural areas that already have a CD program. This commitment to a separate program also reduces the availability of CD resources for MDU work.

The MDU field headquarters has other forms of follow-up. It is constantly loaning its equipment to headmen and district officers who devise a reasonable development activity. It may also arrange to move farmers, on a volunteer basis, to government-operated Self-Help Land Resettlement Centers (*nikhom*) where they are given assistance in building a home and establishing a new farm. Some of the newer *nikhom* appear very prosperous, including amenities such as schools, health stations, and water systems, and they are usually established in areas where upland crops are grown, i.e., the soil is good, but not suitable for traditional rice-farming. The *nikhom* at *Amphur* Kuchinerai, Kalasin, for example, is so successful that there is a long waiting list of new applicants.[30]

MDU field commanders also spend a lot of time in meeting with local schoolteachers. They believe that real progress is dependent on the youth of the country and that schoolteachers are obviously crucial in influencing the young. The teacher may also have considerable prestige in village adult society, although I resist generalization because in my experience it seems that the headman, abbot, teacher, elder citizen, specific clan groupings, or any combination thereof can predominate in the affairs of any given village. Keyes unmistakably assigns the teacher, who is a civil servant in the Thai system of government, a crucial position:

> Those most susceptible to the lure of anti-government and eventually leftist or communist opposition are not, however, the politically apathetic peasantry. Rather I would postulate that the group to which

[30] The *nikhom* idea has also been tried among the hill tribes, with considerably less success. See Hans Manndorff's paper in this volume.

Communist and leftist propaganda appeals the most are lower echelon bureaucrats—village school teachers, clerks, etc. It is this class of people which feels that it does not have salaries commensurate with its positions, as was stated to me by village teachers in the area in which I worked on many occasions. It is also a group which is in a position to be aware of and able to evaluate the inequalities present in the system. . . . . The lower level bureaucrats, particularly the village school teachers, stand in a crucial position in their ability to influence the mass of the population should there be a direct threat to the Northeast in that it is this group which has more immediate and intense contact with the villagers than any other group within the bureaucracy. (Keyes 1964A:3–4)

MDU recognizes the potential significance of the teachers, sees them as natural allies, and tries to assist them as much as possible.

The central headquarters (MDU-HQ) in Bangkok also contributes to the follow-up. When it is convinced that a particular project or program has merit, and the responsible ministry cannot support it completely, MDU frequently allots funds from its own budget for it. These "special fund" expenditures may reach several hundred thousand baht per year per MDU and they provide a critical margin of flexibility which doubtless is one of the strengths of the MDU concept, assuming wise use of the funds. There are also certain more specific MDU-HQ activities. Annual Youth Camps have been instituted to bring young boys (twelve to sixteen years) from the rural areas to Bangkok for a few days. This program is well handled, and about the only question raised concerns just how much the boys are listened to when they return home. Some argue that it would be wiser to entertain young adults in this manner because they have the ability to influence village opinion more strongly and are likely to play a leadership role in the village sooner. There seems to be merit in both approaches.

MDU-HQ arranges so-called staff visits to MDU areas every month, sending several headquarters personnel out to the field to learn about problems firsthand. About three times a year, these visits are done on a large scale (perhaps thirty to forty people) and include representatives of all the participating ministries. The visits may last one week and amount to a full review of the MDU in question, on site. A second technique involves the sending of follow-up mobile teams, twice a year if possible, back to each MDU area. Several of the men who led or participated on mobile teams in the area in the Phase I, forty-five-day effort, go back and visit villages on a sample basis to find out what is taking place. Villagers, of course, are very impressed to see a familiar face, and the practice lends credence to the government's claim that it is seriously interested in their welfare. Valuable lessons about the impact of MDU work and suggestions for improvement are gained.

The above-mentioned three MDU Construction Units also give the organization a significant increase in its ability to influence follow-up activity unilaterally. While these units will be used often to do preparatory road work in new MDU areas, they will also be available for rapid commitment to older areas when a special need arises. This greatly strengthens the hand of MDU staff left in the field.

Experience gained from living in the rural areas also leads to the evolution of new concepts for improving the government's response to need. The shortage of Buddhist monks in remote border areas was noticed, and in January of 1965 over three hundred monks were mobilized by the Prime Minister to spread the teachings of the Buddha to the people living there. Apparently it is planned to send out over six hundred of these missionaries to be "part of a campaign against Communist infiltration and subversion" (*Bangkok Post,* November 23, 1964). The Prime Minister reportedly "stressed the importance of religion in the battle against this hostile ideology" (*Bangkok Post,* November 23, 1964; *Bangkok World,* November 23, 1964; cf. Huff 1963:32–33).

The exact nature of future relationships between MDU field representatives and local officials, and hence the nature of the follow-up itself in a long-term context, is unclear. The ultimate MDU goal is to phase itself out of a job. Eventually local province and district officials, in collaboration with the several central ministries responsible for long-term economic, social, and political development, will have to take over. At present, these follow-up programs are operated in the MDU areas by the ministries in question, in general coordination with MDU. They face a difficult but challenging task, especially as development becomes less a matter of public works and more a matter of changing the habits and attitudes of village populations. The MDU approach to "followup" in the remote areas it is concerned with has been, and is likely to remain, best characterized by the notion that any government service is in fact a follow-up service if it is there and is efficiently conducted.

EVALUATION

The impact of MDU on villagers who have been exposed to it for a reasonable period of time has not been researched in depth. The art and science of eliciting valid information about attitude formation and change, and the relationship of attitudes to the behavior of people, is one of the least understood aspects of the behavioral sciences. We also tend to believe that opinions, attitudes, and beliefs (OAB) change much more slowly than actual behavior because:

> Behavior, being visible, is more responsive to extreme pressures and accommodations. OAB's, being private until expressed, can be maintained without even being subject to question or argument. And there is no necessary reason for OAB's and behavior to be in harmony: we are polite to acquaintances we really don't like, we go along with the majority in a committee action rather than make a fuss, we go to the polls even though we really don't care about the outcome. (Berelson and Steiner 1964:576)[31]

Assuming the validity of this statement, one cannot tell, even in the face of observed enthusiastic villager response to MDU, just how deeply the MDU message has penetrated. Some very exciting research awaits the professionally qualified person who would try to make such an evaluation.

It should be stressed that very few of the generalizations made about the people who live in the rural areas of Southeast Asia have been substantiated by research. Opinions are formed and acted upon from among the extremes represented by those who feel the behavior of farmers and tribesmen is complex and can never be predicted and those who feel it is simple and can always be predicted. For instance, it is commonly assumed that groups known to be fatalistic and pessimistic about life are not likely

[31] These authors also note (p. 8) that much of their inventory "is limited, strictly speaking, to Western cultures and even to the American scene," which makes generalization about rural villages in Asia somewhat hazardous.

to be interested in economic progress. It seems logical that fatalists who believe that mens' lives are determined by forces beyond their control will not participate actively in community development work and, similarly, that those who do "make" such progress will overcome their pessimism. Logic unsupported by evidence can be dangerous. Some very preliminary results on this issue reported by Whyte and Williams on the basis of study in Peruvian villages, including some in which "dynamism seemed to be so rampant that we were hard pressed to balance our sample," completely shattered the assumed pattern (1964:17). They concluded, in general:

1. The expected negative correlation between fatalism and community well-being and progress certainly is not a universal phenomenon. Further research may show that no such relationship exists or that there is a relationship only under certain conditions which remains to be discovered.

2. In practical terms, this suggests that a fatalistic outlook on the part of the inhabitants of a community is not necessarily an obstacle to development efforts. We may eventually conclude that this orientation toward life, [at] this very level, is simply irrelevant to the development process. Apparently it is quite possible for people to hold a very dark and forbidding view toward life in general, while being quite optimistic about the prospects for progress in their village. (*ibid*:19–20)

In fact, Whyte and Williams appear to have found that there is a significant difference in the views and behaviors of people in dealing with "philosophy of life" abstractions and in dealing with more immediate experience and expectations. There is a heavy flavor of this in Piker's thesis that Thai villagers have not let the Buddhist emphasis on other-worldliness and the deprecation of material strivings interfere with their concern for economic improvement in this world, and have indeed managed to rationalize the two positions by suggesting that the achievement of wealth and power is indicative that one has in fact already reached a significantly higher station on the road to salvation. In short, "next worldliness should not under any circumstances be confused with non-worldliness" (Piker 1964:10).[32]

[32] Piker argues that the rich man can donate more money, obtain an education more easily, and do less work, therefore freeing the mind for contemplation. Material success, then, tends to confirm one's ethical standing and also serve as a platform for improving one's position in the future.

In another context, events in recent years have confirmed that there is widespread lack of understanding of the relationship of various Asian groups to force and violence. Westerners, in particular, have been amazed by the political initiatives of monks in Burma and Vietnam and the willingness of many Buddhists to engage in the bloodshed associated with insurgency movements. Leach has argued that "The practical consequences of Buddhist ethics are greatly misunderstood by Europeans. Statistics make it quite clear that in all countries where Theravada Buddhism is the official religion, the incidence of murder and crimes of violence is quite exceptionally high" (Leach 1963:131–132).

These brief examples are cited to suggest that very little is known about the basic characteristics of target audiences exposed to government development programs. In particular, there is inadequate recognition that many of the populations involved have been undergoing considerable change and that perhaps older "basic characteristics" have indeed been replaced by new ones. Therefore, measurement of the success of MDU-type programs in effecting transformations in the attitudes, opinions, and beliefs of the people exposed to them is not an inconsequential task. Really proper assessment will require village-level research in depth by professional anthropologists, sociologists, and psychologists.

It should be said that this is a two-way street. Governments, on the one hand, must recognize the value of research and encourage it. But the social scientists, on the other hand, must also accept some responsibility for acquiring and analyzing, at the highest level of professional competence, data which can shed light on the fundamental socio-cultural factors affecting and perhaps controlling urban-rural and central government-minority relationships. Unfortunately, too many of us are inclined to define our right to the freedoms of research and fail to recognize some of the responsibilities which are their proper counterpart. One can at least pose the question: Is it entirely appropriate for researchers to insist, for personal or professional satisfaction, on the right to study only the couvade for eighteen months in a given tribal cultural setting which is undergoing the trauma of serious change, directed or natural? Should they not also now and then undertake the objective study of factors quite relevant to this or similar change situations, especially where the adjustment of fundamental relationships between majority and minority social and cultural groups is concerned? To be very specific, the Royal Thai Government has been especially lenient in admitting foreign social scientists to work in Thailand. Seldom, however, have the latter developed and reported information which could be used to better inform and structure public policy. Had this been done, the severe adjustment problems involved in rural development might be much better understood than they now are.

Despite the difficulties of direct measurement, the record suggests that MDU is having a positive effect. Physical changes are clearly evident. Locally generated village development projects continue to arise long after the mobile teams have come and gone. Local people ask for help from MDU, confide their troubles to patient MDU staff, and generally demonstrate active cooperativeness as distinct from passive acquiescence or indifference. An increased and sustained level of local initiative and interest after, say, two years involvement with MDU clearly suggests that MDU has had some desirable influence on people in the areas in which it operates.

There are several other rather encouraging signs of success. These emerge from discussion with MDU personnel with long field experience. They often take pride in and cite as their major accomplishments things other than kilometers of road built, schoolhouses roofed, or dams dug. Physical measures of "development" are important. They may be a necessary condition for success, but they are rarely a sufficient condition. The promising achievements are: (1) an enhanced understanding of the nature of the Communist threat, (2) an ability to deal with the rural crime problem, and (3) stimulation of local officials to operate efficiently and "be friendly with the people."

Enhanced understanding of the potential threat merely means that MDU people have found that by living and working in an area for extended periods, they can learn to tell quite accurately the difference between a purely local grievance or dispute and bona fide Communist-inspired troublemaking. The result of this discernment is a much reduced propensity to misinterpret a local incident in a remote area as Communist activity. This in turn reduces the need for hasty action or reliance on indiscriminate police sweeps to "find out" what is taking place. They have learned that innocent villagers very much fear the police-sweep method and that it should be used only as a very selective technique. This experience doubtless has application elsewhere.

Similarly, MDU officials have become aware of the cattle theft problem which exists in some parts of the Northeast. Wealth is usually measured in terms of the number of buffalo a farmer owns. The animal is also the primary beast of burden and often the principal means of transportation. Loss by theft is a major economic and emotional issue, and when it occurs villagers will become sufficiently concerned to band together to form village patrols, and if they live close enough, even travel to Bangkok to petition the Ministry of Interior.[33] I visited an area not involved in the MDU program in 1964 in which thirty-eight of forty villages had or recently had had such village patrol systems—self-led and self-equipped (see Blakeslee *et al.* 1965, for details). MDU personnel have quietly taken steps to energize and assist local police (sometimes inefficient, often understaffed) and arrange for random security patrols by regional army units that also engage in civic action work. MDU-sponsored roads and intra-area radio communications and the continuing travel of MDU personnel throughout the villages in their area also operate as a serious brake and deterrent to thieving. The roads alone and a vehicle or two enable local officials to reach in half an hour parts of their jurisdiction that used to require half a day or more by bicycle or walking. The villager is impressed. This is a government service he very much wants, needs, respects, and understands.

The third significant achievement is bolstering the performance of the district office. One does not develop an acquaintance with Thai administration without soon learning that the district officer or *nai amphur* is acknowledged to be "the most important single link of the government with the people" (Sutton 1962:53; also see n. 23, p. 71 for additional references

---

[33] See, for example, *Bangkok Post*, November 5, 1964, which describes the visit of a delegation of five hundred villagers from Prachinburi Province to appeal to the Prime Minister for help against a crime wave.

supporting this observation). His office *is* "the government" in the rural areas, and its performance largely sets the image villagers have of their government and its policies. District offices also have serious problems. The more remote they are, the less likely they are to have a full staff, and many of the men who are assigned are sent from a Bangkok functional ministry, e.g., Agriculture or Community Development, and have divided bureaucratic loyalties and responsibilities. The most serious and "conspicuously noticeable" of these is the rivalry between the *nai amphur* and the police assigned to his district, thereby compounding the police issue mentioned above (Arsa Meksawan 1962:224–233). *Amphur* officials also complain about lack of vehicles, fuel, and per diem for travel, all of which hampers their movement and reduces their effectiveness.

MDU has stepped into these local loci of power—formidable as a whole in appearance to the villager outside, but internally fractionated or liable to fractionation—with highly interesting results. Unquestionably, a number of *amphur* officials have taken their cue from MDU personnel and have developed more aggressive, positive attitudes in their work. The assistance, advice, and encouragement of MDU men can stimulate local leaders, especially those who are quick enough to see the prestige which accrues to them personally in their jurisdiction if they associate themselves with MDU. This means that an energetic *nai amphur* who can define worthy village development projects is likely to receive a friendly hearing from the MDU field headquarters, which may support him with a piece of equipment, tools, materials, or a small budget allotment in order to encourage local self-help in the follow-up period. It was noted above in the discussion on agriculture that MDU assisted other members of the *amphur* staff in a similar fashion. The *nai amphur* who shows the ability to negotiate such arrangements gains status in the eyes of his villagers, who in turn are likely to show renewed interest in village development. Furthermore, the MDU commander who succeeds in energizing a *nai amphur* makes his own job infinitely more rewarding because he is freed from routine worries and can think about the larger and longer-range aspects of his mission. It is clear at all times, however, that although the *nai amphur* is free to make suggestions and his views are solicited, final control over distribution of the largesse rests with MDU.

Amphur officials who have witnessed the generally very friendly relations between MDU personnel and villagers, month after month, have begun to see what kind of behavior is expected of them by Bangkok and are learning the importance of developing a base of cordiality in the villages if they are to produce the type of accomplishment, in a development sense, that Bangkok (at least as represented by MDU) increasingly expects. It is a long, hard job to change attitudes, but MDU officials believe they are encouraging some important changes in the atmosphere at the *amphur* office.

The role played by MDU personnel and their effect in the field cannot be overestimated. In general, they conduct themselves admirably in dealing with both villagers and officials. It is known that their program receives high-level support. It is also becoming known on an increasing scale that they produce results. Accordingly, they represent progress and command respect. Withdrawal of MDU from an area too soon, or any serious weakening in RTG support for MDU, could remove the "cutting edge" of this rather useful tool of rural modernization and reform. In particular, the ability of MDU personnel to obtain decisions in a matter of hours on projects which a *nai amphur* might take months to arrange through the traditional line of communication from village to district, to province office and perhaps to Bangkok, makes a terrific impact on local officials. MDU field officials have a great deal of discretion to commit their own resources locally, and direct radio communications with Bangkok can bring approval for larger projects rather quickly. MDU headquarters has confidence in its field staff and relies heavily on its judgment of local situations. The latter do not hesitate to be candid about the situations in which they find themselves. Their mutual relationship very much erodes the traditional image of Thai administrative behavior:

> One characteristic is the extreme centralization of decision-making which leads to serious delays in administration. It is partly due to the reluctance of senior officials to delegate decision-making authority to subordinates, the assumption being that they can't be trusted, and partly because the latter are unwilling to assume responsibility because

this might violate the hierarchy of deference and suggest aggressiveness and also because one dislikes saying "no." (Thomas 1962:29)

It is revealing to find that MDU personnel cite the stimulation or "reconditioning" of local administration as one of their major achievements, while on their side, many of the *nai amphur* and other officials applaud MDU for guidance and support. The potential for trouble between the two was tremendous. It is not hard to conceive of a situation in which MDU might have ruptured, ignored, or embittered local lines of authority. Instead the results appear to have been generally salutary. The above description of the mutually advantageous relationships which have been worked out has a strong flavor of the concept of reciprocity, which students of Thai culture and society feel pervades so many interpersonal social arrangements.

The long-run implications of this situation are thought-provoking. In time of national trouble a strong local government is a crucial asset. If it is weak, the central government must try to replace it, and usually fails because manpower is in short supply or is too inexperienced. The proper policy for a central government then is to make serious efforts to strengthen local government before trouble starts. It appears that MDU is contributing to such a strengthening in those areas where it operates, and it has the potential to play an even more constructive role in the future, in particular systematizing a bit more the informal help now given to *amphur* officials to include help in improving the fundamentals of administration. This merely means taking the next logical step from encouraging initiative and changing attitudes to actual concern with principles and techniques of governing. Certainly in those districts where the *nai amphur* and the MDU staff have developed close friendly relationships, it is possible that the *nai amphur* would be receptive to suggestions concerning improvements in administrative practices (See Huff 1964:8–10).

The factors mentioned here—the security threat, conventional crime, and administration—are being dealt with in a most indirect and perhaps unintentional way. They are the essence of the political organization of a country. In contrast to insurgents, who emphasize political organization in doctrine and practice, political organization is treated very gingerly and uneasily by theorists and practitioners of development and counter-insurgency. Such theorists and practitioners are uncomfortable when it comes to dealing directly with the issue of achieving and sustaining political control, partly because the words themselves have a slightly impure ring, and little more is said beyond vague generalizations about constitutions, democracy, etc. Nevertheless, in its gradual progress in achieving straightforward educational (psychological), social, and economic objectives and impact, MDU is on the threshold of motivating highly constructive advances in administration and government, i.e., in the political framework so crucial to the orderly development of a rapidly changing rural area.

Cultural Tailoring. One of the crucial questions to be considered in dealing with the design of a development program is the extent to which one must tailor it to the cultural backgrounds of the target population. These decisions, of course, are heavily influenced by the relative importance within any given country of views concerning, respectively, the cultural integrity and uniqueness of minorities and the desirability of minimizing diversity in the interest of national unity through some policy of integration or assimilation into the "majority" society and culture.

In Thailand the most obvious instances of ethnic diversity are found among the tribal groups which inhabit the north and northwestern hill areas. Development efforts with respect to these peoples are discussed by Geddes, Kunstadter, Manndorff and Moerman in other papers in this volume. The MDU program will be extended into the North in the second half of 1965. At present, it reaches as far as Loei Province, which forms a transitional geographic bridge between the Northeast and the North; however, in Loei MDU work is confined to the valleys. Hill areas there are not involved beyond the already existing relationships between the tribal population and the Border Patrol Police (BPP), who attempt to teach school, provide medical aid, etc., whenever they can (see USOM 1963). This has been done deliberately because the MDU leadership is not at all convinced that the approach and techniques which have succeeded in the Northeast are suitable for dealing effectively with tribal groups.

The tremendous language variations strike operators first in their priority listing of problems.[34] This is not surprising in a program concerned primarily with communicating effectively. It is realized that no organization can hope to command the dozens of strange languages spoken; hence some agreement must be reached on the few languages which affect the most tribal groups, and then a capability to use them must be developed.[35] Again, the principal source of experience is the BPP. Knowledge of the taboos, habits, beliefs, and attitudes of hill people is almost nonexistent in Bangkok; nor are handy pocket guides available in Chiengmai. It would appear that some level of knowledge about these cultural factors would be essential to the success of an MDU-type program, but it remains for the researcher and the relative handful of people who have lived with tribal groups (mainly medical missionaries, BPP patrolmen and anthropologists) to suggest that level and its substance.

The operator can never know all there is to know about an ethnic group, and probably he need not. But he must have sufficient sensitivity to recognize what is significant to the minority he is dealing with and what is not important. It has been pointed out, for example, that on certain days the Lua? hill tribe hold ceremonies during which nobody is permitted to enter or leave the village on certain trails, and also that their pantheon of spirits resides in known sections of virgin forest high in the hills, which are always off limits for agriculture.[36] The operator needs to know whether these standards of conduct are absolutely inviolable, or are loosely held and considered irrelevant in relation to visitors, or can be compromised under certain prescribed circum-

---

[34] MDU experience in remote areas of the Northeast has led to creation of one extremely significant asset: an appreciation of the difficulty of actually conducting field operations of this type and a consequent tendency not to underestimate or gloss over problems.

[35] It was announced in January 1965 that special programs in the dialects of the Meo and Yao tribes were being tried out experimentally over the government radio station in Lampang. The director of the Public Relations Department said he had been instructed by the government to plan a program of regular broadcasts to the hill tribes in appropriate dialects. "The first step was to make a survey as thorough as possible . . . to find out which are the biggest hill tribes and which dialects are most widely spoken among them" (*Bangkok World*, January 24, 1965).

[36] Based on discussion with Dr. P. Kunstadter during a visit to Ban Pa Pae, Changwat Maehongson, Thailand, in 1964.

stances. Indeed, in the case of a Luaʔ trail violation, payment of a small fine may be sufficient redemption. Encroachment on the spirits' home is far more serious, although Karen agricultural operations in a corner of one such location are leading to the rationalization that if the Karens pay a substantial fine, all will be forgiven. The point is that those responsible for implementing action programs need factual information to improve their judgment in situations in which reaction with minority groups is required. If, as in the case of the Luaʔ, the religious system is viewed by the group "as the central core of their culture," the facts about this religion must be acquired (Kunstadter 1964:10).

It may very well be that careful assessment of tribal behaviors will lead specialists to conclude that governments should not attempt development programs in their areas. The facts of life are such, however, that tribal groups in Southeast Asia are being forced into an inevitable relationship, or "confrontation," with the twentieth century as it exists beyond their small territorial horizons. The task for researchers then is to inform better those who will be required to undertake this responsibility.

As noted earlier, there is a distinctive Malay-Islamic population in the south of Thailand. The MDU program has been extended there by means of a modest effort in Yala and Narathiwat provinces. Prior to arrival, the Secretary of the Muslim Council of Thailand was briefed on MDU, and he wrote letters explaining its purpose and urging cooperation to all the Muslim Committees in the operations area. Adjustments to local conditions have been made, with notable progress in the MDU area directed by a senior Thai military officer who is a Muslim. His staff included four other Muslim officers, and their knowledge of the possible and impossible within the context of Islamic teachings and local custom has been the key to the operation. It is also significant that, over time, this commander has inspired changes in habitual behavior that simply could not have been accomplished in the first instance by fiat—or by a non-Muslim. For example, he learned of the importance of sewing to the families in the area and arranged to have sewing courses taught. In order to attend them, however, the women had to appear on the street and go to school. The men in the area finally gave in to the demand for the course, doubtless recognizing that the new training could increase income. The changes are hardly earthshaking, but some improvement in skills supporting the local economy has been made, the social position of women has been liberalized slightly (and the fact that the increased activity of Muslim women in the village has had no untoward consequences had led to some relaxation of the formalism in relations between Muslim and non-Muslim), and the government has succeeded in showing its ability to assist its citizens. The team leader has also brought Muslim and non-Muslim together in social functions, catering to the dietary requirements of each, and has become a featured speaker in the mosques in the vicinity. Undoubtedly, further MDU activity in the South will be modeled after this experiment.

The Northeast is different from the North and South. It lacks the complete strangeness of the other areas. To make three gross generalizations, prior to initiation of the MDU program Bangkok knew almost nothing about its hill tribe populations; very little about its purely Malay-Muslim districts; but, in contrast, it seemed to know a lot about the Northeast—the problem was to get people up there to apply this knowledge. Subsequently, the Thai government generated the motivation, and MDU has performed the function. The relative ease with which it has done so suggests that the above generalizations are not too farfetched.

In the introduction to this paper it was noted that ethnically and linguistically the Thai of central Thailand and the Thai-Lao of the Northeast appear to be very close relatives indeed, particularly when compared to the distance separating each of them from the hill tribes and the Malays. As weak as they have been historically, ties between Bangkok and the vast Northeast area have existed for a long time, and the sum total of contact has been extensive. Within the context of MDU, the Thai military is no stranger to people from the Northeast, drawing many recruits from that area. Whenever possible, military officers who come from the Northeast are used in MDU operations. These factors have meant that probably less "cultural tailoring" has been necessary and that more knowledge has been available to do sensibly what has been required. The intelligent manner in which it was applied has been discussed above in detail. The success of MDU to date, which has been far greater than anyone had a right to expect, is due primarily to recognition of the value of cultural sensitivity in conducting a people-to-people program productively.

Several other problems remain to confront MDU. There have been repeated explicit references and inferences in the body of this paper to the desirability of a much more intensive research effort to determine the economic, social, and attitudinal effects of MDU work. It is hard to overestimate the importance of finding out why both successes and failures have occurred and to distill out of the record of MDU experience the data and understanding required to plan, direct, and implement the constantly increasing number of MDU areas (Huff 1964:20–21, 46–48).

Given the tremendous importance attached to educating and informing the public in both the impact and follow-up phases, more effort is needed to improve information techniques and insure that they receive the broadest possible application (Huff 1963:46–51; 1964:48–49). Similarly, more attention should be paid to devising more productive means of using the armed forces, the largest pool of organized manpower in the country, in MDU or MDU-related work. Clearly, the small group of military officers who have created and led MDU are the source of its success, and it is they who have displayed and insisted upon the cultural sensitivity emphasized above and sparked the work of the civil ministries; however, they are small in number, and the vast majority of military men sit untapped on military posts, uninvolved, and—in this context—unproductive. I argue only that it is in the interests of all developing nations with sizable military forces actively to seek optimal utilization of them in development roles (see Huff 1963:64–66; 1964:49–51).

Finally, a word of caution about the dangers of uncoordinated work. All the MDU achievements on the list could be wiped out by misfortune in other government programs. One cannot conduct a program based on the message that the government has the interests of the people at heart if action in some other sphere of government activity contradicts the message. Then both programs lose. The most likely candidates for causing such difficulties are large economic development projects, especially dams, which require the resettlement of large numbers of people. This is always a delicate issue, and a perfect solution will never be found; however, these situations must never be permitted to go by default. Proper or improper handling of the large numbers of people involved will constitute a highly visible demonstration of government intentions. In the context of MDU, they should be seized as opportunities and conducted carefully to achieve maximum impact (see Huff 1964:41–43).

Conclusion. As a rule, the Thai people are not prone to settle their disputes by violence. Popular revolutions are not part of their experience. Pressures have been resolved by other means and usually by the actions of their rulers. It is interesting that Thomas closes his study of Thai government, which concludes that inevitable domestic and foreign pressures will necessarily force the country to modify the structure and values of its political system, with the following statement. "One thing is certain, however; if change comes it will come from the top, for this is the way of Thailand" (Thomas 1962:33).

MDU is a clear example of this dictum. It may be only temporary, and neither final success nor failure can be claimed at this juncture in time. But this program does represent a deliberate choice on the part of the nation's leadership to induce, direct, or at least channel change constructively. It is an interesting case study in revolution from above.

REFERENCES CITED

AMYOT, JACQUES
    1964   Intensive village study project, April–May 1964, Ban Nonlan, Amphur Uthumphonphisai, Sisaket. Bangkok, Chulalongkorn University. Preliminary report, December 20.

ANONYMOUS
    1963A Duty to the people. Mobile Development 1 (October). Bangkok. USIS/Thailand translation.
    1963B The history of the National Security Command Headquarters. Mobile Development 1 (October). Bangkok.

ARSA MEKSAWAN
    1962   The role of the provincial governor in Thailand. Bangkok, Thammasart University, Institute of Public Administration.

BERELSON, BERNARD, and GARY A. STEINER
    1964   Human behavior: an inventory of scientific findings. New York, Harcourt, Brace and World.

BLAKESLEE, D. J., L. W. HUFF, and R. W. KICKERT
    1965   Village security pilot study. Bangkok, Military Research and Development Center.

FOSTER, GEORGE M.
    1959   Interpersonal relations in peasant society. Human Organization 19(4).

HUFF, LEE W.
    1963   Observations on Mobile Development Unit-2 operations. Bangkok, Joint Thai-U.S. Combat Development and Test Center.
    1964   Mobile Development Unit follow-up. Bangkok, Office of the Secretary of Defense/Advanced Research Projects Agency, Research and Development Field Unit, Military Research and Development Center.

KEYES, CHARLES F.
    1964A Thailand, Laos, and the Thai Northeastern problem. Australia's Neighbours, Fourth Series, 17 (July–August).
    1964B Status and rank in a Thai-Lao village. Ithaca, N.Y., mimeographed.

KUNSTADTER, PETER
    1964   Research on Lua? and S?kaw Karen hill peoples of Northern Thailand: report of research with some practical implications. Bangkok, mimeographed.

LEACH, EDMUND
    1963   The political future of Burma. In Futuribles: studies in conjecture, Bertrand de Jouvenel, ed. Geneva, Droz.

LEBAR, FRANK M., GERALD C. HICKEY, and JOHN K. MUSGRAVE
    1964   Ethnic groups of mainland Southeast Asia. New Haven, Human Relations Area Files.

LONG, MILLARD F.
    1964   Economic aspects of USOM's program in Northeast Thailand. Bangkok, mimeographed.

LUX, THOMAS E.
    1962   Mango village: Northeastern Thai social organization, ethos and factionalism. Chicago, University of Chicago, Department of Anthropology, unpublished M.A. thesis.

METHVIN, EUGENE H.
    1964   Ideology and organization in counterinsurgency. Orbis 8 (1).

MOERMAN, MICHAEL H.
    1961   A Northern Thai village. Bangkok, USIS. Southeast Asia Survey, Regional Research Report 8.

MOSEL, JAMES N.
    1964   Self, role and role behavior of supervisors in the Thai bureaucracy. Philadelphia, unpublished paper delivered to the Eastern Psychological Association meetings.

MURCHIE, GORDON
    N.D.   Report of observations and comments on trip made with Mobile Development Unit II, Information Team One, during period from June 17 to 27, 1963. Bangkok, USIS.

NINTH PACIFIC SCIENCE CONGRESS, PUBLICITY COMMITTEE
1957   Thailand past and present. Bangkok, Ninth Pacific Science Congress.

PAUKER, GUY J.
1962   Notes on non-military measures in control of insurgency. The RAND Corporation, P-2642.

PIKER, STEVAN
1964   The Weber thesis and SE Asia: alternative considerations. Detroit, preliminary draft of a paper delivered at the annual meetings of the American Anthropological Association, November 19.

PLATENIUS, HANS
1963   The North-East of Thailand, its problems and potentialities. Bangkok, National Economic Development Board.

SCHRAMM, WILBUR
1964   Mass media and national development. Stanford, Stanford University Press.

SEIDENFADEN, ERIK
1958   The Thai people, Vol. 1. Bangkok, Siam Society.

SENI PRAMOJ
1965   Political development in Thailand. Bangkok World, January 23.

SUTTON, JOSEPH L.
1962   Problems of politics and administration in Thailand. Bloomington, Indiana University, Institute of Training for Public Service.

THAILAND, CENTRAL STATISTICAL OFFICE
1961   Thailand population census, 1960. Bangkok, Central Statistical Office, National Economic Development Board.

THAILAND, NATIONAL STATISTICAL OFFICE
1964   Household expenditure survey B.E. 2505, Northeast region. Bangkok, National Statistical Office.

THEH CHONGKHADIKIJ
1963   The battle for the Northeast. Bangkok Post, May 10, 13, 16, 20, 23, and 27.

THOMAS, M. LADD
1962   Thai public administration. New Zealand Journal of Public Administration 25(1).

TITAYA SUVANAJATA
1964   Perceived leader role of community development workers in Thailand. Bangkok, USOM/Thailand Communications Media Division. (A Master's thesis for Cornell University.)

UNITED STATES INFORMATION SERVICE (USIS/THAILAND)
1964   The seventeenth Mobile Information Team trip, April 19–May 2, 1964. Bangkok, USIS/Thailand.

UNITED STATES OPERATION MISSION (USOM) COMMUNICATIONS MEDIA DIVISION

    1963   The civic action program of the Border Patrol Police and the USOM Public Safety Division. Bangkok, USOM/Thailand, Communications Media Division.

VELLA, WALTER F.

    1955   The impact of the West on government in Thailand. Berkeley, University of California Press.

WALTERHOUSE, HARRY F.

    1964   A time to build. Columbia, S.C., University of South Carolina. Studies in International Affairs 4.

WHYTE, WILLIAM F., and LAWRENCE K. WILLIAMS

    1964   The use of questionnaire surveys for community studies of culture change and economic development. Detroit, a paper delivered at the annual meeting of the American Anthropological Association, November 21.

WILSON, DAVID A.

    1961   Bangkok's dim view to the East. Asian Survey I(4).

    1962   Politics in Thailand. Ithaca, Cornell University Press.

YATSUSHIRO, TOSHIO

    1963   Some aspects of village life in Northeast Thailand. Bangkok. Outline of a talk to the USOM Technicians Meeting, September 24.

Periodicals

BANGKOK POST. Bangkok.

BANGKOK WORLD. Bangkok.